You & the Law in Spain

The complete and readable guide to **Spanish Law for foreigners**

David Searl

NEW CHAPTERS prepared by Alex Radford, English Solicitor & *Abogado*

You & the Law in Spain
(2018 Edition)

Published by Alex Radford Books
Camino de Camoján 7, Edificio Camoján
Oficina 17, 29602 Marbella (Málaga) Spain

Tel: (0034) 951 203 094
E-Mail: aradford@mylawyerinspain.com

www.mylawyerinspain.com

First published in September 1985
Second Edition – March 1986
Third Edition – October 1987
Fourth Edition – April 1988
Fifth Edition – May 1989
Sixth Edition – June 1990
Seventh Edition – May 1993
Eighth Edition – January 1996
Ninth Edition – June 1997
Tenth Edition – March 1999
Eleventh Edition – April 2000
Twelfth Edition – March 2001
Thirteenth Edition – May 2002
Fourteenth Edition – March 2003
Fifteenth Edition – March 2004
Sixteenth Edition – March 2005
Seventeenth Edition – March 2006
Eighteenth Edition – May 2007
Nineteenth Edition – May 2008
Twentieth Edition – May 2009
2011 Edition – March 2011
Twenty-Second Edition – April 2013
2015 Edition – August 2014
2018 Edition – February 2018

Designed & Produced by Next Idea, S.L.

Printed in Spain by Solprint, S.L.

ISBN: 978-84-697-8589-8
Depósito Legal: MA 84 – 2018

IMPORTANT NOTICE

You and the Law in Spain is meant as a guide to Spanish Law as it applies to foreigners. It is not, however, a substitute for personal, professional legal advice, and it cannot be a basis for any claim against the author or Alex Radford Books.

This book is dedicated to **Manuel Úbeda Castañeda**
For 30 years of support and friendship

ACKNOWLEDGEMENTS

We would like to express our sincere gratitude to all those people who have taken time from their busy schedules to answer our questions. Among these helpful people, we offer our special thanks for service beyond the call of duty to:

Lawyer Manuel Úbeda Castañeda of Úbeda-Retana & Asociados legal services in Fuengirola for always being on the other end of the telephone with the right answer.

Lawyer Jorge Retana Alumbreros of Úbeda-Retana, for his knowledge of Spanish tax legislation affecting foreigners.

Jesús Úbeda Castañeda, gestor specialist in traffic matters.

Sergio Llull Cejudo of Llull & Goldschmidt tax consultants in Fuengirola.

Marbella gestor **Ricardo Sánchez Bocanegra** for his many years of experience with foreigners.

Tax consultant and property administrator **Juan José López Guzmán** in Fuengirola for his familiarity with communities.

Anette Skou and **Katja Thiron** of the Mijas Department of Foreign Residents. They are ladies who help.

We are grateful for the help of:
Ubeda-Retana & Asociados – Fuengirola
MyLawyerinSpain.com – Marbella

CONTENTS

INTRODUCTION TO THE 23rd EDITION

YOU & THE LAW IN SPAIN
Updated for 2018

Welcome to the 2018 edition of *You & the Law in Spain*, back in the bookshops after a three-year absence, with a new publisher and a new chapter. The new chapter, "When You Have to Go to Court", is written by Alex Radford, Spanish *abogado* and English solicitor in Marbella. Radford is also the new publisher under his imprimatur of AR Books, which will publish *You & the Law in Spain* in successive editions. His law firm, Mylawerinspain.com, provides a valuable new resource, in addition to our long-time collaborator, Ubeda-Retana & Asociados in Fuengirola.

The new chapter covers many situations where you find yourself with no option but going to court. This might involve noisy neighbours, someone who owes you money or a tradesman whose work has been deficient, a dispute over an automobile accident or a property boundary and many other conflicts. In general, lawyers urge you to make every effort to settle conflicts out of court, but sometimes you have no choice.

Official estimates tell us that about two million foreigners own property in Spain and more than four million foreigners hold work and residence permits, meaning that Spain is their real home. Tens of thousands of foreigners buy property here every year and the number is growing as Spain moves out of recession. *You & the Law in Spain* is designed to help these people deal with a legal system unfamiliar to them in a language they probably do not speak. This book is not a substitute for a lawyer or a tax accountant but it should help you to ask your lawyer or tax accountant the right questions and to understand his answers.

I have gathered the information here over 30 years of answering questions in magazine and newspaper columns, at conferences and on my radio programmes. The answers come from Spanish lawyers, government officials, tax advisers, property experts and on through a long list of professionals who keep up with the changes every year.

Experience is essential. And to complicate matters further, practice varies from one of Spain's 17 Autonomous Regions to another as the regions exercise some of their independent powers. Valencia inheritance tax is not the same as Andalusian tax, for example.

Frustration and confusion can arise in any country when you buy or sell a house or move to another town. You may get three different answers to your questions from three different Spanish authorities. Persist, and it will eventually get sorted out.

Changes that will affect you in 2018

Tax System Changed

Just when you finally get used to something, they go and change it. The long-time PADRE computer program for declaring income tax has disappeared, along with the "*Borrador*" or estimated tax, which formerly was sent to millions of taxpayers on their computers. The new "*Renta Web*" system replaces them. The Spanish word *renta* means income of any sort, so do not confuse it with rentals, as in Rentacar. The new system is more flexible than the previous one and can be accessed by smartphone, tablet, laptop or home computer.

2017 Tax Rates Unchanged

The government's plan to cut income tax rates is on hold because they have not been able to pass a new Budget for 2018, so the same rates from 2017 will continue to apply. Politicians in the Spanish Congress wrangled until the November deadline passed, so the same Budget continues.

Time Running Out To Reclaim Overpaid Inheritance Tax

As of January 1, 2019, European Union residents outside Spain will no longer be able to reclaim overpaid inheritance tax on Spanish property. An EU court decision forced Spain to treat EU residents the same as Spanish residents, starting January 1, 2015. This allowed thousands of EU residents to reclaim overpaid inheritance tax. This opportunity ends, however, January 1, 2019, because the Spanish statute of limitations runs for four years from January 1, 2015.

BIG NEWS: Andalusia Raises Exemption To One Million Euros

The big news for 2018 is that the Andalusian regional government has raised the family exemptions on inheritance tax to one million euros per inheritor for children and spouses. Non-resident owners and inheritors can benefit from this exemption if they are residents of the European Union. The Region of Murcia has also installed the one million exemption. Those inheritors who are not EU citizens will continue to pay inheritance tax at the much higher national rates, unless they are resident in Spain. The exemptions are in effect from January 1, 2018. This exemption replaces a former exemption on the first €250,000 of value for each individual family inheritor.

Plus Valia Tax Reclaims Continues

Plus Valia tax is a municipal tax charged whenever property changes hands, even by inheritance. It is based on a scale that depends on how long the property was owned. During the recession property sellers were charged *Plus Valia* tax when they had in fact made no profit on the sale. Finally Spain's high court ruled this practice illegal and thousands of property sellers continue to bring cases against the offending municipalities.

Brexit Brings Bad News

Nothing is certain yet but it looks as if Britons will be treated as non-EU citizens for tax purposes in Spain once they are out of the European Union. This means that they will pay inheritance tax at the higher non-resident rate. It also means they will pay both capital gains tax and tax on the income they make from renting out their Spanish property at 24 per cent instead of at the resident and EU rate of 19 per cent.

SECTION

1

Moving to Spain, Living in Spain

Moving to Spain

BREXIT WILL BRING EXTRA PROBLEMS

We are reasonably certain that the UK will continue to be a formal member of the European Union for this year, 2018, so Britons still come under the heading of "EU Citizens" if they move to Spain now. Also, keep in mind that thousands of non-EU citizens reside in Spain, holding short-term or long-term residence cards. These Americans, Moroccans or Chinese face more bureaucratic hurdles than EU citizens but their problems all can be solved, and the same will apply to Britons after their withdrawal from the European Union. In fact, Spain already imposes most of the same requirements on EU citizens as it does on non-EU applicants, as we shall see below. For pensioners, the medical insurance remains a sticking point, but if the UK is able to negotiate a bilateral agreement with Spain for each country to honour the other's Social Security medical care, this can be solved.

ALL EU CITIZENS FACE REQUIREMENTS

When Spain dropped residence cards for EU citizens in 2007, they also dropped all of the administrative requirements for European Union citizens to reside here officially. An EU applicant no longer needed to show proof of income or medical insurance to justify his residence in Spain. He simply presented his passport and the filled-up application form. His Certificate of Residence was issued immediately along with his NIE, the Spanish tax identification number.

New EU residents then were surprised and pleased by the simplicity of the operation. They no longer had to apply separately for NIE, or assemble documents and photos or have their fingerprint taken or wait for months until the card was issued. The only drawback, they discovered, was that they did not have a nice plastic card with a photo to present as identification when they paid by credit card in Spain.

Old Requirements Restored in 2012

Then Spain took what an EU citizen can only regard as a big step back. As of July 2012, an EU citizen who wishes to reside officially in Spain must show that he will not become a burden on the State.

If the applicant intends to work as an employee, he must present a work contract which includes the name and address of the employer, the tax number and Social Security number of the employer, along with his own registration with the Spanish Social Security.

If the applicant is self-employed, he must provide evidence. This would include registration in the *"Censo de Actividades Economicas"*, a list which assigns a code number to various activities. That is, a plumber has one code and a translator another code. He must also show his registration with Social Security as *"autonomo"* or self-employed, paying a little over €250 a month.

Those who are employed have their Spanish Social Security paid by their employer and those who are self-employed pay on their own so they both are covered for Spanish Social Security health care.

Those who do not intend to work must demonstrate that they have income of at least the Spanish minimum wage, which is just under €650 a month. A pensioner who can show this income will have no problem. However, each case will be examined individually and many other sources of income are also acceptable. This includes property, investments and other sources.

The second important requirement for non-workers is the access to public or private health insurance, equivalent to the coverage of Spain's Social Security health benefits. A pensioner from the European Union who is entitled to health care in his home country can use Form S-1 to transfer this to the Spanish system when he takes up residence, which meets the requirement. Persons who have retired early may need to contract a private medical insurance.

Those EU citizens who already hold the Certificate of Registration in Spain will now have to renew their Certificate after five years and comply with the new measures. (see below).

Why It Happened

We have called this a "step back" because an EU citizen must now carry out a series of bureaucratic procedures that were not necessary before. But let's look at it from Spain's point of view. When they eased the requirements, this drew a flood of immigrants from the new eastern European members of the EU, many of them without jobs or resources. It also allowed many other Europeans to enter the country and work off the books, not declaring their income, with relative impunity. Thousands of these immigrants wound up needing health care or social services at the expense of the Spanish taxpayer.

The European Union rules of free movement, which Spain applied in 2007, already contained the possibility for these requirements, which the individual countries could choose to apply or not. Spain chose the most liberal option, with no requirements. But it did not work out in practice.

Spain Requires Renewal After Five Years

Furthermore, the Spanish authorities have ruled that the Certificate of Registration for EU citizens must be renewed after five years. This means that EU citizens who already hold the Certificate must meet the new requirements.

When questioned by annoyed EU residents, the information service of the European Commission replied that the Certificate has no expiry date and does not need renewing.

Their answer goes on to say that, if the Spanish authorities are requiring EU citizens to renew their registration certificates, "This would appear to be incompatible with both the Directive and the Spanish transposition measure (RD 240/07)."

Here they are referring to European Union Directive 2004/38 which abolishes residence "permits" for EU citizens, and Spanish Royal Decree 240/2007, which transposes the Directive into Spanish law.

Confusion can arise for several reasons.

First, the law says that, after five years of continuous legal residence in Spain, an EU citizen can apply for "permanent" residence. This could lead you to believe that their original certificate expires. Not so. The EU answer says, "Applicants have the option of applying for the Permanent Residence Certificate, but they are not obliged to do so."

Then we have the web site of the Spanish National Police, the "Sede Electronico", which says that the Certificate expires after five

RESIDENT IN SPAIN MUST OBEY SPANISH RULES

If you wish to continue residing legally in Spain, you must follow the Spanish regulations, even if they are in conflict with EU rulings. So you should renew your Certificate after five years and meet the new requirements. You have the right to protest to the European Commission.

years. They cite Article 7 of RD 240/2007 as the legal justification for this. Unfortunately, nothing in Article 7 refers to the expiry of the Certificate.

But remember that Spaniards themselves must renew their National Identity Document every five years or ten years depending on their age. So why should foreign residents get a better deal?

S-1 FORM FOR PENSIONERS

EU pensioners can transfer their rights for health care and medicines to the Spanish Social Security medical system. This was formerly done by obtaining Form E-121 from the pensioner's home country for presentation to the Spanish Social Security system. Form E-121 and other European forms have now been replaced by the S-1 Form. These "E" for "European" forms are readily available in all EU countries. You must obtain it, however, in your home country before you come to Spain. In the UK, they are available from the post office.

OBTAIN EHIC FROM HOME COUNTRY

If you are an EU citizen simply visiting Spain, you should obtain the European Health Insurance Card before you leave your home country. The EHIC is valid for five years so you do not have to renew it each year just to go on holiday. This EHIC replaces the old E-111 form which entitles EU citizens to emergency health care in another EU country. Here is a further note for pensioners in particular. If you now live in Spain and receive your health care from the Spanish system, you will need an EHIC when you return to your home country should you need emergency treatment. You need the EHIC because you have gone off your home country's system.

Formerly, EU citizens resident in another EU country obtained their EHIC from the country of residence, where they received their health care. Now they must apply in their home country, where they originally qualified for health benefits. This means that a UK or French pensioner residing in Spain and receiving his medical care on the Spanish system must apply to the UK or to France for his EHIC.

EU WORKERS

An EU citizen intending to work or start a business in Spain can simply arrive in the country and begin his paperwork immediately.

EU citizens looking for work can apply for employment at the national employment service under exactly the same conditions as Spaniards. When they get a job, they will be required to pay into the Spanish Social Security system in return for medical care and an eventual pension.

Those intending to start a business will face a labyrinth of permits and licences, just as Spaniards themselves do, but it can all be overcome (see section on Working and Starting a Business for details.)

CONSULATES HAVE INFORMATION

Ask the Spanish consulate for a copy of the "C" leaflet, which explains many details about moving to Spain. The leaflet number varies from country to country but it is Leaflet C16 in the UK. This leaflet explains about importing your household goods, and gives information about driving licences, for example. It also lists requirements for obtaining the Visado de residencia, the residence visa, which is necessary for non-EU citizens intending to reside in Spain (see below).

Most consulates have a great deal of information available besides that contained in leaflet C16. The Spanish government produces many publications to inform visitors and investors. If you are interested in doing business in Spain, or travelling about, or in the arts, or in specific data on a certain region, be sure to ask if they have any pamphlets. They can often order them for you if they do not

SELL YOUR UK HOME BEFORE YOU MOVE

Here is a tip for Britons moving to Spain. If you wish to sell your principal residence in the UK, do so before you take out a residence Certificate in Spain. You may be free of UK capital gains tax on the sale, but if you then reside in Spain, the house is no longer your principal residence, making the sale subject to tax. Worse, it will also be subject to Spanish tax because you now reside in Spain. In addition, as a resident, you will be required to file Spanish Form 720 which lists your assets over €50,000 held outside Spain.

have them in stock.

You may also be surprised at the information available from your own government. They publish pamphlets on doing business in Spain, explaining import and export restrictions and currency controls, for example. They probably have data about what is produced and what is needed and current information about how money flows between Spain and your country.

Ask at your country's Foreign Ministry or Commerce Ministry about any subject that particularly interests you, whether it be teaching or onion farming. There is probably a government publication bearing on it.

NON-EUROPEAN UNION CITIZENS

First, go to the Spanish consulate in your home country. If you are from a non-EU country, you will need to obtain the *Visado de Residencia*, a visa you must present when you apply for a residence permit after you have arrived in Spain.

The visa can only be obtained from the Spanish consulate in your home country before you leave for Spain.

There are, in fact, seven different types of visa, depending on whether you are a retired pensioner, an investor, an executive of a multinational company, or carrying out a cultural or sporting activity. Make sure you request the right one for your circumstances.

Second, go to your bank and make sure they understand exactly how your money is to be sent to you. Make absolutely sure they know a corresponding bank in the area of Spain where you will live. Transfers of money can take weeks when not properly handled.

You will need to establish that the bank you choose in Spain has a working relationship with your bank at home and can readily receive funds from them. Transfers have been known to get stuck in a main office in Madrid and not reach their destination until weeks later.

Once you have a bank account in Spain, you can deposit your foreign cheques, or make direct transfers to receive your pension to make payments on your new property, or your rent, making money matters much easier.

Holding a Spanish bank account will also work in your favour when you apply for your visa at the consulate in your country. It is not, however, strictly necessary.

For non-EU persons, this application for the visa is your first legal step towards acquiring residency in Spain. It gives the Spanish authorities a chance to examine your financial situation before they decide whether you will make a useful resident. Once you have the visa, you are practically assured of obtaining the residence permit.

Information sheets issued by Spanish consulates in various countries will show how much income you need in order to get this visa.

If you have this income, you are all right. If you haven't, do not assume that you will be denied the visa. Many other details also come into the picture. You may have capital which is not at the moment producing income, for example, or your income may not start until some future date.

The consular officials will judge each case on its merits. But they do want to be sure that you have sufficient means to support yourself in Spain. If you intend to start a business, for example, you will need to show that you are bringing into Spain enough money to do so, unless you are from an EU country.

VISADO DE RESIDENCIA

When you are ready to apply for the visa, you will need to present a valid passport and evidence supporting your source of income. You may also be asked to show that you have made some arrangements for remitting this income to Spain.

You will also need a *Certificado penal*, a criminal record report, which shows you have no prison record. The Spanish consulate in your country can tell you exactly how to obtain it in your area. United States citizens will need two of these certificates, one from the state of last residence and the other from the FBI.

You then fill out the visa application form in duplicate. If you are a couple, each of you must sign the form. Make it clear that you intend to take up residency, as this affects your right to import your furniture into Spain free of duty (see section below on "Importing Your Possessions").

You will be asked to provide a reference in Spain and one in your home country. If you have bought or rented property in Spain, your seller would make an excellent reference. Or your new bank manager or lawyer in Spain. You will need two passport photos.

You must enter Spain and have your passport stamped within 60 days of the time the visa is issued to you. So it is best to gather all your information and the necessary documents in advance, but leave the final application until a month or so before your intended departure date.

The visa sometimes is issued quickly, but it's best to ask.

NOTE: If you are a non-EU citizen already established in Spain but still on tourist status, it is possible to apply for exemption from the visa requirement so that you do not have to return to your home country. However, authorities have cracked down on this exemption and it is almost impossible to obtain.

With the visa in hand, you can then apply for duty-free import of your furniture. Your removal company should be able to handle all the paperwork involved (see the next section).

IMPORTING YOUR POSSESSIONS

European Union citizens may skip this section, as duties on importation of household goods have disappeared with free circulation of goods within the EU. If they are moving to Spain, and bringing all their possessions, their moving company will know how to handle the forms required. For details on importing automobiles, EU citizens should see chapter on You and Your Car.

NEW RESIDENT FREE OF DUTY

When you come to Spain from outside the EU to take up residence, the Spanish government grants you the privilege of importing your household effects and personal possessions free of customs duty. This privilege is a one-time grant and is only available to those who take out an official residence permit.

You do not have to purchase property in order to justify this privilege, but you will have to show a residence permit, and you will have to make a prior deposit, which will be returned to you within a year.

For those who wish to import furniture for a second residence or holiday home, there is a second form of importation. For this *vivienda secundaria* exemption, you need not become a resident. You must make a deposit, however, just as the resident does. The non-resident must wait two years, however, for the return of his money.

In both cases, the deposit will be about 50 per cent of the estimated value of the goods.

The conditions are that you have not been a resident in Spain during the two years prior to the importation of the goods; that your goods enter the country within three months of your own arrival in Spain; that the goods are used, being at least six months old, and that you undertake not to sell them for two years.

Under this provision you can import, among other things, furniture, books, works of art, personal effects and collections, musical instruments, food and liquor, washing machines, electric or gas cookers, refrigerators, vacuum cleaners, floor polishers, radios and television sets.

The Spanish authorities remind you that the electric current in Spain is 220 volts and 50 cycles. This difference is especially important for Americans and Canadians, who will find their stereo sound equipment needs various adaptors to function properly and that their television sets will not function at all because the European system is different from the North American television system.

All the appropriate information is presented in Spanish leaflet C16, which you should request from the Spanish consulate in your home country at the beginning of your application to come to Spain to take up residency. See section "Before You Leave". (This is leaflet C21 for Americans and its number varies from country to country.)

At the consulate or through your removal company, you fill out a form requesting the Head of the Customs Office, *La Dirección General de Aduanas*, to allow your goods to enter Spain free of duty. You will need a complete list, in duplicate, of all your possessions. The list must be in Spanish. The consulate will legalise your application and list by stamping them, for a small fee.

You can obtain the forms by writing to the nearest consulate or you can collect them in person. Your removal company should include most of this paperwork in its services. Be sure to ask them.

REMOVAL COMPANIES

The selection of a removal company is extremely important. Some companies are familiar with the paperwork, have experienced agents at the borders and customs depots, and know how to keep your property from winding up in Barcelona in the customs shed for three months, which quite often happens when all the papers are not in order. Make enquiries among people who have moved to Spain until you find a company with satisfied clients.

There are a lot of things that can go wrong with international removals, so take your time in finding the right company. You must also present a photocopy of the first five pages of your passport, correctly legalised by the Spanish consulate, to your removal agents. They need to show this at the customs office at the Spanish border when they enter with your goods.

Make sure that your removal company guarantees delivery to your door in Spain. There have been cases where goods were held up in customs and a different removal company brought them from the Barcelona depot or a Spanish port, collecting more money for the distance travelled within Spain.

ONE-YEAR TIME LIMIT TO RECOVER DEPOSIT

From the time your goods enter Spain, you have one year to present a residence permit to the customs authorities and request the return of your deposit.

Be warned. If you wait more than 12 months from the time your furniture enters Spain, you will not be able to claim the return of your deposit. Some unwary foreigners have allowed the time limit to lapse and lost their deposits.

You might think that the professional customs agent employed by the removal company or by you personally to handle the deposit guaranty would inform you when this time limit was near, but you would be wrong in many cases. You yourself must be alert and must see your customs agent to make sure the procedures are correctly carried out, on time.

When you have your residence card in hand, you need to obtain a certificate from your local town hall that the furniture is still in your possession. They will send a policeman or an inspector to visit you. He will check the list against the furniture itself and sign the certificate. With this document and your residence permit — along with the receipt given you showing that this is your first application for a Spanish residence permit — you can claim the release of your deposit.

The deposit will have been made into a Spanish bank, which in turn will issue a certificate that is presented to the customs office. The certificate guarantees that the funds have been deposited in the Spanish bank for the purposes of the customs guarantee. When the customs office releases the deposit, you present that paper to the bank, which releases the funds back to you.

This deposit system also applies when a foreign non-resident purchases or rents property in Spain and wishes to import goods to furnish this property, even though the foreigner will not reside there full-time. You can do this, duty-free, by following the same procedure outlined above. This time, however, you have a time limit of two years.

At the end of the two years, you obtain the document from the town hall certifying that the goods are still in your possession, and the customs office will authorise the release of your deposit. This is called a *vivienda secundaria* plan, for a second home.

One condition for obtaining this exemption is that you must not let the property to others. It must be for your own personal and exclusive use.

Bride's trousseau exempt: A foreign woman who marries either a Spaniard or a foreigner officially resident in Spain may bring into Spain free of duty her wedding gifts and trousseau. This is not a genuine regulation, but a courtesy granted by the Customs Office upon special application. It is only granted in cases where reciprocal treatment is given to a Spanish woman who marries a citizen of another country.

IMPORTING YOUR PET

What about Rover? Yes, of course, you can take your faithful pet to Spain with you, but it's a bit complicated. You want to obtain the standard European Union form for a Pet Passport, whether you are coming from the EU or not.

In order to obtain this passport, you need a health certificate for your pet issued by a veterinary authorised by the appropriate ministry in your country. This certificate must be issued not more than 15 days before you enter Spain with the pet.

In addition you will need a certificate of vaccination against rabies, also issued by an authorised veterinarian. Animals less than two months old do not require this. Animals between two and three months of age must have been vaccinated not less than one month before they are imported. Animals of three months or older must have been vaccinated not less than one month and not more than 12 months before being imported. If the animal has no anti-rabies certificate, it may be quarantined for 20 days.

Finally, you will need a certificate declaring that the area in which the animal was normally kept is free from animal diseases. This certificate usually comes from your agriculture ministry.

All these certificates must be stamped and legalised by the Spanish consulate, for which they charge a small fee, and you will have your authorised pet passport.

Once you have arrived in Spain, you will want to have your pet fitted with a new microchip which gives your address in Spain. UK pet owners can now take their dogs back with them when they return home. They must start the procedures in Spain at least a month before their trip, however, in order to obtain the required certificates.

"DANGEROUS DOGS" LAW IN EFFECT

But wait. If your pet is on Spain's "potentially dangerous dog" list, you will face a series of requirements after you arrive. These requirements are the same ones that Spanish animal owners must meet, so do not feel that you are being made to suffer for being a foreigner.

Our first problem here is that the "potentially dangerous" list is not the same in all of Spain's individual regions and can differ even from one town to another. When you arrive with your dog, you must enquire at the Town Hall where you live, to find out the exact local requirements which will permit you to own and walk your dog legally. Registration of the animal will be required, along with a special insurance policy.

We can, however, take a look at what is common to almost all of the local and Regional regulations. First, we have the Spanish national law Ley 50/1999 that applies throughout the country. Then we have the Valencian Regional law and the Andalusian Regional Law, passed in early 2008. Even though the national law dates from 1999, it was modified in 2002 and 2007, and none of the regulations have been strictly applied until recently. You are likely to find many veterinarians and other officials confused about the requirements. So we repeat our advice above. Go to your *Ayuntamiento* and ask about the local requirements.

You can be quite sure that a Doberman, a German Shepherd, a Rottweiller, a Pit Bull and similar dogs will be on any list. The list also includes crossbreeds of the "potentially dangerous" dogs. Most of the lists also specify measurements of jaws and musculature, making some breeds dangerous simply because of their size.

You will need to obtain a Spanish *Certificado Penales,* which shows that you do not have a prison record and you will need to take a simple exam at an authorized medical centre, rather like the driving medical test, to show that you are in a condition to control the animal.

If someone tries to tell you that nobody is paying attention to the law yet, because it is too new, be advised that in many municipalities the registration and licencing system has been functioning for several years. The fines for failure to comply can run into thousands of euros.

The national law specifies an insurance covering damages up to €120,000 while the Andalusian law requires €175,000. Both of the laws allow only one month after the arrival in Spain or the acquisition of the animal to register for the municipal licence.

CARS, CARAVANS AND BOATS

For information on importing cars, caravans and boats, see the section on "You and Your Car".

GLOSSARY

Agente de Aduana – licensed customs agent
Certificado de Registro – New form of residence document
Dirección General de Aduanas – General Customs Directorate
Certificado penal – certificate of criminal record
EHIC – European Health Insurance Card
Visado de residencia – special visa obtained from Spanish consulate for persons taking up residency.
Vivienda secundaria – second home, holiday home

Resident or Tourist?

If you live more or less full-time in Spain, you should hold the Certificate of Registration if you are an EU citizen or an official residence permit if you are not. The law specifies that a person who has been present in Spain for six months must either leave the country or apply for a residence document.

The disadvantages of being an official resident are largely imaginary, and it is becoming more and more difficult to remain on tourist status when you are really a resident.

Furthermore, some real tax savings are available for residents who sell property or who bequeath Spanish property on their deaths (see final section below on Resident Tax Savings).

Let's take a look at both possibilities.

YOU AS A TOURIST

First of all, what is a tourist? When you visit Spain for a short holiday, you are a tourist. If you have a holiday home or a second home in Spain where you spend months at a time, you are still a tourist of sorts, as your principal residence is in another country

If your principal residence is in Spain and you spend most of your time here, you can still have — technically — tourist status if you do not take out a residence permit. But the Spanish authorities are growing stricter about allowing people to retain "tourist status" when they really live full-time in Spain.

> **The concrete definition is this: a tourist is a person who spends less than six months in Spain in one calendar year.**

The "tourist" stay in Spain for EU and non-EU citizens alike is limited to 90 days. To stay another 90 days, you are required to obtain a *permanencia,* which is an extension that is stamped in your passport (see below).

Anyone who stays more than six months must apply for a residence permit.

PERMANENCIA

It is possible to get a 90-day extension, called a *permanencia*. However, you are entitled to only one permanencia in a calendar year so — even with this extension — you have a total of six months.

The word *permanencia* means a temporary stay, not a permanent one, as you may think when comparing it to the English word. In fact, the verb permanecer in Spanish means "to stay" or "to remain", not "to be permanent".

You apply for this *permanencia*, which is stamped in your passport, by going to the foreign department of your local police station, or comisaría. You need your passport, a couple of photos, and some evidence of your ability to finance your continued stay in Spain.

One *comisaría* requires that you have €1,800 in a Spanish bank to grant the 90-day extension. Ask locally, as practice varies. With these papers in hand, the *permanencia* is routinely granted, and you can stay another 90 days as a tourist.

BENEFITS OF TOURIST STATUS

With Spain's entry into the European Union, most advantages of remaining on tourist status have disappeared. Formerly, only a non-resident could hold bank accounts in freely convertible pesetas or other currencies. With the introduction of the euro, currency exchange restrictions no longer exist, for Spaniards or residents.

Formerly, only a non-resident could own an automobile on tax-free tourist plates. Now, as European Union citizens, no EU person can do this, as he is not a "tourist" in the EU. Non-EU citizens, however, continue to enjoy the right to the tourist registration, without paying Spanish taxes.

So there aren't really many advantages to remaining on tourist status when in truth you are a resident.

People sometimes think that a person on tourist status does not become liable for Spanish income tax. It is simply not true. A person who lives in Spain more than 183 days in one calendar year — whether or not he holds a residence permit — becomes legally liable to pay Spanish income tax. A non resident is also liable for Spanish tax on any income arising in Spain, such as income from renting his flat to holidaymakers.

In many cases, European Union citizens with Spanish residence can continue to use their EU national driving licences until they expire. (see chapter On the Road in Spain for details).

YOU AS A RESIDENT

On balance, if you really reside in Spain, it seems wiser to take out a formal residence permit. If you are an EU citizen, we should not call it a "permit". As of 2007, it is a simple one-sheet Certificate of Registration which only needs to be renewed every five years.

For non-EU citizens it is a different story. Perhaps we should call it the same old story. They need residence permits and work permits, and they face other complications as well.

TAX ADVANTAGES FOR RESIDENTS

Foreigners often think that taking out an official residence permit in Spain will cost them money and expose them to Spanish taxes which non-residents can avoid.

The truth is often the reverse. The resident property owner has a number of tax advantages over the non-resident.

1. If you are a resident and more than 65 years of age, and you have lived in your home for three years, and you pay income tax in Spain, you will not be subject to Spanish capital gains tax when you sell it, no matter how great your profit.

2. If you are a resident and you sell your property, you are not subject to having 3 per cent of the total purchase price withheld and deposited with Spain's Tax Agency as a guarantee against your tax liabilities. Also, you do not pay your capital gains tax until the following year. A non-resident must declare in 30 days.

3. If you are a Spanish tax resident and you bequeath your home to a spouse or child who is also a resident, you can probably avoid Spanish inheritance tax on 95 per cent of the valuation up to €120,000. The conditions are that you have owned and lived in your home for a minimum of three years. The inheritor must be a resident and must undertake not to sell the property for 10 years. Top limit for the 95 per cent reduction is €120,000. Over that, you must pay.

Non-residents pay from the first euro of valuation. (See chapter on Spanish inheritance tax for details)

4. Spanish property owner's imputed income tax does not apply to the owner's principal residence. If a husband and wife jointly own a property worth €120,000 and they are non-resident, they will pay a non-resident property-owner's income tax of about €600 each year. The resident is exempt from this tax on his principal residence. (see section on Taxes for more details).

5. If you really live most of the year in Spain, you are violating the law if you do not obtain a residence card. The law says that your tourist stay, even as a European Union citizen, is limited to 180 days per year. You can be fined €300 if you over-stay this limit.

FORM 720 – A NEW DISADVANTAGE

However, there is one new disadvantage of holding Spanish residence. Since 2013 a resident is required to declare his assets held anywhere in the world to the Spanish Tax Agency on Form 720. It comes in three parts: bank deposits, real estate, and shares and stocks. If your assets in any one of these categories are worth more than €50,000, you must declare them, wherever they are located. See section on You and Your Money for full details.

EU CITIZENS GET CERTIFICATE OF REGISTRATION

In April, 2007, Spain ended the need for EU citizens to obtain a residence card. EU citizens now are issued a sheet of paper called a *Certificado de Inscripción en el Registro Central de Extranjeros*, a Certificate of Registration. The sheet also contains the EU citizen's NIE, his *Numero de Identificación de Extranjero*, which identifies him to the Spanish tax authorities. It is almost impossible to carry out any official or banking transaction without this number. All computer programs are designed for it. For Spaniards, it is the NIF, and it is the same as the number on their national identity document.

In some areas the Certificate is issued as a plastic card.

PROOF OF INCOME AND HEALTH CARE

As of 2012, European Union applicants are required to provide proof of income and access to health care. If you are an EU pensioner with a reasonable income, and the right to transfer your home country health care to Spain, you have no problem. Take your pension documents and your S1 form with you. (See First Chapter on Moving to Spain for details).

If you have found work, you will have a contract and registration with the Spanish Social Security. If you intend to set up your own business, you will have other papers to present. (See Chapter on Working and Starting a Business for details.)

Once you have assembled your documentation and the application form, EX18, along with your passport and one photocopy, you discover that there is one thing that has not changed. You must get Form 790, which is only available at the police station, and take it to the nearest bank. At the bank you pay €10, the bank stamps the form, and you take it back to the police station. This irritating form 790 is the only way to pay the official charge. You can obtain the form in advance, with no waiting on line, and have it ready when you come to get your Certificate of Registration. Or a friend can pick it up for you.

At most police stations, there is a telephone number to call to make an appointment. You call, make your appointment, and show up at the right time. You will probably have to wait a few weeks for your appointment.

You can download the application form EX18 from the Ministry of the Interior web site at www.mir.es.

Who is entitled to a certificate?

Only citizens of the European Union are entitled to the Certificate of Registration. This includes citizens of the European Economic Area and Switzerland. All others must apply for cards as before. This includes non-EU family members of an EU citizen.

These family members are: Spouses, of the same or opposite sex. Spain, Belgium and the Low Countries permit same-sex marriage. Children of the EU citizen and children of the spouse.

Parents and grandparents of the EU citizen and of the spouse.

It applies to couples who are not married but are registered in a State registry of couples. Spain has no such registry nationally but Germany, France, the UK, Denmark, Finland and Sweden have them.

These family members are entitled to residence, but they must apply for a card as before.

NON-EU CITIZEN

If you are a non-EU citizen, you face a number of hurdles when you apply for Spanish residence. Now you will need that *Visado de residencia* which you obtained from the Spanish consulate in your home country before you came to Spain to settle. Obtaining the visa gave the Spanish authorities a chance to check you out, along with your financial means, even before you arrived.

In addition, you will need:

1. Proof of financial means. European citizens can be accepted to live in Spain without working on minimum financial means but non-EU persons will be required to show higher incomes.

2. *Certificado de Antecedentes Penales* (Certificate of Criminal Record). This certificate shows that you have no criminal record. You can request this from your local police authorities. Ask the consulate in your home country for the proper form.

3. Medical certificate.

4. Consular inscription. This a letter from your own nation's consulate in Spain showing that you are registered with them.

5. Medical Insurance. Your private medical coverage must be contracted with a company which has an office in Spain.

6. Passport and photocopy.

7. Marriage certificate and official translation.

8. Three passport-size photos.

9. Payment of fee in differing amounts, depending on your country of origin. The fee is not high.

10. Statement from your Spanish bank showing that your income is

BUY A HOUSE, GET RESIDENCE

As of 2013, a person from outside the EU can also obtain a residence permit in Spain by purchasing real estate worth half a million euros. If a husband buys a house, his wife and children may share in the permit. The permit will be good for two years, renewable as long as the investment is maintained. The house purchase comes as part of a law to encourage various types of investment. The purchase of two million euros worth of Spanish State Bonds or an investment of one million euros in a Spanish company will also entitle the investor to a permit. Other countries, such as Portugal and the United States, have already put similar measures into place.

arriving from abroad and being deposited in Spain.

11. Title deeds to Spanish property or a rental contract, with photocopy.

12. Birth certificates of children under 18 if they are included in the residence application. Translations.

13. The filled-up form requesting the residence permit.

BE ADVISED: To pay the small administrative fee, you must first obtain Form 790, then take it to the bank and make the payment. All European Union citizens pay the same €10. Other nationalities pay differing amounts. The bank returns to you the form stamped as paid. If you can obtain the form from your police station beforehand and pay it in advance, you will save yourself waiting time. If you can't, ask for the form as soon as you arrive, take it to the bank, and then join the queue.
Try to find out in advance just what you will have to present. We try to keep this book up to date, but some offices may want four photos instead of three, for example. Well-organised offices will actually give you a list when you make your first enquiry.

If you are not an EU citizen and are requesting the unified work permit / residence permit, you will have a number of other documents to present, relating to your employer in Spain, or the money you are bringing in to start a business, if that is the case. See the section on "Working and Starting A Business" for more details.

TAX IDENTIFICATION NUMBER (NIE)

Your residence permit will include your *Número de Identificación de Extranjero* (NIE), which identifies you to the Spanish tax authorities. The number is necessary for practically any transaction in Spain, such as paying your taxes. Even a non-resident who has any relation with the Spanish tax system, either by owning property or by drawing interest from a bank, also needs this NIE.

All this sounds complicated but if you speak just a little Spanish and want to have some direct contact with official procedures in your new country, you can handle your request for a residencia yourself. Assembling the necessary documents and dealing with the different people and offices involved is an education in Spanish ways of doing things.

You can also use the services of a *gestoría* to lead you through the process. The *gestor* is licensed by the government as an official middleman between you and the state and provides, for a reasonable fee, many useful services. It is his business to know which little window to go to at what time, and a good one can save you much time and trouble. This Spanish institution is more fully described in the section on "You and Your Legal Advisers".

EU CITIZENS CAN VOTE

Finally, if you are an EU citizen, you will be able to vote in Spain's municipal elections even if you are non-resident. Not only can you vote, you can be elected to office. If this prospect appeals to you, be sure to present yourself at your town hall immediately to be registered in the *padrón*, the list of municipal inhabitants, which is the basis of the voter list. Obtain a *Certificado de Empadronamiento* proving that you have registered. (See section on voting in You and the Spanish Authorities)

Some months before the elections check to make sure that you appear on the voting list, or you will not be permitted to cast your ballot. Perhaps the Popular Party (equivalent of the Conservatives) or the Socialist Party will ask you to stand for office.

GLOSSARY

Autorización de Residencia – residence permit
Certificado de Antecedentes Penales – certificate of criminal record
Certificado de Empadronamiento – certificate of registration in municipality.
Certificado de Registro – new EU residence document
Formulario – form
Gestoría – professional administrative agency
Número de Identificación de Extranjero (NIE) – tax identification number
Padrón – registry of inhabitants in municipality
Permanencia – 90-day extension of tourist visit

Birth, Death, Marriage and Nationality

As all nations do, Spain requires that births, marriages, divorces and deaths be officially registered.

A baby born in Spain needs a Spanish birth certificate, regardless of the nationality of its parents. If the parents are not Spanish, they should also register the birth at their own country's consulate.

A death must also be registered, both in Spain and with the consulate of the country of the deceased.

A civil marriage between foreigners can be celebrated in Spain and will be recognised in other countries as valid. One of the partners must be an official resident of Spain.

Married foreigners can be divorced in Spain, regardless of where they were married, as long as one of the parties is resident, and the divorce will be recognised in other countries.

Let's take a look at each of these events and the necessary formalities in Spain.

BIRTH IN SPAIN

By law, all births in Spain must be reported and registered. Even if you unexpectedly have your baby while you are on holiday in Spain, the birth must be reported here.

This is done at the *Registro Civil*, the civil registry, of the town where the birth takes place. The attending physician or other official of the hospital certifies the birth, though a registered midwife may also do this if the birth takes place at home with only the midwife in attendance.

The report must be made within eight days and include the hour, date and place of birth, the child's first and last names, the full names of both parents, and the doctor's certificate. This information will go on file at the civil registry.

The parents can then request for their own records one of two forms of the birth certificate. One is called the *Extracto de Inscripción de Nacimiento*, which gives the birth date and inscription number and the names of child and parents. This abbreviated "extract" form is sufficient for most legal purposes.

You can also get a *Certificación Literal*, which is more complete and contains all of the items in the declaration, such as the exact place

CHILD BORN IN SPAIN HAS TWO LAST NAMES

When you register the birth of your child, you will come in contact with the peculiarly Spanish practice of using two last names. If you are John Smith and your wife's maiden name was Betty Jones, your son will be registered in Spain as James Smith Jones. The Spanish rule is that the last name of the father comes first, followed by the last name of the mother. A child may choose to use his mother's last name first when he comes of legal age.

and hour, the attending physician, and so on. This one will cost you a little more, but neither of the forms is expensive.

Armed with this certificate of birth in Spain, you can then go to the consulate of your home country in Spain and report the birth. Some countries, such as Great Britain, require the literal certificate before they will issue a birth certificate of their own country. You may also need your passport, your own parents' birth certificates and your marriage certificate. Procedure and necessary documents vary somewhat depending on your country of origin. Your consulate will then issue a certificate of the birth of a citizen abroad.

NATIONALITY OF CHILD BORN IN SPAIN

A child born to foreign parents in Spain does not automatically acquire Spanish nationality.

If both parents are foreigners, the child will be a foreigner even if the parents are residents.

However, if the child should, between its 18th and 19th birthdays, choose to apply for Spanish nationality, it will certainly be granted, particularly if the child has been living in Spain during most of that time.

If either of the child's parents is Spanish, a child born in Spain is automatically entitled to Spanish nationality.

A child born in Spain out of wedlock, where the paternity is not disclosed, is also entitled to Spanish nationality, regardless of the nationality of the mother.

The laws about nationality vary from country to country and can be quite complicated in their attempts to cover the various possible combinations, such as a citizen-and-foreign wife or citizen-and-foreign husband, or a father born in that country who has since taken another nationality.

Make enquiries at your own consulate. Sometimes a country requires that a child of its own nationals who is born abroad must return to his parents' country for a certain time period in order to justify his nationality, for example.

DEATH IN SPAIN

If you are resident in Spain and have no plans to return to your home country near the end of your life, you should take these steps:

1. Make your Spanish will with your lawyer.

2. Select a cemetery where you wish to be buried.

3. Make contact with a Spanish funeral director.

4. Share your arrangements with your partner and family members.

5. Perhaps take out Spanish burial insurance if you are not already covered.

Procedures in Spain are just about the same as in your home country, but it helps to be familiar with them.

If the death occurs in a hospital, a doctor on the staff will prepare and sign the death certificate, which must be officially issued by a Spanish judge. If death occurs at home, the attending physician can prepare the certificate.

THE FUNERAL DIRECTOR

The funeral director is probably the first person you'll want to contact if you are in charge of arrangements for a death.

Funeral directors in Spain, just as in other countries, are aware that family members are distraught when a loved one has died. So they aim to provide full service, including all the necessary paperwork, and you may need to make only one telephone call to set the process in motion.

Funeral directors in areas with many foreign residents usually have at least one English-speaking staff member. When they receive a call, they respond quickly.

If no doctor has officially pronounced the person dead, they will locate a doctor to do so and they will inform both the Spanish judge who officially issues the death certificate and the consulate of the person's nationality, as the consulate must issue a death certificate for that country.

You need both these death certificates for any insurance forms and for executing the will of the deceased. The funeral director takes the passport data of the deceased and of the person who is responsible for the body in order to prepare his own reports. He sees that the necessary official certificates are delivered to the family.

If necessary, the funeral director can then take the body to the nearest cold-storage vault. Such vaults exist in most larger towns in Spain.

Cemeteries are usually owned by the towns where they are located and a foreigner can be buried in most of them, whether or not he is Catholic.

Perhaps we shouldn't say "buried" as most cemeteries in Spain are, in fact, above ground, and the bodies are placed in niches. At a burial, the casket is eased into the niche and a pair of masons brick it in.

MAKE A "LIVING WILL"

The idea of the "living will" or *Testamento Vital* in Spanish is gaining popularity. In the province of Málaga, for example, more than 5,000 people have filed this document with the Health Department. You can specify officially just what treatment you want if you are thrown by illness or an accident into a situation where your life is no longer worth living. In Andalusia you can download the official forms from www.jundadeandalucia.es/servicioandaluzdesalud. But you will have to phone 902 505060 to make an appointment to sign and file the form in person at the health service. Other regions have their own versions of the "living will".

You will probably find that you need to be registered as an inhabitant of your municipality in order to be buried in the local cemetery. This is another reason to obtain that *Certificado de Empadronamiento*, or municipal registration, which we have mentioned before.

This does not represent any discrimination against foreigners. A Spaniard may not usually be buried in the municipal cemetery if he is not registered, either.

If your new home-town cemetery doesn't suit you, there are others available. In Málaga, for example, there is an English Cemetery and in Benalmádena there is an International Cemetery. These have the sort of burial plots to which northern Europeans are more accustomed. Funeral directors can make arrangements for the cemetery plot or niche. They can also contact a British, Danish, Swedish or German pastor, as appropriate, to perform the burial service.

If the body is to be returned to the deceased's home country, funeral directors can make the arrangements for the air transport as well as the embalming. Embalming is not a standard practice in Spain, but it can be done. The Spanish funeral director will see to the body's transport to the airport in the home country, after which you will have to make other arrangements to have the body picked up. A few funeral directors have corresponding agents in other countries who will see to it that the body is delivered to any town in that country.

CREMATION IS AVAILABLE

If your preference is cremation, you will find crematoriums available in many areas of Spain. Cremation — *incineración* — was almost unknown a few years ago but is now quite common. One peculiarity of the cremation procedure is that family members are not allowed to attend the cremation itself. They may hold a religious service before the cremation, with the body present, or after it, with the urn.

Cremation itself costs only around €500 as a minimum, but it does not really save anything on the total price of funeral services (see below).

For those who choose to donate their bodies to medical science, any medical school in Spain will be very pleased to make the arrangements in advance. Simply telephone the medical school and declare your intentions. You can either visit them to fill out the forms or they will send a representative to you. They will arrange with your funeral director for collection of the body. Their only conditions are that the body be available within 24 hours of death and that the death was not caused by an infectious disease or an accident which requires autopsy.

FACT: In the province of Málaga more than half of all bodies, Spanish and foreigners, are cremated.

The usual custom in Spain, where it's hot and bodies are seldom embalmed, is to bury the day after death. This is custom, not law. The law says only that a body may not be interred sooner than 24 hours after the death has occurred.

Where there is no cold storage, it must be buried within 72 hours. Where there is cold storage available, this limit does not apply.

FUNERAL COSTS

What will all this funeral service cost you? A basic rate would be around €3,000, but this can rise quickly when transport costs, embalming fees, cold storage and cemetery fees are added in. The absolute minimum charge including only cremation and delivery of the urn, plus paperwork, will be around €2,000.

You should know that most Spanish cemeteries usually let their niches for varying time periods. The municipal cemetery rates are quite inexpensive, but it isn't the same as purchasing the plot forever.

One Málaga cemetery quoted rates of 300 euros for the first five years, dropping to about half that rate thereafter, around 30 euros per year, or 1,500 euros for 50 years. If the rent is not paid, after a time the body is removed to a common grave-site within the consecrated cemetery grounds.

If you wish to purchase a plot, it can cost more than 3,000 euros for a double plot, for example, at the Benalmádena International Cemetery on the Costa del Sol. You can ask at your own town hall for prices *en perpetuidad*.

If you wish to repatriate a body to the deceased's home country, you will find that prices for air transport of bodies are high. They go as freight and are charged by the kilo. Air transport costs within Europe can range from 1,000 to 2,500 euros. Prolonged storage will also add to your costs. Embalming costs around 1,500 euros.

It pays to plan ahead. Check now with a Spanish funeral director for his rates and services. If the first price quoted you seems high, don't hesitate to visit another funeral director and compare rates.

Burial insurance is also available in Spain.

MARRIAGE IN SPAIN

It is perfectly possible to be married in Spain — people do it every day. But remember that one of the parties must be a resident.

There is quite a lot of paperwork, however. Some evidence must be provided that the two parties are single, such as a certificate from the civil registry of your home country. Birth certificates are required.

A widow or widower will have to present both the original marriage certificate and a death certificate for the deceased spouse. A divorced person will need to present evidence of a valid divorce.

All of these documents must be officially translated into Spanish and accompanied by the Certificate of Apostille, which verifies them. This internationally recognised certificate is issued by different authorities in different countries, so you will have to ask.

The marriage is held at the Spanish Civil Registry office, with the local judge presiding, although town mayors and deputised municipal councillors are also authorised to perform civil wedding ceremonies. It has become rather trendy, in fact, for couples to be married in places like Marbella, where the town hall has arranged a special and attractive wedding site in a municipal park.

If you are interested in being married in Spain and are not resident, be warned that you will have to come in person to present and sign all the forms and it will take about 30 days before these are processed and you can be married. And remember that one of the parties must be a resident. To avoid these formalities, non-residents often get married in their own countries then simply have the union

WIFE DOES NOT TAKE HUSBAND'S NAME

When a woman marries in Spain, she does not take her husband's last name. Mary Smith remains Mary Smith when she marries Robert Jones. And their children take the two last names of their parents, with the father's name coming first. So a son, for example, would be Christopher Jones Smith.

blessed at a ceremony in Spain.

Roman Catholics, even though not Spanish, may also be married in church, following the practice outlined above for civil marriage along with the usual practice of the Roman Catholic church. Each partner will present a baptismal certificate and a declaration from their former parish priest that they adhere to the Roman Catholic faith and they are free to marry. After the ceremony, the priest gives the couple a certificate of marriage, which makes them man and wife, but they must still present this certificate at the Civil Registry to get an official marriage certificate.

If you marry a Spaniard, you receive a *Libro de Familia*, the "Family Book", which is a very important document in Spanish life. It is the official registration of husband and wife and their children. Spaniards present it: when they come of age and get their own identity cards; for identification to the Social Security officials; when they marry; and when they die.

If you marry a Spanish subject, you do not automatically become Spanish. A husband or wife will have to apply for Spanish nationality, which should be routinely granted, but does not come automatically.

MARRYING IN GIBRALTAR

Gibraltar is a less complicated alternative for wedding-bound couples of most nationalities.

Forms are available at consulates in Spain, or in your home country on which the parties to the marriage enter their personal details and apply for a special marriage licence from the Governor of Gibraltar. Again, the divorced or widowed will need to produce the appropriate certificates.

When the licence is granted, the couple may go to Gibraltar and be married in the registry office there. They will need two witnesses.

GAY MARRIAGE LEGALISED IN 2005

In 2005 Spain joined the few countries in the world to legalise same-sex marriages under the same terms as marriage between a man and a woman. Hundreds of couples have already been wed.

Thousands of other couples, gay and straight, have chosen to register their union in special registries created in various municipalities and autonomous regions. These registries record a *pareja de hecho*, partners, of the same sex or opposite sex, living together as families.

Registration in this list confers no legal rights, however. Same sex pairs have the same inheritance problem as unmarried parents (see below). They can leave their property to their partners but the inheriting partner will be subject to Spanish inheritance tax at double the percentage that an immediate family member pays.

In some autonomous regions, such as Andalusia, an exception is made.

COMMON LAW COUPLES

There is no "common law" marriage in Spain. That is, a couple may live together for many years as man and wife and have children together, but this establishes no legal rights for either the man or the woman.

If the man dies, the woman has no claim to inherit any share of his property or to collect his pension. In the eyes of the law, there is no legal relationship.

Unless the man has formally recognised the children as his own, he is not required to bequeath his property to them.

The law regards these children as offspring of a single mother. Their births must be registered as such and they take their mother's two last names because she is their only legal parent.

If the unmarried father of the children chooses to leave parts of his estate to his unrecognised children, they will not have the right to apply the lower inheritance tax rate enjoyed by children of married parents, except in some autonomous regions, such as Andalusia.

If, however, the father chooses to recognise his children, which is by far the most usual case, then he becomes responsible for their maintenance. If the unmarried couple separate, a court will normally award custody of the minor children to the mother and will order the father to pay towards the cost of their maintenance.

DIVORCE IN SPAIN

Through the Franco years there was no divorce in Spain. This was out of deference to the regime's special relationship with the Roman Catholic Church.

In 1981, however, the first divorce law went into effect and it is now possible to obtain a divorce in Spain on various grounds. The law has since been amended and modernised several times. The latest version, enacted in 2005, has made divorce by mutual consent speedier and easier.

Even foreigners who have been married in other countries can, if they are now residents in Spain, obtain a divorce here which will be recognised in their home country. In fact, only one of the parties need be resident in Spain.

If a man's wife leaves him and returns to her home in Belgium, say, he can, after a time, petition in Spain for a divorce. The couple must have been married for one full year before a petition for divorce will be heard, which seems reasonable enough.

The simplest sort of procedure is for the couple to request by mutual consent — or for one of the pair to request with the formal consent of the other — a legal separation. The separation document must be formalised before a Spanish *Notario*. The couple will need a lawyer.

Under the previous law they then had to wait one year in the state of legal separation. Under the 2005 revised law, procedures can be completed within three months.

At the time of requesting this legal separation, the couple will be required to settle their financial arrangements about who gets what share of their property, any child support or maintenance payments, visiting rights of children, and so on. At the end of the separation, there is a brief hearing, and if nothing has changed, the final divorce will be processed.

The 2005 revised law also offers the easiest and quickest divorce of all. The couple, by mutual consent, can settle their arrangements and proceed immediately to a full divorce with no period of legal separation required. This is popularly called *divorcio exprés*.

In addition to this "no-fault" sort of procedure, the standard grounds for divorce familiar to most Europeans also apply. They include adultery, desertion, cruelty, alcohol or drug addiction and mental problems.

You will want to consult a Spanish lawyer when seeking divorce on these grounds. If your income is modest, you may be entitled to free legal assistance, which you can find out by inquiring at your area's *Colegio de Abogados*, the law society (see chapter on Your Legal Advisers for more details).

NATIONALITY

If you move to Spain, install yourself here, take out a Spanish residence permit, pay taxes in Spain, raise your children here and do business here, that does not make you or your children Spanish. You remain a Norwegian, American or Briton, unless you choose to formally renounce your nationality in order to take another.

At this point complications arise. Some countries permit dual nationality, and do not mind if one of their citizens takes on another nationality in addition to the one he was born with.

A British citizen, for example, can take another nationality without renouncing his British citizenship. The United States of America formerly did not permit dual nationality but has now changed. If one of its citizens takes Spanish nationality, this is no longer grounds for loss of his United States citizenship.

An American woman who marries a Spaniard does not lose her American citizenship, nor does she automatically become Spanish. It is also possible for a child born in Spain of a Spanish father and

American mother to have Spanish nationality through his father and place of birth and American nationality through his mother.

Until he reaches the age of 18, that is. Then he must make a choice. Spanish law does not recognise dual nationality for adults, so the child must then either renounce his American nationality, making a declaration to the authorities, or he will lose his Spanish nationality.

But if Spain does not recognise dual nationality, what about the British citizens who take Spanish nationality, but still are regarded as British in the UK? Well, Spain does not regard them as even the slightest bit British. They are now Spanish, all Spanish and only Spanish. If the UK chooses to regard them as British, that is no business of Spain's.

Marriage is another tricky area. In general, marriage to a foreigner does not automatically change the nationality of the partner. So a British woman who marries a Spaniard remains British unless she applies for Spanish nationality, which she can do immediately after the marriage and which will routinely be granted. A British man who marries a Spanish woman, however, will have to wait out a two-year residence requirement before he can apply.

Each nation has somewhat different rules regarding the retention and loss of nationality. Where marriage partners of two different nationalities are involved, perhaps living for long periods in yet a third country, it is best to make careful enquiries at your own consulate. When there are children, it can be even more complex, so it is best to get good advice.

The basic requirement for applying for Spanish nationality is a residence period in Spain of 10 years, even if you are a European Union citizen. This varies for South Americans, for example, who need not wait so long, and in the case of marriage. A number of Europeans who have settled here have taken out Spanish nationality, although members of fellow European Union nations have practically the same rights as Spaniards, and can now even vote in municipal elections.

If you decide to apply for Spanish citizenship, you will need your own birth certificate, your parents' birth certificates and marriage certificate, all translated into Spanish by official translators and authenticated by your own consulate.

You will need to show, by means of previous residence permits, that you have held a *residencia* for 10 years. The process will take up to a year before everything is cleared, and you will do well to have a skilled *gestor* or *abogado* handle your application, as they know the ins and outs of the paperwork.

Finally, you will be required to renounce your former nationality and you will swear an oath of allegiance to the Spanish Crown.

Then you will be Spanish, a citizen of a proud nation which once ruled vast portions of the globe and is today the world's ninth largest industrial power.

Your last will and testament must provide for your family according to Spanish law.

GLOSSARY

Apellido – last name
Certificate of Apostille - internationally recognised form by which the authorities of one country validate a document to another country.
Divorcio - divorce
Incineración – cremation
Inscripción de Nacimiento – birth certificate, comes in two versions, a short form called an *extracto* and a complete form called *literal.*
Libro de Familia – "Family Book" in which the names of husband, wife and children are inscribed.
Nombre – first name
Matrimonio - marriage
Pareja de hecho – unmarried partners living together as family.
Registro Civil – Spanish Civil Registry, where births, deaths and marriages are officially recorded.
Testamento Vital – Living will

Working and Starting a Business

EU citizens settling in Spain will be issued a Certificate of Registration. The certificate also contains the NIE, the Spanish tax identification number needed for almost all official transactions and it includes permission to work in Spain. Non-EU citizens who want to live and work in Spain face a series of bureaucratic hurdles before they can obtain a Residence and Work Permit. As of this writing in 2017, we do not yet know the situation of British citizens when they leave the EU.

EU WORKERS

Let's look at the EU situation first. Council of Europe regulations provide that European Union citizens can work in Spain under exactly the same conditions as Spaniards. The key words of the regulations are "equal treatment" and "non-discrimination".

Spain cannot refuse a work or residence permit to any family members of the EU worker. Spouses and children under 21 years of age, or who are dependent on the worker, have full rights both to reside in the country and to obtain employment, either as hired persons or as self-employed.

This right applies even to family members who are not EU nationals. If a German working in Spain is married to a United States national, for example, the non-EU spouse will have full rights to residence and employment in Spain. However, the non-EU family members must apply for residence cards instead of the simple Certificate of Registration.

All of these rights, and more, are set out in EU Regulation 1612/68, regarding the free circulation of workers within the European Union.

Among these rights are:

The children of foreign workers will have the same rights to trade school education and apprenticeship programmes run by the state as nationals of that state.

Any clause in the employment contract or in any trade union agreement which is discriminatory against EU citizens will be considered null and void. EU workers in other countries may vote and be elected to office in unions at a local level.

Article 9 of Title II of the regulation notes that such EU workers will enjoy the same priority of access to public or subsidised housing as Spanish nationals. That is, where low-cost housing is available to workers, the EU member will be able to enter his name on the waiting list under the same conditions as a national.
Title I of the regulation specifically prohibits any country from applying rules that limit or put unusual conditions on the employment of EU foreigners, or that set out any different or special rules for hiring foreigners, or that oblige employers to advertise jobs differently for foreigners and nationals, or that force foreigners to register with employment offices before they can obtain work, or that make any obstacles for the hiring of EU nationals who may not yet reside officially in that country.
Article 5 of Title I requires that any EU foreigner looking for work in another EU country shall receive the same help from state employment offices as its own nationals seeking work.

All of these regulations add up to non-discrimination and equal treatment for all workers throughout the EU. They even mean that the foreign worker, should he lose his employment in Spain for reasons beyond his control, can have access to unemployment payments — the Spanish dole — just like a Spanish worker.

European professionals who want to work in Spain now find it much easier to have their professional qualifications standardised to Spanish regulations and to set up their practice in Spain.

Doctors, dentists, nurses, veterinarians, architects, lawyers, insurance agents and hairdressers now experience fewer difficulties when they want to render their services in Spain. Other professions also will find restrictions relaxed.

The recognition of foreign qualifications has been greatly simplified and speeded up. Even the professional colleges can no longer act as either open or covert obstacles to the practice of professions by EU citizens who hold the proper titles in their home countries.

Once our EU jobseeker has found employment, he will then need to obtain his Spanish Social Security card. All workers, absolutely all, must register and pay into the Spanish Social Security system.

If you are a hired employee, you will register for *cuenta ajena,* which means "on another person's account". If you are starting a business or working on a self-employed basis, you will register as an *autónomo,* or *cuenta propia,* "on your own account". All workers, Spanish or foreign, EU or non-EU, in work or self-employed, must register and pay Social Security.

The EU worker in Spain no longer has to obtain a separate work document. The Certificate of Registration, which contains his NIE or tax identification number, is all he needs, along with his Social Security card.

NON-EU WORK APPLICANTS

Cuenta ajena

Any newcomer, EU or non-EU citizen, who is looking for a job may enter Spain without any more formalities than the presentation of his passport, and remain as a "tourist" for a time, until he finds work. The jobseeker can present himself at the nearest office of the INEM, the *Instituto Nacional de Empleo,* the National Employment Institute, where he registers as a *demandante de empleo,* a person looking for work. This is exactly the way Spaniards do it. The time limit for this is the normal tourist visit of six months.

This state employment office has different names in the different regions of Spain, as it is administered by the Regions rather than the national government.

When our job-seeker obtains employment, if he is non-EU, he must present his work contract and Social Security registration to the Spanish police and to the national government's sub-delegate office of the province, as well as to the *Delegado de Trabajo,* the provincial director of the Labour Ministry, who issues his residence and work permit. He will also need that visado de residencia we mentioned earlier and other documents listed in the following section on Non-EU Requirements in this chapter.

The first work permit will be for one year and renewals will be for five years. Your new employer will make the arrangements for your registration and payment into the Spanish *Seguridad Social*

(Social Security) scheme. Remember that it is illegal to work in Spain without being registered for Social Security.

There are short-term permits as well, called *Permiso A*, running for three-month, six-month, or nine-month periods. The normal work permit is called *Permiso B*.

Those who have found jobs in Spain should also read the next chapter (Employing others) for a full discussion of their rights as workers.

Cuenta propia — autónomo

The other sort of work permit applies to persons like plumbers, carpenters or business operators, who wish to work as self-employed. This is called working "on your own account" the *cuenta propia*. It is often called *autónomo* as well, because the self-employed worker pays into the Spanish Social Security system under a different plan from the employee.

Unfortunately for these self-employed persons, their situation is a little more complicated, but it is no more complicated than it is for Spaniards themselves. Those persons applying for self-employed permits will have to go through a series of fiscal licences, opening permits and inspections just like Spaniards trying to start a business. The red tape has driven more than one Spaniard round the bend and foreigners will find the same frustrations (see the section of this chapter entitled How to Start a Business for more details).

ILLEGAL WORKER FINED 3,000 EUROS

Be warned. Those who work illegally can be fined 3,000 euros. Working illegally means not paying into Spanish Social Security and not paying taxes. The man and van, or mobile mechanic, or British plumber with a mobile phone number are working illegally if they do not charge IVA, or pay their Social Security, or declare their income. If they use a UK-registered vehicle for their business, the vehicle can be seized by the police.

BEFORE YOU LEAVE

Unfortunately for those citizens of non-EU nations, their situation has not changed. Such third-nation citizens as Americans and Canadians still need the *Visado de residencia*, the special visa which they must obtain from the Spanish consulate in their home country even before they come to Spain. As of this writing, we are not sure if all of the following requirements will apply to Britons now out of the EU.

There are seven classifications of these visas, so be sure you get the right one when you apply. There are visas for people who only want to retire in Spain, visas for people who are going to start a business, visas for those who have found employment, visas for top-level executives, visas for students and visas for teachers.

Applicants who intend to take up employment will have to show a proper work contract, along with proof that the position has been advertised with the Spanish employment institute and that no adequate Spanish candidate can be found for the job.

In many areas this is a serious obstacle, but in specialised fields such as computers the Spanish authorities accept that the outside worker can make a positive contribution to Spain's development. Executives in sensitive positions and teachers usually have few problems in obtaining work permits.

Those non-EU applicants who wish to go into business will have to demonstrate that they have a substantial sum to invest in their Spanish business and that they will provide work for Spanish nationals. Often enough, the Spanish consulate will insist that the investment be made, the employees hired and the business ready to operate before they will grant the visa. Remember that you need this visa even before you go to Spain to apply for the work permit itself, so things can get complicated.

These restrictions seem harsh, but try to understand the point of view of the Spanish labour authorities. Unemployment is at record levels, around 25 per cent and even more in some areas. The Ministry of Labour is also concerned by an influx of EU citizens from Eastern Europe, particularly Rumanians, and a flood of immigrants from North Africa. If your business idea will bring employment to three or four Spaniards, your application will be looked upon most favourably.

Is there any way you can earn a living or supplement your pension without having a work permit? Not really. The law says that anyone who carries out any activity with *fines lucrativos*, i.e. to gain money, is required to have a permit.

Painters may paint in Spain without a work permit. But, if they sell any of their paintings, they must have a permit. An established painter selling his work through a Madrid gallery will have no problem getting a permit. A young street artist who peddles his works to the tourists in the restaurants will probably never get a permit.

A musician contracted to give one concert does not need a work permit, though he is liable for Spanish income tax on any money he earns in Spain. A musician contracted to perform regularly in a nightspot will require a work permit.

There are also temporary work permits, up to six months, for people such as tour guides and specialists who work in Spain for short periods without intending to take up residence. This is the sort of permit often arranged for those timeshare sales people, the OPC, or Off-Premises Contact. The company that hires you should provide you with this permit.

NON-EU CITIZENS WORK PERMIT

If you are a non-EU citizen, first you obtain your visa from the Spanish consulate in your home country. Without it, you will never obtain the residence and work permit.

You will need a police certificate from your home province or state stating that you have no prison record. Americans may need one certificate from their home state and another national certificate from the FBI. This is called a *Certificado penal*. If it is not in Spanish, it must be translated and legalised by a Certificate of Apostille before the Spanish authorities will accept it. Ask the Spanish consulate in your country for the proper forms.

Once in Spain, you need to get your health certificate, the *Certificado médico*. It shows that you have no contagious diseases. Forms are available from the gestorías and government offices, as well as the authorised medical centres.

Then you need a certificate of registration with the consulate of your home country in Spain, showing that you are registered with their office.

Then you need photos, five of them if you are a non-EU citizen. One photo stays with the police, one with the *Sub-Delegado del Gobierno* office of your province, one with the *Delegación de Trabajo* file, one goes on the document itself, and I forget what happens to the other one.

As one veteran resident of the Costa del Sol remarked: "They must have nearly a hundred photos of me by now. I wonder what they do with them?"

They keep them. They really do. I asked a labour official that same question and he led me to a room lined with shelves. On the shelves were the files. In every file were the photos.

This is a complicated, time-consuming and frustrating procedure. You will need some expert advice from the *gestoría* or a lawyer.

AUTÓNOMO PERMIT LIST

Not all of the items on this list will be required in every case, thank goodness, but it gives you an idea.

1. Title or degree. If you wish to practise medicine or architecture, you must present your titles and certificates from EU institutions. If your titles are from outside the EU, they will have to undergo a lengthy process to be validated.

2. *IAE or Impuesto de Actividades Económicas.* This is your business licence, formerly called the *Licencia fiscal*. Now it is called the Tax on Economic Activities. This was formerly a municipal tax but is now administered by the central tax office. The IAE costs nothing if your turn-over is under €600,000, but you must register for it to obtain the correct code number (*epígrafe*) for your specific activity.

3. Your registration with Social Security as a *trabajador autónomo*, a self-employed worker. You register at your nearest *Seguridad Social* office, and in 2018 you will pay about €275 every month as a minimum. It is illegal to work in Spain without paying into its Social Security system.

4. A *Licencia de Apertura*, an opening licence, will be necessary if you have business premises, such as a shop or a workshop installation. This municipal licence comes from your town hall and authorises you to operate your particular business in that particular location.

5. A written explanation of the activity you will carry out. This is called a *memoria de actividades*, and it describes just what work you will do as a self-employed person.

6. Passport and photocopy.

7. Four photos.

8. Title deed and lease contract for business premises and photocopy.

9. If a company has been formed, the incorporation charter.

10. Filled-in form (*solicitud*) requesting permit.

11. Any other permits relating to your special profession. If you are going to work as a cook in a restaurant, you will need a food handler's certificate, for example.

WHAT IT WILL COST

The cost of a work permit depends on a number of factors, principally on whether you use a *gestoría* or a lawyer or feel that you can handle the application on your own, and whether you have found a job or will work on your own account.

If you have a job, your employer will pay most of the expenses and will probably steer you through the entire process. If you are self-employed, you had better figure €500 to €700, including all the taxes and fees.

If your Spanish is reasonably good, you can handle the matter yourself. Obtain the forms from your local police station or from the *Delegación de Trabajo*, fill them out, and wait to see what happens. The first step is for the police to clear your residence permit application. This can take a month or more. Then the papers go to the Labour Ministry office in your province, where they rule on your work permit request. The Government Sub-Delegate (formerly Civil Governor) office also vets it. If granted, you then receive a combined work and residence permit.

The application forms themselves, the *solicitud*, are free, but they are the only item on your list that is. By the time you have added your first Social Security payment of €275, plus any possible costs for opening permits and other fees, you are looking at a real expense.

Few foreigners, however, will feel confident enough about their

Spanish and their familiarity with bureaucratic ins and outs to handle their work permit application on their own..

Perhaps you will turn to a competent *gestoría*. The only way to find one is to make enquiries among people who have work permits and who recommend a particular *gestor*. Their advice can be invaluable.

As in any country, there are right ways and wrong ways to go about things, and a good *gestor* will know the right way. He will also be up to date on recent rulings of the Labour Ministry, and can advise you on whether or not you are likely to get a permit. He may suggest that you word the application in a certain way, for example.

For a work permit, one *gestor* recently charged the rock-bottom figure of €300, with the taxes and fees added to this.

Or you can use a lawyer. This, of course, can cost you €500 or more, in addition to the fees and taxes. Nevertheless, if you are starting a business, employing others, purchasing property for commercial use, or if you feel your particular case may need a little extra explaining, this fee can seem quite reasonable.

A lawyer will be able to advise you on many questions outside the competence of the *gestoría*, such as aspects of investment procedures. Again, make enquiries among people working already to find a lawyer who has given satisfaction.

SOCIAL SECURITY — SELF-EMPLOYED

All those European workers who are now free to seek employment in Spain on equal terms with Spaniards will want to know what the Spanish Social Security system will cost them and what it has to offer. It's never too soon to start thinking about your old age.

Many complications arise in the calculation of Social Security payments and benefits, depending on the age of the worker, time of payment, dependents and other factors, but the short version goes like this:

If you are a self-employed worker such as a plumber or a business operator, you are required by law to pay into the Social Security system in the *autónomo* scheme. In 2017, the minimum rate was €275 per month. You can choose to pay more each month in return for a higher pension later.

RETIREMENT AGE WILL RISE TO 67

Be warned: Over the next few years, Spain's retirement age will rise to the age of 67, being phased in gradually. Workers will also have to pay into the system for a longer period in order to justify a full pension. In addition, the pension amounts will be calculated over a longer time period, meaning that a worker must include his early periods of employment, when he is earning a lower wage, into the total base. This in turn will lower his eventual pension.

The minimum time to qualify for a minimum retirement pension is 15 years, but you need to pay for 35 years and nine months to get a full pension.

If you had paid into the Spanish system at this minimum rate for the last 35 years and nine months, reached the age of 65, had a wife — or husband — under your support who received no other State pension, then you would receive a pension of €786 a month during 2017. A single person receives somewhat less. Most employed workers have paid more over the years, so the average pension is closer to €1,000 a month.

But watch out. If you paid only 15 years, yes, you still qualify for a pension, but it is reduced by the number of years fewer than 35 that you have paid into the system. So, a married person who paid 15 years will get half of €1,000 per month. There is a provision for persons who have no other pension income to have their sub-minimum pension raised to the level of those who paid 35 years. This is called a *complemento por minimos.*

Remember that you will receive 14 of these payments, not 12. It's just like workers' pay. You get an extra month each at Christmas and in the summer.

SALARIED WORKER

If you are a normal salaried worker, your Social Security payments and benefits can vary widely.

WHAT TO DO IF YOU ARE UNFAIRLY DISMISSED

One frequent abuse is the unfair dismissal of workers, along with failure to pay the employer's part of their Social Security payments. This happens to foreign workers and Spaniards alike, but foreign workers are more vulnerable because they are not familiar with the system.

In many cases, the employee is working without a contract and without Social Security and is simply told not to come to work on Monday. He is not paid his last month's salary either. Even with a proper contract and Social Security payments, an employer may let him go with no explanation, figuring the foreigner will disappear without protest.

Or a worker may discover, much later, that his Social Security has not been paid for the past year so he is not covered.

In any of these cases the worker has recourse to the Spanish labour court, Magistratura, but he should obtain legal advice first.

Join the Union: One of the simplest ways to to do this is to go to one of the Spanish trades union organizations. The two major unions are the CC.OO, Comisiones Obreras, and the UGT, the Union General de Trabajadores. These unions are called Sindicatos and they cover all branches of employment.

Don't worry about not being a member. You join when you walk into the office. Fees vary, but it will cost you less than €50 and less than €50 for your yearly dues. Now you are a union member with a powerful worker's organization behind you. And your union dues are tax deductible.

Explain your case and ask for a labour lawyer. The union will assign you a specialist labour lawyer who will go with you to the labour tribunal. In the situations we have described above you are sure to win your case.

If you have been illegally employed, you declare that you, the poor worker, have been abused by the capitalist employer. If the employer has failed to pay your Social Security or your wages, he will be ordered by the court to pay them. The labour courts are usually more favourable to the worker. The union lawyer either will cost you less than €100 or can be assigned a small percentage of the award.

Graduado Social: Or you can consult a Graduado Social. He is a university trained expert in labour law and Social Security. See box in the next section, Employing Others, for details.

The minimum salary base to calculate payments into the system for most workers is €875.70 and a basic percentage of about 30 per cent of this is calculated as the monthly payment for Social Security

A very small part of this is deducted from the worker's salary. The employer pays the greater part directly to the Social Security system in the name of the worker. These payments, with their extra charges, come to an absolute minimum of just over €300 a month that the employer pays for a low-salaried worker.

The system is much more complicated than the outline above and amounts and percentages vary according to the type of employment. Domestic workers, farm employees and street-market workers have special systems.

Once the salaried worker has paid into the system at the minimum rate for the same period of 35 years, he also will receive the same minimum pension of €786 a month as the self-employed worker who retires at 65 with a spouse to feed.

So far we have discussed only the minimum payments and benefits of Spain's Social Security system, but workers may pay more into the system and qualify for higher pensions at 65. A self-employed worker can choose to set his salary base as high as €3,597 a month, meaning he would pay more than €1,000 a month into the system, in order to qualify for the maximum permitted pension of €2,573 a month after 35 years and five months. A salaried worker can also pay the maximum in order to get the maximum.

Those fortunate enough to be earning higher incomes find that no more Social Security payments can be made on the additional income.

The employed worker's monthly contributions include the possibility of unemployment payments if he should lose his job for reasons beyond his control. Self-employed workers only receive payments if they are medically incapacitated for work.

Recent cutbacks in benefits mean that many unemployed workers receive only 75 per cent of the minimum wage as their unemployment benefit. The minimum wage in 2017 was set at €707.60, so that unemployed who had not paid into the system for a full year would receive only about €450 a month. What is worse, they lose their credit towards a retirement pension as well.

Both *autónomo* and *cuenta ajena* workers are entitled to medical benefits through the Spanish National Health scheme, which is going through the same sort of financial and overburden crisis as national health plans in most European countries.

Nevertheless, Spanish Social Security hospitals are just as modern and well equipped as those in other countries and their medical staff are just as well trained. If the Social Security hospital on the Costa del Sol was good enough for Melanie Griffith to have her baby there, it should be good enough for you.

If a worker is ill, he will also continue to receive a portion of his salary, depending on various factors. The self-employed person can also receive sickness pay, at the same rate of 75 per cent of the minimum wage, as long as he can present a doctor's certificate testifying that he is incapacitated for carrying out his profession.

The Social Security system also sets out a schedule of payments for major disability, such as losing your legs in an industrial accident, for orphans and for other areas, and generally functions much like the system in other European nations.

INTERNATIONAL TREATIES

For most foreign workers in Spain, not only EU citizens, there are treaty agreements with many nations to ensure that a worker who has laboured in several different countries does not wind up without enough years of paying Social Security to qualify for a pension in any country.

These agreements usually provide that the total number of years paid into social security systems in various countries be added together to enable the worker to qualify for a pension, which usually is paid proportionally by each country.

STARTING A BUSINESS

The first thing you should do if you are starting a business in Spain is to bring money — lots of it — and open a bank account.

Make contact with a good gestoría to advise you on all bureaucratic procedures. Find a good *asesor fiscal,* the tax consultant, to handle your bookkeeping. Consult a lawyer to make sure you understand your contracts. A good adviser in one of these categories will save you time, trouble and money. Many speak English.

Leasehold: Locate your premises and arrange to purchase, rent or lease. The Spanish lease was formerly called a *traspaso* and is now called a *cesión*. It can be bought and sold under certain conditions.

When you buy a going concern with a *traspaso* or *cesión* for the premises, be aware that the operator of the business who sells you the leasehold may not own the premises. The actual owner will have a right to re-negotiate the *traspaso* when the lease is up. If you lease directly from the owner, you have the right to renewal when the term is up.

Should you wish to sell a business you have started, along with the lease for the premises, you must offer it to the landlord first at the same price as your prospective purchaser has offered. The landlord always has first refusal. The whole business of *traspasos* and *cesiones* has many ins and outs and you will need expert legal advice to avoid pitfalls.

Begin to purchase your equipment and stock and decorate your premises. Also begin to keep careful records of your start-up expenses because the costs, and the IVA that you have paid, will become deductible from your taxes on your business earnings later.

Apply for your *Licencia de Apertura,* your opening licence for the business, which is granted by the town hall. This can cost you as little as €100 for a small shop, €200 for a bar or restaurant, and up to €5,000 if you are opening a bank branch. Be prepared for sanitary and technical inspections, and in some localities be ready for long waits as well.

SIX-MONTH WAIT FOR LICENCE

In the city of Málaga, some establishments have waited as long as six months before receiving their licences. Many of them, of course, simply opened without the licence after a time. In fact, in Benalmádena, on the Costa del Sol, it was recently discovered that more than 1,000 of the 5,000 businesses operating there had no licence at all. Municipal authorities have begun to increase their inspections as a result.

In addition to the other papers, you may need a food handler's medical certificate or other document, depending on the business you choose. You will also be assigned your NIE, your foreigner's tax identification number, which identifies you to the Spanish taxman. Spaniards have a number, too. You can obtain this NIE without having a residence permit if you need it for your operations before your final permit is issued.

You need to acquire two more documents at this time. One is your Spanish Social Security card. As a self-employed businessman you will be called a *trabajador autónomo* (see above). You also need to register yourself as a businessman or professional for the IAE — the I*mpuesto Sobre Actividades Económicas* — the tax on economic activities.

This IAE has replaced the former *Licencia fiscal*, the fiscal licence, though many people continue to call it *Licencia fiscal*. In a move to stimulate small business, the government has:

1. Reduced the tax to zero for professionals and businesses that turn over less than €600,000 a year.

2. Removed the administration of this tax from local municipalities and returned it to the central Tax Agency. Now you must apply to register at your *Hacienda* office, not your town hall.

You must still register for IAE because you must have a tax code assigned to you for your business or profession. A dentist has a different code number (*epígrafe*) to a plumber or travel agency.

COMPANY TAX DOWN TO 25 PER CENT

Company tax has been lowered from 30 per cent to 25 per cent. This tax is called *Impuesto de Sociedades*. In addition, the company tax for startups will be only 15 per cent for the first two years. You need specialist advice here.

If you employ others, you will find that a worker costs you at least €1,200 a month. This is based on the low salary of €750, plus Social Security payments of about 30 per cent of that, plus extra payments at Christmas and in the summer, and assorted other expenses. See next section on Employing Others for more details.

There are many complications with hiring workers and making contracts. Remember it is illegal to hire any worker without paying his Social Security. Perhaps you can take advantage of some of the tax breaks offered to those who create new jobs for younger or older workers or for workers who have been unemployed for long periods. Be alert as to how much it will cost you to make the worker redundant if your business fails to prosper.

Keep accurate books of expenses and income, noting all your payments of IVA, Spain's Value Added Tax, plus your expenses for *gestoría*, accounting and legal advice, and get ready to make your first quarterly tax payment, your *pago fraccionado*.

Modulos or Estimación directa

Many small businesses that deal directly with the public, such as bars and restaurants, will find that they can use a system called *módulos*, or modules, to pay their business tax. The standard system is called *estimación directa*, or direct estimation.

In the case of bars and restaurants the Tax Agency itself decides what your income should be, based on a complex analysis of how many tables you have, how many waiters you employ, your location, the square metres of your premises, and other factors.

You will be charged business tax on this assigned amount each quarter. At the end of the year you file your complete return of actual income, making deductions for business expenses. If the Tax Agency owes you money in return, and they probably will, you claim the refund.

One advantage of this system is that you do not have to maintain a detailed set of accounts in order to present your quarterly statements. This is helpful for small operations dealing in hundreds or thousands of little transactions every day. If you run your business carefully and things go well, the business may produce more profit than the number of tables would indicate, meaning you pay less tax than expected. Of course, you must present your totals at the end of each year.

You can later decide if you wish to pass to the direct estimation system, which requires complete book-keeping, with every *factura* in its place. The advantage, of course, is that you are paying tax on your real business earnings each quarter.

It begins to sound as if you definitely need the services of a tax consultant and business specialist here. Very few can handle this paperwork on their own.

FORMING A SPANISH COMPANY

If you intend to carry out any large-scale activity, you may wish to form a Spanish company, or a branch of a foreign company, in order to do business in Spain. You are permitted to do this as either a resident or a non-resident. If you have €60,000 in capital to invest, you can form a Spanish *Sociedad Anónima,* the equivalent of a British limited company (a plc), or an American corporation (an Inc.), where liability is limited to the amount of capital each investor has subscribed. These companies have "S.A." after their names.

S.A. companies must have their books audited yearly and register these audited accounts with the Mercantile Registry as public documents, available for inspection by any citizen. Thus you can consult the Mercantile Registry for information about any Spanish company with which you intend to do business. You can find out the names and addresses of the principal officers of the company and see its profits and losses for the previous year. Failure to file such an audited statement or to falsify any information it contains is an offence, punishable by fines.

Under the old system, which required very little capital for the formation of a company, hundreds of thousands of companies were constituted with no obligation to publish their accounts. It was easy for an unscrupulous businessman to form a company, conceal its profits, and later disappear, owing money to his creditors, which they had no way of recovering. The present system is designed to correct these abuses.

You can also form in Spain a *Sociedad Limitada,* a simpler form of incorporation with a reduced number of shareholders and capital, or you can undertake a legal partnership or make a Spanish branch company, a sucursal, of a parent company already existing in your home country.

BUYING A SPANISH COMPANY

You can also purchase a functioning Spanish company, but you must be extremely careful to check the *Registro Mercantile,* the commercial registry, for company details and have your lawyer make sure there are no pending lawsuits against the company, such as a demand from a former employee for unpaid wages.

If you form a company, its articles of association must be signed and registered with a Spanish Notary and of course the Mercantile Registry. Formerly, one needed three shareholders and three directors to form a company, but under the new legislation, a single person can incorporate himself.

If you form a company, you may be employed by it as a director, even if you own the company completely. The company will be liable for Spain's corporate tax of 25 per cent on its profits.

You will need the best legal advice you can get — in your home country before you start your Spanish company and in Spain before you form the company — to make sure you get the best tax and business breaks available when you transfer funds. There are many tax complications and opportunities when you set up a company, so study the requirements carefully before you begin.

Such questions as whether you set up your company while you are still a non-resident of Spain and whether you liquidate your foreign holdings before or after becoming a resident will become important considerations.

There is a maze of regulations and opportunities around foreign investment, and you will need a lawyer skilled in these matters. The foreign investment will be vetted by the *Dirección General de Transacciones Exteriores,* the general directorate of foreign transactions, better known as the DGTE, the authority which continues to keep a controlling eye on foreign exchange, even though it has fewer powers to deny money transfers.

You want to be sure that your Spanish company will be able to take its legal profits out of Spain, and also that it will have access to bank credit just like any Spanish company.

Spain's *Ministerio de Economía y Hacienda* publishes several booklets in English which are "must" reading for anyone thinking of starting a business here. The series is called "A Guide to Business in Spain". Among the titles are Foreign Investments, Forms of Business Organisations, and Labour Legislation. Try checking their web site at www.meh.es.

GLOSSARY

Autónomo – self-employed

Certificado de antecedentes penales – certificate of criminal record

Certificado médico – medical certificate, for work permit application

Cesión – leasing of any sort

Cuenta ajena – "on another's account", an employed worker

Cuenta propia – "on your own account", a self-employed worker.

Delegación de Trabajo – provincial office of Ministry of Labour

GLOSSARY

Demandante de trabajo – job-seeker

Dirección General de Transacciones Exteriores – General Directorate of Foreign Transactions, regulates foreign investment

Estimación directa – direct calculation of income for tax purposes.

Impuesto sobre Actividades Económicas – tax on business activities

Instituto Nacional de Empleo – National Employment Institute

Licencia de Apertura – opening licence

Memoria de actividades – description of activities, when applying for business licence or permit.

Ministerio de Economía y Hacienda – Ministry of Economy and Finance

Módulos – modules, a form of estimating business income for tax purposes.

NIE (Número de Identificación de Extranjero) – foreigner's tax identification number.

Pago fraccionado – quarterly tax payment for businesses

Registro Mercantil – Mercantile Registry, where companies are inscribed.

Sociedad Anónima (S.A.) – limited liability public company, plc, or corporation.

Sociedad Limitada (S.L.) – limited liability company, simpler form of incorporation than an S.A.

Solicitud – application

Sub-Delegado del Gobierno – provincial representative of national government.

Sucursal – branch office

Employing Others

Many foreigners will at some point employ Spanish or other foreign workers. Property owners need odd jobs done and the growing number of foreign residents starting their own businesses needs employees. Here are a few things you should know about labour relations in Spain.

REVISED LAW FOR DOMESTIC CLEANERS

Though Spain is no longer the low-priced paradise it once was for northern Europeans, many new residents find they are still able to afford at least a part-time cleaning woman and perhaps a gardener.

As in many countries, most part-time maids, cleaning women and garden workers in Spain are working illegally, whether they are employed by foreigners or by other Spaniards. By "illegally", we mean they are not covered by Social Security, and are not making payments into the system. These workers do not make a lot of money anywhere, and their work is easy to hide.

In Spain the law says that all workers — absolutely all — must be covered by Social Security. After several tries, the Spanish government has come up with a reformed system to regulate domestic employment.

The new system replaces the former law of domestic employees and puts domestic workers under the regular Social Security system, with a few special provisions. The new regulations require a written contract, which can be for a fixed period or an "indeterminate" period and can be part-time or full-time up to the legal maximum of 40 hours per week.

Spain's official minimum wage for 2017 is €707.60 euros a month, times 14 payments

The rules specify that domestic workers be paid at least the official Spanish Minimum Wage, which for 2018 is €707.60 a month, plus two extra month's payments. This wage, which comes to less than five euros an hour, will simply draw laughter from foreign residents in coastal areas, who cannot find a girl to clean for less than ten euros an hour anyway. However, we must remember this is for full-time employment.

The domestic worker can now be registered in the Social Security system, with the right to unemployment payments if she is left without work and the right to medical care, as well as a final pension.

The payments are set at 22 per cent of the wage. The employer pays 18.5 per cent and the worker the rest. If the cleaner works two days a week, the payments cover only those two days.

How do I register?

One of the reforms grants domestic workers the right to a written contract and to Social Security payments made by the employer.

Under the previous law, a verbal agreement was acceptable and the worker could be responsible for her own Social Security payments. No longer.

If you want to be legal, here are the steps you must take.

First, go the nearest office of the *Tesorería de la Seguridad Social* to register for your *Código de Cuenta de Cotización*. This registration establishes you as an employer and sets up an account number to keep track of your payments. The "Treasury" office of the Social Security is not your local administration office. It is where they handle the money. Ask in your area.

You will need your contract with the worker, which specifies the hours to be worked and the amount of payments. These contracts can be "indefinite" or for a fixed period. The contract means the employee becomes a protected worker, with the right to indemnity payments. If your worker already has a contract with you, she will be paid seven days salary for each year worked. A new contract provides 12 days of salary for each year worked before she is let go.

What will it cost you? In an example provided by Social Security, they suppose a part-time cleaning woman who comes once a week for three hours and who is paid about 10 euros an hour, or a little over 120 euros a month. Her Social Security payments from her employer will come to a little more than 16 euros a month.

We urge you to employ a Spanish tax consultant, an *asesor fiscal*, or a labour specialist, a *Graduado Social*, to make sure you get it right.

Labour legislation requires that all workers have Spanish Social Security. Some foreigners have been slapped with stiff fines and been forced to pay Social Security payments for years back when reported by the maid or gardener who seemed so nice at first, so be wary.

In one case, a homeowner who employed a gardener in his village for many years without any papers at all, decided to sell his property and dismiss the gardener.

The gardener, who had always seemed so pleasant, and so ignorant, went to the Labour Court on the basis of the implicit verbal contract and obtained a settlement of almost €18,000. The owner could not sell his property until this was paid.

WARNING TO EMPLOYERS

One veteran labour expert at a *gestoría* in Marbella warned employers of maids and gardeners in the following way:

"Let's imagine that a villa owner decides to sell up and leave Spain. He has a maid and gardener who have never had a contract or in fact anything at all written down. He simply paid them in cash each month or each week.

"Now the maid and gardener come to see me. To be blunt, I just might suggest to them that not only do they put in their case for Social Security payments, but they sue the owner for a year's wages.

"In reality, they have been paid these wages, but there are no receipts to indicate this. For my nasty cleverness, I just might take a commission of 20 per cent of whatever they are able to get. Unscrupulous agents do this every day.

"And that is why I urge all employers of Spanish domestic help to require that at least the employee sign a receipt for his pay each time, even if he doesn't have a contract."

HANDYMAN NEEDS INSURANCE

You may also become an employer of Spanish nationals when you have some work done around your property, such as building a wall in a corner of your garden. If you hire a man on an hourly basis to carry out this work, as is often done, you will probably have no problem.

But take care. Such hiring in theory makes you an employer and the worker an employee, and can make you liable if there is an accident on the job.

Your best protection is to ask any such worker for a *presupuesto*, a bid, for the job you want done. This bid should include the worker's NIF, which is his tax identification number, and it should specify the price, along with the amount of IVA, or value added tax.

That, technically at least, makes him an independent contractor, responsible for his own insurance and Social Security. This written *presupuesto* is a good idea in any case to make sure that both parties understand the terms of your agreement.

As with the maid or gardener, the hitch here is accident insurance. As the property owner, you could find yourself sued if the worker suffers an accident.

Your homeowners' insurance policy will not cover a worker injured on your property. Your protection against this is to ask to see the worker's Social Security card when you contract him for the job. Even better, deal with a registered building contractor. This will surely cost you more, but it is the only way to be completely safe.

Remember also that you must have a proper bill — a *factura* — including the fiscal identification number of the contractor, the price and the IVA, if you wish to deduct the cost of home improvements from your profits when you sell your Spanish property.

Sometimes the friendly offer of "no bill, no IVA" represents a false saving in the end.

BUSINESS EMPLOYEES

Whether your employees are Spanish or foreign, they will be entitled to all the benefits of Spanish labour legislation. This means that you will pay Social Security payments for your employee, and redundancy pay if you let him go. It confronts you with all the changing complexity of Spanish labour law.

One surprise for employers from other countries is that Spaniards are often paid 14 months' salary for 11 months' work. This is because the custom of an extra month's pay at Christmas and again in July persists in many cases, with the employee also entitled to a month's vacation. This is in addition to his 14 paid holidays.

Another of the principal problems of employing workers in Spain is the difficulty of firing a worker. Spain is only beginning to relax its

GRADUADO SOCIAL CAN HELP BOTH WORKERS AND EMPLOYERS

A *graduado social* is a university-trained professional who navigates the bureaucratic minefields of Spain's complex labour laws and Social Security regulations. He knows how much vacation time a worker is entitled to and he knows what outside income may affect a Social Security pension, and a thousand other things.

For the employer he can calculate the correct Social Security payments for the workers. For the worker he can explain the grounds for seeking compensation for unfair dismissal or how much his pension will be.

Gestorias and accountants can do many of these things for you but when they are in doubt, they consult a *graduado social*. He can save time and money for both workers and employers.

strong protection of the worker's right to job security. In response to the present economic crisis, however, the government has imposed labour reforms that allow employers to reduce salaries, change working hours, and make workers redundant.

Many Spanish businessmen have pointed out that the rigidity of this system actually works against full employment because it makes bosses reluctant to take on extra employees when things are going well for fear of being stuck with them later.

It also makes life difficult in seasonal businesses like hotels, and generally cramps enterprise, especially in small concerns where the wages of one or two employees make the difference between profit and loss.

The government has passed a series of measures to make the labour market "more flexible". They include provisions for hiring workers on short-term contracts. The employer must pay the usual Social Security contributions, but he is liable only for a very small redundancy payment should he choose to let the worker go.

Further measures were then enacted to discourage the short-term contracts and encourage long-term hiring. They added an indemnity of eight days' pay for each year worked on such temporary contracts, and relaxed the indemnity for workers let go from long-term contracts from 45 days' pay per year worked to 33 days' pay per year. Another plan provides tax breaks for employers taking on workers over 45 years of age who have been out of a job for more than one year. There are many plans designed to help small businesses, and the foreigner starting an enterprise in Spain could find them quite useful. Unless you get competent legal advice, however, you could miss out on the benefits. In many cases, Spanish labour law continues to regard the relation between employer and employee as legally binding, even if there is no written contract, and the worker becomes protected from dismissal, no matter how poorly your business goes.

BEWARE OF "INDEFINITE" CONTRACTS

Be wary, in particular, of "temporary" contracts which do not give a definite time period or state a date on which the contract lapses unless renewed. In some cases Spanish employees have taken advantage of this type of contract in the following way:

The employee works for a time at his new job. One day he simply fails to show up for work and the employer is unable to contact him. Months later the employer receives a notice from the Spanish labour court that he is being charged with unfair dismissal by the missing employee.

The former employee wants his Social Security paid for six months or a year and he wants an indemnity of €10,000 or so to make up for his suffering.

All this is an invention of course, but the Labour Court (see below) has a long history of favouring the employee against the employer, so some unscrupulous workers have learned to take advantage of this, and the employer faces a long and expensive process to prove he is right. Very often the employer will simply give up, even though he is being taken for a ride, and will make an out-of-court settlement to the "worker".

The employer's only protection here is to formally dismiss the worker when he fails to appear. He must be informed at his home address — a telegram constitutes legally acceptable notice — that he has been fired for failing to appear at his job.

Whether he responds or not, a copy of this telegram will help the employer in his court case later. Some employers have failed to make this official dismissal for cause, to their later sorrow.

Make sure your contract is clearly understood when you take on any new employees.

FINES START AT €3,000 FOR UNREGISTERED WORKERS

You will be right if you think that situations like the above have produced a sort of paranoia in small business owners, who in turn are tempted to hire workers without any contracts or Social Security or any papers whatsoever.

This is illegal, however, even though thousands of Spanish as well as foreign employers are doing it right at this moment.

Labour inspectors do check on establishments and fines start at €3,000 for such unregistered employees, whether they are Spaniards or foreigners. Especially in coastal bars and restaurants, inspectors discover hundreds of cases every year, and fine the owners.

RIGHTS OF EMPLOYEES

Among the rights of employees is included the payment of the official minimum wage, which differs according to the type of work. The absolute minimum in 2017 is €707.60 per month, with 14 months of payments each year. This is quite low, however, and most employees are paid more.

The standard work week is 40 hours, though this varies from one occupation to another. There is an official 40 per cent increase for overtime, with double time for Sundays and national holidays.

In a changing Spain, one is never quite certain what the national holidays will be next year. They even differ from Catalonia to Andalusia.

Workers are entitled to 14 paid holidays a year, 12 of them national and two of them local, such as the town's *fiesta*. The annual vacation is a minimum 23 days. In many cases, "fixed" workers are entitled to a leave of absence with pay of 15 days should they get married, and two days when a relative dies or is seriously ill. A woman may be entitled to 16 weeks' leave for child-bearing, but the Spanish Social Security system will pay a large portion of her salary during this time. A new father gets two weeks off and the mother can choose to pass up to two weeks of her maternity leave to the father.

These are guidelines which do not apply to all workers and you should consult a competent gestoría or lawyer who is expert in labour law to find out just what applies in your individual field.

The Spanish custom of special payments in July and at Christmas, or even more often in some cases, continues to apply. These are called *pagas extraordinarias* and their original purpose was to make sure that workers had some funds in hand for Christmas and summer holidays. These payments are often stated as one month's pay each time, but the actual amount depends on a number of factors, such as seniority, the type of work, and individual contract.

EMPLOYER PAYS SOCIAL SECURITY

The principal expense you will have with any worker you employ in your business, whether on one-year contracts or "fixed", will be the payment of his Social Security contributions. As an employer, you will have to pay this for yourself, as well.

The payments are split between the employer and the worker, but the employer pays by far the greater share. Your payment is based on the *nómina,* the official salary for your type of work, not on the real salary you pay. If you employ a waiter or a shop girl at the minimum wage of €707.60, you will find that your payments are based on the lowest official nómina, which in this case is €875 and you will pay about 30 per cent of this, more than €250 each and every month in addition to your worker's salary. This is a rock-bottom figure. Most employers pay higher wages and higher Social Security payments.

Remember that this includes complete health care, accident and disability insurance, unemployment payments, and the worker's state retirement pension.

Spain, like most other modern industrial nations, is concerned about its Social Security system and where the money will come from as the number of pensioners in the population steadily increases.

An employer can fire a worker without compensation if the worker is repeatedly absent or late, if he does not obey reasonable orders, or if he is drunk or otherwise in a condition which affects his work.

A worker can quit and seek compensation if he feels that the employer has not held to the contract, has substantially altered working conditions for the worse, or has not paid the agreed wages.

LABOUR COURT DECIDES

Disputes about these matters are taken to the *Magistratura de Trabajo,* the Labour Court, which will decide who it thinks has the right and make judgement accordingly. Compensation payable to a worker varies, but he might get 33 days' pay for each year he has worked if the court rules he has been unfairly dismissed.

If a company goes out of business, one guideline holds that its employees are entitled to 20 days' pay for each year they have worked.

The labour laws are complex and vary widely according to the field of work. You will do well to consult a specialist to find out what rules apply to your specific situation.

GLOSSARY

Factura – bill, invoice
Fijo – "fixed", a worker on an indefinite contract
IVA – VAT, Value Added Tax
Jardinero – gardener
Magistratura de Trabajo – labour tribunal
Mujer de limpieza – cleaning woman
Obrero – worker, labourer
Paga extraordinaria – special payment
Presupuesto –estimate for a job of work
Régimen Especial de Empleados de Hogar – Social Security special scheme for domestic employees
Salario Mínimo Interprofesional – minimum wage
Seguridad Social – Social Security
Trabajador autónomo – self-employed worker

You and the Spanish Authorities

In your home country you are probably familiar with the various official authorities you come in contact with. These include the town hall, the state or provincial or county government, the police, the courts and judges, the Social Security system, the national government. Spain is organised in very much the same way as most European countries.

YOUR TOWN HALL

Your town hall, or *ayuntamiento*, will be important to you in many ways. You pay your annual motor vehicle circulation tax here. If you build a house, it is here that you apply for a building permit. It is here — in the urbanismo department — that you discover how much your Plus valía tax will be before you buy or sell property. It is here that you register as an inhabitant of the town in order to exercise your right to vote in municipal elections if you are an EU citizen.

All you have to do is find the right window or *ventanilla*. If your town is located in an area with a large foreign population, you will probably find someone in your town hall who speaks English.

Towns with many foreign residents, like Mijas and Fuengirola on the Costa del Sol, maintain special departments to assist the foreigners. If you are fortunate enough to live in a town with a foreign residents' department, this will be your starting place for most queries.

The mayor is called the *alcalde* and the members of the town council are called *concejales*. You may make any complaints you have to these officials.

Individual *concejales* are responsible for each area of municipal services, rubbish collection, building permits and so on. Ask for the appropriate one, and he or she will give you a hearing.

As foreign residents make up a large part of both the population and the income of many towns, officials generally try to keep them happy.

They are now aware that European Union citizens resident in Spain have the right to vote in local elections, and even to be elected to the municipal government, which ought to establish your credentials. (See next page).

If your town hall does not have a foreigners' department or

anyone who speaks your language, you should get some Spanish assistance and present your complaint or request in writing. This will be stamped as recibido, "received", when you present it.

Spanish regulations on local administration declare that all cases presented in this way must be acted upon, either positively or negatively, in a reasonable period of time. This "reasonable period" of time can seem quite long, but complaints about things like burning rubbish or noisy bars are read and registered. And, when enough of them pile up, something eventually gets done, just as it does in your home country.

REGISTER TO VOTE

If you are a European Union citizen, you are entitled not only to vote in the municipal elections in the town where you are registered but to be elected to office as well. This right applies even if you do not hold a Spanish residence permit.

Can you see yourself at the meeting of the town council as you propose the death penalty for riders of noisy motorbikes? At last you will be in a position to do something about it. Don't laugh too hard. Local Spanish politicians have started to recruit foreign candidates in towns along the Costa Blanca and the Costa del Sol where there are large foreign populations. A few have even been elected in recent municipal elections.

First, however, you must be registered as residing in your town and then you must make sure your name is on the list of voters. Go into your town hall with your passport, your residence permit or some evidence that you live in the municipality, such as a rental contract or a property deed.

EMPADRONAMIENTO

You wish to inscribe yourself in the *padrón*, the list of local residents. You want to be *empadronado*, or inscribed, and receive a *Certificado de Empadronamiento*, a registry certificate for this municipality.

Town halls are generally happy to inscribe anyone residing within their limits because their slices of the national or regional tax pie are bigger when they can demonstrate a larger population. However, they will not register just anyone who walks in.

The principal requirement is that you spend more than six months residing in the municipality. This rule applies to both Spaniards and foreigners. Persons are prohibited from being *empadronado* in two municipalities at the same time. This requirement also applies to Spaniards and to foreigners. If you are from the UK, for example, but you register as an inhabitant of a town in Spain, you will be required to vote for your European Union representative in Spain, not in the UK.

EU VOTERS IN SPAIN

14% of all citizens with the right to vote in municipal and European Parliament elections in the Province of Málaga are European Union citizens resident here. This number will drop sharply when Brexit is complete.

Once you are *empadronado* you can then request that your name appear on the *censo electoral*, the voter registration list, and you will be ready to vote for your local European parliamentary representative and for candidates standing in the next municipal elections, whether for mayor or councillors. Or you may even stand for office yourself. A number of non-Spanish EU citizens now sit on municipal councils.

In modern Spain where regional autonomy has become the order of the day, you may find, as Spaniards also do, some confusion above the town hall level. Many responsibilities formerly handled by the central government in Madrid have been passed down to the regional governments such as the *Junta de Andalucía* or the *Generalitat Valenciana.*

Provincial authorities: Each of Spain's 50 provincial authorities has its own legislature, called the *Diputación Provincial*, which is responsible for various areas, such as consumer complaints and some secondary roads. Through their tourism departments they promote the local attractions and they organise cultural events. They oversee projects which affect various municipalities, such as a province-wide sewage system, for example, or an urban development plan cutting across town boundaries.

Regional authorities: These regional governments set standards for property development and building. They usually operate the health care system and have the power to make changes in a number of national taxes. This means that a resident in Marbella gets health care from the Andalusian health service, not the national health service, and that inheritance taxes in the Valencia region may differ from those in Madrid. Both the Basques and the Catalans have their own special statutes granting them various degrees of autononmy, including the teaching of their own languages in the public schools and their own regional police forces. The governments of the autonomous regions also fight with the central government in Madrid over things like their share of the national taxes and whether they will get a high-speed train next year.

National authorities: The central government in Madrid has gradually been devolving powers to the autonomous regions. This includes the assignment of a share of the national taxes to each region to meet their expenses.

The Madrid government's chief representative in each province is called the *Sub-Delegado del Gobierno*. He is in charge of residence permits, among other matters, because immigration is a national policy.

Sometimes there are areas where municipal, provincial and regional authorities conflict and overlap. You may find that you are dealing with the national government when you could easily think it's the provincial one.

When you apply for a work permit, for example, you deal with the *Delegación Provincial* of the *Ministerio de Trabajo*. This is the office of the Labour Ministry located in your province, but it is not a provincial organ. And so it goes, with various state organisms in charge of different areas. Some will be important to you and others will not.

POLICE FORCES

Three different kinds of police, and sometimes four, may operate in the same areas, which can be confusing.There are municipal police, national police and the Civil Guard. Some autonomous regions, such as the Basque Country and Catalonia, have their own regional police as well.

WARNING: Costa crime is rising

Although Spain is still a much safer place to live than the UK, for example, crime is on the rise, especially in coastal areas frequented by tourists. Be alert for persons who try to distract your attention in supermarket parking lots and at cash machines. Often, one of the gang will pretend to be a Spanish police officer in plain clothes. Another ploy is to puncture one of your tyres. The thieves offer to help, then snatch a handbag. Statistics show that the crime rate in Mediterranean tourist towns like Torremolinos is more than seven times higher than the national average. Police claim they are more than 25 per cent under-strength for the job.

You most likely will come into contact with the local police when a young municipal policewoman puts a 60-euro parking ticket on your illegally parked car. The *Policía Nacional* (National Police) are in charge of applications for a residence card at your local police station, or *Comisaría*. If you drive too fast, you may be pulled over by a motorcycle officer of the *tráfico* division of the *Guardia Civil*.

Municipal police: First, there are the municipal police of your town, called *Policía Local*. They are in charge of matters such as directing traffic and making sure bars close on time. As a general rule, you will find them polite and helpful.

In a situation where another citizen's activities disturb you or damage your property, you may make an official complaint or *denuncia* to the police. This could be neighbours fighting at the top of their lungs or when a bar plays loud music late at night.

If your polite protests to the offending parties are disregarded, call a cop. One visit from a policeman will show your neighbour that you are seriously annoyed, and this ought to take care of the problem.

The police have a device which measures the decibel level of the noise coming from a bar, and they can fine the proprietor if this noise is above permitted levels. They have even been seen in the streets applying this meter to the motors of those small 50cc motorbikes that infuriate Spaniards and foreigners alike.

People often say that police do nothing about the noisy bikes, but in fact they confiscate hundreds of them every year and do not return them until they are fitted with proper silencers.

WHAT TO DO About barking dogs & noisy motorbikes !

If your neighbour's dog barks all night and keeps everyone awake, it can be a real problem. Perhaps the owner does not listen to reason and the barking goes on. Or maybe you live in a rural area and you do not even know the name of the owner. Or maybe your problem is the infamous noisy motorbikes.

Nobody likes to make the kind of protest that may infuriate the offenders and cause even worse problems, but, if you are serious, here is the way to bring official action.

Simply calling the cops generally is not enough. You will have to bring a *denuncia*. The word only means "report". If you can get some of your neighbours to sign it with you, this will help. Go to the *juzgado de guardia*. This is the duty court, where you fill in the proper forms. You do not need a lawyer for this, although it might be a good idea to have one prepare the papers in the most effective way. You do not even need to identify the culprits. A general description can suffice.

The court is required by law to take action. They will assign police to the case. We make no promises, but wouldn't it be nice if the riders of the noisy motorbikes found two policemen with decibel measuring meters waiting for them the next time they passed?

National police: The *Policía Nacional* are more thoroughly trained and are in charge of dealing with most crime. There are National Police posts in towns of any size. Here you find the *extranjeros* or foreigners' department where you apply for a residence card. The National Police are charged with the documentation and control of foreigners in Spain, including the wave of illegal immigrants pouring in from Africa. The National Police have specialised units dealing with matters such as organised crime rings, drug smuggling and money laundering. Organised gangs from Eastern Europe are the most recent threat.

Civil Guard: Finally, there is the *Guardia Civil*. This body was originally organised to provide police protection in country areas, and they have little to do with large cities or even big towns. If you live in a village, though, there will be a *Guardia Civil* post instead of a National Police unit, and you report crimes to them.

Your principal contact with them will most likely be through their mission of patrolling the highways. They assist motorists in difficulty. On the other hand, they might be around a curve with modern radar equipment that times your speed, and identifies your licence number. You won't even know you have been clocked until you get the multa, or fine, in the mail.

You can choose to protest it or pay it, at the *Jefatura de Tráfico*, the provincial highway department. You can usually pay a speeding fine by *giro postal*, a post office money order, which will save you a trip. You may also have contact with the *Guardia Civil* when they mount a checkpoint along the highway, picking drivers at random to apply a breath test for alcohol. The *Guardia Civil* have specialised units at borders, at sea where they pursue drug-smugglers and boatloads of illegal immigrants. They have bomb disposal experts and anti-terrorist specialists, and they also have teams of high-tech computer experts who try to keep tabs on sophisticated computer crimes.

REPORTING A THEFT

You need to contact the police in case of a burglary in your home, a stolen car or a stolen purse on the street.

In large towns, you report thefts to the *Policía Nacional* rather than to the municipal police. In small villages or in the country, you will report to the *Guardia Civil* post. Procedures for reporting theft are much the same in Spain as in any country.

You may have to wait with others for the chance to make your report. A police clerk records the details. The sad reality in all countries is that most stolen items are never seen again. Nevertheless, every year the Spanish police recover thousands of stolen cars, and other items which can be viewed at the police station.

Remember that you must make this report and obtain an official copy of it if you are going to make an insurance claim. In tourist-area towns, you may find the report forms available in four or five languages. In some cities, like Málaga or Fuengirola, there will be interpreters on the spot.

REPORT BY PHONE Call police on 902-10-21-12 and report a theft or loss. This report will be sent to your local police station where you must later sign it to obtain a copy.

IF YOU ARE ARRESTED

If you are arrested by the Spanish police, you have the same basic rights you have in any modern democracy: the right to remain silent; the right to hear the charges against you; the right to legal counsel; the right to contact a lawyer.

You can be held for three days before being taken before a judge, but the judge must be informed of your arrest within 24 hours. That three-day provision may seem overlong but keep in mind that the judge must be informed within 24 hours, so at least one other official besides the police knows that the temporary, uncharged, prisoner is in *gaol*.

In practice, the police hold very few suspects for 72 hours without bringing them before the judge to be formally charged or set free. The police use this power normally to harass small-time crooks or offenders whom they are morally certain have violated the law but who will probably be freed by the judge either on technical grounds or for lack of solid evidence.

WHAT IS A *DENUNCIA*?

Sooner or later, you will hear the Spanish word, *denuncia*. Because it sounds so much like the English verb "to denounce" it is often thought by foreigners to have some special Spanish legal significance. It sounds threatening to them.

In Spanish legal terms, the word *denunciar* means only "to report, to declare". When your wallet is stolen, you go to the police post and make a *denuncia*, a report. So, when someone threatens to have you denounced, it only means he's going to have you reported, as one might report a neighbour's noisy television set or a wall being built which will cut off your protected view.

You should be aware that reporting an infraction to the police

WHAT TO DO In any emergency – Call 112

The telephone number 112 is gradually coming into effect as the standard European Union all-purpose emergency number.

Your call goes to a regional centre where they should speak English and other languages, too. They are equipped to trace your call and find your position. If you can describe the nature of your emergency they will immediately contact the appropriate emergency service, whether it is medical, fire or police.

is not the same as bringing charges in court. If your neighbour's barking dog is disturbing you throughout the night, you can call the police and they may or may not pay him a visit. In most cases, the matter ends here. But, if you go in person to the *juzgado de guardia* (the duty court) to present a formal charge of disturbing the peace, this is more serious. You must sign the charges and be prepared to back up your case. The judge will order the offending dog-owner to appear, along with yourself, to hear both sides of the story.

COURTS AND JUDGES

With a little luck, you won't have anything to do with courts and judges in Spain. Taking a case through a court can be frustrating and time-consuming. The mills of justice grind exceedingly slowly. Spanish courts have been reprimanded and fined by the European Union for the slowness of their proceedings.

The Spanish courts do function, however, and lawsuits are settled and judgements awarded. If you intend to sue someone in Spain, you consult a lawyer, who explains either that you have no case in law for this or that reason, or who says that, yes, you have an excellent chance of getting the damages you seek. Your lawyer then prepares the papers and the process is set in motion.

Justice of the Peace: Maybe a neighbour in your village has begun to build a wall on your property or your landlord has denied you access to the roof terrace when your contract clearly states that you are entitled to it. The *Juez de Paz*, the Justice of the Peace, is often

WHAT TO DO If you are abused

The Spanish legal system has finally begun to take spouse abuse seriously. Until just a few years ago, most spouse abuse was classified as a simple infraction and any action to protect a battered wife was extremely difficult.

This has changed, both in public opinion and in the legal system. If you are in immediate physical danger, call the police. You should get a rapid and sympathetic response. If you have been beaten, go to the hospital for treatment. Have photographs taken.

You can then go yourself to the duty court, the *Juzgado de Guardia*, and present charges against your attacker. If you have a lawyer, talk with him first.

There are centres of attention for battered women in all major cities, with telephone help lines listed in the newspapers. If you are of low income, you have the right to free legal assistance.

In most cases, a court will rapidly issue a restraining order against the offending spouse. If the spouse violates the order and approaches his victim, he can face prison.

the first-level court in small disputes of this type.

At this level, neither party need be represented by counsel. Often enough, just the fact that you have gone to the Justice of the Peace and cited your neighbour to a hearing will be sufficient to solve the problem peaceably.

These Justice of the Peace courts exist only in small towns where there is no higher court locally available. They are empowered to settle only very minor matters.

Court of First Instance: The next step up in the court scheme is the *Juzgado de Primera Instancia*, the Court of First Instance. Here you can bring suit to recover unpaid debts and deal with more serious matters, such as breach of contract or divorce. A lawsuit is called a *demanda* and to sue is *demandar*. Now you need a lawyer.

In the First Instance Court you might sue a business client who has not paid his debts to you for goods and services. If your case is sound and the amount of the debts not too great, you may get a ruling in your favour within six months or you might wait three years — depending on the caseload.

Here also you can sue the contractor whose work has not met the standards specified in the contract or a repairman whose bill seems too high.

***Perito judicial*:** In many cases of this type, your lawyer may ask for the appointment of a *perito judicial*, a court-appointed expert on plumbing, electrical installations, or whatever the subject of the dispute. This expert will evaluate the quality of the work and the price paid. Again, in situations of overcharging a client, very often the mere threat of this *perito judicial* will be enough to cause settlement of the case.

Provincial Assizes & Supreme Court: Legal action usually begins in the Court of First Instance. Any case, however, can lead to a series of appeals and counter appeals to higher courts, such as the *Audiencia Provincial* (Provincial Assizes) with its four separate branches or salas for civil, criminal, administrative or labour cases, and right on up to the *Tribunal Supremo*, the highest court of all. If questions about basic constitutional rights are involved, the case will go to the *Tribunal Constitucional*, the Constitutional Court.

A case might even begin in one of these higher courts when serious criminal activity is involved or where large sums of money are disputed in civil matters.

So, there is a functioning legal system in Spain, which you can make work for you by obtaining skilled legal counsel. Just as in most countries, some Spanish courts function quickly and effectively, but most are slow and overloaded. Do not give up on the system. Even when you are told that the courts are so terrible that you may as well forget about your loss, do not believe this.

Plenty of horror stories exist about taking nine years to settle an accident claim against an insurance company, for example, but there is legal recourse for you, and the Spanish state is spending millions of euros to expand and modernise the court system.

WHAT TO DO If you are accused of abuse !

The other side of the issue of spouse abuse is that wives sometimes use the new laws as a weapon against a husband who may have angered them but has not really abused them.

A husband will then find himself in a difficult position. Basically, in today's new climate, no one will believe him. The police will haul him into court even if the wife retracts her earlier charge.

The principal danger for the falsely accused spouse comes if he accepts a *juicio rápido*, the quick hearing. This type of hearing, without full legal preparation or the presentation of much evidence, is useful in many cases, such as drunken driving or petty theft.

However, it can lead to a hasty judgement where the court simply accepts the wife's declaration and rules the husband guilty. He is issued with a restraining order that forbids him to enter his own home, a fine, and a gaol term of 90 days.

The fine and gaol term are suspended but the husband is now on record and will be a second-time offender if he comes again before a court. The husband's only defence is to insist on a full hearing at a later date.

The court will seek more severe penalties against him at this full hearing, but the husband will have his own lawyer and the full protection of the law if he is truly innocent of the charges.

LAWSUIT WITHOUT LAWYER – *PROCESO MONITORIO*

Spain's revised Law of Civil Judgement has made it much easier for businesses and services to pursue their cases against debtors who just won't pay up.

The law allows you to make your claim without a lawyer or procurator, filling in a simple form at your nearest court, for debts up to €30,000. The words to remember are "*proceso monitorio*". This is the equivalent of a small claims court in the UK.

The creditor presents himself at the court with some evidence of the debt, such as an unpaid bill or a work order, preferably with the signature or stamp of the debtor, though this is not strictly necessary. The creditor must have the address of the debtor for official notification, and he must bring his case in the court district where the debtor resides.

The two principles of the new system are immediate action and rapid verbal hearings. Once you have presented your case, the judge should order a hearing within a short time, citing both parties to appear. At the hearing the two sides give their arguments in the presence of the judge and the process is recorded on videotape. Yes, you will be filmed.

If the debtor does not appear, or if the judge decides he has not presented a valid reason for not paying the debt, he will order the debtor to pay within 20 days. If the debtor does not pay, the judge will order his assets seized by the court in an amount sufficient to cover the debt.

These assets will be seized even if the debtor appeals to a higher court. It is now easier for courts to act against assets such as bank accounts, which can speed up the seizure process. Yes, all this sounds very well for creditors, but will it work in practice?

Most Spanish courts are simply unprepared to put the new law into effect. Not enough courtrooms have the required videotape and recording equipment, and there are not enough judges to handle all of the verbal hearings.

The process can be started very simply for debts up to €9,000, but if the amount is more than €9,000, and the debtor decides to contest the case, lawyers and procurators will be required, meaning extra expense for the creditor.

Nevertheless, the new *"proceso monitorio"* should be a useful tool for small businesses and self-employed persons with outstanding debts.

It also enables communities of property owners to proceed immediately and effectively against owners who do not pay their community fees.

JUICIO RÁPIDO

The *juicio rápido,* or "quick judgement" procedure, is another recent attempt to speed up Spanish court operations.

It can be applied to a number of situations, including hearings for traffic violators who face suspension of their driving licences, for those accused of spouse abuse and for most petty crimes.

One positive effect has been the rapid resolution of hundreds of serious traffic violations which formerly had to go through long court procedures, as well as the disposal of many petty crime cases. In spouse abuse cases the law has aided in speeding up injunctions against husbands who have committed physical abuse against their spouses.

An accused offender can choose to insist on a full hearing if he feels the abbreviated procedure will not bring him justice.

CITIZENS' BILL OF LEGAL RIGHTS

Whenever a poll is taken, Spaniards rate their justice system at the bottom of the list. In response, all political parties together have backed a "Bill of Rights for Citizens before the Administration of Justice", or *Carta de los Derechos de los Ciudadanos ante la Justicia.*

This 41-point list is designed to make the administration of justice seem more user-friendly and we can only hope that it is put effectively into practice. Any attempt to improve the present poor relations between citizens and their justice system can only be praised.

Some of the major points are:

Information: Citizens have the right to be informed by the court of any proceedings involving them and be advised of the probable length of time they will take.

Direct contact: Citizens have the right to direct contact with the judges and court secretaries involved in their case.

Compensation: Citizens' claims for compensation from the state for judicial errors shall have preferential treatment.

Lawyer's Estimate: Citizens may require a cost estimate from their lawyers in order to know approximately how much a legal proceeding will cost them.

YOUR CONSULATE

Consulates generally carry out routine paperwork with your home country's government, such as the renewal of your passport. They usually have lists of English-speaking doctors, lawyers and so on. They help persons in distress, who have lost their passports and money, for example.

What your consulate cannot do is solve your personal problems in your new country. If you are accused of a crime and put into gaol, your consular representative may visit you, but he is not in charge of handling your defence.

If you have a dispute with your Spanish neighbour, this is not the consulate's line of work. They do, however, try to be helpful and often go far beyond the call of duty in emergencies.

YOU AND THE SPANISH CONSTITUTION

Since King Juan Carlos I signed it into law in December, 1978, Spain has had a constitution similar to that of other European countries, enshrining all the normal rights and obligations of a modern, democratic state.

It guarantees the basic liberties of free speech and belief, equality before the law, freedom of religion, the right to due process of law for anyone accused of crimes, and abolishes the death penalty. It states that human freedoms will be protected by the law as set out in the Universal Declaration of Human Rights.

It declares that a person has a right to privacy and that his home may not be entered or searched without a warrant unless a serious crime is suspected. It establishes the right to a proper legal defence by a lawyer, and so on.

In Article 13, it declares that foreigners in Spain shall also enjoy all the rights established in the constitution. Article 13 first opened the door for the possibility of foreigners to vote in municipal elections where they reside in Spain.

SPAIN'S LAW FOR FOREIGNERS

Foreigners in Spain can be forgiven if sometimes they are not quite sure where they stand under the law. Or even what law they stand under.

In January of 2000 the Spanish Congress passed a sweeping law called the *Ley de Derechos y Libertades de los Extranjeros en España*, the "Law for the Rights and Freedoms of Foreigners in Spain".

The law replaced the Foreigners' Law passed in 1985 and greatly liberalised the requirements for obtaining work and residence permits for non-European Union citizens. EU citizens already enjoy almost all of the rights of Spaniards themselves.

Together with the new Foreigners' Law came a complete programme designed to help the thousands of illegal immigrants, largely from North African countries, to legalise their situation in Spain, obtaining permits and access to Spanish health care and other services.

Then the Congress, fearing the wave of illegal immigrants pouring in from Africa, turned around and made the law stiffer again. In early 2005 they changed the law yet again. The Socialist government enacted measures to allow any immigrant with a work contract and already in the country for six months to apply for a legal permit.

FELIPE VI: SPAIN'S NEW KING

With the abdication of King Juan Carlos I and the proclamation in June, 2014, of his son as King Felipe VI, Spain has a new king and a continued Constitutional Monarchy. In today's modern political times we tend to forget that Spain is in fact a Kingdom.

Hundreds of thousands of illegal immigrants applied, clogging the system so badly that thousands of "normal" foreigners find themselves waiting up to a year for a simple renewal of their residence card.

The Foreigners' Law deals with many of the areas discussed in this book, including entry formalities, resident status, work permits and penalties for foreigners living or working in Spain illegally.

It sets the criteria to use in granting a work permit, listing circumstances that will work in favour of the applicant, such as having been born in Spain, or being the spouse or child of a foreigner who already holds a work permit.

Another important section lists the circumstances under which a foreigner can be expelled from Spain, which include working without a permit, or having been convicted of a serious crime, either in Spain or abroad. The foreigner can appeal the decision. If he doesn't, he can be given 72 hours to leave Spain, and he will not be able to return for at least three years.

It also establishes a new system of "permanent" and "temporary" work and residence permits, especially designed to ease the situation of the immigrant workers, but which can also be applied to other non-EU citizens as well, such as Canadians and Australians.

GLOSSARY

Alcalde – mayor
Ayuntamiento – town hall
Censo electoral – voter list
Certificado de Empadronamiento – certificate of residence in the municipality
Comisaría – police station
Concejal – municipal councillor
Demanda – lawsuit
Demandar – to sue
Denuncia – report to authorities of an infraction
Derecho - right
Diputación – provincial legislature
Juez – judge
Juicio – trial, hearing
Juzgado – court
Multa – fine
Perito judicial – expert witness
Plus valía – municipal capital gains tax
Proceso monitorio – procedure to recover debt without lawyer involved
Querella – criminal charge
Reclamación – complaint
Votar – to vote

When you have to go to court

NEW CHAPTER by Alex Radford, English Solicitor & *Abogado*

WHAT CAN I DO ABOUT NOISY NEIGHBOURS?

Below are some answers to the most frequent questions asked, the rules and laws that govern this area and how to act when noisy neighbours do not respect the noise levels or the rules agreed in the community.

What rules and regulations are there in place where you live? What are the permitted noise levels and times when noise can be created and not? Noise regulations can be found in local, regional and state laws. These give times when noise is allowed, what intensity and up to what level of decibels. Most of these rules are specifically found in local regulations known as *Ordenanzas Municipales*.

You should be able to find your local town hall noise rules by searching for example for *Ordenanza Municipal Reguladora de la Emision y Recepcion de Ruidos y Vibraciones* on the internet.

For example the Marbella Town Hall rules can be downloaded from their official website. These rules divide the day into two noise level periods. The first is from 0800 to 2200 and the second from 2200 to 0800. In these rules it states that, during the day, with the windows closed, the permitted noise levels inside buildings, lounges and bedrooms is 30 decibels (DBA) and 28 decibels at night. So if your neighbour is playing loud music, have a look at the permitted noise levels in your area.

If it is not your neighbours causing the noise but their pets, then there will also be a local regulation governing this. For example in Torrox there is a local regulation governing noise caused by pets. Yes, we mean barking dogs. This regulation sets out that people who own domestic pets are obliged to adopt the necessary measures to ensure the tranquillity of their neighbours. From 2300 to 0700 it is prohibited to leave pets in terraces, patios, balconies or other open spaces where noise can be created.

In addition to the local regulations, other rules and laws govern permitted noise levels.

— Article 325 of the Spanish Criminal Code states that causing excessive noise is punished with up to two years in prison in extreme

cases. Fines are applied in less serious cases.
— Article 45 of the Spanish Constitution refers to protection of the individual and improvement of their quality of life. This article would be the backbone of any criminal proceedings against someone.

— Public bodies can take action against activities considered annoying, unhealthy and damaging using Decree 2414/1961 of 30 November known as the *Reglamento de Actividades Molestas, Insalubres, Nocivas y Peligrosas.*

— If the offending noise takes place in a building or an urbanisation with a Community of Property Owners, proceedings can also be issued in the Civil Courts as regulated by the Law of Horizontal Property, which punishes annoying activities caused by neighbours. All these regulations are backed up by the Constitutional Court which has ruled in cases of noise and established a fundamental right of freedom from sound contamination.

So if you have noisy neighbours, where do you start?

- First collect information about when the noise is created, what time of the day, what type of noise (music, television, shouting) and build up a body of evidence.
- Speak to your neighbour or the person causing the noise politely and calmly, explain how their noise is affecting the quality of your life and refer them to the local regulations if necessary. It you are uncomfortable talking to the neighbour or offending person on your own, take a friend or fellow neighbour who also is suffering from the same noise.
- You can visit your local police station and place a *denuncia* (official complaint) against your neighbour for committing a crime against the environment. This measure could result in a criminal sentence for the offender;
- Call the police and ask them to speak to your neighbour to reduce the noise levels. A knock at the door from a local policeman asking you to turn your music down is never a welcome knock. If the noise

continues, call the police again so there is a record of the persistent behaviour. The police or local Town Hall can check if there is excessive noise and see if the local regulations are being complied with. If the noise is being caused by a bar or disco, then the police will check the local opening licence, the number of people permitted inside and they can take action to halt the activity immediately;

- Measure the noise. For example, on your smart phone you can download a noise measuring application which can be used to show the persistent noise levels being created. Or purchase a noise-measuring device to help you build up your evidence.
- If you are going to court, it is likely that you will have to instruct a noise technician to measure the noise at different times of the day and produce a report which can be used in the legal proceedings.
- Submit a complaint at the Town Hall so that the municipal technicians are instructed to measure the noise.
- If you live in a Community of Owners you can ask the President to request the offender to cease the noisy activity. Raise the issue on the agenda for the next meeting of the community of owners;
- If you have taken some of the above steps without success, then it may be time to visit a lawyer to consider legal proceedings. Your lawyer will ask you for proof of the offending behaviour including proof of who is causing the noise, when, at what level, noise reports, and names of witnesses. Before issuing legal proceedings, be sure to obtain a full quote from your lawyer for the cost, and ask him how much you may have to pay out if the case is not successful.

GOING TO COURT IN SPAIN

Most lawyers will advise you to make every effort to settle conflicts out of court, but sometimes there is no alternative. If you have been in an accident, if you are owed money or are in dispute with your neighbour, then ask the following questions before you issue legal proceedings.

1. Do you have a valid claim? What are the prospects of success? How strong is your case? What are the weak parts?

2. Do the research on your opponent. Who are you suing? If you win, can they repay you? What assets do they have?

3. Appoint a lawyer who is experienced and used to litigating and dealing with Court agents and Judges. Don't be afraid to ask your lawyer if he has handled similar cases.

4. Make sure you can understand your lawyer. Does he speak your language? If not, consider finding a lawyer who does speak your language.

5. Appoint a lawyer who specialises in the area of law you intend to litigate in.

6. How much is your lawyer going to charge? Ask for a written quote for the legal costs of the proceedings at first instance and also for enforcing the judgement. When are the costs payable during the proceedings?

7. What other costs will you incur in the legal proceedings such as expert witness costs and court agent fees (*Procurador*).

8. If the claim is successful, will you recover all of your costs?

9. If the claim is unsuccessful, how much will you have to pay your lawyer and the other side?

10. If settlement is reached before you get to court, how much will your lawyer charge you?

11. A Spanish lawyer (*abogado*) should be registered with their local college of lawyers, the *Colegio de Abogados*, (Law Society) and have professional indemnity insurance. Ask them to confirm the level of professional indemnity insurance cover and their college of lawyers' registration number.

12. How long will the proceedings take? Can you wait that long?

13. If you are owed money, can charges be placed on the assets of the other side?

Before litigating, obtain answers to all of the questions you may have and only issue legal proceedings once you are aware of the risks involved and how much it could cost you if the claim is unsuccessful. Remember that, unfortunately, litigation is not an exact science.

PERSONAL INJURY LAW

If you have been involved in an accident in Spain or are the victim of medical negligence, or if you have stepped into an unmarked hole in the pavement and broken your leg, once liability has been admitted by the other side, then your injuries must be valued. Yes, you need a lawyer to make sure you get your fair compensation.

The Spanish legal system uses the Baremo Tables to value compensation for personal injury. These tables were first introduced in 1995 and were significantly updated in 2016 to raise compensation awards by as much as 50 per cent in some cases.

The principle of the Baremo Tables is to restore the victim, as much as possible, to his condition before the accident.

The tables are divided into three main categories. 1) Compensation for death 2) Compensation for long lasting injuries 3) Compensation for temporary injuries. Those entitled to compensation are known as beneficiaries. Below we take a look at each of these categories.

1) Compensation for death

In the event of a person being killed in an accident the following beneficiaries would be entitled to compensation:

- The widowed spouse
- Parents
- Children
- Siblings
- People who lived with the victim for a minimum period of 5 years
- Economic dependants

Compensation is calculated according to the financial loss suffered by those who depended financially on the victim. The tables are very complicated. For example, a spouse less than 67 years old who has been married 15 years and whose husband is killed in a traffic accident, has a base compensation of €90,000. Then there are the children who will get more or less depending on their ages. And on and on.

2) Compensation for long lasting injuries

This compensation is for those victims who leave hospital and continue to suffer from their injuries. For example, if their quality of life is not as good as it was before the accident, or if they continue to suffer from their injuries or are affected psychologically.

Injuries are subdivided into categories of light injuries, moderate, serious and very serious. In order for the compensation to be calculated correctly, detailed medical reports are necessary, on how the injuries affect quality of life, prognosis for the future, whether the victim will ever recover from his injuries, amount of days in hospital, days off work and other factors.

Further reports list the effects of the accident on members of the family or people close to the victim who support and may give up work or dedicate time to looking after the victim, as they are also entitled to compensation. If works are necessary to the family home to adapt it for the victim's injuries, then these costs could also be recovered.

One recent comparative study took the example of a man 41 years old left completely paralysed by an accident, with a wife and two children. In Spain the family was awarded a total of 1.2 million euros. In France the award was six million euros and in the UK it was eight million euros.

3) Compensation for temporary injuries

This part of the Baremos Tables sets out compensation for specific injuries, such as a broken leg. Like the injuries covered in part 2, these also are divided into subcategories of very serious injuries, serious, moderate and basic.

The general principle of Spanish Law is to restore the victim or their family members to the condition they were in prior to the accident. Therefore any costs reasonably incurred can be recovered. Spanish insurance companies, however, can be frustrating and obstructive to deal with when claiming compensation. If you have been involved in an accident you should instruct an experienced personal injury lawyer and qualified experts to prepare reports supporting your claim.

WHO PAYS THE JUDICIAL COSTS?

Let's suppose that you have won your case, but who pays for the costs you have incurred in the proceedings? These judicial costs could be your lawyer's fees, the court agent's fees (*Procurador*), costs of witnesses, expert's fees, costs of certificates and searches.

In the Spanish legal system, there is the general principle that whoever wins the case has the right to insist on payment of the judicial costs incurred. However, in order to recover those costs, it is necessary that the court sentence expressly states that the other side has to pay the costs. Without this express statement in the sentence, judicial costs cannot be recovered.

If one party is only partially successful in the legal proceedings, then it is not unusual for there to be no statement regarding judicial costs, which means that each side pays its own costs. Even if your case has been successful, if the other side has been declared insolvent, then it will be difficult to recover judicial costs. So try to make sure you only sue someone who can pay.

If you lost the case, then you will pay your own team's legal costs and also, potentially, the judicial costs of the other side.

Unless a court sentence states the exact amount of legal costs to be paid to the winning party, then the parties proceed to what is known as the valuation of costs (*tasación de costas*). The procedure values the judicial costs payable to you. If the losing side does not pay those costs voluntarily, then proceedings can be issued to enforce payment.

IF YOU HAVE AN ACCIDENT

If you have a traffic accident where other cars and drivers are involved, as soon as possible after the initial shock, you need to assemble the names, addresses, car registration numbers, contact information and insurance policy numbers of all drivers involved, details of anyone injured and of other passengers. If it is clear who is responsible for the accident and you and the other drivers agree, you can sign the form known as parte amistosa, which means a friendly report, in which you will draw a diagram of the accident, explain how the accident occurred, insert the details of the drivers as well as their insurance companies and state who is responsible for the accident.

If blame for the accident is not clear, state that responsibility for the accident is not agreed. Even though this report form is standard in Europe, be extremely careful about signing anything you do not completely understand. The document is admissible evidence in court.

When the emergency is dealt with, inform your insurance company as soon as possible and they will send you a claim form to repair the damage to the car.

Claim up to one year

The good news is that you have one entire year to make or to modify your claim for injury or damages. It might be a back injury or even some twisted part of your car which is not immediately apparent and only comes to light months later.

Article 7 of the *Ley sobre Responsabilidad Civil y Seguro en la Circulación de Vehiculos a Motor* establishes that the injured person or their heirs shall have a direct action against the insurer for all compensation, which shall lapse after one year. Therefore it is important to notify the insurance company and person who caused the accident of the claim within one year of the date of the accident. Otherwise you could lose your right to compensation.

DEBTORS IN A COMMUNITY OF OWNERS

If your Spanish property is in a *Comunidad de Propietarios*, a community of owners, then you are legally bound to pay the Community fees. If you fall behind in the payment of the fees, then the Community can take legal proceedings against you. The list of debtors will be published at the general meeting of the owners, the AGM. In the same meeting the assembled owners will vote to approve the appointment of lawyers and court agents, after which they can bring a case against you to recover the fees.

Legal proceedings for recovery of Community debts move a little more briskly than other cases because there is usually no dispute about the fact that payment is due. Once judgement is obtained, the Community of Property Owners can place charges against your property for the debt owed and for the judicial costs. They can seize the amount of the debt from your Spanish bank account. In extreme cases, the property can be sold to pay the Community debts. If you are in debt with your Community, do not bury your head in the sand. Talk to the President and attempt to make some regular payments.

GLOSSARY

Abogado – lawyer, attorney, solicitor
Actividades Molestas – bothersome or annoying activities
Baremo – tables to evaluate injury compensation
Denuncia – official complaint
Hoja de Encargo – work order, for lawyer or plumber
Ordenanza Municipal – Municipal Ordinance
Parte Amistosa – "Friendly" accident report
Procurador – administrative court agent
Perito Judicial – Expert authorised by court
Tasación de Costas – valuation of costs

You and Your Legal Advisers

Who are these legal advisers we keep telling you to consult? What can the Spanish *abogado*, the *gestor*, the *asesor fiscal*, the *Notario* and the *administrador de fincas* do for you?

They can do a lot to steer you right and save you money while protecting you from a load of problems and headaches. Let's examine each of them.

YOUR *ABOGADO*

Abogado means lawyer, solicitor or attorney. Do not be afraid to consult a Spanish lawyer. They are trained professionals whose job is to serve their clients within the law.

Many of them who practise in areas with many foreigners speak excellent English or German and are accustomed to dealing with foreign residents in Spain and their special problems.

Foreigners make up more than half the clients of many lawyers in Marbella and the surrounding area, for example. In Fuengirola, more than 40 per cent of all court cases involve foreigners. These Spanish lawyers make their living by serving their foreign clients, and they are prepared to serve you as well.

If you are purchasing property in Spain, starting a business, attempting to get a work permit, investing in a Spanish business, or making a Spanish will, you need a Spanish lawyer to advise you.

A lawyer will check the title of property you wish to buy in order to discover if the seller really holds clear title or if there are unpaid taxes on the property. He will vet your contract to make sure the provisions are the normal ones and do not contain any tricky clauses working to your disadvantage.

In a country where you do not speak the language, do not have any local knowledge and are not familiar with the law, it seems basic common sense to get expert help, for your own protection.

Doing it yourself is often penny-wise and pound-foolish. Yes, you can get a standard form to make a Spanish will and have the Notario register it for a small fee. But only the *abogado* will explain to you whether you can legally make such a will or not. Your terms may not be valid in Spanish law.

In any case, when it is time to probate the will and distribute the estate, a lawyer's services will be necessary, and the lawyer who prepared the will in the first place will be familiar with its terms and prepared to see they are carried out.

Spanish lawyers work with another professional, called a *Procurador*, who handles much of the complicated routine of preparation and presentation of documents to the court. The *Procurador* charges his fees separately. If a lot of paperwork is involved, they can be substantial.

If you instruct a lawyer to act for you in your absence, you can be sure that your taxes, fees and other matters will be correctly handled while you are away. If you employ a lawyer for one transaction, you will later find it easy to ring him up for five minutes of consultation. There are dozens of ways a lawyer can help you.

LAWYERS' FEES

Lawyers' fees vary widely because they depend on the amount of work involved. A half-hour consultation with a lawyer may cost you 60 euros and save you hundreds of thousands. Or it may cost you nothing, depending on the situation.

Handling a property purchase may cost you as little as €500 or it could run into the thousands if the lawyer discovers complications that need sorting out.

One rough estimate for property transactions is one per cent of the amount involved, although many lawyers will try to charge more.

Ask in advance, and try to establish an agreed fee or percentage before you assign your case to a lawyer. Many of them will agree to this and you can avoid unpleasant surprises later.

The *Colegio de Abogados* publishes a list of guidelines, setting minimum recommended fees.

Property purchase: One per cent of the total price is standard.

Residence and work permit: €300 for a married couple.

Disputes over money: There is a sliding scale. To claim €600,000, a lawyer will charge 10 per cent. For €300,000, the base fee is 5 per cent.

Divorce: Where there are no children and no property at stake, and the divorce is by mutual agreement, a minimum of €1,000.

Will preparation: Minimum €100, plus about €60 to Notary.

These are rock-bottom fees, remember, but they give you an idea. A "Bill of Rights for Citizens before the Administration of Justice" (*Carta de Derechos de los Ciudadanos ante la Justicia*) provides for the *hoja de encargo*, a work order, which lists the services that the lawyer will provide and the fees he will charge.

The work order provision is part of a 41-point programme to make the citizen's contact with the legal system more user-friendly (see section on Courts for more details).

As lawyers are notoriously reluctant to tell clients what their fees will be, we can only hope that this laudable initiative works out in practice. On the lawyer's side of the case, it is difficult for them to know in advance just how complicated a case may turn out to be.

Nevertheless, it is certainly worth mentioning this Bill of Rights when you try to find out how much your lawyer will charge you.

HOW TO COMPLAIN

If you find that your lawyer is not giving you proper service, is there anything you can do? Suppose you have waited two years for your title deed and you hear nothing from the lawyer, and you wish to make a formal complaint. Or perhaps you have received an extremely high bill for services not correctly rendered.

The professional organisation which watches standards and defends the interests of its members is called the *Ilustre Colegio de Abogados* (the Illustrious College of Lawyers). You can complain directly to this body, which has branches in each province, about the activities of one of its members. A simple letter to the *Colegio* stating your problem should draw a response and they may even question the lawyer about his practices or charges.

As in any country, one finds that the lawyers' watchdog committee is reluctant to condemn a fellow attorney, but they will hear your complaint and look into it. The *Colegio* is perfectly aware of the normal fees for various legal services, and they may decide that you have a good case for claiming that you have been overcharged for some particular service.

Even so, it is not wise to depend entirely on the *Colegio* to act on your behalf. You will probably want to consult another lawyer, who will help you prepare a letter of complaint to the College. The College will question your original lawyer about the problem. Your original lawyer will then have to explain the basis for his fees.

If the explanation does not satisfy the College, you will get a reduction.

In serious cases, the College takes stronger action. A number of Spanish lawyers have been charged with failure to perform the services for which they were instructed, or for using their clients' money for their own purposes, or for participating in schemes to cheat their clients.

These lawyers will be fined, disbarred and even imprisoned. It does happen, so do not hesitate to make your complaint if you feel that you have been wronged.

Remember that it also helps to have your agreement with your lawyer written and signed. This will help both in negotiating fees and in establishing the facts if you have a complaint.

FREE LEGAL ASSISTANCE

If you are a resident of modest means, you may even find that you are entitled to free legal aid in Spain.

The poor have been guaranteed free access to legal defence since the granting of the Spanish Constitution in 1978. Nevertheless, the system has been sharply criticised for the limited service provided, for abuse by persons falsely claiming to be poor, and for the fact that the state paid the public defenders too little and too late, which did not encourage them to work hard for their clients.

A new Free Legal Assistance law has been enacted to remedy these defects.

The law of *Asistencia Jurídica Gratuita* provides easier access to legal help, greatly widens the scope of the help available, and attempts to check the abuse of the system by persons who in fact have sufficient means to pay their own private lawyer.

For the foreigner, the good news is that even a non-resident of Spain may qualify for free legal aid. Resident foreigners of course are entitled.

Persons of incomes below 2.5 times the official minimum wage are entitled to free legal aid. As the Spanish minimum wage is about €8,000 a year, this means families with incomes under €20,000.

Furthermore, the *Colegio de Abogados* has installed its own offices in each judicial district in Spain. Those who are seeking free legal aid can present themselves at their local office and request the forms to apply for aid.

You will find the legal aid offices in your local court building, usually called the *Palacio de Justicia*. We say it's easy, but filling in the forms can be complicated.

In an attempt to identify false applicants, the forms require copies of your Spanish income tax declaration, or a certificate from *Hacienda* that you do not pay income tax. The form also requires a certification from your town hall listing any properties you own, and even a note from the Traffic Department giving details of any automobiles you own in Spain.

Workers and beneficiaries of the Spanish Social Security system also have the right to free representation before the labour court, so anyone who feels he has been mistreated by his Spanish employer can be sure of professional assistance to plead his case.

For the first time, the legal aid includes advice and planning before any court action takes place. This means that a poor person who feels that he must bring a lawsuit against a neighbour who has built a road across part of his garden can get legal advice and help before he takes any action.

Perhaps a pointed letter from the lawyer will settle the matter out of court, thus saving time and money for the taxpayers as well as the persons involved.

The law also provides free access to the services of court-appointed experts, those professionals who evaluate the costs of a botched plumbing or carpentry job, for example, so the judge can assign a value.

In Spanish such an expert is called a *perito judicial*. Even the threat of calling one can often make the offending supplier back off on his attempts to collect a bill for substandard work.

Even more important, the free legal aid law provides an exemption from the deposits necessary in many legal actions.

Often, you must make a deposit of a certain percentage of the amount you are seeking in order for the court to accept your suit. Although this aims to discourage people from making idle lawsuits simply for the nuisance value, it also has the effect of preventing persons of modest means from bringing some justified legal actions.

So, the exemption from deposit empowers them to sue when otherwise they would not be able to do so.

A false declaration of poverty or the concealment of financial resources can bring an order to repay to the State any expenses incurred on behalf of the person who has requested free legal aid. This is to prevent abuses of the system, which occurred all too frequently under the former law.

YOUR *GESTORÍA*

All countries have bureaucracies and red tape, forms to fill in, certificates to be obtained, licences and permits but some people say that Spanish red tape is in a class all its own. Not only foreigners in Spain have to deal with this *papeleo*, or paperchase. Spaniards themselves have the same forms to deal with and are driven just as mad by their own bureaucracy. This situation has given rise to the *gestoría*, a peculiarly Spanish institution licensed by the government.

The *gestor* is the middleman between you and the bureaucracy. When you are standing in line waiting to present the papers for your residence renewal and you see a man with a folder of papers pass directly behind the counter and engage the attention of one of the clerks while you and the rest of the people wait, that is the man from the *gestoría*.

He is doing exactly what you are doing, but he is doing it for half a dozen or so people who have paid him to handle the matter. He receives prompt attention from the clerks not because he pays them bribes, but because he saves them work. They know that his forms will be properly filled in and all necessary documents present.

The *gestoría* can save you a lot of time and trouble, usually for a rather small fee. The *gestor* has no official powers, but he must pass an exam and is licensed by the authorities as a professional. He can be held to account if he mishandles your applications or charges for services he does not perform.

The *gestor*, if he is experienced, can do a great deal more than save you time in the queue. There are *gestorías* in large cities with 30 or 40 employees, where you find experts on one floor arranging the Social Security payments for a restaurant's waiters, while on the next floor someone is processing the papers to renew the tourist licence plates for a foreigner's car, and on the ground floor a messenger is picking up clients' property purchase contracts to take along to the registry office.

They carry out all the operations described in this book, and many more besides. They can advise you on all sorts of transactions.
If you are starting a business, you will definitely need a good *gestoría* to steer you through the complexities of licensing, administration, bookkeeping and taxation. There are also small *gestorías* which simply do not have the expertise to handle a lot of the often complex problems involving foreigners, so it is necessary to ask among old hands for a *gestoría* which has given them satisfactory service.

The *gestor*, as a licensed professional, also has a *colegio*, and if you feel that you have not received satisfactory service, you may lodge a complaint. Ask in advance what the fees are for the service you require. If they seem high to you, try another *gestoría*. The *colegio* sets fees, but these are minimums, not maximums, unfortunately, as their primary aim is to prevent a price war.

One note of warning: Although a good *gestor* can provide many services, including the arranging of rental contracts and the hiring and paying of employees, we advise you to use the services of a lawyer and a tax consultant as well, to make sure that you are fully protected.

Sometimes a busy *gestor* will apply a standard contract in a situation where legal or tax complications can later arise, so do not be lulled into a false sense of security when he says that your contract is the one everyone uses. He is probably right, but check with the lawyer and tax consultant just to be sure.

YOUR *ASESOR FISCAL*

Literally translated, this is a "fiscal adviser", basically an accountant and tax consultant.

In the first stages of your residence in Spain, you may not need an accountant. But when it is time for you to declare for Spanish income tax, you should certainly consult an *asesor fiscal*. If you have any investments in Spain or are starting a business, you will also need an accountant or financial consultant.

He can save you money and see that you keep on the right side of the ever-changing tax laws as well. Again, you should ask among veteran residents to find a satisfactory *asesor fiscal*.

Otherwise, you may have the frustrating experience of one resident who, out of curiosity, consulted three accountants, two *gestorías*, and the information office of *Hacienda* about his income tax, and received six different answers.

As discussed in the section on You and Your Taxes, the income tax situation in Spain is gradually becoming stricter, and foreigners have the additional complications of taxes paid outside Spain or income arising outside Spain, which require expert advice.

In business, you will need to know things like just how much holiday pay your workers should get, what expenses you can deduct, how to reclaim Value Added Tax you have paid.

Most of these accountants are also familiar with labour legislation and can advise you on whether or not you may dismiss a worker, and how much compensation you will have to pay him.

Unlike the *gestor* or the *abogado*, anyone may set himself up as a tax consultant as there are no legal requirements. This means that, if you suffer loss through bad advice or service from your adviser, you have no easy recourse to a professional oversight body. Your only remedy will be to bring a civil lawsuit against him in the normal courts for the loss.

THE *NOTARIO*

The *Notario*, public Notary, is a public official, like a judge, and you cannot employ him as your agent or instruct him to act for you in the same way you engage a lawyer or accountant, although he can give you useful advice.

His principal mission is to make sure that certain matters are officially noted and registered. These include wills, as discussed in the section on Making A Will, and various sorts of contracts, such as your purchase contract when you buy property. He will register your foreign money contribution when you buy your property. He also registers the charters of companies, and the official book of minutes of a community of property owners is presented for his stamp, which makes the book an official matter of public record.

You might also need a notarised letter when you notify the tenant of your property that you wish to end the rental when the contract term ends, or to make some other official notification.

The Notary receives fees from you for these services, but you cannot instruct him to act for you in the same way as a lawyer or an accountant. These fees are fixed by law.

They currently run about €75 for a will and about €500 for a property sales contract.

For most foreign property purchasers, their big moment comes when they sign their contract at the Notary's office. The Notary or your lawyer then passes the contract to the Property Registry for inscription.

The original of your property contract, the *escritura*, stays in the Notary's office, where you can always request an authorised copy. He also keeps the original copies of Spanish wills made before him.

In the past, Spanish notaries did not hesitate to register sales contracts which obviously under-declared the real amount of the purchase price, nor did they involve themselves with payment of taxes.

Now, however, they are required to warn the parties to contracts that if they undervalue the purchase significantly, they will be subject to fines if *Hacienda* discovers this.

As part of enforcing Spain's campaign against tax fraud, the Notary is now obliged to take much greater care when he identifies the source of funds used to purchase property.

If you have a Spanish bank account and you get a bank cheque for the seller to pay for your new property in Spain, you will be fine. If you wish to pay for the property in pounds to a non-resident seller in the UK, you may do this but you should obtain a copy of the bank transfer or cheque beforehand to present to the Notary.

They must also verify that three per cent of the purchase price is withheld and paid to *Hacienda* when property is sold by a non-resident, as a guarantee against the capital gains tax.

THE *ADMINISTRADOR DE FINCAS*

This licensed professional is a property administrator. He can handle all of the matters that come up with your property, such as seeing that taxes are paid, managing rentals and making sure that books are properly kept. He is licensed to serve as a paid administrator for property owners' communities.

Although there is no legal requirement that a community administrator be a licensed professional, it is often a good idea to employ an administrador de fincas because he will see that the community's affairs are handled professionally.

"*Finca*" in this case does not mean a little house in the countryside. It refers to all property in general. He can advise you about any aspect of owning and purchasing property.

Like the other professional groups, there is a *colegio* which oversees standards for these property consultants, and you can formally complain to this college if you feel your administrator has not given you reasonable service.

HOW TO CHOOSE A LEGAL ADVISER

Walk into the nearest bar or hairdresser and ask them to recommend a lawyer or a tax consultant. Anybody in business will have an opinion, whether they are foreign or Spanish.

Visit three establishments and you will have a list of professionals whom people love — and another list of advisers to stay away from. You will also have a fund of useful practical information about how things really work in Spain, because every new settler has a story and loves to tell it.

The consulates of all nations maintain lists of lawyers, tax consultants, doctors and other professionals who speak the language of their nation. These lists are not necessarily professionals whom the consulate is recommending. They are simply noted as speaking your language.

GLOSSARY

Abogado – lawyer, attorney, solicitor
Administrador de fincas – licensed property administrator and manager
Asesor fiscal – tax consultant and accountant
Asistencia jurídica gratuita – free legal aid
Colegio – official college of professionals
Gestoría – licensed administrative office
Hoja de encargo – work order, either for a plumber or a lawyer
Notario – public Notary
Perito judicial – court-appointed technical expert
Procurador – legal expert who works with lawyer

How to Complain

Sometimes people will put up with mistreatment because they are confused and ignorant of how to go about protesting in their new country. But even though consumer protection in Spain still lags behind many countries, you can usually get a hearing when you have a complaint.

TOWN HALL

Town halls maintain offices where you make a *reclamación* in writing if your complaint has to do with municipal services such as poor rubbish collection or cuts in the water supply.

The Law of Local Administrations requires the town hall to accept your complaint and register it as received for consideration. They are supposed to respond within a relatively short period of time, even if their answer is a refusal of your demand, but in practice we find that many complaints are slow to produce results.

If your town hall has an office for foreign residents with staff who speak several languages, this would be your best starting point, of course. More and more towns with many foreign residents are opening these offices and some of them give excellent service.

You may follow up by asking for the appropriate concejal, or council member. Each councillor is assigned a particular area of responsibility, such as rubbish collection or street maintenance, and he will probably give you an appointment so that you can discuss your problem in person with him or her. If you don't speak Spanish, take an interpreter with you.

Sometimes you may even be pleasantly surprised when a simple telephone call about the broken streetlight brings a repair crew the same afternoon.

OMIC – THE PLACE TO START

This is the big one. Most towns maintain consumer information and complaint offices called *Oficina Municipal de Información al Consumidor* which can inform you about prices, quality requirements for merchandise, and also process complaints. These offices are sometimes located at the municipal market and sometimes they are in the town hall itself.

The OMIC offices are usually very helpful and make an effort to see that action is taken. The offices themselves have no legal power to compel the return of an item or punish offenders, but they see that the proper authorities are informed.

This is where you present your complaint sheet for processing almost any complaint about a commercial establishment, from a restaurant to an auto repair garage (see below).

We recommend the OMIC as the place to start almost every sort of complaint. Even if the problem does not come under their competence, they will help you to find the most effective method of dealing with it.

The OMIC is not limited to basic consumer problems such as defective goods or abusive prices. They can process complaints about timeshare, rentals, mobile phones and property purchase, too.

HOJA DE RECLAMACIÓN

Most foreigners first become acquainted with the *Hoja de Reclamación*, the complaints sheet, in a restaurant or bar, where a notice proclaims in Spanish and English that the sheet is available. All establishments are required by law to keep this official complaint sheet.

When a customer complains, they must produce the sheet for him to register his complaint. If the establishment refuses to produce the complaint sheet and you are really serious about your problem, you go outside and find the nearest policeman. Return to the shop with the policeman. If they do not produce the complaint sheet in his presence, they can be fined up to €6,000.

The sheet comes in three copies. It is in Spanish with a brief English translation (see the example on another page). Our example is the Andalusian one. Forms may differ from region to region. The establishment keeps one copy and the customer takes the other two, one to retain and the other to present at the local OMIC office for processing.

If you do not like confrontation with the establishment owner, you can simply go to the OMIC, where they have the forms on file. Staff will help you prepare your complaint correctly. You can then return to the establishment and drop off a copy for them. If the manager refuses to sign the form, this is not strictly necessary.

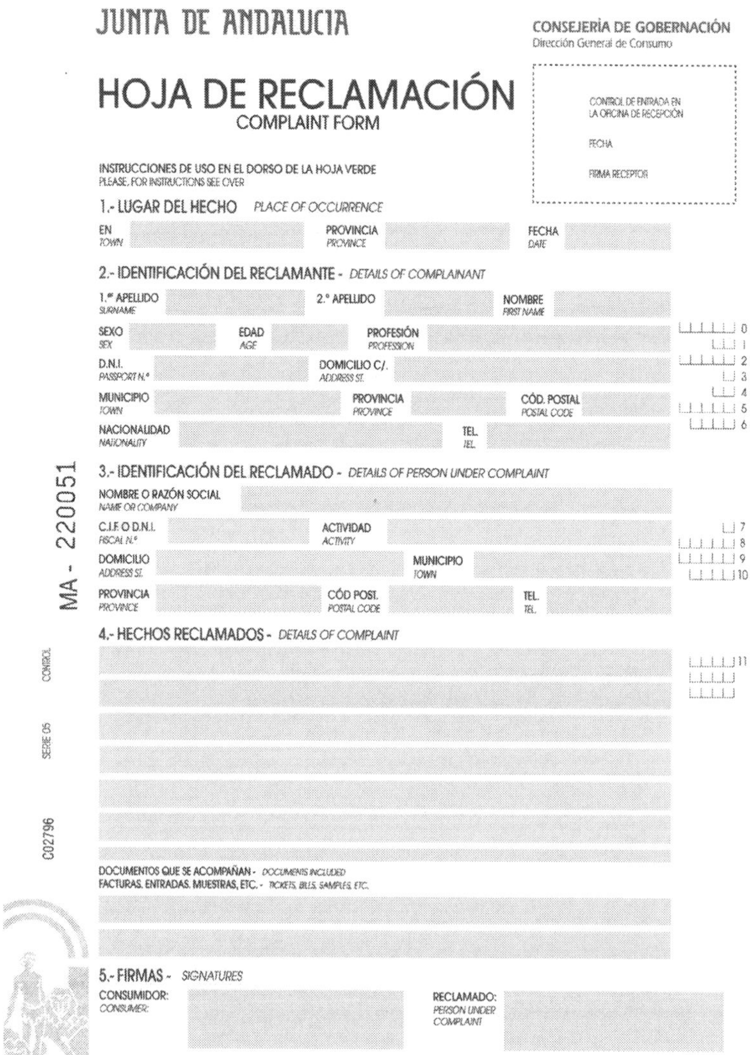
JUNTA DE ANDALUCIA

CONSEJERÍA DE GOBERNACIÓN
Dirección General de Consumo

HOJA DE RECLAMACIÓN
COMPLAINT FORM

CONTROL DE ENTRADA EN LA OFICINA DE RECEPCIÓN
FECHA
FIRMA RECEPTOR

INSTRUCCIONES DE USO EN EL DORSO DE LA HOJA VERDE
PLEASE, FOR INSTRUCTIONS SEE OVER

1.- LUGAR DEL HECHO *PLACE OF OCCURRENCE*

EN *TOWN* — PROVINCIA *PROVINCE* — FECHA *DATE*

2.- IDENTIFICACIÓN DEL RECLAMANTE - *DETAILS OF COMPLAINANT*

1.er APELLIDO *SURNAME* — 2.° APELLIDO — NOMBRE *FIRST NAME*

SEXO *SEX* — EDAD *AGE* — PROFESIÓN *PROFESSION*

D.N.I. *PASSPORT N.°* — DOMICILIO C/. *ADDRESS ST.*

MUNICIPIO *TOWN* — PROVINCIA *PROVINCE* — CÓD. POSTAL *POSTAL CODE*

NACIONALIDAD *NATIONALITY* — TEL. *TEL.*

0 1 2 3 4 5 6

3.- IDENTIFICACIÓN DEL RECLAMADO - *DETAILS OF PERSON UNDER COMPLAINT*

NOMBRE O RAZÓN SOCIAL *NAME OR COMPANY*

C.I.F. O D.N.I. *FISCAL N.°* — ACTIVIDAD *ACTIVITY*

DOMICILIO *ADDRESS ST.* — MUNICIPIO *TOWN*

PROVINCIA *PROVINCE* — CÓD POST. *POSTAL CODE* — TEL. *TEL.*

7 8 9 10

MA - 220051

4.- HECHOS RECLAMADOS - *DETAILS OF COMPLAINT*

11

CONTROL SERIE 05 C02796

DOCUMENTOS QUE SE ACOMPAÑAN - *DOCUMENTS INCLUDED*
FACTURAS, ENTRADAS, MUESTRAS, ETC. - *TICKETS, BILLS, SAMPLES, ETC.*

5.- FIRMAS - *SIGNATURES*

CONSUMIDOR: *CONSUMER:* — RECLAMADO: *PERSON UNDER COMPLAINT*

Each province has a consumer affairs department. If you want to make sure your complaint is heard, you can follow up your *Hoja de Reclamación* by checking back with the OMIC to see whether they have examined the sheet from the offending establishment.

Consumer laws in Andalusia, for example, require absolutely all businesses to keep such complaint sheets. They must respond directly to the client's complaint within 10 days. If they do not, the client can continue his case through the OMIC.

This includes automobile repairs, sales of appliances and restaurants, to name three typical areas of complaint.

You can also make a complaint to the tourist office which most towns maintain. Although these offices are primarily there to give information, they will direct you to the appropriate place for making your particular complaint known.

If you have a complaint about a shop regarding weight, quality, service or prices, you can direct this to the *Jefatura Provincial de Comercio Interior*, the Provincial Department of Internal Commerce, in your province.

This office is charged with seeing that weights are honest, that prices are within certain margins on controlled items, and that merchandise is up to standard. Although they probably will not oblige a market stall to replace the kilo of rotten oranges they sold you, these offices maintain a staff of inspectors who will visit an offending establishment. If they find any violations, the shopkeeper will be warned or fined.

EUROPEAN CONSUMER DIRECTIVE

When you buy a washing machine or any home appliance in Spain, you should know that European Union consumer directives prescribe an obligatory guarantee for two years. This replaces Spain's former requirement of a six-month guarantee. Remember that you must fill in your guarantee form and have it stamped to assure this.

When you wish to return a defective appliance to the shop which sold it to you, they sometimes declare that they are not responsible and that you must deal with the manufacturer directly. This is simply not true. Recent Spanish consumer legislation obliges the seller to make good on the guarantee.

If you do not get satisfaction, you have recourse to the OMIC. If you are a serious consumer, you might consider one of Spain's consumer organisations, as described below.

See What To Do section for an example of how things might work.

CONSUMER ORGANISATIONS

There are a number of national consumer organisations, as well as others which operate in the various provinces or autonomous regions. These organisations generally require that you become a member and pay their yearly fees, which are not high, in order to benefit from their services.

One of the largest and most effective of the national organisations, with a good record of assistance to consumers, is the OCU, the Organización de Consumidores y Usuarios. Their head office is in Madrid and their telephone number is 91-300 00 45. Or send them a fax at 91-388 73 72.

WHAT TO DO If you buy a lemon

Mrs. García bought a shiny new washing machine, but only five weeks later it stopped working. The machine was covered by guarantee so a repairman came and re-did the programme. But a few weeks later the motor stopped and had to be replaced. Then it de-programmed itself again.

These breakdowns continued, and Mrs. García knew she had bought a "lemon", a unit or an automobile that comes with factory defects. It would never be right.

Her initial attempts to have the machine replaced with a new one instead of endlessly repairing it failed. The shop simply refused. Mrs. García obtained the *hoja de reclamación*, the complaints sheet, and filed a complaint with her local OMIC, or consumer office.

Her complaint was being processed but it got no immediate result. She still had no washing machine. Then she contacted the consumer organisation she had joined the previous year. They contacted the manufacturer directly and within two weeks Mrs. García had a new washing machine.

The shop itself was required by law to replace the defective machine, but they refused to do this. The manufacturer would have eventually replaced her machine in any case, but it seems clear that the call from the consumer organisation had some effect.

Mrs. García feels that her annual dues of 40 euros to the consumer group is money well spent.

They offer an advice service weekdays from 10am to Ipm on 91-388 74 24. Their Barcelona office also offers consumer advice on 93-218 06 11 from 10am to 12 noon.

The OCU publishes a magazine called *Compra Maestra,* which analyses different products, and another called *Dinero y Derechos,* which concentrates on legal and financial matters. Both of these publications are excellent sources of information for this book.

Another excellent national group is *Facua* – Consumers in Action. You can visit their web site at www.facua.org and find information in English. They have been particularly active in forcing Spain's electric companies to make refunds on bills they overcharged. Other consumer organisations are found in the telephone book of your area. These locally-based consumer associations may be particularly effective in different areas. We give details on the OCU simply as one example.

WHAT TO DO To fight the electric company !

A recent study showed that something like 20 per cent of all electric metres in Spain do not function correctly. Nevertheless, this could actually work in favour of the consumer.

One problem area can arise when you buy a re-sale property from a private owner, who still owes an electric bill. Sometimes the company does not even read the metre for months and months, charging only the base fee. Then they read the metre and charge for four months or even six.

If you are a new owner, you are not responsible for the bills of the preceding owner. The company will try to charge you for it, however, saying they will cut off the electricity.

Let them cut it off. Then make a new contract with the company in your own name. This new contract starts from zero.

The company cannot deny you a new contract, no matter what they say.

Another problem is damage arising from power cuts. This could be food in the freezer or damage to your electrical appliances. You go first to the company itself with some proof of the damage. If they do not pay, you go to the consumer office, the OMIC, and file a claim there. Spanish electric companies pay out millions in damages every year. Recent consumer legislation requires them to give your five hours of free consumption for every hour you have been without power.

Other defenders of consumers' and citizens' rights include:

OMBUDSMAN

If your complaint to the town hall, as mentioned above, fails to bring the desired result, or if you feel that you have been unjustly treated by any government agency, you may have recourse to the *Defensor del Pueblo*, the regional or national ombudsman. You must have exhausted all normal administrative channels before he will accept your case. This Defender of the People is the last resort when you are convinced that justice has not been done.

BANKING COMPLAINTS

Every Spanish bank has its own central Defender of the Customer (*Defensor del Cliente*), who will hear your complaint when you do not get satisfaction from the branch office. If you are still unsatisfied, you have recourse to the complaints department of the Bank of Spain.

Your first step is to talk to your local bank manager. If this does not produce results, you need to make your complaint in writing to your bank's *Defensor del Cliente*. If they do not respond within two months or if their answer is negative, you can then go to the Bank of Spain, the *Banco de España*, with full documentation of your complaint. If your complaint refers to a delayed response or a negative decision from your local bank, they promise to resolve your case within six weeks. Their web site is bde.es.

DOCTORS AND HOSPITALS

If you have a complaint against the treatment given you by a private doctor, you can present this to the *Colegio de Médicos*, the College of Physicians, which is the professional body overseeing doctors. If you feel that you have a case for malpractice, you can bring a civil suit against the doctor for damages and suffering. If you are not properly treated in a Social Security hospital, you can also claim against the regional health system. These cases are now appearing with more frequency in Spain, and courts have made large awards. There is also an association for the defence of the patient which has branches in major cities.

LAWYERS

As mentioned in the section on lawyers, the Law Society, or body which controls professional standards and fees, is called the *Colegio de Abogados*. Your best bet is probably to consult another lawyer and explain your case to him. The new lawyer will help you put your complaint in proper form. Nevertheless, you can go directly to the *Colegio* office in your province if you feel you have been overcharged or improperly treated.

REAL ESTATE AGENTS

In some European countries, the responsibilities of real estate agents are very carefully regulated. Unfortunately, in practical terms, this is not the case in Spain. Anyone may mediate in property transactions and "buyer beware" is the only advice we can give. There are professional bodies for registered agents such as the API, the *Agente de la Propiedad Inmobiliaria*, which enforces standards. However, many property agencies are not registered and the law does not require this.

TAX CONSULTANTS

If your Spanish *asesor fiscal*, or tax consultant, has given you bad advice which has cost you money, your only remedy is to bring a civil lawsuit against him. Many tax consultants have advanced training and are members of the various associations, but there is no professional oversight body so anyone can hang out his shingle and call himself a tax consultant.

GLOSSARY

Ayuntamiento – town hall
Compra – purchase
Comprador – purchaser
Concejal – municipal councillor
Consumidor - consumer
Demanda – lawsuit
Demandar – to sue
Factura – bill, invoice
Hoja de Reclamación – complaint form required of all businesses
OMIC - Oficina Municipal de Información al Consumidor – municipal consumer information office, receives complaints
Reclamación – complaint

SECTION

2

Property in Spain

Buying Property

2018 – PROPERTY MARKET PICKING UP

The property market in Spain has been picking up for the past few years, based on increasing demand from Europe and very low mortgage rates. The base lending index, the Euribor is at practically zero, meaning home mortgages at minimal interest. Prices are rising a little for both new and resale properties, but most experts feel that this is not the start of another real estate boom. British buyers in particular are being held back by doubts about Brexit and by the pound's dropping value against the Euro.

The foreign buyer needs to take care. Too many purchasers seem to leave their common sense at the airport when they enter Spain.

You need sound legal advice from a Spanish professional who may be a lawyer, a registered estate agent, a specialised *gestor*, or an *administrador de fincas*, any of whom is qualified to act in your interests and make sure you are protected and well-advised in the transaction. It's foolish to depend entirely on the seller of the property to make sure you are treated fairly.

REAL ESTATE AGENTS

Let's start at the beginning. Your first contact when you decide to buy property in Spain will almost certainly be the estate agent.

In many countries, an estate agent is a registered professional who can be held financially responsible if he acts as intermediary in a sale and the terms later turn out to be falsely based.

In Spain there is no law regulating real estate agents. Anyone may act as intermediary. This means it is difficult to hold an estate agent responsible when a purchase goes wrong. Citizens of Scandinavian countries, or the UK, for example, where consumers are more carefully protected, even from their own mistakes, should be warier in Spain.

There are, however, two professional associations which require examinations and set standards for their members. One of these offers the title of *Agente de la Propiedad Inmobiliaria*, or API for short. The other is the *Gestor Intermediario de Propiedades y Edificios* (the GIPE). You will do well to deal with an estate agent who holds one of these titles.

Even so, if your Spanish estate agent causes you to suffer loss, either through negligence or honest error, you will have a hard time obtaining any recompense. Ask your agent if he carries professional indemnity insurance, and, if so, how much. You may again be surprised to find that most estate agents have either no insurance at all or a minimum amount required by the official Spanish agents' association. Ask your agent if he operates a Bonded Clients' Account, into which any deposits will be placed, and which is untouchable except for the stated purpose of the deposit.

Example: sellers make off with deposit

Here is what can happen if you pay your deposit directly to the seller.

A British couple found an apartment they liked on the Costa del Sol. They agreed a price of €280,000, and they transferred a deposit of €28,000, 10 per cent of the price, to its German owners to reserve the villa.

The British couple used a Spanish lawyer plus the advice of a British property agent working in Spain and they felt all was well. They sold their home in the UK, shipped their furniture to Spain, wound up their business, and came to Spain for the closing of the sale, when they would pay the rest of the price and sign the deed.

Just before the date with the Notary, their lawyer received a message from the German sellers, saying they could not make it that day and that they would be in touch later. This set off alarm bells with everybody involved. It turned out that the owners had in fact sold the property a month earlier for €310,000 to another buyer, had kept the €28,000 deposited with them, and had left Spain for parts unknown.

Of course the unfortunate British buyers have a clear case against the German sellers for breach of contract, with the right to recover their deposit, plus damages and loss, but how are they going to find them? In fact, they have the right to a sum twice the amount of the deposit if the seller backs out of the deal.

In many European countries, the buyers would also have a case against the estate agent and perhaps the lawyer as well for negligence in performing their services. In Spain they also have a case, but here standards are less strict and the lawyer and estate agent may declare that they simply followed accepted practice and were just as dismayed as their clients, and a Spanish court may well accept their arguments.

So, be sure to take care that any deposit you make goes into that escrow account, a blocked account, where neither party can get at it until the sale is closed.

Unscrupulous agent can take advantage

In a few cases, unscrupulous estate agents have taken advantage of distressed or innocent sellers, telling them that they can obtain only a very low price for their property. This might be a widow who has returned to her home country and wants to sell her Spanish property because she needs the money. The agent tells her he can get only €190,000 for the property.

She had the idea it must be worth €250,000 or more in today's market, but she lets herself be convinced. The agent also convinces her to sign an agreement which authorises him to keep anything he can get over that price. The agent then sells the property for €250,000, just as he knew he could, making himself a "commission" of €60,000.

The buyer makes out the cheque to the estate agent, who puts €60,000 in his own account and €190,000 to the owner. All legal and in order. He never tells the seller what he sold it for, and since the buyer and seller never come into contact, the truth is never discovered. Even if it was, the agent has done nothing illegal. After all, the seller signed the agreement, didn't she? This sort of sharp practice becomes a great temptation for agents where owners are often absentee and ignorant.

Even the final figure of the purchase price on the sales contract may be the under-declared amount of €190,000. In any case, since the agent is acting with a power of attorney to sign the contract for the absentee seller, nothing can be done about it after the fact.

These cases and others like them make a powerful argument for using a Spanish lawyer when you buy property. I will say it again and again: you should use a Spanish lawyer when you buy property in Spain. You should use a lawyer in your own country when you buy property. Why should it be different in Spain?

Having stated this warning, we find that most Spanish estate agents and foreigners selling property in Spain, are both registered and honest. They only want to make a fair commission by selling good properties which will make their buyers and sellers both happy. Be careful anyway.

COMMISSIONS HIGH IN COASTAL AREAS

Most Europeans will be surprised to find that estate agents dealing with Spanish holiday property take commissions starting at 5 per cent and going up to 10 per cent. These high commissions, say the agents, are justified because they have to deal with many unusual factors in a market where a buyer comes from one country and the seller from another and the transaction takes place in Spain, a third country. They also cite high marketing expenses from international advertising.

Let's just say that, when you are in the final stages of negotiating your purchase price, even the amount of the estate agent's commission might come on the table for a little reduction. Keep in mind that the API, for example, recommends 3 per cent commission for its agents in most areas of Spain.

Spain has all sorts of estate agents, ranging from the small office in the High Street, who has been in the town for many years and knows everybody personally, to the most modern international real estate offices, filled with computers. Some of the major agencies can contact their offices in Frankfurt or London by Internet, and screen you five views of their offerings right there on the computer. In addition, there are many "Euro agents" of all nationalities who quite legally operate in Spain, although their credentials may not be as well established.

One of these agents should be able to find the property you are looking for. Very few agents in Spain are exclusive, so you could find two agents showing you the same property.

The estate agent is working for the seller, so his presentation of the property will be the most favourable one, and you should check the facts carefully through your own representative. A reputable estate agent will be very happy to have you verify any of his information through your own lawyer, for example.

YOUR SPANISH LAWYER

Many Spanish lawyers working in areas popular with tourists speak excellent English or other languages. They are accustomed to dealing with foreign residents and their special problems, including property purchases.

How to find a good Spanish lawyer? Good question. Here is perhaps one of the few areas in which you can ask advice from people you know. Ask around until you find some satisfied clients. You can try walking into a bar and asking the people if anyone knows a good lawyer. Everybody in the place will have a story about either a good one or a bad one.

Consulates also maintain lists of lawyers who speak the language of their nationality, English, German, and so on. These lists do not mean that the lawyers are the most highly regarded.

How much will it cost? Figure the lawyer to charge you around one per cent of the value of the transaction, unless there are some unusual complications. Settle this with him before you start.

WHAT TO WATCH OUT FOR

Let's give the basic "Buyer Beware" warning first. It goes like this: **Believe Nothing. Check Everything.**

When they say there is no outstanding mortgage, check the Property Registry. When they say it measures 145 square metres, measure it. When they say the terrace is included, check the plans. Any reputable seller will be perfectly happy to have his offers checked. Spoken words do not count. Only pieces of paper count.

Both the European Union and the Spanish government have investigated fraud reports in holiday property, revealing the presence of illegal urbanisations where unwary buyers end up having problems of unpaid taxes, unregistered title deeds, and difficulty in obtaining municipal services or building permission. Spaniards have also been defrauded and problems with house purchase make up a principal area of complaint for the Spanish consumer associations.

To make sure your urbanisation is legal and registered, ask to see the *Plan Parcial* approved by your *ayuntamiento,* the town hall. The *Plan Parcial* is not a partial plan, as it sounds, but the plan of parcelas, or building plots, which must be approved. This assures you that your urbanisation is legal. If the developer cannot show you this approved plan, you may have a problem.

If the development is on the beach, make sure it is approved by the *Jefatura de Costas* as well as the town hall. Spain's 1988 *Ley de Costas*, or Law of Coasts, empowers the authorities to restrict building and to control height and density within 100 metres of the high-water mark, and a revised law to protect the shoreline threatens even many existing properties. Check this with your lawyer.

NEW PROPERTIES

In the case of a new property, you want to make sure that the property has been declared to *Hacienda* for IBI (*Impuesto sobre Bienes Inmuebles* or annual real estate tax), as you can incur more fines for not registering it. You want to see the *Licencia de Primera Ocupación*, the First Occupation Licence.

Until you have this, you will face difficulties in getting your water and electricity connected.

Make sure that your developer has made a *Declaración de obra nueva*, a declaration of new building, and has paid the small tax associated with this, as well. Make sure that your escritura mentions the house you have purchased as well as the plot of land on which it stands. Sometimes the deed only refers to the land.

This makes you the owner of anything standing on the land, of course, but you may find yourself subject to taxes and fines relating to an undeclared building. Even worse, you may have bought an illegally constructed house which can never be registered because of zoning regulations. It has happened to thousands of unwary buyers all over Spain. Check this at your town hall's *urbanismo* department (next page).

Sometimes, the purchase of an undeclared building can even work in your favour, but you will need expert advice to make sure you stay within the law. Once you are sure that the building can in fact be registered, you make a contract to purchase only the land from the seller. That's all he has title to, anyway.

The price for the land alone is much lower than the price for the land and house together, for a considerable saving on the property transfer tax of eight per cent. You purchase the house separately by a private contract.

HOW TO BE SAFE

But what about those building permits issued by the Town Hall which seem perfectly legal, but later, often years later, are revoked by the Regional government planning authorities? This is the situation of thousands of homes all over Spain. The house is already built, sold and inhabited by its new owner when the decision making it illegal arrives. The only way to be absolutely safe is to see the *Certificación de Convalidación* from the Regional authorities such as the *Junta de Andalucía* or the *Comunidad Valenciana*. It is published in the Official Bolletin of the province.

The Town Hall *urbanismo* department requests this certification, because it validates their building licence. The reason nobody carries through with this procedure is because it can take a year for the regional government to respond. Nevertheless, it is the only way to be absolutely safe. (See Chapter Five on building your house for more details)

You want to see the *Licencia de Primera Ocupación*, the First Occupation Licence, which the Town Hall issues after an inspection of the finished work.

Then the new buyer makes the *Declaración de obra nueva*, just as if he himself has built the house. Building permits and other papers are necessary for this, but it can all be arranged, and the buyer will pay only one half of one per cent, compared to the transfer tax of eight per cent. It has been done but sound legal advice should be taken because the plan will not work in all areas and situations.

PGOU – TOWN PLAN

It is also important to have a look at the town planning maps of the area around you. A newly prosperous Spain is improving the road system all around the country. What if one of those highways is planned for the bottom of your garden? You can find out from the town's urban plan. This plan is called the *Plan General de Ordenación Urbana*, the *PGOU* for short. If you yourself cannot read plans, and few of us can, have your lawyer do it.

BEFORE YOU SIGN ANYTHING

Before you sign anything in Spain, even a small reservation deposit agreement when buying from a private re-seller, there are some pieces of paper you should see. These include:

1. The seller's own title, known as the *Escritura Pública*, and a report from the Property Registry called a *Nota Simple.*
2. The paid-up receipt for his annual property tax, the *IBI.*
3. The *Catastral* certificate giving the exact boundaries and square metres of area.
4. Paid-up receipts for the annual fees of the community of property owners, the statutes of the community, and the minutes of the last AGM.
5. Paid-up receipts for all utility bills.

ESCRITURA PÚBLICA

The *Escritura Pública* is the registered title deed of the property. It is inscribed in the *Registro de la Propiedad*, the Property Registry, and it is the only iron-clad guarantee of title in Spain. If your seller cannot produce an *Escritura Pública*, something is wrong. In this title deed you will find a description of the property, the details of the owner. If any mortgages or court *embargoes* exist against the property, they will be registered here as marginal notes. You want to see the seller's title deed, if only to make sure that he really is the owner of the property being sold to you.

Your lawyer can obtain a *Nota Simple* from the Registry, containing the pertinent details and notes of any mortgages against the property. Your lawyer can obtain a *Nota Simple* very rapidly on the Internet if he is entered in the Registry programme. However, it would be best if you could see a copy of the complete deed as well.

Strange things can happen with deeds. In one recent case, a widow was selling her property in Spain. However, living in another country, it had never occurred to her to declare the death of her husband in Spain, and his name was still entered on the title deed as half owner of the property. This was done in perfect innocence, because she simply considered herself the full owner of the property when her husband died.

By Spanish law a property held jointly in two names cannot be sold without the signatures of both parties. Because no one had seen the full *escritura* before the scheduled closing and final payment, the fact did not come to light until both parties were ready to sign at the Spanish Notary.

The signing had to be postponed for months until the widow could declare her husband's death, which had happened 10 years before, prove that she was the heir, formally accept the inheritance, re-register the property in her own name, and finally sign to sell it.

One fortunate consequence of her error was that she did not have to pay any Spanish inheritance tax, because the demand for the tax lapses after five years. Some people do this deliberately, but her lack of action was inadvertent.

All this inheritance settlement could have taken place early in the negotiations if the title deed had been available for examination. You will do well to insist on seeing the complete *escritura*. After all, it's important to know that the seller is really the owner of the property. This applies to a flat in a new apartment building as well as to re-sales.

CHECK *IBI* RECEIPT

One very important paper you must see before purchasing any second-hand Spanish property is the *Impuesto sobre Bienes Inmuebles* (IBI), the municipal real estate tax. When purchasing from the second or third owner, you must always ask to see the latest paid-up receipt for the IBI before you sign any contract with the seller. If not available, something is amiss. Really, you want to see the IBI receipts for the last five years, not just the current one, because you can be liable for five years of back tax.

Here again your lawyer or property consultant will have valuable advice. A new property bought from a developer will not have an IBI receipt yet and it will be your responsibility to register the property for this tax.

The IBI receipt will show the property's catastral reference number and also your *valor catastral*, the official assessed value of the property. This is a very important figure because various taxes are based on it (see section on Taxes). The assessed value is almost always considerably less than the real market value, but it has been steadily raised over the last few years.

Your annual real estate tax is charged by the municipality, It can be as low as €200 if you own a small cottage in a village, or as much as €3,000 a year if you own a new luxury villa on acres of land near Marbella.

A surcharge of 20 per cent will be added to the bill if it is not paid on time. You can arrange to have this bill paid directly through your bank, in order to avoid forgetting it. Fill out the forms authorising the bank to pay it and the tax people will send the bill directly to the bank. In many municipalities those who pay their IBI tax early get discounts of 10 per cent, and a standing order at the bank will ensure that this is done.

The current IBI receipt must be presented to the Notary at the signing of the contract, because it contains the *catastral* reference number, but you as the buyer want to see it well before that.

REFERENCIA CATASTRAL

Every property sale must include a mention of the *Referencia Catastral.* As noted above, this reference number appears on your IBI receipt.

The *Catastro* is a second system of property registration, concentrating on the exact location, physical description and boundaries of property, unlike the Property Registry, which focuses on ownership and title. The *Catastro* is also concerned with the valuation of property and is the source of the famous valor catastral, the assessed value of property for tax purposes.

These two systems, strangely enough, have never even communicated with each other, and we find that the *catastral* description of a property sometimes differs greatly from the one in the Property Registry.

As a first step in trying to bring the physical reality into line with statements people sometimes make in contracts, the Spanish authorities have begun to require that all property transactions now include at least a mention of the *Catastro* reference number in addition to the *escritura.*

It is a very good idea for the buyer to request the actual certification from the Catastro with a full description of the property. If it matches the data given in your contract, you are all right. If there are large differences, perhaps something is wrong.

The certification itself comes in two parts, one being a description in words of the property and the other being a graphic representation, either a plan or an aerial photo. Get both of them. It costs only a few euros, although it can take up to two months for the *Catastro* to deliver the certificates, so you had better start early.

It is astonishing how often the boundaries and square metres of a property can differ so much. This is because people through the years have simply accepted the vague descriptions made in the title deed, and do not check any further. Be warned that, when you ask the seller or the estate agent for this *catastral* certificate, they will pooh-pooh the idea, saying it is not legally necessary yet, although it will be in the future. Do not pay much attention to them. Insist on getting it, so you can be sure of your real boundaries and the real size of the property.

The Notary is also empowered to call attention to the fact that discrepancies exist between the *Catastro* and Property Registry descriptions. The buyer and seller can go ahead with their transaction, but they have been advised of the discrepancy.

COMMUNITY FEES, STATUTES AND MINUTES OF AGM

If you are buying a flat, a townhouse, or a villa on an urbanisation, ask also to see the latest paid-up receipt for community fees. These are the fees charged by your *Comunidad de Propietarios,* the Community of Property Owners, which is the Spanish term for "condominium", meaning the legal body that controls all the elements held in common. In a building this would be the lift, gardens and pool for example.

In an urbanisation, the community as a whole jointly owns the roads, gardens, pool, lighting system and other elements as well. Each owner is assigned a quota, or percentage of the expenses, which he must pay, by law. See the section on Communities for full details.

Just remember that you become a member of the community, with legal rights and obligations, just by purchasing your property. Only those who buy a country property or a house on a normal street in a town will not have to deal with community problems.

The receipt for community fees assures you that the fees are paid and gives you a good idea of your monthly charges in the future. Read the statutes, the regulations of the community, too, as they will be binding on you once you have signed the purchase contract. If the basic statutes that rule the community prohibit the keeping of pets in the building or on the estate, you will have real problems if you want to keep your dogs, for example. Get a copy of these statutes in a language you can read, even if the Spanish regulations are the only valid ones.

Then you want to see the minutes book, the official record, of the last annual general meeting of the community. Decisions are taken by majority vote of the owners at each year's AGM, and these actions are recorded in the minutes book, the *Libro de Actas*, which is an official document. If you find that the principal point at last year's meeting was how to solve the community's chronic water shortage, then you will know you are going to have problems in your new house. Talk to the community president if this is possible. A well-run community can add thousands of euros to a property's value, and a community with problems is a source of endless aggravation.

UTILITIES BILLS

You want to see paid-up receipts for the owner's electricity, water, rubbish collection and even telephone. These assure you that the bills are paid and also give you an idea of what it will cost to run the place.

If you should get stuck with unpaid bills by the previous owner, be aware that these are personal bills from private companies. They do not attach to the property, only to the person who signed the electric or water company contract.

The company will insist that they will cut off the service if the bills are not paid. Let them cut it off. For a reasonable fee, you simply go into the company office and sign a new contract, starting fresh without the previous owner's bills. This fee is exactly the same as the charge for changing the electricity contract into your own name in any case.

Once you and your lawyer or adviser are satisfied with these checks into the situation of the property, and you and the seller have arrived at a price, you can factor into your calculations the amount of taxes and fees that will be paid on the transaction.

PROPERTY TRANSFER COSTS – TWO TAXES, TWO FEES

What are the taxes and fees going to cost you? They will probably be a minimum of 10 per cent of the purchase price if you buy a second-hand property from a private seller but they can go higher if you buy a new property from a developer. This is because IVA, or value added tax, is charged on sales of new properties, rather than the property transfer tax charged on sales between private individuals. This IVA tax has recently been raised to 10 per cent for residential properties and 21 per cent for plots of land and commercial properties when bought new from a developer.

So you have two taxes and two fees to pay on the transfer of property. The two fees are for the notarisation of the deed and for its registry in the Property Registry. The two taxes are the transfer tax or the IVA and a sort of capital gains tax based on the increase in the rated value of the land, usually called the *Plus valía* tax. This tax is a municipal tax.

Notary: You pay the *Notario* a fee fixed by an official scale. The fee varies according to the amount of land, the size of the dwelling and its price, but let's say between €500 and €1,000.

Property Registry: Then there is a fee for the inscription of the property in your name in the official *Registro de la Propiedad*. This will be a similar amount. Your lawyer or property consultant can tell you exactly how much these fees will be before you buy.

Transfer tax: The transfer tax, called *Impuesto de Transmisiones Patrimoniales* (ITP) in Spanish, is eight per cent of the value declared in the contract for private sales, in Andalusia. This ITP varies from Region to Region. If you purchase new property from a developer, this tax will be IVA (value added tax) at 10 per cent because the sale is a business operation, not a private deal between two individuals.

In addition to this, you pay a documents fee, or stamp duty (*Actos Juridicos Documentados*) of 1.5 per cent, so buying a new property in Andalusia will draw tax of 11.5 per cent. A resale property is taxed at 8 per cent. In fact, the tax can be even more, because it is 8 per cent only up to €400,000. The next €300,000 is charged at 9 per cent, and any price above that pays at 10 per cent. The Balearic Islands Region uses the same system.

The ITP is different in Spain's autonomous regions. In the Canary Islands, for example, the transfer tax is only 6.5 per cent. In Madrid it is 6 per cent and in Catalonia and the Valencian Region it is 10 per cent.

If you buy a building plot without a house on it or a garage, you will be charged the regular rate of IVA, which is 21 per cent.

Plus valía: The other tax on property sales is the *Arbitrio sobre el Incremento del Valor de los Terrenos*, the municipal tax on the officially calculated increase in the value of the land since its last sale. This is usually called the *Plus valía* for short, and it can vary widely. In the case of an apartment or a townhouse in a new urbanisation, where little land is involved and where there has been no real increase in value because such a short time has passed since it was developed, the tax can be very low. It will be much higher if you buy a house with several thousand square metres of land, which has not changed hands for 20 years and which has been recently re-zoned from rural to urban land, thus jumping greatly in value.

RECLAIM OVERPAID *PLUS VALÍA* TAX

People who sold their Spanish property at a loss over the past four years, and who paid the *plus valía* tax to their Town Hall are now able to claim back the tax payment. The Town Halls collected the tax because it is based on an official and artificial increase in value and not on the real selling price. The Spanish Supreme Court has now ruled that collecting a tax on a profit that does not exist is illegal. This opens the door for something like half a million property sellers to seek recompense. Those sellers who actually made a profit must still pay it.

DON'T CONFUSE *PLUS VALÍA* WITH CAPITAL GAINS TAX

Do not confuse this municipal *Plus valía* tax with the property seller's 21 per cent capital gains tax on profits from the sale (see Tax section). You have to pay them both.

This tax is based on the official or rateable value of the land, which was always lower than the real market value. In today's depressed real estate market, the real value has sometimes dropped to below the official value. The tax varies from 10 per cent up to 40 per cent of the annual increase, depending on the length of time between sales and the town where it is located. The land is officially re-valued periodically for this purpose.

You can find out exactly how much your *Plus valía* will be simply by going into the municipal tax office in your town and asking. They keep the records there for each property and will be glad to tell you the assessed value, so you can find out in advance. Or have your lawyer or property consultant do it.

The *Plus valía* tax can be charged directly against the property itself, meaning that an unscrupulous seller might promise to pay it and "forget", leaving the new owner to pay it.

WHO PAYS WHAT?

In deciding who pays what, the buyer and seller are free to contract whatever terms they choose. There is no Spanish law which requires that one of the parties must pay any particular tax.

Traditionally, the seller has paid the Notary's fees and the *Plus valía* tax, as he is the one making the profit on the increase in the land's value, while the buyer pays the *Impuesto de Transmisiones* and the Registry fee, as he is the one who is interested in making sure the property is truly registered in his name. Spanish consumer regulations state that this should be the normal division of costs.

It is a frequent practice, however, for the contract to state that the buyer will pay *todos los gastos*, all the expenses arising. There is nothing illegal about this. Remember that the two parties are free to make any contract they choose.

This practice, which may seem unfair to the buyer, has come about because tax bills, especially the *Plus valía*, have often gone unpaid, especially by non-resident sellers. By the time the new purchaser realised this, the seller was gone and the buyer stuck with the taxes anyway, as they were billed to the owner of the property if the seller did not pay. Charging the new owner with all the taxes is at least straightforward and avoids complications.

Nevertheless, you can use this point in negotiating your final price. If the contract you are offered states that you as the purchaser must pay all taxes and fees, you could suggest that the seller take something off the price.

HOW MUCH TO DECLARE?

Formerly it was the practice to declare a ridiculously low amount for the value of the house, in order to minimise the transfer tax, but now Spanish lawyers advise sellers and buyers to declare the approximate market value, normally the real value of the sale. Spanish tax inspectors will make their own assessment if they feel the declaration is too low.

Spain's Tax Agency, *Hacienda*, maintains its own tables of values on property, and they are empowered to set a higher value on a sale if they judge the declaration to be under market value. More than one property purchaser has been disconcerted to discover that he has to pay extra taxes when he gets a new tax bill six months after the sale.

CHECK *OFICINA LIQUIDADORA* FOR OFFICIAL TAX VALUE

If the buyer is responsible for the Property Transfer Tax of 8 per cent, he may find a hidden danger. In today's depressed market, more than one buyer has been dismayed to receive an extra tax bill months after the sale. This is because the real value of the sale at today's price is less than the official tax valuation of the property. This official valuation is the lowest amount the Regional tax authorities will accept for tax purposes. They apply this official value and send you a bill for the difference.

The tax office applies several factors, such as location, size, quality, age and others to set the value.

You want to apply to the *Oficina Liquidadora* of the Regional tax office for an official statement of valuation. Your lawyer can probably do this on the internet. This value tells what your final tax will be. You may do well to declare this value on the sale, even if the real price is lower. If you choose to declare the real and lower price, at least you know what your extra tax bill will be.

THE CONTRACT

Let's suppose that you have found a property that suits you, that all of the pre-purchase checks have satisfied you, and you have negotiated the price down to what you can pay. Keep in mind that most sellers will come down on the price. Make an offer and see what happens.

Terms of the sales contract will be your next concern.

Because most buyers take some time to assemble the cash needed for the purchase, it is usual for the buyer and seller to make a "private contract" first, with the buyer putting down a non-returnable deposit of, say, 10 per cent. This reserves the property while the buyer brings his money into Spain or perhaps obtains a Spanish mortgage. If the buyer fails to complete the sale, he loses the amount of his deposit.

If the seller finds another buyer in the meantime, willing to pay more, and sells the property, the first buyer can claim twice the amount of the deposit back.

Remember never to pay the deposit directly to the seller. Make sure that it goes into an escrow account, a blocked account called a Bonded Client Account, from which it will not be released until the sale is final. Insist on this.

The seller, through the estate agent, will certainly have a prepared private contract all ready for you to sign. The contract they offer may suit you perfectly, but it is quite likely that it will contain some clauses more favourable to the seller than to you, the buyer. This is when you want your lawyer to read the contract and make suggestions.

BUYER BEWARE

When you go to resell your property, you will be charged Spanish capital gains tax on any profit you make. If you are a resident, you pay it as part of your income tax at 21 per cent for the first €6,000 and 24 per cent up to €24,000 and 27 per cent above that. If you are a non-resident EU citizen, you face 19 per cent capital gains tax on your profit or 24 per cent if you are a non-EU resident, regardless of the amount. If you declare a low value now, you will be liable for tax on a much bigger profit when you sell later. It is in your own best interest to declare the full amount of the sale.

It is a very good idea to have the contract made in Spanish, with a translation into English or German or your native language, so you can be absolutely sure about what you are signing.

Although most property sales between individuals follow this system of private contract and deposit, followed by closing and final payment, there is nothing binding about it. If you like the property and have the price ready, you can proceed directly to the Notary, pay over the full price, and get your title deed.

ESCRITURA DE COMPRAVENTA

This private contract, although it sets out all the details of the agreement, such as payment terms and who pays what share of the taxes, is not the final document for the sale.

This final document is the *escritura de compraventa* and it must be signed by you and the seller in the presence of a *Notario* in order to make it legally binding. You can make a *poder* — a power of attorney — allowing another person to sign for you if you cannot be present (see section below for more on Power of Attorney). The Notary keeps the original document in his files in case any question arises later. The *Notario* is an official of the state, not a private lawyer, who makes sure that contracts are legal. His duty is to certify that the contract has been properly signed, the money paid, and that the purchaser and seller have been advised of their tax obligations.

He does not verify or guarantee the accuracy of the statements made in the contract. Too many people think that the *Notario* assures them that all statements made in the contract are true. This is not so. The Notary can, however, give useful advice to both parties.

Contracts can be quite simple or very complicated. If you are paying one lump sum and the property is to be delivered at once, there remains only the question of who is to pay the taxes and fees.

If you are paying in stages, there will be a number of further provisions in your contract, relating to the timing and amount of the payments. The buyer may find that the seller offers him a contract which states that he loses all sums paid out if he fails to keep up the payments, as well as having to vacate the property immediately. In fact, this is always negotiable. If a buyer who cannot keep up the payments takes his case to court, the court will almost certainly allow him to receive some of his money back in exchange for vacating the property, which he loses.

This will depend on how many payments the buyer has already made, for example. If he has already paid more than half of the full price, the court will not allow the seller to keep it all.

The buyer really needs a Spanish lawyer to make sure this sort of complicated contract is fair to him.

POWER OF ATTORNEY

A "general power of attorney" or *poder general*, is frequently used in Spain. The power comes in a standard form, which lists all of the actions that can be carried out by the holder. These include buying and selling property, handling bank accounts, spending and receiving money, taking out a mortgage or other loan, and just about anything that the granter of the power can himself, or herself, do with their assets.

The form contains a clause declaring that all of these actions shall be taken for the benefit of the granter of the power. This means that, if you decide to take the money and run, the granter has a case against you for defrauding him, if he can find you.

There are also other forms of power of attorney, limited to carrying out certain specific actions in the name of the granter, such as signing a contract for the sale of a specified property at a given price, during a given time period, after which the power lapses.

But the general power is the one most used, simply because situations change and unforeseen complexities arise in any transaction. This can mean that the holder of the power is unable to act because the power does not mention the specific circumstance which has arisen, such as signing at the bank to obtain the money transfer from abroad.

The wide powers of the general power of attorney avoid these problems. In an international property market, we often find that a seller or a buyer cannot be physically present at the moment of signing a purchase deed at the Spanish Notary, so he gives his lawyer or some other trusted person a general power of attorney to sign for him.

Once the deed is accomplished, the granter then revokes the power of attorney, again at the Notary, and all goes on as before.

A power of attorney can also be very useful for persons who have aged parents in Spain because it allows the child to manage the property and finances of the granter of the power. The only possible hitch is whether your aged parent wishes to grant you all of these powers. In the usual circumstances, however, the aged parent is only too glad to have all these matters taken off his hands.

You make the *poder general* at the Notary. Although it is always a good idea to consult a lawyer before taking any important legal step, it is not necessary. The Notary has the power of attorney forms, probably in his computer, which will print copies for you while the Notary himself retains the original authorisation. A reminder: you need copies authorised by the Notary in order to use the power of attorney at a bank or in a property sale. The simple copies you can also obtain are for information only.

The only documents necessary are the national identity document or the passport of the maker of the power. He will need the name and identity document or passport details of the holder.

The entire operation should not cost much more than €60. Yes, it all seems too simple and too cheap for such a wide-ranging document, but there you are.

The recipient of the power of attorney does not need to appear at the Notary. The document requires his signature, but he can do this at his own convenience. So the maker of the power can simply post it to the recipient.

Contract must describe property accurately

The contract must accurately describe the property being sold. This is one area where the *catastral* certificate is important. Too many buyers have discovered too late that their boundaries are not what they thought, and the hedgerow at the bottom of their garden, an obvious division, is not the legal line at all, but belongs to their neighbour. This sort of error does not necessarily imply bad faith on the part of the seller. He may have happily accepted the boundaries and square metres set out in his title deed, and never checked them.

Remember that we mentioned the *Registro de la Propiedad* is concerned mainly with ownership of property, while the *Catastro* is concerned mainly with the physical measurements and characteristics. The Property Registry is quite often wrong, so get the *Catastral* certificate and be sure.

If you really have problems with boundaries, you should have an official surveyor, a *topógrafo*, come and survey the plot. On a transaction of €200,000, the €500 or so that he charges is very little.

Even those buying apartments will do well to measure their square metres of enclosed space and terraces, to make sure they match the description offered. It is astonishing how often the flat actually has fewer square metres than stated. If you discover this, it may make a bargaining point for getting the price down.

Buyers of rural land will certainly need a property surveyor to measure the land and identify its boundaries. In these cases, even the *Catastral* department may not have the correct data. The titles to many rural properties state only that the finca borders on the north with Juan García's farm, and that is simply not good enough.

Contract must identify buyer and seller

The contract must also fully identify the seller and buyer. Remember that the seller is the owner of the property, not the estate agent handling the deal. It is always a bad practice to make your cheque out to an agency. You should know exactly who the seller is and make your cheque directly to him. If the seller insists on anonymity, meaning a bearer cheque, make sure that no money changes hands until you are actually at the Notary, where you will sign the final contract.

Make your cheques out only to the name of the seller. In the case of reserve deposits before the sale is completed, and where you may never have met the absentee seller, insist that your cheque be deposited in an escrow account, a Bonded Client Account. Then the money can be paid out only to the seller and only when the specified time limit has elapsed.

FREE OF CHARGES AND LIENS

One extremely important item in your contract is the clause stating the property is sold free of all charges, liens and mortgages. Fine, you say, but how do you really know this is true? This is where your lawyer comes in. He can make a check at the property registry, the *Registro de la Propiedad,* where any such mortgages or liens must be registered against the *escritura*. The *Registro de la Propiedad* is an extremely important office for the property purchaser.

Any mortgage on the property must be registered there, and the true owner of the property is listed. For a small fee, the *Registro* will give you a nota simple for any property. This is a summary of the property's entry into the registry books, which would include a reference to any mortgages pending on the property.

Such a check-up can avoid problems. One horrible case occurred when a British owner returned to Spain to find that the house he had just bought had been seized by court order and auctioned off to pay an outstanding mortgage left by the seller. The locks had been changed and the house was no longer his. His only remedy was to sue the fraudulent seller for breach of contract and fraud. That is, if he could find him.

He could also have solved the problem if he had been aware that his property was under threat. If he himself had been present in Spain to receive legal notice of the coming seizure and auction, he could have arranged with the court to pay the mortgage, which attaches to the property itself, not to the previous owner.

Paying the mortgage would have been an unpleasant experience but much cheaper than losing the entire property.

Notices of such legal actions appear by law in the *Boletín Oficial*, the official legal gazette, and often in the local newspapers as well. If the new owner cannot be located by the court, these published notices constitute sufficient legal notice to make the seizure of the property correct in law. Overworked Spanish courts have been severely criticised for failure to make sufficient attempt to locate the absentee owners, but the practice continues.

A lawyer will also check to make sure that no back taxes are owed on the property and that its original registration is in order. Back taxes must be checked with *Hacienda* or the town hall. They are just about the only debts not listed at the Property Registry.

FINAL TITLE AND REGISTRATION

In fact, even the *escritura de compraventa* contract does not fully assure your title until it is registered with the Spanish Property Registry, thus making it an *escritura pública*, a public document. It is, in fact, the same document, now registered and with the stamps of the *Registro de la Propiedad* on it.

Notice of the contract signed can be sent by fax directly from the Notary's office, at the time of signing, to the *Registro de la Propiedad*. This notification will ensure that no one else can register the property, until the full contract is presented at the Registry. Or you can have someone deliver the signed contract directly to the Registry. Normally, this will be someone from the Notary's office.

You yourself will never have the original of your *escritura pública*. The original document is stamped at the Property Registry, which converts it from a sales contract into a public document, the famous *escritura pública*, which is your final and definite title, proof against all comers.

The document is then returned to the Notary, where it is kept safely on file. If you, or any official body, needs a copy of it, you request it from the Notary, who produces an authorised copy. The copy is what you take home.

In fact, you no longer sign the contract itself. In these modern times of easy and foolproof copying, the parties to the contract sign a blank sheet of paper, and the Notary keeps these samples in his files for later authentication when necessary. So, nobody can copy your signature from a copy of your title deed because it isn't there.

In cases where the same piece of property has been fraudulently sold two or three times, the purchaser who first has it registered will be the owner, regardless of the dates of the other sales.

Slow as the administrative bureaucracy may be, your deed should be registered within a few months. Usually your lawyer or whoever is handling the matter will ask you for a deposit of money in advance to cover the estimated taxes and fees, and will either bill you for the remainder or refund to you the overpayment when the deed is registered. This is normal and acceptable practice.

If the matter seems to drag on for months, you had better look into what is happening. There was a case a few years ago where one property consultant took people's money, put the cash into his own bank account and the compraventa deed into a drawer. He used his clients' money for a year or so, enabling him to make down payments on Costa del Sol property, and then, at last, presented the deeds for registry. The registry came through in due course and he notified his clients, who often got a small refund, which made them happy. Everyone mistakenly assumed that it took a year and a half for the registry to process the papers.

WHAT CAN GO WRONG: UNPAID MORTGAGE

The reason for haste in delivering the sales contract to the Property Registry is simple. As long as the property continues to be registered in the name of the seller, he can use it to take out a mortgage, for example. The bank checks the Registry, finds the property correctly listed, and grants the seller a mortgage of, say, €120,000 on the apartment valued at €180,000. He then disappears to some other country with the €120,000.

Our criminally-minded seller has prepared this operation well in advance with the innocent bank, but he does not execute it until after the sale has taken place, in the time between signing the *compraventa* contract and the new owner's registration of it as an *escritura pública*. Otherwise, the buyer would have found the mortgage listed against the property in the Property Registry when he got the *nota simple*. This is also why it is a good idea to get the *nota simple* immediately before signing the contract.

The unknowing buyer is perfectly happy with his new property, convinced that pre-purchase checks have assured that the title had no charges against it (which was true at the time).

Happy, that is, for a few years, until he suddenly discovers that the property has been sold at a court auction — *subasta* — without his having been informed, and the police are coming with a court order to put him in the street.

How can this be? The bank foreclosing the unpaid mortgage of €120,000 and repossessing the property will inform only the person registered as owner when the mortgage was taken out. The court has no reason to inform the new owner because he does not exist as far as they are concerned. They are repossessing the house of the person who failed to pay the mortgage. These cases have happened.

The buyer may find out about the mortgage because the bank in fact checks at the house and finds him there instead of the mortgage-holder. No matter how he protests, legally, the new owner has no case. The bank acted in good faith and their mortgage claim has preference. The only choice is whether to pay €120,000 more or to abandon the property. It's possible, of course, to bring suit against the seller to recover the money. If he can be found.

Such cases are rare, but they happen.

METHOD OF PAYMENT

Give some thought to your method of payment. One point to consider is whether you are buying from a resident or a non-resident.

In the old days before the European Union, property buyers had to pay Spaniards or residents in pesetas, and had to prove importation of foreign currency if they later wanted to export the money from Spain. With the lifting of exchange controls, this is no longer necessary, although a report must be made to the bank.

You can pay for your Spanish property in euros, through a bank cheque, from your Spanish bank, along with a bank certificate that you have imported foreign currency for this purpose. You can also pay by a cheque in foreign currency. Or you can pay by direct transfer from your foreign bank to the seller's foreign bank, so that no money enters Spain.

Spain's law to control money laundering and other types of financial fraud stipulates complete identification of buyer, seller and means of payment. If the transaction takes place in Spain through Spanish banks, the presentation of the transfer document or a certified bank cheque to hand to the buyer make full disclosure If you want to pay in Norwegian krone in Norway to a seller from Norway, you can do this, too, by presenting the bank transfer documents at the Spanish Notary.

If you want to pay in cash or gold bars, you will have to obtain the new Form S-1, on which you register the source of the cash, how it came into Spain, and to whom you are delivering it.

Three per cent tax deposit if you buy from non-resident

If you buy from a non-resident, you must deposit 3 per cent of the total purchase price with *Hacienda* in the seller's name, as a guarantee on his taxes.

You pay the seller only 97 per cent of the price. You pay the other 3 per cent directly to *Hacienda*, presenting Form 211 to justify your payment. The Notary will want to see your copy of Form 211, showing that you have made the payment and filed the form with the Tax Agency.

This amount serves as a guarantee against the non-resident seller's Spanish capital gains tax liability and for his payment of the annual Spanish wealth tax and non-resident property owner's imputed income tax. Non-resident owners of Spanish property are required to declare 2 per cent of the official rated value, or, if recently raised, 1.1 per cent of the *valor catastral*, of their property as if it were income each year. They then must pay income tax on this imaginary income at 24 per cent for non-EU residents or 19 per cent for EU residents.

If *Hacienda* discovers that the non-resident seller has failed to keep up his yearly imputed income tax payments, they can retain this amount from the deposit of 3 per cent.

The deposit is mainly designed, however, to cover the non-resident's liability for Spain's non-resident capital gains tax of 21 per cent on his profit. See Taxes on Property for details.

BUYING OFF-PLAN

In theory, buying Spanish property off-plan sounds like a very attractive proposition. It means that you start to pay for the property when you have only seen the plans, even before construction begins.

Because you are paying up front, you can save a good deal of money at the end. The builder gives you favourable terms because you are financing his project, and the flat is worth perhaps 25 per cent more when it is finished, a year or more later.

When prices are rising rapidly, off-plan purchase also becomes an attractive investment. Investors make the first payments with the intention of selling on the contract, even before the flat is finished, for a quick profit of 15 or 20 per cent. Perhaps they should be called speculators in this case. Thousands of buyers, both Spanish and foreigners, took advantage of the plan, sometimes in fast-growing cities and sometimes in the coastal areas.

In today's depressed real estate market, construction has practically vanished and off-plan buying has disappeared with it. In addition, a thousand things can go wrong with off-plan buying, so it is best to be very cautious.

A recent study shows that more than 80 per cent of all new properties in Spain are delivered late, sometimes very late, like six months or even a year. Further, more than half of all new properties have defects when they are occupied by their new owners.

So, what should you watch out for and what are your options if you find yourself in this situation?

First, you want to make sure that the builder actually has a building permit. This is so basic that buyers can be forgiven for not thinking of it. There have been cases where the developer had begun selling properties before he was able to obtain the permit.

Your purchase contract must state a delivery date, meaning that you can take occupation of the premises, with all work finished and all legal documents in order. It should also have a penalty clause which obligates the builder to make a payment for each day over the deadline.

ANDALUSIAN LAW REQUIRES SELLERS KIT

Since February, 2007, property sellers in the Andalusian regional community are required to provide a complete information packet to possible buyers. Developers, private sellers, estate agencies and landlords who let are affected.

In the case of new properties this seller's kit is called the *Documento Informativo Abreviado,* the abbreviated information document. This identifies the builder, the planner, the project manager, the developer and any intermediary in the sale. It includes plans of the flat, the building, the specifications, the usable square metres, the delivery date and the conditions of the contract. If the project is completed, the document includes the Property Registry data and information on the building insurance that protects the buyer even if the builder goes bust. If the property is not finished, the packet includes the building licence

The buyer can also request an information sheet which includes all terms of payment and full details of any mortgage offered. All of the relevant documents themselves must be delivered to the buyer three working days before the signing.

For a private re-sale, the packet is called the *Ficha Informativa,* an information sheet. It includes the address, description of the flat and building, or of the house, details of the owner, the year of construction, and any charges against the property.

For rentals, a landlord must offer the details of the property, the square metres, the monthly rent to be charged, the deposit, usually of one month, and whether the tenant must pay Community fees.

In real life, many estate agencies in Andalusia have failed to put up the notice that these information packets are available and many do not even know they exist. Even so, it is a step in the right direction.

Spanish law specifies that a purchase contract must contain a date of delivery. Insist on it.

What you as the buyer want is a specific date, such as January 3, 2019, with a penalty clause obligating the seller to pay a certain amount of money for each day he is late.

In practice, sellers often ignore this completely or fudge it by putting in a clause which says the property will be delivered within 90 days after the issuance of an extremely important document called the First Occupation Licence, the *Licencia de Primera Ocupación*. This is issued by the municipal building department when they verify that all requirements are met for inhabiting the building.

WHAT IF THE BANK REFUSES TO PAY THE BUILDER'S GUARANTEE?

So your builder went broke in the financial crash and failed to finish the apartment. You saw the bank document that guarantees the return of any money you have so far paid in. You go to the bank and they don't pay. They give one excuse after another. Your only recourse is to go to Court. You can take heart from a recent decision on the Costa del Sol. In this case, the flat was actually built, but no First Occupation licence was granted because the entire building was ruled illegal. The Court ruled that an illegal flat did not constitute full completion of the contract and ordered the bank to pay up. It took two years.

This licence can be delayed for a number of reasons. In one recent case, the new building was located in a newly developed zone where the town had failed to complete some of the necessary services, such as access roads. This meant that the first occupation licence was not forthcoming from the town hall, which gave the builders their excuse for late delivery.

There is little you can do about late delivery if you do not have this clause. Of course you have the final protection of the money-back guarantee. This clause states that, if the property is not delivered to you under the conditions of the contract, you have the right to your money back. The builder is obliged by law to hold bank guarantees for this amount.

PROPERTY PURCHASE CHECK-LIST

1. Advice from a Spanish lawyer or property consultant.

2. The seller's *Escritura Pública*, or title deed, as registered in the *Registro de la Propiedad.*

3. A *nota simple* from the Property Registry, showing that no mortgages are registered against the property.

4. *Referencia Catastral.* The number itself appears on the *IBI* receipt, but you want the full certification document, the *Certificado Catastral*, that describes the property in detail.

5. A check on the legality and *Plan Parcial* if you buy in an urbanisation, and assurance of a building permit if you buy a plot.

6. A paid-up receipt for the *Impuesto sobre Bienes Inmuebles*, or the *Declaración de Obra Nueva.*

7. The *Licencia de Primera Ocupación*, the First Occupation Licence, which allows connection for electricity and water.

8. Receipt for paid-up community charges and a copy of the Statutes and the Minutes of the AGM. Copies of owner's bills for electricity, water, and rubbish collection.

9. A contract, in Spanish, and a translation into your own language, with terms you understand.

10. A decision about your form of payment, whether in euros or other currency, and be sure to insist on declaring the full amount.

11. An *Escritura de Compraventa* signed before a *Notario.*

12. Payment of fees and taxes, and the 3 per cent deposit to *Hacienda* if you buy from a non-resident, using Form 211.

13. The new Certificate of Energy Efficiency.

Another option might be to strike a deal with the developer to occupy the flat without the first occupation licence. In cases where the property was complete and ready to live in, but the licence was delayed for some outside reason, thousands of flat-buyers have talked with the promoter and simply moved in. Some of them have continued to use the builder's electric and water supply for up to a year before the paperwork was complete.

Watch these points for any new property

1. When you first look at a new property, the developer must show you the plan of the apartment, the plan of the building and gardens, and the construction specifications, the *memoria de calidades*. These specifications will form part of your purchase contract, and you have recourse if they are not met.

2. By law, the information offered in any advertising material for the flat forms part of the contract. That is, if the photo shows a pool and gardens and these are not provided, you have action against the seller.

3. All amounts paid to the developer must be guaranteed by a bank. The developer must show you the document for this. He may not charge you a fee for it.

4. At the very beginning, the developer must provide a copy of the contract you will sign so that you can study it. Make sure the contract includes a provision that the developer pays his own *Plus valía*, a municipal tax on the increase in value of the property.

5. *The Licencia de Primera Ocupación*, the First Occupation Licence. Without this, you cannot contract electricity and water services.

6. The developer or builder will probably offer you a mortgage which he has already constituted on the property. You may choose to acceptthis or handle your own arrangements. You may not be charged acancellation fee if you do not accept the builder's mortgage.

7. Under Spain's recent building laws, the developer is responsible forany finishing defects for one year, any minor defects in the apartmentfor three years and for structural defects during 10 years.

8. The new consumer protection law stipulates that the developer or builder must take out a 10-year insurance policy to cover those structural defects. This policy remains in effect even if the developer or builder goes out of business after a few years. You want to see it. The new-build property cannot be registered without it.

Finally, it is always wise to use a Spanish lawyer, if only to vet your contract.

BUYING WITHOUT ESCRITURA

Sometimes the seller does not have an *escritura pública,* for perfectly legitimate reasons, or at least for reasons which will not affect you, the purchaser. Perhaps he has not completed his own purchase yet, or it has taken a longer time than usual.

One reason for owning property on a private contract only, without a public title deed, is that the property cannot be seized by the court in order to pay a debt of the owner. Only registered property can be attached by a court. Another reason is simply to avoid the payment of the transfer taxes and fees, which can total 10 per cent or even more of the value. A third reason is, of course, to conceal assets, either from a creditor or the tax man, or an ex-wife, for example. When the Property Register is checked, there is nothing listed under that name.

On the Spanish Costas, where there was a freewheeling property market for some years, many properties changed hands so quickly as buyers sought quick profits that they simply did not register them. They just waited for the next buyer to carry out all the formalities, thus avoiding transfer taxes.

It is possible that a house you fancy has had two or three owners in the last five or six years and that not one of them ever got his final *escritura pública.* It might be that the house does not legally exist, as it has never been declared to the tax authorities in a *Declaración de obra nueva.* The only legal document for the property simply refers to the plot of land and does not even mention the house.

Or you might buy a tract of land in the *campo,* the owners of which are seven brothers whose family has owned the land for a hundred years but never had a written document.

There are perfectly legal ways of solving all these problems.

Maybe you can have the piece of land made over to you by the original seller, three owners back. You yourself can make the *Declaración de obra nueva*, even though you did not build the house.

But be careful. If you want to establish the title through a series of private contracts, you may find that you are liable for quite a lot of back taxes, perhaps two or three *Plus valías* which have never been paid by the previous owners. This tax may be charged to the present owner of the property.

205 PROCEDURE

One completely legal and frequently used solution for property which has no registered title at all is called a 205 procedure, after the number of the regulation which controls it. In this process, you obtain from the Property Registry what is called a "negative certification". This means that the Registry has searched its files and finds no registered owner for the property. Here again you will find the *Certificado Catastral* useful, because it will have an accurate physical description.

You then request that the property be registered in your name because you have bought it from whoever is the seller, who, in turn, justifies his title by whatever document or evidence he presents. This transaction must be published and posted publicly in case anyone wishes to protest. If no protest is made against your claim, at the end of about a year's time you will get a solid title.

If you are going to buy under these conditions, be sure to hold back a percentage of the price until the property is registered in your name. No matter how simple the procedure appears when you start, there is always the possibility of some unknown person coming forward with a claim to the title. There is an element of risk.

EXPEDIENTE DE DOMINIO

This process, roughly translated as an ownership proceeding, requires more time and expense than the 205 procedure, because it involves more investigation and court action. The *Expediente de Dominio* can also be used to establish title when the property is in fact registered, but in the name of a person who no longer claims it either because he has sold it to someone on a private contract, who has never registered the sale, or perhaps because the original owner has died. This will take about two years.

The claim must be published in the official bulletin and evidence taken in court. Finally, the court will rule on the title and it will be solid. There is always the chance of some nephew who should have inherited the property making a claim of his own against the present purchaser, and the court will decide where the best claim lies.

In any of these procedures to establish title and register the property, be warned that you will be unable to obtain any mortgage funding, and you cannot borrow against the property for two years after its registration. In any of these cases, you need sound legal advice. Ask around among older residents for an abogado or an administrador de fincas or a gestor whom they trust.

PROPERTY OWNED BY OFFSHORE COMPANY

You might be offered property already owned by an offshore company registered in one of the many "tax havens" around the world.

This means that the property is not registered in the name of the owner. It is registered in the name of a company located in Gibraltar or Panama or the Caiman Islands. The owner of the company owns the property.

These "tax havens" earn their name because they are legal jurisdictions where taxes on locally registered companies are nil or very small, and secrecy is assured from the owner's own tax jurisdiction.

The advantages are clear. When you sell your Spanish property, it is only the company that is transferred. The same company continues to own the same Spanish property, so no Spanish transfer taxes are charged. Only the offshore company has a new owner. The same applies for inheritance tax when the company is bequeathed to an inheritor. The offshore location charges no tax on this.

The disadvantages are that Spain, keenly aware of the tax loss, has placed a flat tax of 3 per cent per year on any property held by an offshore company. They have a list of tax havens. European Union authorities have also placed restrictions on these companies, so it is becoming a doubtful proposition.

Spain is also ending the tax advantages of companies which exist simply to hold property. Such a company is called a *sociedad patrimonial*, a holding company. If they are Spanish companies, 2007 was a transitional year, when the companies could be wound up and ownership transferred to the individual owners or some other form of company at a low tax rate. Starting in 2008, such companies are treated as any other company doing business and taxed at the higher company tax rate of 25 per cent instead of the 21 per cent capital gains tax charged to individuals. There are moves to treat the off-shore companies as Spanish companies if their only asset is Spanish property.

In the Spanish property boom of the 1980s, these companies became very popular, but they don't look so good now. In Gibraltar, one of the most popular havens, the tax-exempt companies ended as of December, 2010. (See Tax chapter for details). As a buyer, you have a choice between purchasing the off-shore company itself or buying as an individual and paying the transfer taxes. See section on Taxes for advantages and disadvantages of offshore companies.

BANK REPOSSESSIONS

In 2018 we are looking at a property market which is picking up but starting from a low point where prices had dropped by more than 50 per cent in some cases from the previous boom highs. There still remain millions of properties unsold over the whole country.

As a result, the sunshine coasts and inland offer many bargains. Some of these bargains are on sale by people who could not keep up the payments on their property, some of them are offered at cut-rate prices by developers who are stuck with stock they couldn't sell, and some of them are villas and apartments that have been repossessed by banks. By the way, bank foreclosure of mortgages is one of the few Spanish legal procedures that works quickly and effectively.

One of the easiest ways to make a stab at buying a cut-price property is simply to walk into the offices of bank managers in an area where you would like to live. Go into the bank, say that you would like to speak with the manager about a business matter. He will probably speak English and he will probably receive you after a short wait. Say to him: "I am interested in buying a repossessed property. *Reposesión*. Do you have any on your books?"

It may just happen that he points to a stack of *escrituras* on his desk and says: "How about one of these?" If the bank is a bit more modern, he may punch up a list on his computer terminal and inquire about the price range that interests you. The bigger banks have even started their own real estate agencies to move the thousands of properties they have repossessed in the last few years. So, you look at their brochure and pick a villa or an apartment that seems promising. You view it, like it, and buy it from the bank for maybe half what it used to fetch on the market. It can be that easy.

If you are willing to make an effort to search them out, some great bargains are waiting for you. Be prepared to haggle with the bank and be sure to have your lawyer help you. If the bank says they will take €120,000 for the property you are told is worth €150,000, offer them €90,000. Keep in mind that the next bank will also have some repossessions available.

COURT AUCTIONS

If you really feel like getting into the system, you could even try the court-ordered auctions of property being sold to satisfy debts. These auctions, called *subastas*, can offer some incredible buys to those who get into the inside of how they work. Properties have been sold at one-tenth their real value, for example. Yes, in northern European countries this simply cannot take place, but under the Spanish system the court is obliged to take the highest offer, no matter how low, after the property has been offered several times.

You are right if you think that this system attracts abuses. In many courts, there are professional *subasteros* who work together, sometimes in collusion with corrupt court officials, to offer low bids. Later, these professionals split the take among themselves. They often assign the properties to third parties, who are not real buyers, but who also get their share of the profits once the property is sold on again.

CAPITAL GAINS TAX

Today's buyers of Spanish property need to be warned that Spain has removed an important deduction from its system of capital gains tax.

As of January 20, 2006, no property seller is exempt from capital gains tax. Those long-term owners who bought before 1986 had reduction factors which reduced their tax to zero after 10 years. Now, however, they must pay capital gains tax on the part of their profit calculated since January 20, 2006. All other reduction factors on any asset at all have also been cancelled, retroactively, as it were.

This means that all sellers of property can now apply only a coefficient of reduction that more or less matches the inflation rate, meaning that your Spanish property purchase will certainly attract capital gains tax when you sell it, no matter how long you have owned it (see section on Taxes on Property for more complete information).

MORTGAGES

You as a resident or non-resident can qualify for a Spanish mortgage, but you are not going to find any more of those loans of 120 per cent of value that got us into this trouble in the first place. However, do not believe that Spanish banks have completely turned off the credit tap. They are definitely more careful about the amounts they will lend on a property and they now vet their applicants much more thoroughly, but you can still get a mortgage if you qualify.

You will find interest rates in Spain are low. This is because they are based on the Euribor, set by the European Central Bank, just as UK interest rates are based on the Libor, the base interbank rate set in London. The Euribor is actually below zero in today's warped economy. As a result you see variable-rate mortgages now offered at rates between one per cent and two per cent. Be careful, however, because clients are usually required to domicile their salaries or pensions with the bank, and also to purchase insurance or investments from the bank. Also, these low rates are almost certain to rise in the next few years.

Fixed, variable, or mixed?

This can be confusing. Should you take a mortgage with an interest rate that is fixed for, say, 20 years? Some Spanish banks are offering fixed-rate mortgages at two per cent for 30 years, with all the conditions mentioned above. Or should you choose a mortgage which has an interest rate that varies along with the central bank base rate? Perhaps you should pick one of the mixed products, where the rate is fixed for the first few years and then changes each year as the central bank adjusts the base rate.

Most Spanish banks will mortgage no more than 80 per cent of assessed value for a non-resident buyer. This means you will need a substantial down payment for your Spanish property.

WHAT IF I CANNOT PAY MY SPANISH MORTGAGE?

If you realise that you cannot continue paying your Spanish mortgage, you must immediately talk with your bank. Do this before you have missed even one payment. It is important. Here is why.

First, in these unusual times, you may find your bank open to negotiation. This would include:

- Setting a longer term on your mortgage to lower your payments.
- Granting you a short time with no payments at all.
- Or perhaps an interest-only mortgage for a time.
- The bank might even find someone to buy your property by taking over your payments.

If none of this works out, you may find that your only way out is to give the property back to the bank. Well, you can do this if you meet two conditions. First, you must be current in your mortgage payments. Second, you must not be in "negative equity". This means that your property is worth less than what you owe on your mortgage, and many UK homebuyers will know the term from their own last property crash.

The Spanish for giving back the keys is: *Dación en Pago*. This is a far better option than repossession, and here is why. If the bank goes through the legal procedures for repossessing your property and having it sold, the return from this may not clear your total debt. If the property, in today's low market, is worth less than the debt, the bank can come after your other assets, even in another country.

Two magic words

In addition to all this financial strategy, you will need to examine a Spanish mortgage contract carefully to determine the opening commission, the closing commission, the survey fee, whether you are required to take a life insurance policy for the value of the mortgage, study charges and other fees. If these charges are high, they can spoil the effects of a low interest rate.

This is when you need to learn the two magic words that will help you and your financial advisers sort it out. These words are "*oferta vinculante*", a binding offer. Spanish consumer regulations oblige the bank to present you with such an offer, which lists every term in the mortgage contract. The offer is binding on the bank and is valid for 10 days. This gives you time to study the offer. If you get two or three of these offers from different banks, you can compare them.

The offers will list such items as:

Tipo nominal – This is the listed interest rate.

Tipo anual efectivo - This TAE is the real effective interest rate, taking into account that your charges and fees reduce the real amount of money available to pay for your property.

Opening commission – This is often charged at one per cent of the amount of the mortgage, though some of the new offers charge half of one per cent or even less.

Evaluation charge – This is for the property surveyor's report by which the bank decides the value of the property for mortgage purposes. Figure around €300-€500.

Redemption penalty – This is the cancellation charge for early repayment of the mortgage in its entirety. This commission is usually about one per cent but it varies. It is based on the amount remaining.

Home insurance: You may be required to take out home insurance through the bank.

Cancellation fee, too: Even when you have paid off your mortgage, you have one final responsibility. You must make sure that the mortgage entry in the Property Registry is cancelled. If you do not, your inscription will continue to show that a mortgage is outstanding. The bank will handle this but you must remind them, and pay the fee.

THOUSANDS SUE BANK TO RECOVER MORTGAGE OVER-PAYMENTS

When the bank issues a variable-rate mortgage, the terms are usually based on the Euribor interbank rate for the Euro. The bank will offer "Euribor plus two per cent" for example. These mortgage contracts have included a "ceiling" provision and a "floor" provision. That is, the interest rate can never go above a certain figure, like 12 per cent, and it can never drop below a certain figure, like four per cent, no matter what the bank exchange rate does. The floor provision is called the *Cláusula Suelo*. Recently, with the Euribor rate at figures like one per cent, the "floor clause" means that people paying four per cent are paying interest rates one per cent higher than "Euribor plus two per cent". Spanish courts have now ruled that these floor and ceiling clauses are "abusive" and must be annulled. Further, new rulings order the banks to pay back the amounts overcharged by the clauses. One per cent difference does not sound like much, but when it is applied to a mortgage of €200,000 over a few years, it can be substantial. In the first sentences to be final, mortgage holders are being awarded sums between ¢4,000 and €9,000. There are now about 15,000 cases underway in Madrid and thousands more in Malaga and Valencia. If you are a victim of this clause, now is the time to start legal action. In the overloaded courts, the process will probably take about two years.

Life insurance: It is quite common for the bank to insist on your taking a life insurance policy through them to cover the amount of the loan. They have no legal right to force this on a client but many banks insist on it.

Mortgage insurance: This is a new development in Spain, with only some of the new offers incorporating a scheme which insures the mortgage repayment if the holder loses his job or falls ill. You can also insure your mortgage against sharp rises in the interest rate. It costs extra, of course.

Spanish banks and building societies make no formal distinction between mortgages and re-mortgages, and the idea of a buy-to-let mortgage does not exist. If you wish to re-mortgage a property you already own, the bank will study your ability to re-pay the loan just the same as mortgage to purchase. You are always free to change your mortgage from one bank to another, and Spanish law has recently lowered the charges for this change.

In addition to the costs noted above, you will have a notary fee and a Property Registry fee. The mortgage is a legal document and must be signed by you and the bank's representative before the Notary. The mortgage is also a property document and must be registered in the Property Registry against your property.

This list of charges sounds quite daunting and many property purchasers have been upset to discover that they actually receive €8,000 or €10,000 less than the amount. Prepare yourself and do the numbers.

EQUITY RELEASE

Spanish banks and other lending institutions are finally catching on to the idea of equity release, or "reverse mortgage" on the home you already own in Spain. As mentioned above on re-mortgages, these products are now becoming better known. A bewildering variety of possibilities is on offer.

Be very wary of schemes which promise to re-invest the cash sum and produce enough income to pay off the loan with no cost to you. Hundreds of people have fallen victim to these plans when the stock market drops and the investment does not produce the promised returns. Some are in danger of losing their homes entirely.

Perhaps the simplest form is where you are, say, 70 years old and you own your home free and clear. The Spanish bank will pay you in cash perhaps 50 per cent of the value, with no re-payments at all. When you die, the loan and all the interest come due, with the property as security. Your heirs can either pay off the loan and interest to keep the property, or they can sell the property to pay off the loan and keep whatever is left.

Spain is now preparing new legislation to ensure that such products are correctly regulated and explained, especially to elderly homeowners, both Spanish and foreign. The new regulations will include tax breaks for the elderly.

SUBSIDISED HOUSING

In Spain, as in most countries, the government subsidises some types of housing. Ordinarily, this housing is destined for the poor and is offered to them on favourable terms.

Such housing is known in Spain as VPO, or *Vivienda de Protección Oficial*. You may think that this housing is not meant to help well-to-do foreigners purchase vacation homes, and you would be right. But there are several classes of VPO projects. One class, operated by the Spanish government, is available only to the poor, who must make a declaration of poverty in order to obtain it.

The other class, more frequently seen, is based on the provision of cheap government financing to the project developer, and these apartments are available to foreigners, although controls are becoming stricter. Purchasers now must be residents and they cannot have incomes of more than about €1,500 a month.

Nevertheless, especially if you are an EU citizen and an official resident of Spain, earning a living here, with a modest income, you may qualify for government assistance in buying your home, just as Spaniards do.

Remember, when purchasing VPO flats, the offer will stipulate that you make a very small down-payment, but if you can make a larger payment of €20,000 or so, and thus totally clear the constructor's own financial contribution to the project, this will be very advantageous. The balance, payable over 15 years or more on favourable terms, will then repay only the cheap government loan and not contribute further to the constructor's profit.

There are, of course, controls on the resale of such flats, which block speculators profiting at the expense of the government.

INSURING YOUR HOME

As in any country, it is sound practice to carry home-owner's insurance protecting you against damage to the building itself, damage or theft of its contents, and against claims from others who may suffer injury or damage resulting from your ownership.

This is especially important when you are absent from your Spanish property for long periods, but be alert to clauses in your contract which render your insurance invalid if you are away from the property for more than a stated period of time. Often, by paying an extra premium, you can be covered even though you are absent much of the time.

Both Spanish and international insurers offer various policies at various prices. Make enquiries among older residents to find a company which has given good service.

You fill out a form in which you state a value for your house and its contents. Remember that, should you choose to insure your property for only half its real value, the insurance company, which makes its own evaluation, will pay you only half the value of any individual items which are stolen or damaged. People sometimes think they can insure half and then get full value when only two or three items are stolen or damaged, but this is not so.

The company will also ask you to report on whether your property will be unoccupied for lengthy periods, how old the building is, how many doors and windows there are, whether they are guarded by *rejas* (iron bars), if there is a burglar alarm system, and so on. If you do not respond truthfully to these questions, there can be grounds for a later denial of any claim you make. Your premiums will vary according to your situation.

Be sure to read the fine print in your policy. Often, insurance against theft of the contents of your property will not pay unless entrance has been forced and there is evidence for this. If a "guest" at one of your parties makes off with your wife's jewels, you will not be paid. If there is no copy of the contract available in your language, have someone translate for you.

What will insurance cost you? Policies and conditions vary, but you can estimate that about one euro per year per thousand euros of value will cover the building itself against damage by natural causes or fire or explosions if the building is in a town. An older house in the country, far from fire-fighting services, would cost more.

Insurance of your furniture and household effects will be

somewhere around €2.50 per thousand euros of value if you live in an apartment; up to €3.50 per thousand if you live in a detached villa. This covers fire and theft.

If one of your steps collapses and the postman breaks his leg, or you leave the bathtub water running until your downstairs neighbour's apartment is flooded, they can claim compensation from you as the owner. You can cover yourself for claims up to €50,000 for less than €50 a year.

Most Spanish companies offer a comprehensive policy covering the building, the contents and third party claims. One company quoted a figure of €1,200 per year for comprehensive coverage of a villa and contents valued at €240,000. An apartment or townhouse would be less costly.

TIMESHARE LAW

A comprehensive Spanish law regulates important legal aspects of timeshare itself and provides consumer protection that brings the country into line with European timeshare regulations.

Putting a crimp into the high-pressure selling techniques of the timeshare touts around bus stations and tourist spots, the law provides a 14-day cooling-off period during which no deposit may be taken and the buyer can withdraw from the contract he has signed without any penalty.

Furthermore, the law requires that the timeshare operator provide full information and a contract in the buyer's own language. If any element of the purchase does not meet the brochure or written description or match the contract terms, the contract may not be enforceable.

The law also provides that any loan which the buyer may have taken out to purchase the timeshare will also be cancelled. This has been one tricky aspect of hard sales, in which the timeshare seller offers a low-interest loan to the prospective buyer. All well and good, but if the buyer later wants out of his contract, he finds that he still owes the loan to the bank, a third party, and it must be paid off. This practice is ended by the new law.

The law also provides that all contracts will be subject to Spanish law. That is, even if the buyer's contract states that its terms are subject to the laws of some distant offshore jurisdiction, where the timeshare company's headquarters is located, this provision is not valid and the contract will be subject to interpretation in Spanish courts.

This has been a thorny point in many timeshare contracts because the buyers found it difficult to dispute any point when the court was thousands of miles away.

Even the service companies which maintain the resorts have, until now, often been registered in offshore tax havens. This made it difficult for timeshare buyers to bring action against the companies when they failed to keep the resorts in good condition.

Under terms of Spain's new law, the service companies must have a permanent establishment registered inside Spain, where they can be held legally responsible.

Furthermore, the new law makes the resort owner finally responsible for proper maintenance of the resort, and action can be taken against the resort owner if the service company fails to perform.

On the other hand, the resort operator can repossess an owner's holiday weeks if the owner fails to pay one year's maintenance charges. The operator must give 30 days' certified notice before he can do this, and, unless this right is specifically renounced in your contract, he must pay back the owner the value of his remaining weeks in the scheme.

That is, a timeshare plan may run from a minimum of one year to a maximum of 50 years. If an owner has used his weeks for 25 years in a 50-year plan, and then defaults, the operator must pay him back half of his original price, as well as assuming the debt owed by the owner to the service company.

However, it is also possible for the timeshare contract to contain a penalty clause which will let the company keep the entire amount originally paid. Watch out for this clause in your timeshare contract.

The law also provides that timeshare contracts can be registered in Spain's Property Registry as a special right, although the law is also very careful to note that timeshare is not a property right as such, that it is a service contract not a property sale.

The full name of the law in fact is The Law Regulating the Rights

TIMESHARE TIP - Get your deposit back

A fast-talking salesman convinces you to put down a deposit on a Spanish timeshare, holiday club or similar plan. But later, after you return to the UK, you change your mind.

The timeshare company will not want to return your money. So you send them a letter cancelling your agreement within 10 days. Guess what? If you paid by credit card, you will find that all major credit card companies have agreed that they will "claw back" the payment when you show them your letter and proof of postage. Your only dealing with the timeshare company is the posting of the letter of cancellation.

of Rotational Enjoyment of Real Estate for Touristic Use, and it forbids any mention of property rights in timeshare publicity.

Unfortunately, the law does not mean that all timeshare sales are now regulated and controlled to protect the consumer. Timeshare companies have already come up with new schemes relating to "vacation plans" and "point systems" to move their products out of the area controlled by the law.

EXPROPRIATION OF PROPERTY

For most people, any improvement of the road system or flyovers and bypasses to increase safety is good news.

It may not be such good news if your property borders a projected highway or is affected by a new bypass, because the authorities — represented by a public works department such as the *Ministerio de Obras Públicas y Transportes (MOPT)* — can expropriate your property and put you off it.

They must pay you, of course. The *doctrine of justiprecio* applies, meaning they must pay you a fair price. You may have to fight them to get it, however.

There are legal avenues open to you to protect your rights in the matter. First, the authorities must officially inform you that expropriation proceedings are about to begin against you. They will send you an official letter inviting you to attend the *acta previa a la ocupación*. This is a hearing, usually held in your town hall, at which you may present any protest you have about the extent of your property being expropriated.

Money is not discussed at this first hearing, only the amount of land being taken. You should take skilled legal counsel with you when you go to this hearing.

If the authorities are only interested in a few square metres of your vast *finca*, then you have no real problem. If, however, they want to put the road through the kitchen and reception area of your popular restaurant, or if the amount of land they take will leave you with too few square metres to be buildable, then there must be some negotiating.

In such a case, some lawyers advise that you attempt to make the authorities expropriate your entire property and not just part of it. This obviously is because the property, once divided, becomes all but worthless and such a situation is manifestly unfair to the person involved.

In these negotiations, the authorities are usually reasonable and fair, but they will be even more fair and reasonable when confronted by skilled counsel.

Your chances of resisting expropriation altogether are very poor indeed. The entire concept of expropriation or Eminent Domain exists because sometimes the public good takes precedence over private ownership. They are going to build the highway and your chance of moving the route away from your private property is very small. Once the amount of land being expropriated is agreed, the authorities take the situation under analysis and then communicate their offer of payment to each owner. If the offer is acceptable, you inform them and the deal is done.

If, however, as is more frequent, you are not satisfied with their offer, you negotiate again. The doctrine of *justiprecio* is not just a word and it can be enforced. You will need to prepare a case for a higher price on your property, including sales prices of land around you, improvements you have made, and so on. You will need expert advice for this. If you are unable to come to an agreement with the authorities by negotiation, you have recourse to the *Jurado de Expropiaciones*, which is a special court set up for this purpose only.

The presiding members of this tribunal are not only judges; real estate experts are also included, and decisions it has rendered have ensured that fair market value is paid to many owners.

Beyond that, you can appeal this tribunal's ruling to the normal courts all the way up to the Supreme Court.

To sum up, in any expropriation proceedings, you have little chance of resisting entirely the order. But you do have two opportunities to protest both the amount of land being taken and the payment offered. Skilled counsel can make sure your interests are protected.

GLOSSARY

Abogado – lawyer, solicitor
Administrador de fincas – licensed professional property administrator
API – Agente de la Propiedad Inmobiliaria – real estate agent, member of long-established association.
Arbitrio sobre el Incremento del Valor de los Terrenos – municipal tax on property sales, see Plus valía.
Boletín Oficial – Official state gazette, where laws are published
Catastro – Land Office, concerned with measurements and physical description
Certificado Catastral – catastral certificate describing land and buildings
Cláusula Suelo – "Floor" provision in Spanish mortgages
Comunidad de Propietarios – Community of Property Owners
Contrato – contract
Dación en Pago – giving property back to the bank
Declaración de Obra Nueva – declaration of new construction
Escritura de Compraventa – sales contract
Escritura Pública – registered title deed
Expediente de Dominio – ownership proceeding, to establish title
Factura – bill
Finca – any plot of land or property
Gestor – licensed administrative expert in Spanish procedures

GLOSSARY

GIPE – Gestor y Intermediario de Propiedades y Edificios, title awarded by association of estate agents and property administrators.
Hipoteca – mortgage
Impuesto sobre Bienes Inmuebles (IBI) – annual real estate tax
Impuesto de Transmisiones Patrimoniales (ITP) – Property Transfer Tax
IVA (Impuesto sobre el Valor Añadido) – Spanish value added tax, charged when developer sells new property to first buyer
Jurado de Expropiaciones – special tribunal for expropriations
Justiprecio – doctrine of fair price by the state in forcible purchase
Ley de Costas – law protecting coastline
Ley de Tasas – law of public fees
Ministerio de Obras Públicas y Transportes (MOPT) – Ministry of Public Works and Transport
Nota Simple – certificate of registration from Property Registry
Notario – Notary
Plan General de Ordenación Urbana (PGOU) – town development plan
Plan Parcial – plan of building plots on urbanisation
Plus valía – municipal tax on property sale
Poder – power of attorney
Registro de la Propiedad – Property Registry
Reja – iron grillwork protecting windows and doors
Reposesión – repossessed property
Seguro Decenal – 10-year building insurance guarantee
Subasta – auction
Subasteros – professional auction buyers
Tasación – evaluation of property
Tasador – property surveyor, evaluator
Topógrafo – property surveyor
Urbanismo – town planning department
Valor catastral – assessed value of property for tax purposes

Selling Your Property

TAX WARNING

Sellers of Spanish property should be aware that they are subject to Spanish capital gains tax on the profits from their sale, whether they are resident or non-resident.

Furthermore, a sale of Spanish property attracts transfer costs that can total as much as 20 per cent of the price, in addition to that capital gains tax.

In some areas, real estate agents charge commissions of 10 per cent, although the Spanish estate agents' association recommends 3 per cent. Add to this taxes and costs that total about 10 per cent and you are looking at some very high transfer costs.

Non-residents pay Spanish capital gains tax at 19 per cent on their profit from the sale. As of 2017, residents pay 19 per cent on profits up to €6,000, 21 per cent from €6,000 to €50,000, and 23 per cent on amounts above that. The Spanish Tax Agency requires that a buyer from a non-resident seller withhold 3 per cent of the price and pay it directly to the Tax Agency as a guarantee against the seller's capital gains liability. The seller never sees it. So remember that, if you are a non-resident seller, you will receive only 97 per cent of the agreed price.

The non-resident must then file Form 210, on which he calculates his real Capital Gains liability. If that 3 per cent deposit is less than the real amount the seller must pay more. If the deposit exceeds the tax due, the seller can claim it back. Residents' tax is calculated as part of their income tax, paid the year after the sale. Residents are not subject to the withholding of 3 per cent.

You may be exempt from capital gains in two cases:

1. You are 65 years old, a tax resident, and you have lived in your home for a minimum of three years.
2. You are tax resident and you use the full purchase price to buy another principal residence in Spain or in another European Union country.

For full details on taxes involved in selling property, see the following section, Taxes on Property.

PROPERTY SELLER'S CHECKLIST

1. Your real estate agent

First, read the section on Estate Agent in the previous chapter. One rule often cited by those who have sold their homes in Spain is: Don't try to do it yourself. Get an estate agent, or several, and let them handle the showing of the place and dealing with prospects. Otherwise, you go crazy. There may be exceptions to this rule, but most sellers are in agreement.

Very seldom do Spanish estate agents demand the exclusive right to market your property, so you will probably list your sale with several agents in your area. Each agent will have his own form of agreement with you, in which his commission is stated if he brings the client who eventually buys your property. This agreement will contain the commission charged. Some agents charge as high as 10 per cent. Five per cent is more frequent. You make your own deal on this.

An agent can help you get your price right. He will know what the market is in your area. You can then decide if you want to put a higher price and wait longer to sell, or a lower price in order to attract an immediate buyer. Be warned that an agent will not work very hard to market your property if he thinks it is overpriced and unlikely to sell.

A good estate agent will see you through the entire process of finding a buyer, negotiating the price, making the contract, securing the payment, signing before the Notary, paying the necessary taxes, and all the other details that arise.

The usual sequence is:

1. Seller and buyer to agree all the details of the purchase on what is called a "private contract", at which time the buyer makes a substantial deposit, usually 10 per cent.

2. This deposit takes your property off the market and holds it while the buyer assembles the full amount of the purchase price, either from his own resources or by obtaining a mortgage. This deposit should be paid into a Bonded Client Account held by one of the lawyers involved, for release when the deal is completed. It should not be paid directly to an estate agent or the seller. If the buyer does not complete the sale, he loses his deposit. If you, the seller, accept a higher offer in the meantime, you have to return double the amount of the deposit. Be warned. It is astonishing how often an apparently serious purchaser is unable to come up with the cash. Don't count your chickens before they have hatched. Be warned also that some buyers will try to make stage payments and get possession. If they do not complete the payments, you will have plenty of trouble getting them out and recovering your property. (See section below on Lawyers).

3. When the two parties are ready to complete the sale, they go to the Spanish *Notario* and sign the sales contract at his office. The contract can also be signed by proxy. This often happens with an absentee seller. He gives his lawyer a power of attorney, called a *poder* in Spanish. This poder empowers the attorney to sign in the name of his client. A seller who does not wish to return to Spain can even make this proxy at the Spanish consulate in his own country (see Power of Attorney section in Buying Property chapter).

CAN I SELL MY HOUSE WITHOUT A FIRST OCCUPATION LICENCE?

What about those thousands of houses without First Occupation Licences, or with dodgy building permits annulled by the Regional Government, or with no building permit at all and with the danger of a demolition order at any moment? Can they be sold?

Yes, is the cheering answer in most cases, especially in Andalusia, where the government has created a sort of halfway legality for houses under threat.

If your house meets some basic requirements and is not on land classed as flood plain or parkland, you should be able to "regularize" it. If you have a building permit, even though annulled, or a *Declaraciòn de Obra Nueva* and perhaps a *Certificado de Antiguedad*, meaning the house is more than five years old, you probably can do this In Andalusia you want to obtain a Certificado de Asimilado a Fuera de Ordenación, a "Certificate of Assimilated to Outside the Planning Regulations". A structure that is classified as outside the town plan is considered irregular rather than illegal. If this confuses you, you are not alone. It is a sort of halfway step but it lifts the threat of immediate demolition.

It means you can sell your house, if you can find a buyer. In Part One of this Section I advise purchasers not to buy a house without a First Occupation Licence. Many real estate agencies will not accept such properties for sale. This is the most prudent course, but if you offer a very good price and can find a buyer with a taste for risk, then there is nothing illegal about the sale. The buyer must be informed that the house will never be completely "legal" until the law is changed.

4. This sales contract is stamped by the *Notario* and it should be immediately taken to the Property Registry office, where it is converted into the famous *escritura* — the title deed. The contract is called an *escritura de compraventa,* a purchase contract, and the title deed is called an *escritura pública,* because it is a registered document of public record. They are exactly the same document, before and after its registration. The original deed is then kept at the Notary's office. You yourself never have it. You have only an official copy. It is only this public deed that makes the buyer the new owner, with a title proof against all comers. Discuss the entire procedure step by step with your agent, so you know what is going on at each stage.

The steps listed above are the most usual form of property transactions, but there are many possible variations. If your buyer has the cash ready and you have your title deed clear, there is no reason why you cannot go directly to the Notary and complete the sale immediately, for example.

Don't forget that you want a proper bill — a *factura* — from your estate agent, listing the amount of the commission and adding 21 per cent IVA to this sum. Make this clear at the beginning of the transaction. The entire amount is deductible from your profit as a legitimate expense when you go to calculate your capital gains tax.

2. Your Spanish lawyer

Conventional wisdom says that the buyer always needs a lawyer but the seller may not. We say that the seller, in the complex world of international property transfer, really ought to have a lawyer, too. Your estate agent may be perfectly competent, but complications can arise outside his area of expertise. It is always good to have two people working for you as well so you can compare and contrast their views.

For example, some "buyers" will make you an offer of renting with option to buy but their sole intention is getting a cheap rental. They pay you a low rent, and then they stop paying the rent altogether, and then they leave. They never had any intention of buying the place. And it isn't worth the expense for you to try to collect the last three or four months of rent that they didn't pay, even if you could find them. Furthermore, your property has been off the market for six months or a year.

So, when the term of option to buy is mentioned, you or your lawyer or your estate agent should be aware that it ought to mean that the buyer pays you €10,000 or €15,000 for this option, which will be deducted from the total price when they purchase. If they let the time limit of the option expire, which might be two or three months, they forfeit what they have paid for it.

For all our dire warnings throughout this book, the majority of property transfers are quite clear-cut and no problems arise. Very few turn into nightmares.

Lawyer's fees vary widely. You can take one per cent of the purchase price as a guideline for a standard property transfer. Get this clear with your lawyer before you even start. Ask him how much he will charge you. Your legal fees are also deductible from your profits as a necessary expense in realising your capital gain. Again, you need a bill with Spanish IVA charged at 21 per cent.

3. The sales contract

Your lawyer will also explain to you some things not expressed specifically in the contract.

For example, your contract may state that your buyer pays €50,000 now and takes possession of the property, paying another €30,000 after three months and another €30,000 after an additional three months to complete a total price of €110,000. If he fails to meet any payment, he forfeits the amount already paid and the property returns to you. He promises to vacate immediately. You don't like the idea of the stage payments, but you feel safe because of this clause in your contract.

Your lawyer will warn you that this clause is not strictly enforceable and matters will not turn out so easily if the buyer fails to complete payment. If the buyer can't pay and refuses to leave, you will have to go to court to resolve your contract and get your property back. It will not happen automatically.

The court will probably rule that you indeed get your property back, but that you can't keep all of the money the buyer has already paid you. After the court makes its own calculation of how long the buyer has been in the house, plus inconvenience to you, and a series of other factors, it will decide that you can keep, say, half of the money already paid. Then, after this procedure has dragged out for months, you can again take possession of the property and start again on the process of selling it. This is only one of the many complications that come up in property transactions.

Some other points you want to study beforehand will be the division of payment of the transfer taxes and fees. Will you follow Spanish tradition and charge the Notary and the *Plus valía* tax to the seller and the transfer tax and the registration fee to the buyer? Or will you try to make the buyer responsible for all charges in the transfer? What price will you declare, the real price or a lower figure? (See below for more details on these questions.)

A good contract will help you foresee and avoid some of these complications but even the best contract cannot protect you against every eventuality. The standard contract used by your estate agent is probably as good as any, but your lawyer may have suggestions to make in your own particular case.

4. How much you declare

It was formerly a common practice in Spain to declare a property sale at much lower than its real price, in order to save money on transfer tax and wealth tax later. The Tax Agency is now watching property sales much more closely, however. If they believe that your sale is undervalued — and they have their own tables of market values — they may send you a notice that your sale has been re-assessed by them, along with a bill for how much extra tax you owe.

CHECK PRICE OF SALE AT *OFICINA LIQUIDADORA*

In today's climate of slashed prices for property sales in Spain, both buyer and seller can be dismayed to discover that the regional tax office refuses to accept the real price of a sale. This is because the official value set on the property is higher. A number of recent buyers have been burned this way, receiving the extra tax bill months after the sale. A property seller who wishes to establish credibility can go to the regional *Oficina Liquidadora* and obtain an official valulation on the minimum value you can declare. Your prospective purchaser will be impressed by your attention to detail.

Today, more and more contracts are declared at their real value. Furthermore, as buyers become more sophisticated, they have realised that a low declaration now means that they will show a larger profit on paper when they go to sell later, making them subject to a higher Spanish capital gains tax.

If you want to know exactly how much *Hacienda* thinks your property is worth, you can find out by asking at your regional *Oficina Liquidadora*. They will give you the amount listed in their own tables. Any attempt to declare a value under that figure will probably bring a notice to pay more.

5. Assemble your documents

It will help your sale to go smoothly if you have all your documents in order before you even begin to advertise. It builds confidence in the possible buyer — and his own lawyer — to see all the right papers in order when they consider purchasing. This set of documents is called in the UK a Seller's Pack and is now required by law. In Andalusia, a 2006 law specifies for re-sales a packet called the *Ficha Informativa*, an information sheet. It includes the address, description of the flat and building, or of the house, details of the owner, the year of construction, and any charges against the property. Even where not required, this set of information is a good idea.

DOCUMENTS YOU NEED

Escritura pública: The most basic paper of all is your title deed, which shows that you are the registered owner of record with an incontestable title. In fact, you have probably never seen your real title deed. What you have is an authorised copy. Unlike some systems of property registration, in Spain it is not the piece of paper itself which counts; it is the inscription in the *Registro de la Propiedad*, the property registry office.

If you lose your deed, you can always get another copy from the Notary, where it is on file permanently. Listed on the inscription in the property registry are any liens, charges or mortgages against the property. Back taxes, however, are not listed.

Your prospective purchaser will get for himself a nota simple from the registry, which is an extract showing the basic information and any charges against the property, but he will want to look at your copy of the full deed in any case.

In a few cases, owners have their property only on a private contract and the house may not even be registered. If this includes you, don't panic. This can be solved in various ways, depending on the individual circumstances.

You can offer your buyer the possibility of a Regulation 205 procedure or a full-scale *Expediente de Dominio*, (see reference in previous chapter) in which a court will study the case, publish the proceedings, and finally issue a clear title to the property. You might even find a new buyer willing to run the same risks as you in order to avoid taxes, who will simply purchase the property on a new private contract.

Or you can register the property and pay the taxes.

IBI receipt: Your receipt for the paid-up *Impuesto sobre Bienes Inmuebles*, the Real Estate Tax, is an important item. The IBI receipt shows first that the estate tax is paid for this year. It would be a good idea to have the receipts for the last five years, to show good faith.

The IBI receipt also shows the amount of the *valor catastral*, the official assessed value of the property for tax purposes. This value is almost always less than the real market value, but they are gradually being raised. The IBI receipt also confirms that the house exists and is registered for taxes, which can be an important point when no escritura pública exists and the owner holds the property only by virtue of a private contract. Finally, the IBI must be presented when you sign the contract at the Notary because it also displays the number of the *referencia catastral*, which, since 1997, is a required part of the documentation in property transfers.

***Referencia catastral*:** The Catastral Reference is the file number of the property's registration in the Land Registry, which in Spanish is called the *Catastro*, a word that exists but is rarely used in English.

Property is registered here by its measurements and boundaries and physical characteristics. The Property Registry is concerned only with ownership and mortgages.

You are right if you think that it doesn't make sense to have two separate bodies — which don't even talk to each other — dealing with land and property registration. Now, even the Spanish authorities begin to agree with you and, as a first step, they require that the catastral reference number accompany any property transfer.

Furthermore, the Notary and the Property Registry office are now authorised to make note of the fact if there is any great difference in the physical description of the property given in the *Catastro* and the legal description given in the sales contract and title deed.

This difference might include the fact that the *Catastro* shows a four-bedroom villa and a swimming pool while the sales contract mentions only a plot of land at a very low price. It is yet to be seen just how effectively the Notary and the Registrar of Property will inform the tax office, but the way is now clear, so be warned.

It is a good idea for the seller to obtain the completely detailed *Certificado Catastral* and include it in his documentation. This will add to the prospective purchaser's confidence, and will make it absolutely clear what he is buying.

Land descriptions on title deeds are often quite vague, even misleading. The *Catastro* is usually more accurate, because they have been updating their information for some years now, sending inspectors to check the physical reality of land and houses, and using aerial photographs as well.

It can take several months to obtain the certificate. There's a small fee.

Income tax declaration: If you are resident, and so not subject to the retention of 3 per cent of the price, you may be required to present your most recent income tax declaration when you sign the contract at the Notary. The income tax declaration, or a certification from the Tax Agency that you are current in the payment of your Spanish taxes, is now more important than the residence card in proving your tax status in Spain. This is even more necessary since the introduction of the simple Certificate of Registration for EU residents. Your tax consultant or lawyer can download the tax certification from the Tax Agency web site.

If you are a non-resident, your buyer would like to see your current Form 210, on which you declare for non-resident property owners imputed income tax and wealth tax. This is not to pry into your affairs, but your buyer will feel well-informed about the taxes he will face after he purchases. Non-residents should be warned that any unpaid property owner's income tax can be taken by the tax man from the 3 per cent retention the buyer pays into the Tax Agency in your name.

Consult the chapter on Taxes on Property for discussion on how to calculate your capital gains tax on the sale, and the annual taxes on property that you pay every year.

Non-residence certificate: This belongs to the buyer, not to the seller, but be warned that, if the buyer is a non-resident and the form of payment is not through a bank cheque which identifies the buyer as the issuer, along with his bank, the buyer must obtain beforehand a certificate of non-residence from the Spanish Ministry of the Interior, and it can take as long as two months for this certificate to be issued.

If payment takes place abroad, for example, by transfer from the buyer's account in London to your own account in London, this is perfectly legal, but it offers the Spanish tax man no control over the transaction for documentation purposes. So, they require this certificate if the transaction is not documented, with full details of the buyer and seller and their foreign banks.

If the buyer works through a Spanish bank, he will have a certificate of changing the foreign money into euros for property purchase, and Spain can document the transaction. If the sale takes place in pounds or another currency outside Spain, this is perfectly legal, and acceptable as long as the cheque is presented when the deal is completed at the Spanish Notary.

It is only when the buyer himself wishes to keep the details anonymous and confidential that he must present the certificate of non-residence. Spain wants to know where the money comes from, or at least that someone has made a deal without telling them.

TWO TAXES AND TWO FEES

We have discussed in the chapter on Buying Property the two taxes and two fees on property sales.

The two taxes are the ITP — the property transfer tax of 8 per cent — and the *Plus valía*, a sort of artificial capital gains tax charged by the town hall on the increase in an official set of values for the property.

The *Plus valía* varies widely, depending on the amount of time that has passed between sales, as we mentioned earlier. You can find out exactly how much it will be by asking at your town hall. They have a *Plus valía* office which will tell you the exact amount of the tax beforehand.

Remember, as discussed in the previous chapter, that your Town Hall may wish to charge you this tax on a non-existent profit, simply because of the time which has passed. The Supreme Court has ruled that this practise is illegal.

The two fees are for the Notary and the Property Registry. They will be in the neighbourhood of €500 but can be higher on large transactions. You can find out exactly how much by asking in advance.

If you determine the amount of these taxes and fees on your sale price in advance, you can include them in your sales presentation, impressing the buyer and his lawyer with your professional approach.

COMMUNITY CHARGES AND STATUTES

If you are selling a flat or townhouse that belongs to a community of property owners, you will want to include your last bill for the *cuota* — the community yearly charge, along with a copy of the statutes that regulate your community. The buyer will want to know what the yearly charge is and he will want to see the statutes of the community he is joining. It would be a good idea to have a copy of the Minutes, the *Libro de Actas*, of the last annual general meeting as well, to prove to your prospective purchaser that your community is well run and a nice place to live.

UTILITY BILLS

Copies of your bills for rubbish, water, electricity and even telephone are necessary parts of your sales presentation. Any buyer will want to know how much these charges are on the property, and he will also want to be sure that they are paid up.

Once you have assembled all this paperwork, it would be a good idea to prepare a folder with photocopies of each relevant document, so that you or your lawyer or your estate agent will be prepared to answer any question that a prospective buyer might have.

ENERGY CERTIFICATE NEEDED TO SELL OR RENT HOUSE

All houses sold or rented in Spain since June, 2013, need to have the new "Certificate of Energy Efficiency", which shows how effective the dwelling is in producing and retaining heat and cold. Spain's Royal Decree 235/2013 of April 14, 2013, puts the requirement into effect, thus complying with European Union Directives from 2007. In fact, buildings of new construction after 2007 should already possess the energy certificate. The April decree refers to "already existing" structures, which have been exempt until now.

European property owners will already be familiar with the energy certificate because a number of countries have already complied with the European Directive. In English, it is called the Energy Performance Certificate. Now these owners will need one for their Spanish property as well if they wish to sell or rent.

If you are not selling or renting your Spanish property, the certificate is not required. Also, it is not required for vacation properties which are occupied less than four months of the year, or whose energy consumption is less than 25 per cent of a normal one-year figure.

If you want to sell or rent, however, you must have the certificate of energy efficiency and make it available to the prospective buyer or tenant as part of the property description. It should be referred to in any publicity. If you are already renting out property, the certificate will not be required until it is time to find a new tenant.

If you have not provided the certificate, the buyer or tenant can report you and you can be fined up to €3,000 for a private property.

What is the Energy Certificate?

The IDAE, the *Instituto para el Desarollo del Ahorro de Energia*, is the body charged with developing a standard system for rating the energy efficiency of buildings. They have developed two computer programs which provide a system for rating the energy efficiency. They take into account the insulation, building materials, windows and other openings, plus the production of heating, cooling, hot water, and other factors. The idea is to produce a final number relating to carbon emissions. This then is translated into a rating from A to G, where A is the most efficient and G the least efficient.

Who Issues the Certificate?

Various types of professionals are empowered to inspect properties, make the study, and issue the energy certificate. These include architects, technical architects, licenced industrial engineers and others. You should have no trouble finding an authorized expert. Real estate agencies advertise that they will arrange for your energy certificate if you list your property with them for sale.

How much will it cost?

The estimated cost for this service ranges from about €200 for a small property up to €350 for a large property, but prices will vary according to the complexity of the study and other local factors. There is no standard price. It is quite possible that the expert who inspects your property will have some useful solutions for you to upgrade your rating and even save money on your energy bills.

However, there is no legal requirement for you to upgrade, even if your rating is low.

Once you have the Certificate of Energy Efficiency in hand, you need to present it at the registry established in each of the separate autonomous communities. The Andalusian registry will be different from the Valencia registry, but for the same purpose. You will have to ask in your Region.

GLOSSARY

Abogado – lawyer, solicitor
Administrador de fincas – licensed professional property administrator
API – Agente de la Propiedad Inmobiliaria – real estate agent, member of long-established association.
Arbitrio sobre el Incremento del Valor de los Terrenos – municipal tax on property sales, see Plus Valía.
Boletín Oficial – Official state gazette, where laws are published
Catastro – Land Office, concerned with measurements and physical description
Certificado Catastral – catastral certificate describing land and buildings
Comunidad de Propietarios – Community of Property Owners
Contrato – contract
Declaración de Obra Nueva – declaration of new construction
Escritura de Compraventa – sales contract
Escritura Pública – registered title deed
Expediente de Dominio – ownership proceeding, to establish title
Factura – bill
Finca – any plot of land or property
Gestor – licensed administrative expert in Spanish procedures
GIPE – Gestor y Intermediario de Propiedades y Edificios, title awarded by association of estate agents and property administrators.
Hipoteca – mortgage

Impuesto sobre Bienes Inmuebles (IBI) – annual real estate tax
Impuesto de Transmisiones Patrimoniales (ITP) – Property Transfer Tax
IVA (Impuesto sobre el Valor Añadido) – Spanish value added tax, charged when developer sells new property to first buyer
Jurado de Expropiaciones – special tribunal for expropriations
Justiprecio – doctrine of fair price by the state in forcible purchase
Ley de Costas – law protecting coastline
Ley de Tasas – law of public fees
Ministerio de Obras Públicas y Transportes (MOPT) – Ministry of Public Works and Transport
Nota Simple – certificate of registration from Property Registry
Notario – Notary
Plan General de Ordenación Urbana (PGOU) – town development plan
Plan Parcial – plan of building plots on urbanisation
Plus valía – municipal tax on property sale
Poder – power of attorney
Registro de la Propiedad – Property Registry
Reja – iron grillwork protecting windows and doors
Reposesión – repossessed property
Subasta – auction
Subasteros – professional auction buyers
Tasación – evaluation of property
Tasador – property surveyor, evaluator
Topógrafo – property surveyor
Urbanismo – town planning department
Valor catastral – assessed value of property for tax purposes

Building Your Own House

If you intend to build your own castle in Spain, the first item on your list should be finding a good lawyer. This lawyer should be Spanish and he should be familiar with your area.

This may sound a backwards approach, but when you check out all the things that can go wrong with buying land, getting a building permit, and contracting the construction, perhaps you will agree.

The second item on your list should be a promise to yourself that you are prepared to put a lot of your own time into overseeing the entire project, from beginning to end. Getting what you want depends on your own personal supervision.

Most building projects go up just as planned, with only minor setbacks, but it is best to be prepared and take care before you start.

So, let's suppose that you are determined to buy land and build your dream house. The rewards are great. But be prepared for plenty of exasperation and, above all, don't leap in with your eyes shut. Too often, the aspiring house-builder thinks that all he has to do is pick one model of villa from a selection that the developer or builder shows him, and that it will appear as if by magic a few months later.

Sometimes this method works out perfectly well, but not all of us can read a plan and visualise the final result with accuracy.

Too many people tell their builder that House Type B suits them very well, pay a fat deposit, and go back to their native country. When they return six or eight months later, they find: that House Type B doesn't look anything like they thought it would; that the builder hasn't placed it in the spot they had agreed on; and, furthermore, they absolutely hate the yellow tiles in the bathroom.

It will take your personal supervision to get it done the way you want it. With forethought and patient attention to detail, you can indeed have your dream house. But let me repeat that first warning. You simply cannot walk away and expect to return finding that your house has been built just the way you want it. You will have to be there every day. Let me repeat. Every day.

Or you can hire a Project Manager. His job is to do, for a fee, what you would do if you were there. This profession hardly existed in Spain not very many years ago. But, as residential homes have become ever more expensive, ever more technically sophisticated, and ever higher in quality, the need for professional project managers has grown. A good project manager will save you more money than he charges, in addition to the time, trouble and general hassle. He will also be familiar with the legal aspects involved.

FINDING THE LAND

First, however, you have to find a plot where you can build. Everything mentioned in the previous chapter about buying property applies here, and there is more besides.

Building land is available already divided into plots with all services on many urbanisations, as housing estates are called. This is the easiest way and also the safest because the developer has already arranged the legal details for building permits. You also know what you are getting into because you see the houses that are already there. It is also more expensive because of the work that has gone into the site preparation and the legalities.

Even then, we still find entire estates with dodgy building permits. These permits were often issued on shaky grounds by the Town Hall itself. Marbella on the Costa del Sol is now trying to sort out thousands of these permits, which have been impugned by the Andalusian regional government. In Chiclana on the Atlantic coast, thousands more of these illegally built homes are gradually being legalised. There are similar situations all around Spain, which are now coming to light because the Marbella scandal set off crackdowns by authorities in every part of the country, including the Costa Blanca, Balearics and the Canary Islands.

Country land is also much harder to find than before, and for the same reason. As thousands of foreigners moved inland from the coastal areas, the building departments of the small villages simply looked the other way and allowed construction on almost any site.

For years it was a common practice to build a country house on rural land that was not zoned for residence, pay a fine, and have the property made legal.

So many foreigners and Spaniards themselves did this that development officials have now cracked down on rural building and it has become almost impossible. In most parts of the country small towns and inland villages are now preparing new urban plans which will open up land for building again, but on a legal basis.

Once these development plans have final approval, it should be easier to realise your dream of a cottage in the country. Until then, you must take extra care.

BUILDING PERMIT

The first thing you have to know is, can you get permission from the town hall to build on it? The permit is called a *Licencia de obra or Permiso de obra*. Be advised that building permits cost around 4 per cent of the estimated construction cost. This varies from town to town.

If your land is in a registered urbanisation, or housing estate, with its papers in order, you will probably have no problem. If the site is an empty plot in a village street with other houses already there, you should find permission easy. Sometimes the land comes with the building permit already arranged. This land, of course, is more expensive because it has been prepared for development. But, even on a registered urbanisation, some problems can arise.

There are zoning changes from time to time, and you may find your beautiful property is in the middle of a green zone where no building can take place.

Do not take the seller's word as gospel. Your town hall's *urbanismo* department is a very important stop for you. Go yourself and take someone who speaks Spanish. Your lawyer, for example.

PGOU

You want to see the PGOU, the *Plan General de Ordenación Urbana*. This is the Town Plan. These plans generally are approved every four years. Any interim changes in them must be publicly posted and approved, with a chance for affected property owners to protest or make claims.

In many municipalities, you may find that changes have been made in the building codes and town plans, which though sometimes approved by the town hall still need the final go-ahead from the regional government, which must vet and clear the municipal plans.

In some cases, there are special building codes set up for specific zones. The PGOU analysis is not for amateurs. You need a specialist to make sure you understand it.

If your land is located in an existing and approved urbanisation, the permit will probably be forthcoming, but you must still check on it. You must also be sure that the urbanisation is an approved one.

There are some developments that never received official approval and where building is stopped today because they never met the legal requirements for the services they must provide, such as roads of a certain width, or water supply. You can find out by asking to see the *Proyecto de Urbanización* and the *Plan Parcial*. This is not a partial plan, as it sounds in English, but the plan of parcels, building plots, which is registered at the Town Hall.

In most of Spain's autonomous regions, such as Andalusia, the building permit issued by the town hall must also be vetted and approved by the regional building department. These departments exercise this control over the municipal departments to ensure that regulations are followed.

Be sure to check also the building regulations for plots and areas around your chosen spot. One of the worst, and most frequent, horror stories on the fast-growing coasts of Spain is the nightmare of the cut-off view. That is, you return to your pleasant villa on a hillside overlooking the Mediterranean to discover that a four-storey apartment building now blocks your view, and your new neighbours look right into your bedroom window. Make sure that you know what type of building permits will be issued around you before you buy.

In today's building climate, this check-up may be more complicated than it sounds.

In some municipalities the planning authorities make special deals with developers, whereby land is rezoned to permit greater building in exchange for part of the builder's profits going into the town's coffers. This is neither illegal nor corrupt, as the profits help all residents of the town, but it can harm the interests of those who already have purchased.

These special arrangements are called convenios, meaning simply "agreements". In Marbella, for example, municipal authorities

BUILDING COSTS

These costs are very approximate. So many variations come into building costs that it is extremely difficult to calculate an average price that means anything. Nevertheless, the table should give you some idea of what to expect.

Basic construction: figure 900 € a square metre.

Good construction: 1,500 € a square metre

Quality construction: 2,000 € a square metre and up, way up.

BASIC CONSTRUCTION means walls using large solid building blocks with no cavities and the use of basic flooring and finishing materials.

GOOD CONSTRUCTION at the top end of the price will include cavity walls and some higher-quality finishing materials. No air-conditioning or central heating, however, and no marble.

QUALITY CONSTRUCTION: The sky is the limit here. Remember that the area of location is also an influence. Labour costs are higher in Marbella than in the interior, for example.

issued so many building permits and made so many deals that the Andalusian regional development department finally acted to take building control out of local hands entirely. In complete defiance of the law, some building permits were granted on land zoned for parks and schools.

Country land – rústico

The short version is this: Country land, formerly classified as *rustico,* meaning rural, no longer exists. That is, the land still exists, but it is now classified as *No urbanizable,* meaning that you cannot build on it. End of story.

Formerly, Town Halls could make exceptions in their municipality, allowing building on plots of, say, 10,000 square metres. No longer. The only exception is if you are a genuine farmer. If you purchase a working farm or an olive grove and you wish to put a proper villa on the land to live in, you may do so. The catch is that you will have to show that farming is your main source of income and meet some other requirements.

Nevertheless, you might find a piece of land with a ruin or a house on it already. But is it legal? You can find this out at the local town hall. The urbanismo, or development, department can tell you exactly what will be permitted or prohibited within any area of the municipality. Visit the town hall yourself, taking someone who speaks Spanish, or send your lawyer, to make absolutely sure that a permit will be forthcoming. You want to obtain a written *informe urbanistico* on the status of your land.

The land may also have a *camino real* or a *servidumbre de paso*, an old pathway that crosses the land. It is a right of way and you can't cut it by building. People can pass over your land and it might even be transformed into a road some day.

Or an irrigation ditch might exist, which again is a legal right of way you cannot block, nor can you deny access to it for those who use it. Country land may have water problems, too. Where does the water come from? Can it be cut off? If you intend to drill your own well, you will need a special permission for this.

Have an expert check the town planning maps to see if any new highways are planned for the zone. It can come as a nasty surprise two years later when you see the bulldozers starting work next door, or you are called to a hearing where proceedings are launched to expropriate the bottom of your garden.

Once you have determined that a building permit will be forthcoming and that no special encumbrances exist on the land, you can start to find out just what land you are buying.

LAND MEASUREMENT

The seller must have an *escritura*, a title deed, for the land, just as for a flat or land with an existing house. Sometimes there is no registered title for the land, only a private document. See the preceding chapter for various ways of getting the land officially registered.

But, in the more usual case where official title exists, this *escritura pública* will describe the land, but sometimes the description isn't exact enough to suit you.

Descriptions in the Property Registry often use vague terms like the bare statement that the land borders on the east with the land of Pepe García. Well, Pepe has a big farm. Just what part of it constitutes the border? It could be where the fence is or where the ditch is or where the path is.

Then you need an official survey. Remember that the Property Registry is concerned with ownership, not with exact description. A surveyor is called a *topógrafo* and he will measure your plot exactly.

You can have this done independently but you should also check the *Catastral* registry.

CHECK THE *CATASTRO*

Here again, just as with buying a house, you want to check with the *Catastro* as well as the Property Registry. The *Catastral* office lists the boundaries and measurements and physical characteristics of the land. You want to be sure that this description squares with the description in the escritura.

If not, you may be able to get the *Catastral* reference to square with the reality of the land, and this in turn with the title deed.

The *Catastro* will have a map, a plan of the land, so that you can see that the boundary with Pepe García's farm runs along the fence, just as you thought. Or you may see that your plot includes a piece of land which Pepe García thinks belongs to him. Especially in old country properties, there is often some confusion.

You want to have exact, officially recognised boundaries, and the number of square metres that match the survey and the *escritura*. They probably will not agree, but you can correct this when you purchase, so that your own title and the physical description are in agreement. This clarity will be greatly to your benefit should you later wish to sell your land and house.

Ask for the official surveyor at the town hall. The survey will form part of your escritura when you buy the land. If your land is on an approved urbanisation, there will likely be an up-to-date survey already existing. The survey and the *Plan Parcial* will also show your access and where your water and electricity come from.

SEGREGACIÓN: PERMIT TO SUBDIVIDE

Yes, there may be another paper you need to see before you buy. If you intend to purchase a piece of Pepe Garcia's big farm, you will need to see the segregación document, a permit to subdivide the original piece of land into smaller plots. Only this will allow you to register your land as a separate plot.In some scams, the developer has a piece of land which he marks off into plots. But these plots are not registered officially and never will be without the *segregación* title.

Once you have determined that you can indeed build and you know the exact borders of your land, you had better find out if the seller is in fact the owner of the land.

Are you buying from the developers of the urbanisation, or from an individual? If the land is in the *campo*, does Juan really own it? He may share it with his two brothers, one of whom does not want to sell. Or there may be a mortgage on it. The same rules apply as for any property purchase. Check the *Registro de la Propiedad*.

BUILDING EXPENSES

Architect fee: 8 to 9 per cent (official college says 6 per cent, you can try to negotiate)
***Aparejador* (building engineer):** 1.5 per cent (he supervises building construction)
Building licence: 4 to 5 per cent (varies from town to town)
Topographic land survey: 0.66 per cent
Safety study: 0.8 per cent
Geological report: 0.94 per cent
First occupation licence: 0.5 per cent
Declaration of new construction: 0.5 per cent (you pay this when you register the house for taxes)
Total: 16 to 19 per cent

Finally, you sign the *escritura de compraventa* at the *Notario*, and you are ready to proceed with building. When you checked restrictions at the town hall, you should also have discovered what building code problems you may have. Do you have to leave three metres between your boundary and any building? Can you put a wall closer to the road than one metre? Is two storeys the absolute limit? If you are in an established urbanisation, does the association of property owners require you to submit your building plans for approval?

We repeat that checking the building code sounds simple but in practice it is often complicated. Many municipalities have old building codes in place, with new ones written and approved by the town council, but not yet ratified by their regional governments, which must give final approval.

This means that even official *permisos de obra*, or building permits, are sometimes granted on the basis of shaky legality.

RURAL HOMES THREATENED IN ANDALUSIA AND VALENCIA

Land laws in the Valencian community and in Andalusia have created thousands of "illegal" homes under threat, which may complicate your land purchase even further.

In Valencia, the LRAU outraged country property owners. The initials stand for the *Ley Reguladora de Actividades Urbanísticas*, the Law Regulating Urbanisation Activities. It has come to be known as the "land-grab law". The law provides that town halls may designate private developers as "urbanising agents", with the power to compel private owners either to sell parts of their land at low prices, or to pay high charges for infrastructure.

The law is clearly open to abuse and thousands of buyers, both Spanish and foreign, have suffered. Even the British ambassador has questioned the Valencia government about the protection of citizens' basic rights. Investigators sent by the European Union have issued four devastating reports, each one more detailed and horrifying than the last. There have been petitions signed by thousands of people and protests delivered to the UK government. And still there is no definite action. The European Union can cut off EU funding as a last resort.

In the meantime, citizens' groups such as AUN, *Abusos-Urbanisticos No*, continue to keep up the pressure on Spanish authorities.

The Valencia government has enacted a modification of the LRAU, called the LUV, the *Ley Urbanística Valenciana*, but affected owners charge it is simply more of the same high-handedness. Now the protesters have taken their case to the European Court of Human Rights, where early indications are very positive that some action will be taken against the Valencia authorities.

If you buy in an established urbanisation on the Costa Blanca, you should be all right. If you buy country land or property, make sure you check on any possible urbanisation plans in the area.

In Andalusia, the revised *Ley del Suelo*, the Land Law, has some similar provisions, but authorities affirm that more protections are in place to guarantee the rights of private owners.

The revised law also cracks down on the practice of illegal construction on suelo rústico, or country land. Its principal first effect has been virtually to halt the sale of country plots, as we mentioned above.

DEMOLITIONS: THE LAW NOBODY WANTS ENFORCED

It finally happened. A villa belonging to a retired British couple, constructed with full building permission from the Town Hall of Vera, in Almería province, was demolished. Bulldozers and police officers from the Andalusian regional government appeared at the gates with a court order and knocked down the structure.

Nobody wanted this.

The Priors, whose home it was, did not want it, of course. Their seven neighbours, whose houses also have firm demolition orders against them, now live in fear, wondering when the hammer may fall on their properties. The Vera Town Hall, which issued the permit that has since been legally annulled, did not want it. The outburst of publicity in the UK and Spanish newspapers has given the town a terrible black eye.

Further, Vera's municipal authorities acted with the knowledge that they were infringing the regional development plan when they made their own local rules to allow building on rural plots of 10,000 square metres. They now face lawsuits for being the proximate cause of loss and damage to the Prior family.

The *Junta*, Andalusia's regional government, did not want this. Their own slowness of procedure played a large part in letting the situation develop so far. If they had acted more rapidly and effectively to annul the local permits, the whole process could have been stopped before anyone suffered serious loss.

Nevertheless, it is not quite fair to say that the authorities did nothing and then reacted suddenly, out of the blue, without informing anyone. The Priors' building licence was issued in 2002. In May of 2003 they moved into their finished villa. By that time, the Almería provincial planning commission had issued a report which was unfavourable to the licence. As these reports are not binding, the Vera Town Hall took no action to rescind the licence nor did they inform the Priors. Town Halls are required to submit any building permit they issue for rural land to the Andalusian authorities. As a result, later in 2003 the Andalusian regional government initiated an ordinary court case against the licence. In 2004 the court ruled the licence was null and without effect.

The ruling was appealed to the administrative court in Almería. This is the Contencioso-Administrativo court, which deals with disputes between public bodies or between a private citizen and some organ of the administration. These administrative courts are overloaded with cases, but the court issued a ruling confirming the first sentence that rendered the licence null and void. In 2006 the court also ordered the Vera Town Hall to carry out the sentence, demolish the property, and inform the court and all interested parties of its actions.

The Town Council voted to accept the decision and carry out the demolition. However, it did not put this into action and finally the Andalusian regional government sent its own officials and bulldozers to do the job. The nasty part is that at no point were the Priors informed. Since then, a dozen more demolitions have taken place, each one bringing a wave of outrage by citizens.

So we find the regional authorities are now stuck with having to enforce their own laws in the harshest possible way. It is the only way to ensure that situations like the runaway Town Hall of Marbella do not occur again. When the dust settles from the present conflicts, we can hope that the building laws, for the first time, will be obeyed and enforced at all levels. This will mean that property owners, buyers and sellers can feel safe. In the transition period, thousands of innocent buyers are suffering.

PRIORS GET (SOME) COMPENSATION

Finally, in 2012, the Priors, who are now living in their garage, received some compensation from the Spanish State. In one of their several cases, they were awarded about one-tenth what their property is worth. They continue with their case against the Vera Town Hall for full compensation.

Town Halls all over Andalusia did not want this to happen either. Thousands of properties which have been inhabited for years are facing exactly the same legal situation. Many of them have firm demolition orders already in place, which could be carried out at any time. In the municipality of Mijas, for example, on the Costa del Sol, there are about 3,000 homes, most of them owned by Spanish families of modest means, in an irregular situation. More than 300 of these homes could be demolished at any time. The Town Hall itself is now attempting to negotiate a solution to make the houses legal.

In Marbella the illegal building permits were issued by corrupt Town Hall officials who were after personal gain. This is one end of the scale. In Mijas and many other towns the irregular permits went to local families who desperately needed housing. In most cases, they already owned the farmland on which they built their homes. Many of them did their own building, for that matter. It is a hard choice for a town hall. They must either deny housing to these low-income families or try to get around their own laws. This is the other end of the scale of illegal building.

DEMOLITIONS: HOW TO BE ABSOLUTELY SAFE

The best way to buy with absolute security is to purchase an empty lot on a normal village street, possibly with a ruin on it. You then apply for building permission from the Town Hall and put up a two-flat. Live in one and rent out the other. No community fees, no urbanisation problems, and no British neighbours.

The next best way you will not like, but here it is: You must obtain the *Certificación de Convalidación* from the *Junta de Andalucía* regional planning department. This is clearance from the regional authorities for your building permit issued by the Town Hall. It takes the form of publication in the Provincial Bulletin. Each Town Hall is required to file any building permit issued on suelo rustico, or non-building land, with the regional planning department for clearance. In Andalusia, this has been in effect since 2003, with the passage of a revised and stricter building law for the region.

The main reason you will not like this is because it will take months, perhaps a year, for the clearance to arrive. That is why nobody does it. If any of those innocent buyers in Almeria had been advised to wait for the regional clearance, this would have been denied, and the building cancelled.

Perhaps the planning authorities will find a way to speed up the process and make it easier to obey the law.

ARCHITECT

At last you need an architect. You have your rough sketches but you need someone who can turn them into real blueprints. In fact, you will need architect's drawings in order to get your building permit in any case.

The only way to find a good architect is to ask around. If you prefer to use a foreign architect for your design, you may do so. Since Spain's entry into Europe, EU architects can now practise and sign plans for approval by the official *Colegio de Arquitectos*.

Architects' fees, at least as a minimum, are standard and are set by the *Colegio*. They are about 6 per cent of the estimated cost of construction.

To this you must add another 1.5 per cent for the *aparejador* (see below), so your design and supervision will cost you about 7.5 per cent of your estimated construction cost. This construction cost, by the way, will be less than either your real cost or the real market value of the house when finished.

The price includes final plans that must suit you, and the six copies necessary for approval by the College of Architects and for your building permit. The fees stated here are only suggested minimum charges, as the College no longer has the legal power to enforce the rates. Hence, you may be able to get a cheaper fee by a little negotiating.

MEMORIA IS BINDING AGREEMENT FOR BUILDING SPECIFICATIONS

The price also includes preparation of the *memoria de calidades*, or building specifications, which includes items like the size of pipes, the formula for the concrete, and the type of materials to be used.

You yourself want to have a personal hand in this. You can choose here just what sort of electrical fittings and bathroom fixtures and kitchen tiles you want. This is the time to think of details about shelves and about whether you want wood window frames or aluminium, and so on.

It is important to give this a great deal of thought because the *memoria* is what you will give your builder in order to get his bid on the job. He will set his price according to the materials stated in the memoria, and any changes you may make later, or any additions, will cost you extra. These extras can add up to a lot of money, so the *memoria* is a very important document.

If the builder fails to install any items as set out in these building specifications, he can be held responsible.

The architect's fee includes overall supervision of the construction, but you are not likely to see your architect on the building site once he has finished the design.

The actual supervision usually falls to the aparejador, a professional architectural engineer who sees that the building is carried out to the specifications required. He will visit the site from time to time to check on things and he will take his own fee, about half what the architect charges you. He signs the documents certifying that the house is properly constructed, which you will need in order to occupy your house legally and to get your electricity connected.

Your architect will be able to recommend an *aparejador*. Often they work out of the same office.

Finally, you are ready to find a builder. It is only reasonable to get several bids on your job, remembering that the lowest bid is not always the best deal and that the highest bid does not ensure high quality. Ask around.

Your contract with the builder should include the *memoria*. It should state the total price; whether or not the site grading and preparation and final clean-up are included; the manner of payment; and give a definite completion date, with a penalty clause for late delivery. You ought to have your lawyer vet this contract.

Be advised that many building projects are not finished on time. If your contract contains a penalty clause, well and good. Often, however, the only guarantee is that you can get your money back if the project is not delivered on time.

In real life, you don't want your money back. The apartment or house is already worth 10 or 20 per cent more than you paid for it a year ago, when construction started, so you would suffer this loss. In this case, you simply wait.

PAYMENT SCHEDULES

Payment terms are not standard, but a typical schedule might be:

1. A deposit of 20 per cent when the contract is signed.

2. Another 20 per cent when the walls and roof are completed. (At this point, it is customary to have the bandera party, when a flag is placed on the roof, and the owner invites the workers and his own friends to a *fiesta* at the site.)

3. Another 20 per cent when the door and window frames are installed and the inside is more or less complete.

4. Another 20 per cent when the house is painted and ready to inhabit, with plumbing and electricity installed and functioning.

5. A payment of 10 per cent when all the outside work included in the contract is finished, such as patios, walls, pool.

6. The final payment of 10 per cent should be held back for six months to a year, if you can swing the deal, to cover any defects in construction which don't show up until the rains start, for example. There is always something.

10-YEAR INSURANCE - LOE

Spain's recently revised building law makes builders legally responsible for 10 years for any damage resulting from the foundations, load-bearing walls and other structural elements. The builder is responsible for three years for damages caused by construction material defects, and for one year for the state of finishing elements. The law is called the LOE, the *Ley de Ordenación de Edificación*.

The law requires the builder or developer to contract an insurance policy that covers the possibility of building defects over the 10 years after completion of the project. You need to see the document for this policy. It is a separate document made with the insurance company. Builders want to escape it if they can because the insurance policy itself can cost from two to four per cent of the building cost. If you are building yourself, with a small contractor in a rural area, make sure this policy exists.

For self-builders the trap is that in some cases you cannot have your new house legally registered unless you present the policy. If your builder has not done it, then the responsibility falls on you as the developer of the land. It is not illegal for a self-builder constructing his own home to skip the policy, but if you want to sell, say five years down the road, you must make it clear to the buyer that the policy is not in place.

DECLARACIÓN DE OBRA NUEVA

Before you can register your new house for real estate taxes, you must make a *Declaración de la Obra Nueva*, a declaration of new work, in order to have the structure appear on your escritura. So far, your deed mentions only the piece of land, not the house you have just built.

The declaration of new construction will cost you one half of one per cent of the declared value of the construction. Again, if the Tax Agency does not agree with your declared value, they can raise it.

Your lawyer or property consultant will show you how to register the new house. If you do not register (dar de alta) with the tax people, you can be fined, so take care of it as soon as possible. Two per cent of the value of your house is also calculated as income when you go to file for your Spanish income tax if you are a non-resident (see Taxes on Property).

When you go to make your declaration of new work and register the house, you will need the *Certificado Final de Obra* issued by the architect, the *Licencia de Obra*, building permit, issued by the town hall, and the *Licencia de Primera Ocupación*, the permit to inhabit the dwelling, from the town hall. You will also need the 10-year insurance policy.

Then you will be the completely legal and registered owner of your dream house and you can begin to pay your non-resident property owner's imputed income tax and your annual real estate tax.

GLOSSARY

Aparejador – building engineer
Arquitecto – licenced architect,
Bandera – flag, here referring to "flag party" when house is roofed
Camino real – royal road, meaning right of way across land
Catastro – Land Registry, distinct from Property Registry
Escritura de Compraventa – conveyance deed
Escritura Pública – registered title to land
Certificado de Final de Obra – construction completion certificate
Declaración de Obra Nueva – declaration of new construction
Licencia (or *Permiso*) *de Obra* – building licence
Licencia de Primera Ocupación – licence to occupy the dwelling
Memoria de calidades – detailed building specifications
Plan General de Ordenación Urbana (PGOU) – municipal building plan
Plan Parcial – plan of building plots in housing estate
Proyecto de Urbanización – housing estate development plan
Rústico – country land, not zoned for building
Segregación – sub-division of a piece of land into plots
Servidumbre de paso – legal right of way
Topógrafo – land surveyor
Urbanismo – urban development office

Letting and Renting

REVISED RENTAL LAWS AFFECT LANDLORDS AND TENANTS

The Spanish parliament, the *Congreso de Diputados,* has amended several laws affecting both property owners and rental tenants.

Changes in the law of letting modify the basic Tenancy Act, the *Ley de Alquileres Urbanas,* the Law of Urban Lettings. These changes come in the law, *Medidas de Flexibilizacion y Fomento del Mercado del Alquiler de Viviendas* "Measures of Flexibility and Development of the Market for Rental Dwellings". This mouthful is *Ley 4/2013 del 4 de junio,* for those of you who wish to consult the original.

LIMIT FOR RESIDENTIAL CONTRACT DROPS FROM 5 YEARS TO 3 YEARS

One of the most important changes in the rental law is the reduction of the fixed maximum for long-term contracts from five years to three years. Along with this, the "tacit extension" of the contract, when landlord and tenant do nothing, drops from three years to one year. All this adds up to increased flexibility for the landlord and reduced security for the tenant.

The revised law applies to contracts signed after June 6, 2013.

Tenants may now terminate the contract and leave the property after six months, by notifying the landlord one month in advance. They may not be held liable to pay back the rest of the amount of the contract. Formerly the tenant was liable for the payment of all the rents for the period remaining in the contract. Rarely did a landlord attempt to recover his remaining two years of rent, but the law allowed him to do so.

Landlord may terminate the contract and seek eviction after one month of non-payment of rent. Even so, many months will pass before he is able to obtain an eviction order.

Rents can be raised each year, either by agreement or according to consumer price index.

Provision for tenant to renounce his right to first refusal when property is sold. This right formerly could not be renounced by the tenant. Now we can be sure that a landlord will include the renunciation in his standard contract. If the tenant wants to retain this right, he will have to negotiate.

TENANT: WATCH OUT FOR TWO NEW RULES

Landlord may now recover his property after one year if he needs it for family or wants to sell it. Further, a new purchaser of the property can put the tenant out unless the contract is registered at the Property Registry in the special section for rental contracts. Again, less security for the tenant. If you are renting a Spanish property, you need to make sure your contract is registered. Landlords will also find the tax agency checking this registry to see who is getting rental income.

So we see that a new tenant on a residential, long-term contract must keep his wits about him and be alert to maintain his rights in his contract.

REGIONS CRACK DOWN ON HOLIDAY RENTALS

The revised national law does not even mention short-term or holiday rentals. These holiday lets are now to be regulated by Spain's individual autonomous regions. The Regions, such as Andalusia or the Valencia Community are now acting to tighten restrictions on holiday lets. This means that we could see seventeen different sets of regulations for holiday lets.

One of the most restrictive systems is already in place in the Canary Islands, where it is illegal to rent out a single apartment in an apartment building for a holiday let without registration. (See section on Holiday Rentals for details.)

LONG-TERM RENTALS PICKING UP

In 2018 we are also seeing an increase in long-term rentals. Two factors are important. One is that Spaniards are getting over their long-time prejudice against renting rather than buying. This means that demand is growing. The other factor is that today's low property prices mean that purchasing property and renting it out begins to look like a better deal. So you can profit both from your rental income and the rising value of your property in the future. As a result, Spain's minimal buy-to-let culture is coming alive. Some sources estimate in late 2017 that your rental income should turn a profit of about four per cent after expenses and property prices are rising nationwide at a rate of four per cent. This gives a theoretical gain of about eight per cent per year.

However, plenty of things can go wrong.

Tenants may lose their jobs and cannot pay their rent. Unscrupulous tenants may pay the first few months of rent, stop paying, and then hang on for the six months or year or even more that it takes the landlord to get them out. This has been a dangerous scam for owners on the Spanish coasts. (See section on How to Evict a Non-paying Tenant)

However, if you plan carefully and take time to study the situation in person, you can buy to let today.

Here are some key points to keep in mind:

1. Establish a personal relationship with an experienced local estate agent.

2. Never purchase on the basis of one visit. Make at least three trips to Spain.

3. Buy only property in the best locations.

4. Vet your letting agency with extreme care.

5. Study your mortgage options carefully.

If you follow these steps you should find yourself in an excellent position as the market picks up, both in terms of letting and in an increase in the value of your property.

As we mentioned in the chapter on purchasing property, there are thousands of desirable flats and villas available today at greatly reduced prices. If you have a reasonable down payment and can demonstrate that you are solvent, you will find that a Spanish bank is eager to grant you a mortgage, in spite of what you have seen in the papers. Furthermore, the mortgage will draw rock-bottom interest rates as the Euribor index continues at just about zero per cent. As of 2017 banks are offering mortgages at less than 2 per cent. They are also vetting the applicants thoroughly, to ensure that they are solvent and can meet the payments. The downside is that there are also dozens of problems that arise with rental properties, which we will examine in this chapter.

TENANTS IDENTIFY LANDLORDS

Many foreign owners who let their Spanish property seem blissfully unaware that they are subject to Spanish income tax on their rental income. This applies to both residents and non-residents.

The Spanish tax man has sweetened the rental package recently by introducing a reduction of 50 per cent in rental income for tax purposes. This formerly applied to official residents of Spain but has recently been extended to non-resident landlords who are EU citizens. Non-resident landlords from non-EU countries still have no deductions.

Resident or non-resident EU citizens who are landlords can also deduct expenses for upkeep from their rental income. As a result, many landlords will pay little income tax.

Rental income is declared for Spanish income tax on a special form 210. (See Rental Tax Box for more details.)

Landlords, be warned. Tenants who make tax declarations in Spain are now required to list their landlord's name and tax identification number on their income tax declaration along with the catastral reference of the property they rent.

We all know that many owners rent out their flats and say nothing to the tax man. This requirement to identify has already produced tens of thousands of new tax declarations in its first years.

LETTING LAW: "Old Rent" Ends

Spain's current Law of Urban Lettings, the *Ley de Arrendamientos Urbanos*, went into effect on January 1, 1995, and was amended in the summer of 2013.

The big news for this year, however, is that the provisions of the "old rent" law have finally disappeared. It has taken almost 20 years, but *Renta Antigua* is finally gone for good.

The current law ends the forcible extension provision of the 1964 law, which made rental contracts indefinitely renewable by the tenant. The 1995 law allowed landlords gradually to raise the old controlled and ridiculously low rents of the 1964 law to market prices today, and, eventually, to recover their own property.

THREE RENTAL SITUATIONS

We must distinguish three possible situations for rentals existing in Spain today, depending on when the original contract was made.

1964-1985: Under the terms of the rental laws in effect from 1964 to 1985 tenants were so protected that landlords gave up in despair and stopped building rental apartments. Until recently more than 200,000 apartments in Spain were still occupied under this old law, which protected a tenant so strongly that he could pass on his rights to his children and even his grandchildren. Further, his rent could never be raised, or raised only by a small percentage related to the inflation rate.

Incredibly, there were still thousands of apartments in Spain with tenants paying less than €100 a month. The grandchildren of the original tenants were living in spacious flats in prestigious areas, paying rents of €20 a month. The landlord was helpless to do anything about it, even though his real estate tax was €1,500 a year and his community fees another €1,000. Next door, another tenant paid €1,200 a month for the same type of apartment, having signed his contract after 1985. All this has finally ended.

1985-1995: Revised rental laws passed in 1985 by the Socialist government aimed to remedy this situation in the best capitalist way, by making rental properties good business. The revised law provided that all contracts ended when they said they ended, without provision for forcible extension. The law also ended any restrictions on rent increases. Landlords immediately began to raise rents sharply and to offer short-term contracts with little protection for the tenant. Now it was the tenants who suffered, because they were unwilling to settle into a flat from which they might be evicted in one year's time, or be forced to pay sharp increases.

1995-2018: The 1995 rental law, amended in 2013, now in force is designed to provide a better balance between the rights and needs of tenants and landlords.

CONTRACT RENEWABLE UP TO THREE YEARS

The present law provides that residential contracts, as distinct from short-term holiday lets, are subject to yearly renewals up to three years. Rental contracts are usually made for one year but the law requires that the contract is renewable for a total three-year period of tenancy.

A landlord can offer a contract of two years but, if the tenant decides that he wants to stay on, this contract is renewable for a total period of three years. If the tenant himself wishes a contract ot only two years, this is all right.

The rent can be revised upward by an inflation factor each year. At the end of the three years, the landlord can raise the rent as much as he chooses, either for his new tenant or for his existing tenant, if he decides to stay on at the new and higher rent.

DEPOSIT

The current letting law also establishes the landlord's right to a deposit as a guarantee against damages. The deposit can be held by an agency independent of both landlord and tenant. This agency will not release the deposit until both parties agree.

The deposit consists of one month's rent for a residential unit and two months' rent for commercial premises. Where rentals are scarce, landlords will demand larger deposits. They are free to do this if the tenant agrees.

ACT QUICKLY TO EVICT NON-PAYING TENANT

The only secret to evict a tenant who fails to pay the rent is to act immediately. Do not wait. Tenants always have some reason for not being able to pay. Those who have lost their jobs hope to get work next week, for example. If they intend to defraud you, they are likely to have very plausible stories about how they will pay next month. Pay no attention, in either case.

1. Send the tenant a certified demand for payment as soon as he is even two weeks late with the rent. This can be a notarised letter or a Burofax, which is delivered by the Spanish Post Office. The demand should set an early date, such as two weeks hence, by which you expect payment, and should state in a polite way that you will be forced to commence legal proceedings against the tenant after that date.

2. Now try to reach a friendly agreement with the tenant. Perhaps he can stay and pay with a lower rental. However, even if you and your tenant are on good terms, proceed with the eviction process. This is called a *juicio de desahucio* in Spanish.

3. Here's why. It can take up to a year and a half to complete the eviction formalities and obtain a court order forcing the tenant to leave the property. During this time, he has paid you no rent and your chances of getting it from him are small. So the sooner you set the wheels in motion, the less money you will lose.

4. No, you may not legally take action against the tenant by cutting off the electricity or the water or by changing the locks. The tenant can bring charges of harassment against you in Court if you do this.

5. Now you want to claim back your lost income from the tenant. This is in fact a separate case from the case to evict him. Most landlords do not even bother trying to reclaim the rent owed because it involves extra expense with a low probability of getting anything back.

6. Yes, you need a lawyer to handle your eviction case. This will cost you between €1,000 and €2,000. The justice authorities are opening new courts to specialise in eviction hearings and are attempting to streamline the procedures, but progress is slow. One Spanish lawyer observed that she obtained an eviction order in three months in one case, and another took more than a year

The deposit, called a *fianza,* can be held by the housing department of the regional government. In Andalusia, for example, it is deposited with the *Consejería de la Vivienda* of the Andalusian autonomous government, which has offices in major cities.

HOW TO BE SAFE WHEN YOU LET YOUR FLAT

Sorry, but the only way really to be safe is to know your tenant.

This can be almost impossible on the Spanish Costas, where

rentals are often arranged by Internet and where people move around more frequently than they do in most areas. We have already mentioned above the dangers of the professional rental defaulter.

There are insurance and guarantee schemes for protection of rent when the tenant defaults, but these plans all cost money and do not always function effectively. Knowing your tenant is the only real security.

HOLIDAY RENTALS HAVE SEPARATE RULES

This basic rental law does not affect short-term holiday rental contracts, called arrienda de temporada. Holiday rentals are now regulated by Spain's individual Autonomous Regions, so terms vary from Andalusia to Valencia and so on. (See below)

These holiday contracts do not grant the tenant any right to automatic extension and they require that the tenant vacate when the contract ends. So, foreign property owners can be assured of this legal protection when they let their holiday homes for periods of several months. However, they should still take some care with vetting tenants because the legal procedures for eviction of a tenant who refuses to leave can take more than six months, even when the law is on the landlord's side.

There have been a number of recent cases in which unscrupulous tenants have signed up for holiday rentals, say, for two months, and then simply remained in the apartment without paying any further rent. Four to six months later, the landlord is able to obtain an eviction order, but the tenants have lived rent-free for that period. A court may enter a judgement against them for the amount of rent owed, but they simply move to another town and repeat the scheme.

HOLIDAY RENTALS BY REGIONS

Spain's new national law referring to rentals leaves the regulation of short-term holiday lets to the individual Autonomous Regions. The following list gives an idea of the picture as of the summer of 2017. Some regions, such as the Canary Islands,, are in the midst of making changes while others are contemplating new rules. You must check with your own Region to be sure. In spite of scare stories in the UK press, the new holiday letting rules are not too hard on landlords.

Usually they require the payment of a small fee, the registration for a licence, and the need to meet certain standards.

We may also note that any person who wishes to rent his property on a short-term basis and stay entirely off the radar may do so as long as he does not provide any holiday-type services or advertise on holiday letting web sites. The income from all these lets must be declared to the Spanish tax man.

Canary islands: After years of basically ignoring their own regulations, the authorities are now imposing fines of €18,000, reduced to €15,000 on appeal, for violations of the tourist letting law from 1995. Having no licence, lets of less than three months, advertising as "tourist" or "holiday" lets, offering hotel-type services, all are included as violations. The tourist authorities have carried out thousands of inspections and issued thousands of fines. No new licences are issued to private owners. Only complete complexes are allowed. This is the strictest regulation in Spain, promoted by hotel operators who regard apartments as unfair competition, and private owners are up in arms. A revised law coming into effect soon will ease the restrictions.

Andalucia: New tourist letting law requires registration in the "*Registro de Turismo*" letting section. Those who advertise on tourist letting websites or identify their properties as holiday lets with services will be required to register. Any provision of hotel-type services such as cleaning and fresh linen will means you must register. New law draft requires provision of maps and brochures of attractions in area, air conditioning, heating to 19 degrees centigrade, and Internet connection. No fees yet established. Bed and Breakfast specifically included.

Cataluña: Law of 2012 makes distinction between tourist apartment complexes and private lettings. Owners present form to register at Town Hall where property is located. The form describes the dwelling, the owner's personal details, an emergency telephone number that must always be available, maintenance and cleaning company details. Town Hall will send this information to the *Registro de Turismo de Cataluña*. Since 2012 Cataluña has a tourist tax which is 75 cents a night in Barcelona and 50 cents a night in the rest of the Catalonia.

Balearics: The Balearics tourist law came into effect in 2012, requiring registration and licence for villas and semi-detached properties. However, the law does not include flats. Private owners who wish to rent their flats for short periods must observe the rules we cited in the introduction. That is, they must not provide hotel-type services or advertise the property as a "holiday let". They need to make sure their letting contract does not mention services. Licence fee is about 25 euros per guest. A semi-detached with 4 beds will cost just under 100 euros to register. Fees in other regions are similar or higher. But be alert because revisions to the law which passed in August of 2017 have shifted regulation powers to each individual municipality in the Islands.

Valencia : The Valencian Community, which includes Alicante, permits owners to rent out their property as tourist rentals without being registered or licenced. The only requirement is that the landlord must declare the income, just as in the other regions. However, the owner must note in any advertising that he is not registered, so it might be an advantage to register, which will give prospective tenants more confidence. The tourist rental law establishes three categories of rentals. These are Standard, Primary and Superior. The law also requires registration in order to use an accredited letting agent. So, if your property qualifies as Superior, justifying a higher rent, it will probably be worth your while to register.

LANDLORDS MUST BE WARY

If you are a property owner and you wish to let your own flat or villa in Spain, or go into the tourist accommodation business, you must be very careful about the terms of your contracts and the quality of your tenants.

The opportunity to pay off your property by letting it looks tempting on paper. It can work out to your entire satisfaction, and in fact it often does. Nevertheless, many problems arise and you need to be wary.

Tenants may damage your furniture or harm your plumbing and electrical installations. Letting agents may keep your money and allow your apartment to fall into ruin while you are absent.

The safest way is to let only to people you know and trust. Even then it is a good idea to get the rent in advance and a deposit against possible damages as well. Electric bills always arrive late, so it is best to include an estimated charge in the rent.

If you have a telephone, have it disconnected. There have been many problems with telephones.

A property owner interested in long-term letting should be aware that the residential tenant may have the right to first refusal if the property is put up for sale and the rental contract is formally registered. See Right of First Refusal below.

NECESSARY NOTIFICATION

If you have let your property on a three-year vivienda contract (see above) and you wish to take possession yourself at the end of that time, remember that you must officially notify the tenant well before the end of the contract that you do not intend to renew it. If you do not do this correctly, the contract can be regarded as renewed for one year and at the same rent.

LETTING AGENCIES

If you want to let your property on a casual basis and for only a few short periods each year, you will most likely let by word of mouth to people you know or to people recommended by friends.

If you want to let on a more regular basis, you will probably use an agency or holiday company. You may find that your garden apartment development or your urbanisation office includes a letting service which, for a commission, will handle all the details for you. This could be your solution, but read the agreement carefully and talk to others who have used this service to make sure they are satisfied.

There are also holiday companies which bring people to Spain for two or three-week self-catering holidays. These are becoming more and more popular, especially for young families who prefer to stay away from hotels. These companies are always looking for new properties to let. Because they charge their clients high prices for short stays, they can afford to pay you, the owner, a good price for the use of your property.

Again, be sure to read their agreement very carefully. Remember that a series of holiday tenants can do a lot of damage to your property.

Also make sure that this company is legally registered and that it is paying all the proper taxes. Because, when you provide linens and other hotel-type services, and deal with many tourist visitors on a short-term basis, you move into a new area legally. You are now a business yourself and you should legally declare your property as a tourist letting accommodation. This means that inspectors may come to check the standards and the tax man will be informed.

It also means that you or your holiday rental company must declare the income, and set aside 24.75 per cent of the rent as a withholding tax to the Spanish government. You declare for this tax on Form 210, just as the individual letter does. You or your holiday company must also add an extra 21 per cent IVA, value added tax, to their fees, which must be paid to the Tax Agency as well.

On the other hand, you can now deduct maintenance expenses from your Spanish income tax. You cannot do this when you inhabit the property yourself, but maintenance becomes a business expense when you let out your property regularly.

You may also employ a real estate agency in Spain to handle your letting, but be sure you are dealing with people who are competent and whom you trust. All too often one finds that extra fees and charges from the agency soon add up, or they do not properly see to the maintenance of the place. Figure about 15 per cent fees for property management of this sort.

There have been cases where the agency has rented out the property and told the owner that it was not rented. The agency kept all of the money and the absentee owner assumed that his flat was empty.

Make sure that your letting agent is not empowered to sign extensions of contracts or make new contracts without your knowledge and consent.

NON-RESIDENT RENTAL TAX

Either a resident or non-resident owner of property in Spain may rent out his property. Be advised, however, that you must declare your rental income for Spanish income tax.

Even if your tenant pays you in UK pounds into your bank account in London, legally this income arises in Spain because the property is in Spain. It is true that many owners who let their property occasionally say nothing about it to the tax authorities and the chances of their getting caught are slim. Nevertheless, Spanish income tax is due on any income arising in Spain.

"I was told that, as I am tax resident in the UK, I only needed to declare the rental income in the UK," says one landlord. "My lawyer told me I had to pay Spanish tax," says another.

They are both right.

You are liable for Spanish non-resident income tax of 24 per cent if you are non-EU resident or 19 per cent if you are EU resident, which must be declared quarterly on Form 210. You must also declare this income to the UK or German tax man, where you are resident. The double taxation agreement between the two countries means that you can claim back from Spain what you paid in the UK, so you are not taxed twice but you must declare in both countries.

If you are a tax resident in Spain, you should add your rental income to your other income when you make your annual Spanish income tax declaration. If you register your property as a tourist letting operation, you can put down the maintenance expenses of your property as a business expense and deduct this from your tax.

RENTING IN SPAIN

If you decide to rent in Spain, you will find thousands of apartments and villas at prices to suit almost every pocket.

Some are basically equipped small flats designed for self-catering holidays and often rented through agents in Britain, Holland or Germany. Others are real homes being let by their owners in the hope of making a little money from their property until they can retire to enjoy it full time.

For those who intend to live in Spain, it is a good idea to rent a place in the area where they hope to live permanently.

When you have found a property that suits your needs, you will be asked to sign a rental contract.

HOLIDAY CONTRACT

If you are renting a holiday flat for a self-catering visit to Spain, you will probably find this contract in your own language, to be signed in your own country before you leave with the rental company handling the property.

This is perfectly all right. Just make sure the rental company has a sound reputation. Sometimes the accommodation promised you does not measure up to your expectations, so be alert (see section on How to Complain in Spain).

The contract forms are usually quite standard, including a list of all the equipment and furnishings, and requiring a deposit to cover any damages the tenant may cause. There is not normally any dispute about the return of this deposit if you have left the flat in good condition.

If you have seen the way some holidaymakers leave their rented flats, you would understand why the companies insist on this deposit.

SPANISH CONTRACT: *Vivienda* or *Por Temporada*

If you are already in Spain when you arrange your holiday rental, you will also be asked to sign a contract. It will specify the amount of the rent, the manner of payment, any deposit and the time period.

The contract will be headed *por temporada,* which means short-term. This is to distinguish it from a long-term rental, called *vivienda,* or residence, because long-term tenants have rights which short-term tenants do not.

***Temporada* Contract:** A *temporada* contract might even be as long as one year. There is no specific time limit past which a contract becomes long-term.

However, unless otherwise specified in your short-term rental contract, the landlord may put you out at the end of the period stated, or he may offer you a new contract increasing the rent as much as he likes.

These short-term contracts are designed for holiday rentals, not as long-term or permanent residence. Such a *temporada* contract running for one year would be pushing it a little, but the idea is to show the intention of impermanence, so the tenant does not establish full rights. This does not always work as planned, which we have seen in the example above. Even short-term tenants can sometimes try to claim a longer contract.

***Vivienda* Contract:** The *vivienda* contract, on the other hand, is meant for those long-term lets when the tenant truly makes the apartment his home. The tenant is much more protected and the revised Spanish law requires that a *vivienda* contract be renewable for a minimum period of three years. This gives the tenant some stability, as he knows that he has at least this period, and he must be officially notified well in advance of the end of the period if the landlord does not intend to renew the contract.

11-MONTH CONTRACT

Many people seem convinced that, under Spanish law, a Spanish contract made for 11 months protects the landlord from an unwanted extension of the contract into a three-year "*vivienda*" contract. It simply is not true. If, as we discussed above, the tenant can justify that the place has become his real home, the tenant will win his case. The 11-month contract demonstrates the landlord's desire to avoid a full residential contract, but that is all.

ONE-YEAR FOREIGN CONTRACT

Let's suppose you want to rent a villa in Spain for a year, or even more, and you find that a rental agency in your home country, or even in Spain, has the perfect house at the right price. They offer you a one-year contract, in German or English, with option to renew. This contract, in your own language, will not say that it is either a temporada or a vivienda contract. The agency does not think in terms of Spanish law, and they don't expect that you will, either.

This foreign-language contract is perfectly legal, although it would have to be translated into Spanish for any court proceedings, and it is a perfectly good offer, which, in fact gives you as the tenant more protection than it gives the landlord.

You can renew the contract if you want. If the landlord wants you to leave, you can threaten to go to court, claiming that the villa has become your retirement home. You can say that you will ask the court to have the contract extended to the full three years of the long-term let.

The landlord and the agency will be reluctant to become involved in any legal dispute in Spanish courts first, because they will probably lose their case, and perhaps they are not declaring all the rental income for Spanish taxes.

Even if the tenant pays in pounds in another country, the income derived from property in Spain is still subject to Spanish tax.

NO CONTRACT

Some owners do not want to make any contracts. This can be perfectly all right, too. Just make sure you have clearly written receipts for the rent you pay, which will constitute an implicit contract. Such an implicit rental contract exists even if you don't have the receipts, as soon as the owner cashes your cheque, but it's better to have some piece of paper as evidence.

If you are paying month to month in such a situation, the implicit contract ends at the end of each month you pay, or on the date stated on your receipt.

REGISTERED CONTRACT

For full security in your rental, you also want your rental contract registered with the housing department. This means that you will have full legal protection in the event of any court case about your rental.

Many rental contracts are simply not registered and the landlords are probably not declaring the rental income for tax purposes. Your contract is still valid in court, but only the registered contract, where the landlord is completely legal in his operations, has the full protection of the law.

As we noted earlier, the landlord can require a deposit, usually a month's rent, which can be held by an agency independent of the landlord and tenant. Though it is a common practice, it is never a good idea to pay the deposit directly into the landlord's account, as he then is in complete control over whether to release the deposit or not at the end of the let.

RIGHT OF FIRST REFUSAL

One of the important rights which may be acquired by a long-term residential tenant, unless he renounces it in his contract, is the right of first refusal when the property is put up for sale.

If the landlord sells the property, he is required by law to offer it first to the long-term tenant. He should do this in writing, stating the price and conditions of the sale. If the tenant does not reply or if he refuses the offer, the landlord is then free to sell the property to anyone he chooses.

If the landlord sells the property without informing the tenant in advance, the tenant even has the right to have this sale annulled and to purchase the property himself at the price declared on the sale contract.

As the price of a property sale is often under-declared on Spanish contracts, this means the tenant would buy the property at the lower price which was officially declared. This provision acts as a further deterrent to the landlord.

In Spanish this right is called *tanteo y retracto*. Remember that this right will not apply if your contract is not officially registered in the Spanish Property Registry. It is also possible for the long-term tenant to renounce this right in his rental contract.

COMMUNITY FEES

Long-term, or vivienda, contracts often contain provisions requiring the tenant to pay community fees, that is, the dues charged each year by the property owners' collective for that block of flats, and even the real estate taxes, known as the *IBI*.

An owner is within his rights to make such a contract, but you should be wary and know what you are getting into. Such extra charges can add up. Furthermore, clauses obliging the tenant to pay the community fees and real estate taxes are considered abusive under Spanish law, and you can protest if you choose, even after you have signed the contract.

If these charges are not mentioned in your contract, they are the owner's responsibility and you can refuse any attempt by him to make you pay for them.

To sum up, in strictly legal terms, the taxes and fees are for the property owner's account. However, it is not illegal for the landlord and tenant to agree in the contract that the tenant will pay them. As long as you know what you are getting into, and the amounts of these charges are clear, and you as the tenant are disposed to accept the price, then it is okay.

If, however, you feel that you have been deceived by the landlord into signing the contract, you can protest the clause and you will surely win your case.

FORMAL NOTIFICATION NECESSARY

Be advised that, if you have a three-year vivienda contract and your landlord wishes to terminate your rental at the end of the period, he is obliged to notify you officially, for example, by a notarised letter, well before the end of the period. If he does not notify you officially, the contract can be regarded as renewed for one year and for the same rent.

In any of these situations, most Europeans will find the tenant to have more protection than is normal in many countries. That is, even though the law states that the rental period is finished, a landlord will have some trouble putting out anyone who chooses to stay. He cannot simply summon a policeman and order you out. He must get a court order for this and the procedure will take some time, even when the law is entirely on the landlord's side.

HOW TO COMPLAIN

Finally, if you feel that your holiday apartment does not meet the terms of your contract, or if your landlord has abused his side of the deal, you can complain. If you are a genuine tourist, the tourist office of the province or town where the property is located will hear your complaint. If you are a semi-permanent resident, you will do better at the *OMIC*, the *Oficina Municipal de Información al Consumidor*. This is the consumer information office, usually directed by the regional government. Its mission is to deal with consumer problems and these include rents.

BUSINESS PREMISES

More and more foreigners are coming to Spain to start their own businesses. Not the least of their problems is the leasing, purchase or rental of the business premises. This is an area where you really need the best legal advice, apart from your normal good business sense.

LEASING

A Spanish leasehold, which used to be called a *traspaso* but is now known as a cesión, gives the lessee the right to re-sell it on to a third party, although he must first offer it to the property owner. If the property owner chooses not to buy back the leasehold at the price asked, the tenant can sell it to another person, with the landlord having the right to perhaps 10 per cent of the sale.

The new type of leasehold called *cesión* is less rigid than the old traspaso and there is no exact legal format required. A property owner and a business tenant can agree on any conditions they choose, which often means that the deal is much like a normal rental contract. These business rentals or leases are usually open-ended, with no final cut-off point as long as the tenant continues to pay the rent.

WATCH OUT FOR

Be particularly alert to the terms of any lease or rental contract you purchase from a presently operating business. Sometimes it is presented by the seller as a leasehold when it is simply a rental agreement which gives the tenant no rights to any of the profit from re-selling it.

When you are asked to pay a large sum of money for a "leasehold", you want to be very sure that you are buying something which you will later have the right to sell. If all that is being offered is a rental agreement, then you are paying for nothing.

This has happened to more than one business purchaser in Spain, who sees the term traspaso on the contract heading and believes he is buying a lease, when the contract, when carefully read, turns out to be just a rental. Take legal advice before you get into a Spanish lease.

GLOSSARY

Alquiler – rental
Arrendamiento – rental, lease
Cesión – lease
Contrato de vivienda – long-term residential contract
Contrato por temporada – short-term holiday contract
Fianza – deposit
Inquilino – tenant
Juicio de Desahucio - eviction hearing
Ley de Arrendamiento Urbano – rental law
Propietario – owner, landlord
Tanteo y Retracto – right of first refusal to buy property
Traspaso – old form of leasehold

SECTION

3

You and Your Money in Spain

You and Your Money

For many European Union citizens in Spain, cross-border transactions have been greatly simplified by the introduction of the euro, with no more exchange rates and conversion tables to worry about. UK citizens, however, still have to deal with exchanging pounds for euros. Until recently, this worked in their favour as the strong pound made the purchase of Spanish property very attractive. Now Brits are suffering again as their pound drops against the euro. Scandinavians suffer the same fluctuations.

The answer to your first question is: yes, you can take out of Spain all the money you bring in, and more. If you have made money by selling property at a profit or by working or investing, you are free to take your profits out of the country. This will remain true even after the UK leaves the European Union. There are forms to fill out and the normal Spanish taxes to pay, but you can do it.

Spain has free conversion of currency, but it also has a complex reporting system by which many transactions between residents and non-residents involving foreign exchange and a value in excess of €12,500 must be declared to the bank on Forms B-1 and B-3.

NEW S-1 FORM TO EXPORT CURRENCY

The former B-2 form, required for prior authorisation to take larger sums out of Spain, has been done away with after EU charges that it interfered with the free flow of capital in the EU. It has been superseded by the S-1 form, which is presented to Spanish customs officials when a person is exporting or importing cash or gold or bearer cheques worth more than €10,000 and not made out to a specific person.

The form is not required for cheques made out to a specific person, such as the seller whom you are paying when you buy your house. Such a cheque can be a personal cheque or a bank cheque. The S-1 form contains all data relating to the person carrying the funds, the source of the funds and their destination. The same form is required should you carry more than €100,000 in cash on your person within Spain. All instructions and the form itself can be downloaded from the Tax Agency web-site at www.aeat.es.

The form comes from *SEPBLAC* (the *Servicio Ejecutivo de Prevención de Blanqueo de Capitales*). This is the Spanish agency created to control money laundering.

This S-1 declaration does not mean that the Spanish authorities can deny the exchange, only that it must be reported. Spanish banks have complained about the added paperwork, and it has been reflected in higher bank commissions for routine operations.

Both Spaniards and resident foreigners may hold bank accounts in foreign currencies, either inside Spain or abroad. If a resident opens such an account, he must inform the authorities within 30 days, however, and he must regularly present a form to the Bank of Spain detailing the movements in this account.

This measure makes it convenient for those expatriate residents who wish to retain bank accounts in their home countries, or who do business abroad, or who wish to keep their bank deposit certificates inside Spain but denominated in pounds or dollars. It also helps Spaniards who are doing business with other countries.

IF YOU SELL YOUR PROPERTY

Whether you are resident or non-resident, if you sell your property in Spain and receive payment in Spain, you have the right to take out the money and send it wherever you like.

If the amount is more than €12,500, however, you must have your bank fill in one of the "B" forms to report the transaction. These forms list full identification, details of the source of the funds and reason for the transaction. The forms are required in order to keep some control over laundering operations of black funds, where the source is not known.

The "B" form does not give Spanish authorities the power to refuse the transfer; it is only for information. In fact, our property seller does not need to present the form until 15 days after the transfer has taken place.

So, you can sell your property for €300,000, then change euros into pounds, and send them to your British bank account immediately. Or sell for euros. You can have a bank cheque made out in your name or you can have the bank transfer the funds to your British bank.

When a non-resident purchases Spanish property, he must also fill in the proper form. This is only to show that he originally imported the foreign currency into Spain and is not using black money —

undeclared profits inside Spain — to make the purchase.

The non-resident buyer can also present a certified cheque in foreign currency made out to the seller if he is paying in another country's money. This is perfectly legal if the seller prefers to be paid in his own currency and avoids the need to fill in any forms at all.

MORTGAGES – SUE THE BANK TO RECOVER OVERPAYMENT

If you hold a Spanish mortgage, you may be a victim of the "floor clause" which allows the bank to charge you higher interest than they should when interest rates are very low, as they are in 2018. These clauses have been ruled abusive and annulled by Spain's Supreme Court and thousands of mortgage holders are now suing their banks to recover the overpayment. (See Section Two on Buying Property for full details.)

The important element here is the identification. As long as the *DGTE*, the *Dirección General de Transacciones Exteriores*, the General Directorate of Foreign Transactions, knows who you are, which means that *Hacienda*, the tax ministry, also knows who you are and what you have done, then they are satisfied. If the taxes on the transactions are not paid, at least they know the name of the dodger and where to find him.

The Spanish Tax Agency has another control on non-resident property sellers. If you are a non-resident thinking you can take the money and run without paying your Spanish capital gains tax of 19 per cent on the profit, think again. The purchaser of your property must pay 3 per cent of the total purchase price directly to Hacienda in your name, as a guarantee that taxes will be paid (see tax section for details).

If you are tempted to obtain payment in some more portable and less traceable form, such as cash, bearer cheques, or gold coins, be warned that any such exportation over €10,000 is illegal unless the exporter reports it to the *DGTE*.

To do this legally, you must fill in form S-1, which contains all the pertinent information. You then present the authorisation at the border to be stamped by the Spanish customs agents, if you can find one.

Those caught taking out too much cash without reporting it can face stiff fines. So Spain maintains a check on the amounts of foreign exchange passing across its borders, but you can transfer any amount of funds you choose in any form you choose.

LOANS IN FOREIGN CURRENCY

A Spaniard or a resident can borrow freely from abroad in foreign currency for sums up to €1.5 million without any authorisation. Above that amount, authorisation is needed. The only condition is that the lender not be based in a "tax haven" on the Spanish government list.

This means that a home-buyer in Spain can obtain his mortgage from a lending institution in the UK or any other country, denominated in any currency he likes.

For some people, such loans or mortgages are the perfect solution. When your income is denominated in pounds, it is not a bad idea to have your loan in pounds as well, so you know that any currency fluctuations will not change your payment situation.

Keep in mind also that foreign lenders are always reluctant to lend against property located in another country. European unity has not yet reached the stage where it is as easy for a bank in the UK to repossess a Spanish property as one in York.

TRANSFERS OF CASH, GOLD AND BEARER CHEQUES

Let's take a closer look at the regulations regarding transfers of funds in and out of Spain.

First we will take the rules regarding cash in any currency, gold bars, precious metals and bearer cheques, which you can carry in your attaché case across the border quite legally if you observe the regulations.

Any amount under the value of €6,000 is completely unregulated. You can carry this amount in or out of Spain without mentioning it, whether you are resident or non-resident.

Whether resident or non-resident, when bringing into Spain more than €6,000 in cash or bearer cheques, you are required to declare the sum to the customs authorities where you enter Spain, on form B-1.

This form includes your personal details and a statement of what you intend to do with the funds.

If you are taking out of Spain more than €6,000 but less than €30,000, you must also fill in form B-1. You can do this at the bank where you obtain the cash or cheque, which will give you one copy for presentation to the customs agent at your point of departure, or you can make the declaration directly at the customs.

If you want to take out in cash more than €30,000, you must fill in form B-2 and request permission from the *DGTE*. This is routinely granted. Both of these forms have a validity of 15 days only, so you will want to plan your trip accordingly.

If you are re-importing or re-exporting sums which you have previously imported or exported, you must also make the declarations, as long as they are more than €6,000. If you are bringing into Spain a cheque from abroad made out to the seller of the property you wish to buy, you can declare this on Form S-l to the customs, which will serve as full documentation of the source of the funds used to buy your property.

TRANSACTIONS THROUGH BANKS

The above refers only to cash, gold and bearer cheques. Transactions made through banks — the great majority of all money transfers in and out of Spain — are regulated more closely.

The top limit for absolutely free transfers is €600. That is, a resident or non-resident may obtain a bank cheque in foreign currency from his bank or effect a transfer in pounds sterling or US dollars up to this amount without any control at all, simply exchanging his euros for the foreign money.

In order to make a payment abroad of more than €600, the Spanish resident must declare to the bank the name and address of the recipient of the transfer or payment, and state the reason for the payment.

The resident must make this declaration to the bank before the payment is made, unless the payment is being made by a cheque in the name of the recipient, drawn on the resident's account, in which case the declaration may be made up to 15 days after the transfer.

So, even if you are just sending a cheque for €1,000 for an

SINGLE EUROPEAN PAYMENTS AREA REQUIRES NEW BANK CODE

Any transfers of funds inside your own European country or to other countries now require a few new digits on the code of your Spanish bank account. This is necessary for the new Single European Payments Area, SEPA, which makes banking transactions simpler throughout the 18 countries of the Euro area. It should cut costs and speed up transfers.

encyclopaedia you have ordered from London, you must fill in the form. In fact, the bank does this for you.

A resident who is receiving payments or transfers from abroad must also supply full information to the bank where the transfer arrives, including the name and address of the non-resident who sends the sum, and the reason for the operation.

The same declaration applies to transfers effected by debits and credits in your bank account to or from another bank account.

Residents who receive payments from non-residents, or make payments to them of more than €600 in cash or bearer cheques, must declare these payments on form B-3. This form includes the name, address and NIE of the resident and details of the non-resident and states the reason for the operation.

Note here that the resident who receives or makes the payment must make the declaration even when he is not the final recipient or the person responsible for the operation. This would include a fiscal representative who is receiving funds from abroad to pay his client's tax bill, for example, or a person who is acting as agent for another in making a payment abroad.

So, we see that transactions between residents and non-residents are documented for sums above €600 when they involve bank transfers, but cash and bearer cheques can be freely imported and exported up to €6,000.

We can begin to see why the banks have already complained about the paperwork involved. Even where it is not a question of permission being denied, the simple reporting takes a lot of time.

OPERATIONS BETWEEN NON-RESIDENTS

Operations between non-residents transferring bearer cheques, euros or foreign currency must be reported. The original importation of the means of payment must be justified on form B-1, or declared on form B-3 if such means come from a resident, before the bank can carry out the operation.

This means that, when a non-resident buys a Spanish property from another non-resident, the purchaser must declare his importation of the foreign currency and its exchange into euros, or pay by a cheque on a non-Spanish bank in a foreign currency. This is perfectly legal, and many sellers prefer to be paid in their own currency.

The non-resident property buyer can present to the Notary a copy of the transfer made abroad to the non-resident seller as proof of the source of the funds.

For purposes of foreign exchange transfers, the resident may accredit his status by showing his residence certificate although many Notaries require your latest Spanish income tax form to prove you are a taxpayer in Spain. If you have to prove that you are a non-resident, you must obtain a certificate from the Ministry of the Interior declaring that you are not listed as a resident, and this certificate must be dated at least two months before it is presented.

BANK ACCOUNTS IN SPAIN

Both residents and non-residents may freely open bank accounts in euros. The accounts of residents and non-residents are distinguished from each other, because different regulations apply to transfers for the resident and the non-resident. The non-resident account is called a *cuenta extranjera*, but for all internal purposes it is exactly the same as the resident's account. The only difference is that Spanish withholding tax of 19 per cent is not withheld from interest payments on the non-resident account.

In addition to your normal current account from which you write euro cheques to pay your normal bills in Spain, you may wish to take out a deposit certificate in euros or other currency. The interest rates will vary, because Spanish banks have cut back their interest on deposit certificates, in line with the general drop in European Union interest rates. In fact, the banks cut back their own rates of interest before they cut back the interest rates they charge on mortgages.

Those residents who presently hold time deposit accounts in Spanish banks should check their interest payments now if they are on a variable-rate scheme. It might be time to discuss this with your investment advisers.

If you are a resident, 19 per cent of your interest earnings will be withheld and paid to the Spanish taxman in your name, just the same as for Spaniards. You may be eligible for a refund on this tax (see section on You and Your Taxes). If you are a non-resident, no tax will be withheld, but you will be liable for tax in your country of residence.

IS MY MONEY SAFE IN A SPANISH BANK?

Remember when we trusted banks? In today's climate, people can be pardoned for asking whether their money is safe in a Spanish bank.

The short answer is: yes. Up to €100,000 for each depositor, Spain's Deposit Guarantee Fund will reimburse any account in a registered bank which cannot pay. All Spanish banks and savings institutions pay into the central fund to cover losses.

Each depositor is covered for €100,000 in both cash deposits and other financial instruments, such as time deposits in the bank. If two names are on one account, each will get €100,000. If you have accounts in two different banks, each one will pay the full amount.

Any bank operation involving more than €3,000 requires that the payer and the receiver of the amount be identified.

Your normal current account may be paying as low as a miserable one-tenth of one per cent (0.1 per cent) on its average balance, and you will be paying some of the highest bank charges in Europe for routine services. You may be irritated when you discover that your bank has charged you €5 to make a draft for €60 worth of pounds in order to pay for a magazine subscription in your home country, so be sure to ask in advance what these charges will be.

And remember what we said in the first chapter about making sure of just how your pension cheque or funds from abroad will be transferred to you in Spain, and just how long it will take from the time of sending to the moment you can write a new cheque.

Many people have suffered greatly from delays in the transfer of funds, even when they have been sent from a British bank to its branch in Spain, so ask the bank manager how long it will take. You may wish to use one of the rapid bank transfer systems such as SWIFT, which assures you of quickly having the money sent. It costs a little more, but it is probably worth it.

There have been many complaints about high commissions charged on these transfers, as well. Some people have been charged more than 4 per cent when sending money out of Spain. This would be €4,200 on a transfer of €120,000. Other banks charge fees of around €21 per €6,000 of transfer, a total of €420 on the same operation, or one-tenth of the charge.

NO COMMISSION ON PENSIONS

Spanish banks have even charged exchange commission on direct transfer of British pensions. This is against European Union banking regulations, especially when the British send the pension cheques directly in euros to the Spanish bank.

If your bank is charging commission on your pension cheques, make sure that you are receiving them by direct transfer in euros. If not, arrange to do this — a simple letter is sufficient — and tell your Spanish bank that charging commission on pension transfers is against the EU regulations.

The British will send your pension cheque to you in euros through the Bank of Scotland, leaving the Spaniards no excuse whatsoever for charging commission. Make sure they don't. This rule should hold even after Brexit happens.

Having said the above, many Spanish bank services function very well. Spain has one of the most complete and modern networks of electronic banking services, for example, where you can be sure of using your bank card to obtain cash from the electronic teller in all parts of the country, and in other countries as well.

If you have a complaint with your bank service and your local manager does not give you satisfaction, you will find that almost all banks have a *Defensor del Cliente*, who will hear your case and who must respond within two months.

More than half of all such complaints are resolved in favour of the client, reports the banking association. If you don't get any joy from your own bank, you can also complain to the Bank of Spain's *Servicio de Reclamaciones* in Madrid.

You will have to try your bank manager first, then the bank's own client department, and present your case in writing but the Bank of Spain helps hundreds of depositors every year. You can telephone them on 91-338 5068 for detailed information.

WRITING CHEQUES

Once you begin writing cheques on your normal Spanish account, you will find that many Spaniards prefer a cheque made out *al portador* ("to the bearer" or, as the Americans say, "cash"). The *portador* cheque is preferred by many because there is no record of who cashes it. You can either accept this practice or insist on making the cheque out in the name of the person for whom it is meant.

The post-dated cheque is no longer effective in Spain. That is, if you put a date one month or so in the future on your cheque, the receiver of it will be able to cash it at the bank immediately regardless of the future date you have written.

If you have a cheque written by a person with insufficient funds in the bank, you will be able to collect a partial amount up to the total of funds available. That is, if you have a cheque for €600 and the issuer has only €300 in his account, you can collect the €300 and the bank will note this on the cheque, which you can present again later in the hope that the rest of the money has arrived.

You will also find that personal cheques are not used quite as much as they are in many European countries for routine payments. Spaniards are still not quite used to the idea of personal cheques, though charge and credit cards are widely accepted. For many payments, especially instalment purchases of automobiles or major home appliances, the Spanish system prefers to use *letras*, or bills of exchange.

TAKE CARE WITH *LETRAS*

For example, when you buy a car on instalments, you may sign 24 *letras* of €200 each, one to be paid each month. The auto dealer may send each letra to your bank, where it will be paid directly from your account, a system often used. Or you can go round and pay it yourself in person each month. The *letra* which you sign is a personal debt, so you want to be cautious.

And you want to make sure the *letra* is paying for what you think it is paying. There have been cases where someone selling property insisted that the buyer pay in *letras*, but had them made out to him personally and not to the company selling the property. So our buyer paid the *letras*, which the seller's agent was converting to his own use, and the poor buyer wound up having to pay for the property again, as the company had never received any money.

In another case, a man working for a company signed *letras* for a piece of machinery. The company went out of business but the man had to finish paying for the machinery, as he had signed the *letras*.

In yet another case, a man signed *letras* to pay for his new computer. He sent the computer back to the company because it was defective. The company made no problem, but the distributor who had sold him the computer went out of business, having already disposed of the *letras* to a bank.

The bank now held the bills of exchange and expected payment from the signer. Our buyer's only recourse was to bring a lawsuit against the bankrupt distributor, because the computer company had not received any money from him so could not return it to him, and the bank had made a deal in perfectly good faith to purchase the letras from the distribution company.

This practice of purchasing other people's *letras* is quite legal and normal. The bank or other institution buys them at a discount, because they will have to wait for payment, and the company accepts this in return for immediate cash. In the case above, however, it leaves our purchaser out in the cold.

STANDING ORDER – DOMICILIACIÓN

Another useful service available from your bank will be the *domiciliación de pagos* or the "domiciling of payments".

The word "*domicile*" simply means home, and the domiciling of a payment is a standing order at your bank to pay your electricity bill, for example, or your *IBI*. This service is very useful for people who do not spend the whole year at their property in Spain, as it assures payment of necessary bills while they are away. You fill up a form at the bank. A copy goes to whoever is sending the bill and the bank keeps another copy as their authorisation to pay out directly from your account.

The disadvantage, of course, is that a bill may be paid which you do not want paid. The electric company or the tax authorities may make an error, which you would normally protest and refuse to pay. The bank will pay it unless they notice something terribly wrong.

The idea of *domiciliación* also applies when you are investing in Spain. This is a bit different, however. This official "home account" is one through which all your foreign transactions must pass. When you bring foreign exchange into Spain to make your investment, it comes into the officially domiciled account, and when you wish to repatriate your profits, you also do it through the same account. The *Dirección General de Transacciones Exteriores* can thus keep an eye on all cash movements related to your investment.

INVESTING IN SPAIN

One of the simplest ways to invest in Spain, whether you are a resident or not, is with bank deposit certificates for varying periods of time. These pay different rates of interest depending on the amount invested, the time period fixed and the currency in which they are held. An official resident may now hold his deposit certificates in any currency he likes. At today's interest rates, however, you will not achieve a very high rate of return on your investment.

An official resident will also find that the bank withholds 19 per cent of the interest to cover income tax. You get a receipt for this and when you go to pay your Spanish income tax, you deduct this prepaid tax from any income tax you may owe (see section on You and Your Taxes). If you are not a resident, you may hold these deposit certificates in any currency and no tax will be withheld.

You can also, resident or non-resident, purchase shares in Spanish companies on the *Bolsa*, or stock exchange, which is doing much better than the banks for 2018, and you can purchase Spanish government bonds.

Spain does not tax stock-market profits

Spain does not tax profits made by an EU non-resident investor in the Spanish stock market. These profits from sale and income from interest on bonds are now considered as not arising in Spain. Dividends, however, remain taxable, when paid by Spanish companies.

But even dividends are free of Spanish tax when the EU investor puts his money into a foreign company which is quoted on the Spanish stock-market, and there are many. As of late 2017 the Spanish stock market is doing very well.

This freedom from tax applies only to individuals who are resident in other EU countries, not to companies. It supposes that the non-resident investor is paying his taxes in the country where he resides.

You may also find new investment opportunities open up for you as a non-resident of your home country, such as certain British government stocks which are not taxed at source when the holder is a non-resident.

Expats find new hazards as well as new opportunities, however. If you are tempted to invest your pension capital in offshore funds that promise rapid growth, be warned that the independent financial advisers are completely unregulated in Spain.

Investments in the Spanish stock market are controlled by the *Comisión Nacional del Mercado de Valores*, a board which oversees the stock market. Insurance investment products are regulated by the national insurance board. The offshore funds, however, manage to fall outside the control of these bodies. Many of the funds provide good returns. But the investor should be warned that he has no comeback if things go wrong.

INVEST IN PROPERTY

You can do what thousands of Europeans have done, and invest in real estate, especially on the Spanish coastline. Major international real estate developers have begun large projects to serve a rising market over the coming years. In any case, if you have cash and want to buy Spanish property, you will be welcomed warmly.

You could develop the land yourself and create your own urbanisation. You could chance across one of the last empty building lots in a town by the sea and put up your own apartment block. You will still find opportunities as today's market is just beginning to take off.

Perhaps you want to purchase a few apartments and make some income by letting them to holidaymakers. At some point, your flats will increase in value. This can be a sound long-term investment even though it involves much more administrative work. You will be allowed, as a non-resident, to take out of Spain the rents you receive for your property.

Of course, you have to pay Spanish tax on this income arising in Spain. Non-resident non-EU citizens pay at 24 per cent and non-resident EU citizens pay at 19 per cent. Declare on form 210 and pay to *Hacienda* before you take the rest out of Spain.

If you rent regularly to tourists on a short-term basis, providing linens and cleaning services to holidaymakers, you must also charge *IVA*, or value added tax, at 21 per cent, and register your business as tourist letting.

Your accountant or property consultant or management company can steer you right on these taxes. You also get to make a number of deductions for property maintenance on your income tax which are not available to home-owners who inhabit their property.

AVOIDANCE AND EVASION

"Avoiding" taxes, by the way, does not mean "evading" taxes. To evade a tax that you are legally liable to pay is a crime. But taking advantage of your change of residency in order to avoid taxes is only sensible.

For example, British emigrants should establish both residency and legal domicile (two different things) in Spain before they sell up their business in Great Britain. They can often, though not always, avoid British capital gains tax this way. This advantage does not apply to your principal residence in the UK. There are similar advantages for those of other nationalities, but you need to take expert counsel.

This book cannot replace an individual investment adviser who studies your particular circumstances and plans the wisest course for you. Each person's situation and needs are different, requiring different strategies. The formation of a family trust or corporation based in Andorra or another tax haven, which would own all your property and pay you an income, might be best for some people. Such a family corporation has great advantages in tax reduction, with the useful provision that it attracts no death duties.

All of these schemes have disadvantages as well, remember, and some people have been tricked out of their savings by unscrupulous operators, so be alert.

GLOSSARY

Bolsa – Spanish stock market or stock exchange
Cheque – cheque (see Talón)
Comisión Nacional del Mercado de Valores – national board regulating investments in companies registered with Spanish stock market.
Defensor del Cliente – Defender of the Client, bank ombudsman
Dinero – money
Domiciliación de Pago – standing order to pay a bill
Letra – bill of exchange
Cuenta Corriente – current account
Dirección General de Transacciones Exteriores – General Directorate of Foreign Transactions
Divisas – foreign exchange
Efectivo – cash
Portador – bearer, cheque made out to "cash"
Retención – withholding tax
Talón – cheque
Talonario – chequebook
Transferencia – transfer

Taxes on Property

CAPITAL GAINS TAX FOR 2018

After a series of modifications over the past few years, which lowered rates, Spanish capital gains tax in 2018 is charged by the following scale for residents:

Profit	CAPITAL GAINS TAX
0- €6,000	19%
€6,000 - €50,000	21%
€50,000 – excess	23%

Citizens of European Union countries who are non-resident in Spain pay at the flat rate of 19 per cent, no matter how great their profit. Non-resident sellers who are citizens of countries outside the European Union now pay at the higher rate of 24 per cent.

> **Spanish Capital Gains Tax applies to income from rental properties, as well as to profits on a property sale, so Britons who let their Spanish property will find they pay higher taxes on their rental income after Brexit, as well as the higher rate on their house sale profits.**

LONG-TERM OWNER'S EXEMPTION DISAPPEARS

Until January 1, 2015, long-term owners of property in Spain had the right to a partial or total exemption from capital gains tax. If they bought before 1986, they had no tax to pay on any increase in value up to 2006. After that, they had to pay, but only on the portion calculated after 2006. Now this exemption has disappeared.

INFLATION CORRECTION FACTOR CANCELLED

Furthermore, until 2015, all property sellers were able to apply an Inflation Correction Factor, designed to bring their original purchase price up to date with today's values, which helped to lower their real profit and their Capital Gains Tax. This factor has also been cancelled.

So we see that the lower tax rate will be applied to a larger profit, thus cancelling any good effects to reduce total tax. The only advantage of the removal of these factors is that they make the calculation of capital gains tax much simpler.

Withhold 3 per cent: If you think you get get away with not paying your capital gains tax, remember that buyers of Spanish property from non-resident sellers are required to withhold three per cent of the total purchase price and pay it to the Spanish Tax Agency against the non-resident seller's capital gains tax liability.

Non-resident sellers and persons who buy from non-resident owners should be reminded that they are required to make this retention and declare it to the tax authorities. If they do not, the tax agency can charge it to the property itself.

The buyer from a non-resident seller must file Tax Form 211 (see forms at end of this chapter), on which he declares the details of the sale and deposits three per cent of the total purchase price with the Tax Agency. The Spanish Notary will want to see this form when the sales contract is signed.

Declare on Form 210: The seller then files Tax Form 21O, declaring details of the sale. Non-residents now pay their capital gains tax on Form 210. If the seller owes little or no capital gains tax, he claims a refund of the three per cent deposited in his name. If he owes more tax than the three per cent, he must pay the excess at this time. He has 30 days to declare. The seller is far more likely to owe money to the Tax Agency than he is to be entitled to a refund.

WHO IS EXEMPT?

There are three special situations in which a property seller is not liable for capital gains tax. Let's see if you are among the lucky ones.

TAX RESIDENTS OVER 65 EXEMPT

An official resident of Spain 65 years of age and over, who has lived in his principal residence for three years, is not subject to capital gains tax when he sells the residence.

If you are 65 or over and hold a Spanish residence permit or the EU Certificate of Registration, you can buy a principal residence this year, live in it three years and sell it with no capital gains tax to pay. Remember that you must be able to prove that you are a tax resident by presenting your paid-up Spanish income tax forms for the previous three years.

RESIDENTS GET ROLLOVER CREDIT FOR NEW HOME

An official resident of Spain who reinvests all of the proceeds of his house sale to purchase another Spanish home as his principal residence will get complete relief from capital gains tax. In fact, this resident can get relief if he buys a new principal residence anywhere in the European Union, not just in Spain. He must have lived in his present home for three years to qualify. If he uses only a portion of the total amount of his house sale, he will get a percentage of relief up to the amount reinvested.

One typical situation is where an older couple sell their large villa, which they no longer need, and move into a smaller apartment, using the rest of their profits to improve their life style. If we suppose that the couple originally bought the villa for €120,000 and sell it today for €180,000, they have a profit of €60,000.

If they buy a new flat for the whole of the €180,000 selling price, they will have no Spanish capital gains tax to pay. But if they buy a small flat for €90,000, and keep the remaining €90,000 in cash, they will have used only one-half of their sale proceeds to purchase a new principal residence. Thus, they get to deduct only one-half of their profits. Half of €60,000 is €30,000 free of tax.

HOLDERS OF USUFRUCT

A recent change in capital gains regulations exempts elderly persons who use the "inherit from yourself" or "Equity Release" schemes in which you sell your house but retain the right to live in it until your death.

A person 65 or older who contracts with a company to sell his principal residence in exchange for the lifetime right to inhabit the dwelling, along with a monthly payment or a lump sum, will not be taxed on any capital gain involved. This makes such deals to turn your home ownership into lifetime income more attractive for older persons of modest means. The right to inhabit the property is called a usufructo. This sort of deal can be very tricky, however, so you need to be extra-careful.

If you do not fall into one of these groups, you will be liable for capital gains tax when you sell your property.

DEDUCT EXPENSES, CALCULATE YOUR TAX

To calculate your tax, you need to know your original purchase price. Then add all the official expenses you had in acquiring the property. At the time of purchase you should have attached the receipts for the taxes, fees and other expenses to your title deed for your files. Add to your original price the amount of property transfer tax you paid at the time, at 6 per cent or 8 per cent, or at 7.5 per cent or 10 per cent if you bought a new property from a developer, thus paying *IVA* instead of transfer tax. Enter expenses for notary, property registration, the plus valía tax if you as the buyer had to pay it, and lawyer. You need the official receipts for these payments in order to claim them. If you have a bill from your estate agent, with IVA, you can deduct this. If the commission is five per cent, you deduct it from your price.

RESIDENT PAYS AS INCOME TAX

A resident pays his capital gains tax as part of his income tax. If you sell in 2018, you do not declare this until May of 2019, when you file for Spanish income tax for the year 2018.

In Spanish, capital gain is called *incremento de patrimonio*, and there is a section of the tax form especially designed for it. Under the revised law the resident pays at 19 per cent up to €6,000 and 21 per cent up to €50,000 and 23 per cent over that. If we suppose that you have made a corrected profit of €100,000, this means €1140 on the first €6,000 plus 21 per cent of the next €44,000, say, €9,240, plus 23 per cent of the remaining €50,000, giving €12,000, for a total tax of about €22,380 on a profit of €100,000.

NON-RESIDENT PAYS 19 OR 24 PER CENT

The non-resident seller now pays 19 per cent, if he is an EU citizen or 24 per cent if he is not, no matter how great his profit. He must declare for this tax on the revised Form 210. We see that tax for the non-resident EU citizen on the same profit of €100,000 comes to €19,000, or about €3,000 less than the resident's tax on the same profit. The non-EU citizen, perhaps an American or a Russian, pays €24,000. Once the British are outside the EU, they will have to pay at the higher rate.

Remember that the buyer does not pay the full price to our non-resident seller. He withholds three per cent of the total purchase price and pays it directly to the Spanish Tax Agency, filing form 211. The notary demands to see the paid-up form 211 at the signing of the deeds, so there is no escape.

If we suppose the total price was €300,000 for your profit of €100,000, this three per cent will be €9,000. If the total tax is €21,000, the seller still owes about €12,000 on top of this deposit. He is required to file Form 210 and pay the rest of his tax. If he decides to become a tax dodger, he can leave Spain, owing the Tax Agency €11,000.

If the deposit of three per cent turns out to be greater than the amount of tax owed by the non-resident, he can claim a refund on the same revised Form 210. The Tax Agency promises to return the over-payment within 90 days, but many report that they take as long as a year.

Section Two
Taxes you pay every year

WEALTH TAX CONTINUES IN 2017 AND ENDS (SORT OF) IN 2018

For the tax year 2017, payable in 2018, Spain has maintained its controversial tax on capital assets, popularly known as "wealth tax". It is the last country in Europe to maintain the tax. This tax is formally referred to as the *Impuesto sobre el Patrimonio*, the tax on capital assets. It is charged on property of almost any type, including houses, apartment buildings, yachts, stocks and shares, bank deposits and gold bars under the bed.

The big news is that, starting January 1, 2018, the tax remains in place, but no one will pay it because the government has declared a discount of 100 per cent on any tax owed. This tricky maneuver allows the government to restore the tax at any time simply by removing the discount. They already pulled this stunt in 2007 and later restored the full effects of the tax. So, the tax is in effect for 2017 to be paid in 2018. After that, no one will pay, unless they change it back.

The disappearance of wealth tax will cost the autonomous regions of Spain about one billion euros of revenue.

Confusion about the tax has arisen because its administration has passed into the hands of Spain's individual autonomous regions, which means that its application varies from Andalusia to Catalonia, for example. The Madrid Region in fact has already placed a 100 per cent discount on it, so no one who lives there pays any tax at all. Catalonia has lowered the basic exemption from €700,000 to €500,000 and the Valencia Region has cut it to €600,000. Andalusia keeps the exemption to the national level of €700,000. Furthermore, some regions have made small changes in the tax scale.

Let's stick to the national rules for an example. A subject pays no tax at all on the first €700,000 of valuation of his assets, whatever they are. The best news for non-residents is that they now share in this exemption. Under the previous law they had no exemption at all and had to pay from the first euro of valuation. The official tax resident of Spain has a further exemption on the first €300,000 of valuation of his principal residence. This means that a tax resident can have assets of a million euros before he has to pay anything.

In addition the system of valuation of properties provides for three possible values. These values are the original value of acquisition, the rated value or valor catastral, or the value set by the State regarding some other tax. The tax will be charged on the highest of these three values.

Let's suppose that you are a non resident who owns property on the Costa del Sol. This means you first apply the exemption of €700,000 to your assets in Spain. If you only own one house, let us say that it is valued at €800,000, so you are €100,000 over the limit. You will have to pay two-tenths of one per cent, that is, 00.02, per cent of this amount, for a wealth tax of €200.00. The tax rate increases as the amount goes up, so a person liable for tax on 10 million euros would pay at 2.5 per cent.

If you were a tax resident of Spain, you would have the further exemption of €300,000 on your principal residence, so you would have nothing to pay. Also, if a non-resident husband and wife each own half the house, the tax is personal, so they can own a villa worth

1.4 million euros without any wealth tax.

From these numbers we see that only those with quite serious wealth, resident or non-resident, will have to pay anything under the restored wealth tax. The non-resident has all of the following year to make his declaration and the resident will declare on the re-established Form 714 as part of his income tax declaration in May and June of the following year.

TWO TAXES EVERY YEAR

PROPERTY OWNERS' IMPUTED INCOME TAX:

Spain's property owners' imputed income tax is a tax that homeowners pay simply because they own property. The tax is not charged on the owner's principal residence. A non-resident must pay the yearly tax, however, because he is not resident in Spain, so his principal dwelling cannot be here. Residents who own more than one dwelling are subject to the tax on their second home or other property.

Persons subject to this tax have 2 per cent of the valor catastral, the official rated value, of their property attributed to them as a sort of imaginary income. This is 1.1 per cent if your rated value has been raised sharply since 1994 and many values have been raised. You must enquire locally to check your value.

Residents pay their tax on this notional income by having it added to their other income as if it were more earnings. This means that they pay tax at their normal income tax rate. If their incomes are modest they will pay 15 per cent and if their incomes are high they will pay 30 or even 40 per cent.

The non-resident is taxed at the flat rate of 19 per cent if he is an EU resident or 24 per cent if he resides outside the European Union, on any income arising in Spain, even imaginary income.

If a non-resident husband and wife own a villa which has a *valor catastral* of €120,000 and a real value of €180,000, we find that the Spanish Tax Agency imputes to them separately an ownership of €60,000 each, half of the *valor catastral*.

We then calculate that 2 per cent of €60,000 is €1,200 of imaginary income. Taxed at 24 per cent, this gives a bill of almost €300 each. If

NON-RESIDENTS NOW DECLARE ALL TAXES ON NEW FORM 210

As of 2011, non-residents declare every form of income in Spain, including Spanish Capital Gains Tax charged on the profits from the sale of property, on revised Form 210.

This income includes:

1. Non-resident property owner's imputed income tax.
2. Non-resident owner's income on rental of Spanish property.
3. Capital gains tax on property sale.
4. Business activities in Spain by non-resident owner.
5. Some types of investment and dividend income.

This imputed income tax, explained above, is paid every year. If you do not rent out your property, this is the only tax you pay. If you let your holiday flat, you must pay that same 19 per cent or 24 per cent on your rental profits, as well as the imputed income tax.

Husband and wife as co-owners no longer have to file separate forms. They now can declare together on one Form 210. Spanish Capital Gains Tax is now declared on Form 210 as well. Non-resident capital gains tax is 19 or 24 per cent of the profit. This tax was formerly declared on Form 212, which has been done away with.

Non-resident property sellers now declare and pay their capital gains tax on another Box of Form 210. The non-resident seller has a deposit of three per cent made by the purchaser to the Tax Agency in his name as a guarantee against his capital gains tax. Thus he receives only 97 per cent of the purchase price.

To make sure that the buyer has carried out his obligation to withhold the three per cent and pay it to the tax man on Form 211, the Spanish Notary is required to see Form 211 and there is a box for it on the seller's Form 210.

The seller is required to declare his capital gains tax in 30 days after the sale. However, the new Form 210 is presented quarterly for payment, during the first two weeks of the month after the quarter ends, that is, April, July, October and January. So a sale that takes place early in January, say, does not have to pay until April 1-15.

our owners are EU citizens, they pay at 19 per cent, for almost €250 of real tax on their imaginary income.

PAY BY TRANSFER FROM UK

Perhaps the best of the innovations in the non-resident tax system is the possibility to pay your taxes by Internet from your home country.

As of March 1, 2011, non-residents who must pay tax in Spain can do so by direct bank transfer from their home country.

Even without the "*Certificado Electronico*", which is a digital identity document, a taxpayer can access the web of the Tax Agency, www.aeat.es, to download the forms. The Agency is the *Agencia Española de Administración de Tributos, AEAT*.

In fact, the Tax Agency no longer issues paper forms. Even if you are in Spain and intend to pay the tax in person, you have to download the forms in order to fill them in.

So a non-resident who wishes to pay his Spanish taxes without a visit to Spain at an inconvenient time, or who does not wish to appoint a Spanish tax consultant to handle it for him can do it all in front of his home computer.

ANNUAL REAL ESTATE TAX (IBI)

The annual real estate tax on your Spanish property must also be paid. This tax, based on your *valor catastral*, can vary widely from town to town for the same type of property because it is a municipal tax. You can expect to pay much more for a townhouse in Marbella than you would pay for the same accommodation in an inland provincial town. If you live in a typical village house set back from the coast, your annual real estate tax could be as little as €100. If you have a well-positioned villa on a large lot you could pay as much as €3,000.

This real estate tax is called the *IBI*, the *Impuesto sobre Bienes Inmuebles*. The tax is raised every year, in line with inflation.

If you are a non-resident, the best solution for you is to have the tax *domiciliado* in your bank. This is a standing order to the bank to pay the tax — and you can include any other municipal charges as well. You obtain a form at the bank which authorises them to pay the tax bill, and you deposit a copy of the form with your *ayuntamiento*.

This tells them where to send the bill. You are thus assured that your taxes are paid when they are due, the same as the telephone, water and electric bills.

If you prefer to pay the bill in person, you will have to go to your town hall and pay it each year. Some towns offer a discount for early payment, so be sure to ask.

In addition to the *valor catastral*, the assessed value of your property for tax purposes, the *IBI* also lists your referencia catastral number, which will locate your property at the *Catastro* office, along with its officially measured dimensions. This can be important in buying and selling property because sometimes the physical description does not agree with the description given in the property title.

If you think that you can simply forget about these taxes because you are not a Spanish resident and some day will sell your home in the sun anyway, think again.

The Spanish tax agency, *Hacienda*, will check the books at the time of the property sale. They will be holding that deposit of 3 per cent of your total sale price, remember. It is a guarantee against the owners' imputed income tax obligations for the last four years, as well as against the capital gains liability. You will also be required to present the current real estate tax receipt, the *IBI*, when you sign the sale contract.

COMMUNITY CHARGES

The fees charged annually by your community of property owners, to pay for your share of maintaining the community property, are not taxes of course, but they need to be factored into your totals when you are calculating the annual running costs of your Spanish property. These fees might be as little as €400 a year for a small flat or more like €4,000 a year for a luxury villa on an elegant estate in Marbella.

YOUR FISCAL REPRESENTATIVE

The non-resident property owner of only one property is no longer required by Spanish law to name a fiscal representative who is resident in Spain. Those who own two or more properties must do so, however, under penalty of fines that can go as high as €6,000 if he or she does not comply.

The fiscal representative assures the Spanish tax authorities that they can have a reliable contact inside Spain for the non-resident taxpayer.

Although most non-residents name their tax consultant or lawyer as their fiscal representative, it can be anyone, even a foreigner, as long as he is officially resident in Spain. Any *gestoría* or tax office has the simple forms necessary.

The fiscal representative cannot be held responsible for payment of his principal's taxes.

NON-RESIDENT'S FISCAL IDENTIFICATION NUMBER

If you are a non-resident property owner, you will have the above-mentioned taxes to pay and perhaps a fiscal representative to name. In order to pay these taxes, you must apply for a *Número de Identificación de Extranjero (NIE)*, which is your Spanish tax identification number. Residents, whatever their nationality, also have a number.

In fact, you should apply for this number when you purchase your property. The number identifies you to the Spanish taxman and is required when you pay your taxes or have any dealings with *Hacienda*. To obtain it, simply present yourself at the nearest police post, or comisaría, with a foreigners' department, along with a photocopy of the first pages of your passport. Fill in the form and wait a few weeks for your number to be assigned. You can also have your *gestoría* do this for you.

Then you will be registered with *Hacienda's* central computers just like the rest of us in today's electronically observed society.

If you are an EU citizen coming to live in Spain, you will be assigned your *NIE* number when you obtain your Certificate of Registration, which has replaced the residence card.

SPECIAL TAX ON OFF-SHORE COMPANIES

During the property boom of the 1980s thousands of luxury homes on the Spanish coast were sold on the basis of ownership through a non-resident company. Many of these offshore companies are located in the so-called "tax havens" where little or no local tax is charged and the names of the owners are confidential.

On the Costa del Sol, entire urbanisations were marketed with Gibraltar companies already formed to own the property. The buyer purchased the Gibraltar company, in Gibraltar, and his real name never appeared on any Spanish documents, only the name of the Gibraltar company.

GIBRALTAR TAX-EXEMPT COMPANIES DISAPPEAR

Tax exempt companies formed in Gibraltar to own Spanish property disappeared at the end of 2010. Stiffer European Union controls on tax havens and money laundering have forced the change. The Gibraltar authorities have designed a new "non-resident company" format that offers many of the same advantages.

Other non-resident companies are located in European countries where they are subject to tax like any other company, including tax on their assets in Spain.

There is nothing incorrect about this sort of operation, and it means that all Spanish transfer taxes — which can amount to 10 per cent of the price — are bypassed when property owned by such companies changes hands. This is because only the offshore company is bought and sold, a transaction which takes place outside Spain. As far as the Spanish government is concerned, the property is still owned by the same company, and no change has taken place, so no tax is due. This offshore company ownership also avoids Spanish inheritance tax. The company is not registered in Spain, even though it possesses an asset here, so no Spanish inheritance tax is charged when the company is bequeathed to its inheritor. As far as Spain is concerned, the same company continues to own the property. The new inheritor then continues to own the company through some other country.

This is all perfectly legal. Nevertheless, it is not quite cricket and the loss of tax revenue irritated the Spanish authorities — so much that they finally enacted a special tax on properties owned by offshore companies. They were not the first to do so. In fact they were just about the last country in Europe to tax these operations.

SPECIAL TAX IS 3 PER CENT

This special tax on properties owned by offshore companies is 3 per cent of the *valor catastral*. This means that, if your property is valued at €100,000 (with a real market value of perhaps €150,000), your annual tax is €3,000.

For companies registered in tax havens around the world, there are absolutely no exemptions. Spain's tax ministry has a list of jurisdictions regarded as "tax havens".

When both the company and its real owners are fiscal residents of "normal" countries which have taxation treaties with Spain, the company can claim exemption from the tax of 3 per cent by revealing all details of the owners, and presenting certification that the company pays its taxes in its country of registration. They do this by presenting Form 213 every year to the Spanish Tax Agency.

The law is designed to crack down on those persons taking advantage of secrecy provisions in tax havens while permitting normal EU companies to continue to own property in Spain as long as they pay their taxes at home.

WARNING: RESIDENTS REQUIRED TO DECLARE ASSETS ON FORM 720

As part of this crackdown on assets hidden abroad, Spain has come up with a new tool. If you are a tax resident of Spain, you are now required to declare any assets worth more than €50,000 that you hold outside the country. You do this on the new Form 720. March 1 is the deadline to declare. The penalties are severe for failure to declare. The minimum fine is set at €10,000.

Many foreign residents have investments and property in their home countries. They bring into Spain enough income for their needs and they declare this for Spanish tax. Nevertheless, the majority of their assets are outside Spain and never have been declared to the Spanish Tax Agency, the *Agencia Tributaria*.

This has been perfectly legal until now. The only requirement has been Spain's tax on capital assets, the *Patrimonio* tax. A tax resident of Spain is liable for tax on any assets worldwide worth more than €700,000. So, if you owned a property in Germany worth, say, €350,000, and an apartment in Spain worth €250,000, you had no need to declare or to pay because you were €100,000 under the limit.

However, as a tax resident of Spain, you are liable for tax on your worldwide income and assets. If your house in Germany or the UK is rented out, you are liable for tax in Spain on that income. You can obtain forms from the Tax Agency so you do not pay tax in two countries.

THREE TYPES OF ASSETS

The foreign assets declaration law, passed in November, 2012, does not establish any new tax. The Tax Agency says that the declaration on Form 720 is purely "informative". The law sets out three classes of assets. If the value in any one class exceeds €50,000, you must declare. These classes are:

1. **Bank accounts, including time deposits.**
2. **Shares, stocks, bonds, some types of insurance and pension funds.**
3. **Real property, such as land or houses.**

The amount to declare is the value at December 31 of the preceding year. You present your bank balance for that date, and the average balance for the last three months of the year.

You need the value of each type of stocks in your portfolio. Establishing the value of pension funds or annuities can be complicated. Life insurance policies with a stated redemption value must be declared. Life insurance policies which pay only on death need not be declared. Real property is valued at the original price of acquisition.

The main issue is whether you have any control over the asset. If a company owns a house and you are a shareholder in the company, this means you have some control over the asset and must declare.

Obtaining this data can take time. Remember that the minimum fine for not declaring is €10,000. After that, penalties can mount up to the point where the fine is larger than the undeclared asset.

GET PROFESSIONAL HELP

There is no paper version of Form 720. It exists only electronically. If you wish to declare on your own, you will need to obtain the official Digital Signature, which you install in your own computer to identify yourself to the tax agency. The form is 22 pages long. You will probably need only a few of these pages, but you have to know which ones. Any authorized tax consultant or *gestoria* can file the form for you, which will be the option for most of us. Almost every taxpayer will need professional assistance.

Keep in mind that the requirement is not aimed specifically at foreigners. All tax residents in Spain must declare, and most of them are Spanish. As part of Spain's anti-fraud campaign, the stiff penalties are aimed more at Spain's own tax evaders who have concealed millions of euros in bank accounts in tax havens around the world. If these undeclared accounts are discovered later, the Tax Agency has a new weapon to punish the offenders.

GLOSSARY

Ayuntamiento – town hall, where you pay IBI
Coeficiente de Actualización – inflation correction factor
Contribuyente – taxpayer
Formulario – form, as in tax form
Impuesto – tax
IBI (Impuesto sobre Bienes Inmuebles) – annual real estate tax
Impuesto sobre el Patrimonio – wealth tax, capital assets tax
Incremento de patrimonio – capital gain
Modelo – type of form, as in "Modelo 211"
NIE (Numero de Identificación de Extranjero) – foreigner's tax identification number.
Paraíso fiscal – tax haven
Patrimonio – capital assets, wealth
Referencia catastral – reference number for property inscription in the Catastro Registry
Representante fiscal – official tax representative of foreigner
Valor catastral – rated value of property for tax purposes
Usufructo – usufruct, right to inhabit property

TAX FORM INSTRUCTIONS
210 – 211 – 213

FORM 210

As of January 1, 2011, non-residents of Spain declare any form of Spanish income on the new Form 210. This includes capital gains tax, rental income and non-resident owner's imputed income tax. Form 212 for capital gains has disappeared. The following instructions are not complete, but they give you an idea of the new data required.

Persona que realiza la autoliquidación: If someone else is presenting the form, enter his details here. If it is you yourself, enter "*Contribuyente*".

Número de justificante: This will come when you download the form from the Tax Agency web.

Contribuyente: That's you. Enter your own name, address, and NIE. List your details in your home country, a new addition to the data required.

Fecha de devengo: This is the date the tax falls due. You have until the end of this year to pay your imputed income tax for the previous year, so you put 31-12-15 in this box. The form is now payable quarterly, so put 1T or 2T in that box for the first or second *Trimestre*, which is a quarter in Spanish, if you are declaring rental income or capital gains.

Renta obtenida: If you declare imputed income tax, put 02, if it is rental income put 01 and for capital gains tax put 28. If you pay in foreign currency, divisas, the codes are listed on a separate sheet.

Representante del contribuyente: If you have a tax representative in Spain, either professional or volunteer, put details here.

Pagador/Retenedor: If you are collecting rents and are subject to withholding tax on the rents, enter it here. If you are declaring only your imputed income tax, leave this blank.

Situación del inmueble: Details of property for imputed income, rental or sale.

Determinación de la base imponible: Calculation of your tax base. For imputed income tax in 210I, make the calculation described in the Tax Section.

Rental and dividend income go in 210R, *Rendimientos*.

MINISTERIO DE ECONOMÍA Y HACIENDA

Agencia Tributaria
Teléfono: 901 33 55 33
www.agenciatributaria.es

Impuesto sobre la Renta de no Residentes
No residentes sin establecimiento permanente

Modelo **210**

Persona que realiza la autoliquidación

NIF
Apellidos y nombre, razón social o denominación

Número de justificante:

En su condición de: Contribuyente S · Representante del contribuyente R · Responsable solidario: Pagador P, Depositario D, Gestor G · Retenedor (sólo para autoliquidación con solicitud de devolución) T

Devengo
Agrupación: · Período/Año · Fecha de devengo

Renta obtenida
Tipo renta 2 · Clave de divisa 3

Contribuyente

N.I.F. · F/J · Apellidos y nombre, razón social o denominación
N.I.F. en el país de residencia · Fecha de nacimiento · Lugar de nacimiento: Ciudad · Código País · Residencia fiscal: Código País 1
Dirección en el país de residencia
49 Domicilio
50 Datos complementarios del domicilio · 51 Población/Ciudad
52 Correo electrónico · 53 Código Postal (ZIP) · 54 Provincia/Región/Estado
55 País · 56 Código País · 57 Teléf. fijo · 58 Teléf. móvil · 59 N.º de FAX

Representante del contribuyente o, en su caso, domicilio a efectos de notificaciones en territorio español

N.I.F. · F/J · Apellidos y nombre, razón social o denominación · Representante: Legal · Voluntario
Domicilio
31 Tipo de Vía · 32 Nombre de la Vía Pública
33 Tipo de numeración · 34 Número de casa · 35 Calificador del número · 36 Bloque · 37 Portal · 38 Escalera · 39 Planta · 40 Puerta
41 Datos complementarios del domicilio · 42 Localidad / Población (si es distinta del municipio)
43 Código Postal · 44 Nombre del Municipio
45 Provincia · 46 Teléf. fijo · 47 Teléf. móvil · 48 N.º de FAX

Pagador/Retenedor/Emisor/Adquirente del inmueble

N.I.F. · F/J · Apellidos y nombre, razón social o denominación

Situación del inmueble (sólo rentas de los tipos 01, 02 y 28)

31 Tipo de Vía · 32 Nombre de la Vía Pública
33 Tipo de numeración · 34 Número de casa · 35 Calificador del número · 36 Bloque · 37 Portal · 38 Escalera · 39 Planta · 40 Puerta
41 Datos complementarios del domicilio · 42 Localidad/Población (si es distinta del municipio)
43 Código Postal · 44 Nombre del Municipio
45 Provincia · 60 Referencia catastral

Determinación de la base imponible

210 I Renta inmobiliaria imputada
Base imponible 4

210 R Rendimientos
Rendimientos íntegros 5
Exención aplicada dividendos (límite anual 1.500 euros) 6
Gastos deducibles 7
Base imponible (5 - 6 - 7) 8

210 G Ganancias patrimoniales (excepto bienes inmuebles)
Base imponible 18

210 H Rentas derivadas de transmisiones de bienes inmuebles
C/O · Cuota participación (%): Contribuyente · Cónyuge
Cónyuge
N.I.F · Apellidos y nombre

	Adquisición		Mejora o 2ª adquisición	
Valor de transmisión	9		13	
Valor de adquisición (actualizado)	10		14	
Diferencia	11		15	
Ganancia	12		16	
Base imponible (12) + (16)			17	

Fecha de adquisición · Fecha de mejora o 2ª adquisición
Número de justificante del modelo 211

Liquidación

Exenciones:
* Ley IRNR, excepto dividendos (límite anual 1.500 euros) 19
* Convenio 20

Tipo de gravamen Ley IRNR (%) 21
Cuota íntegra 22
Deducción por donativos 23
Cuota Ley IRNR (22) - (23) 24
Porcentaje Convenio (%) 25
Límite Convenio 26

Reducción por Convenio (24) - (26) 27
Cuota íntegra reducida (24) - (27) 28
Retenciones/Ingresos a cuenta 29
Ingreso/Devolución anterior (*) 30
Resultado de la autoliquidación (29) - (28 + 30) 31
(*) exclusivamente en caso de autoliquidación complementaria

Fecha y firma

Fecha ....
Firma: · Firma:
Fdo: D/Dª .... · Fdo: D/Dª ....

Autoliquidación complementaria

Nº de justificante de la autoliquidación anterior:

Ejemplar para el contribuyente/representante

In 210H, *Rentas derivadas de transmisiones de bienes inmuebles,* you calculate your profit from the sale.

In 210G, *Ganancias patrimoniales,* which is capital gains from sources other than the sale of real estate.

Liquidación: This is payment. In Box 21, *tipo de gravamen,* the tax percentage, put 24 per cent, for all non-resident income or 19 per cent for capital gains.

Fecha y firma: Date and signature.

FORM 211

This is the form used for declaring your deposit of three per cent paid to Spain's Tax Agency when you purchase property from a non-resident.

Datos del adquirente: Here you enter name, address and details of the buyer, including his NIE, his tax identification number in Spain, even though Form says NIF. If you have *Hacienda* stickers, *etiquetas,* you can use these instead.

Devengo: Date of the sale.

Datos del transmitente: Enter details of the non-resident seller. Where it says "*Clave Pais*", a separate sheet gives you a three-digit number code for every country.

Representante: If you have a fiscal representative in Spain (not required if you own only one property), you enter his details here.

Descripción del inmueble: Description of the property, including the address, whether or not it is being transmitted through a private document or a public document signed before a Notary, and, if so, the Notary and his registration number of the contract. Finally, enter the *Catastral* reference number, found on the IBI receipt.

Liquidación: The liquidation is the calculation of the amount. Here you enter the declared price of the sale and calculate three per cent of it.

Adquirente: Buyer signs, with date.

Ingreso: Enter your form of payment, whether in cash or by certified cheque made out to "*Tesoro Público*".

MINISTERIO DE ECONOMÍA Y HACIENDA

Agencia Tributaria

Delegación de

Administración de

Código

Impuesto sobre la Renta de no Residentes

DECLARACIÓN/DOCUMENTO DE INGRESO

Modelo 211

RETENCIÓN EN LA ADQUISICIÓN DE BIENES INMUEBLES A NO RESIDENTES SIN ESTABLECIMIENTO PERMANENTE

261600012187 4

Datos del adquirente

Espacio reservado para la etiqueta identificativa

Devengo

0 A

Fecha de devengo...

N.I.F. | F/J | APELLIDOS Y NOMBRE (por este orden) o RAZÓN SOCIAL | N.º adquirentes

Calle/Plaza/Avda. | Número | Esc. | Piso | Prta. | Teléfono

Código Postal | Municipio | Provincia/País | Clave País

Datos del transmitente no residente

N.I.F. | F/J | APELLIDOS Y NOMBRE (por este orden) o RAZÓN SOCIAL | N.º transmitentes

Dirección Postal

Municipio | País | Clave País

Datos del representante

N.I.F. | F/J | APELLIDOS Y NOMBRE (por este orden) o RAZÓN SOCIAL

Calle/Plaza/Avda. | Número | Esc. | Piso | Prta. | Teléfono

Código Postal | Municipio | Provincia

Descripción del inmueble

Calle/Plaza/Avda. | Número | Esc. | Piso | Prta.

Código Postal | Municipio | Provincia

Doc. público | Doc. privado | Notario o fedatario | N.º de protocolo

Referencia catastral

Liquidación

Importe de la transmisión 01

Total a ingresar (Consultar instrucciones) 02

Adquirente

Fecha:

Firma:

Ingreso

Ingreso efectuado a favor del **Tesoro Público,** cuenta restringida de la A.E.A.T. para la **Recaudación de los Tributos.**

Importe I

Forma de pago: ☐ En efectivo ☐ E.C. adeudo en cuenta

Código cuenta cliente (CCC)

Entidad | Sucursal | DC | Número de cuenta

Espacio reservado para la Administración

FORM 213

This is the form on which you either declare and pay your annual tax of 3 per cent on the *valor catastral*, or rated value, of your Spanish property owned by a non-resident company, or on which you cite your non-resident company's exemption from the tax.

Entidad sujeta: Either paste in your Tax Agency label, or fill in the details of the non-resident company. "*Código extranjero*" is the tax number, if it has one, in the country of registration.

Devengo: Enter year for which tax is being paid.

Representante: If the company has a fiscal representative in Spain, enter his details here.

Exenciones: Companies which are exempt from the tax check the appropriate box here. If your company is not located in a tax haven, and it pays its taxes in a "normal" country, check Box 1, and so on. Only those non-resident companies located in tax havens must pay.

Liquidación: Your *base imponible* is the *valor catastral* of the property. Tax rate is 3 per cent of that value. If you have owned the property less than a full year, you will have a proportional reduction. Otherwise you pay the full tax. When a company has several owners, some of whom are entitled to exemption and others not, there is a reduction as well.

NOTE: FORM 213 has two other sheets, one of them for listing all properties owned by the company, and another for entering the details of persons owning the company when exemption is requested because the company pays its taxes in a normal jurisdiction and discloses the names of its real owners.

MINISTERIO DE HACIENDA

Agencia Tributaria

Delegación de

Administración de | Código

Impuesto sobre la Renta de no Residentes

Gravamen Especial sobre Bienes Inmuebles de Entidades no Residentes

DECLARACION-LIQUIDACION/ DOCUMENTO DE INGRESO

Modelo **213**

GRAVAMEN ESPECIAL SOBRE BIENES INMUEBLES DE ENTIDADES NO RESIDENTES EN EUROS

263100004912 4

Entidad sujeta al gravamen

Espacio reservado para la etiqueta identificativa

(Si no dispone de etiquetas, haga constar a continuación sus datos identificativos, así como los de su domicilio fiscal)

Devengo

Ejercicio ....

N.I.F. | Razón social de la entidad

Calle/Plaza/Avda. | Número | Esc. | Piso | Prta. | Teléfono

Código Postal | Municipio | Provincia

Domicilio de la entidad en el país de residencia | Código extranjero

Residencia fiscal: país | Código país | Nacionalidad

Representante

N.I.F. | Apellidos y Nombre o Razón social

Calle/Plaza/Avda. | Número | Esc. | Piso | Prta. | Teléfono

Código Postal | Municipio | Provincia | Fecha otorgamiento poder

Exenciones

Entidades exentas (artículo 32.5 de la Ley 41/1998, del Impuesto sobre la Renta de no Residentes):

1) Entidades con derecho a la aplicación de un Convenio para evitar la doble imposición que contenga cláusula de intercambio de información, en los términos y con los requisitos del artículo 32.5.b) de la Ley 41/1998.

2) Entidades que desarrollan en España, de modo continuado o habitual, explotaciones económicas diferenciables de la simple tenencia o arrendamiento de los inmuebles en los términos del artículo 7.2 del Reglamento del Impuesto sobre la Renta de no Residentes. Epígrafe del Impuesto sobre Actividades Económicas

3) Sociedades que coticen en mercados secundarios de valores oficialmente reconocidos.

4) Entidades sin ánimo de lucro de carácter benéfico o cultural, en los términos del artículo 32.5 e) de la Ley 41/1998.

Liquidación

Base imponible 01

Cuota (3% de 01) 02

Porcentaje de reducción .... 03 %

Reducción en la cuota 04

Cuota a ingresar 02 - 04 05

Negativas

CUOTA CERO

Declarante

Fecha:

Firma:

Ingreso

TESORO PÚBLICO. Cuenta restringida de Caja de la Delegación o Administración de la A.E.A.T.

Forma de pago: Dinero de curso legal | Cheque conformado y nominativo a favor del Tesoro Público

Importe: I

Spanish Income Tax

NO BUDGET FOR 2018

Spain's coalition government was unable to pass a new budget for 2018 by the deadline last November, so the 2017 budget continues in place as of our writing in early January 2018. This means that planned tax cuts will not take place this year. The government had hoped to install a plan that saved workers about €800 a year and meant that incomes under €14,000 would pay no tax at all after deductions. However, other changes have been introduced into the system.

PADRE TAX PROGRAM AND *BORRADOR* DISAPPEAR

Another change is the disappearance of the *PADRE* computer program for declaring tax, along with the "*borrador*" or estimated tax. The Tax Agency calculated the citizen's tax for him, based on his salary or other income and the normal deductions. This estimated tax was formerly sent to millions of taxpayers on their computers. They checked the figures, and if the numbers were correct, that was all they had to do. Of course, they then had to pay their tax or wait for a refund through their bank. In many cases, however, changes during the year had gone unregistered. These included things like the birth of a child, meaning a new deduction, or a salary raise, meaning a higher tax. So the taxpayer had to correct the original estimate. He could only do this through his home computer.

RENTA WEB

Both *PADRE* and the *Borrador* have been replaced by the *Renta Web* system. The new system is much more flexible than the previous scheme. It can be accessed through a telephone, tablet, laptop or home computer. It allows the taxpayer to stop in the middle, go back and change data, and can even be started at home and finished later through a tablet. It is easier to make changes as well.

English speakers may be befuddled by the name "*Renta Web*" and its similarity to Renta Car. The word *Renta* in Spanish means "income" of any sort. It has nothing to do with rentals. The income tax system is often referred to as *IRPF*, which stands for *Impuesto sobre La Renta de las Personas Fisicas*, the tax on income of individual persons.

Taxpayers can access *Renta Web* by having the Tax Agency's Electronic Signature, another key code called *Cl@vePIN*, or by a reference number called *RENO*, which the Tax Agency assigns after the citizen enters a series of identification factors. The secure electronic signature, or *Firma Electronica*, has various advantages in dealing with the Tax Agency, but it requires one visit in person to your nearest *Hacienda* office to establish the code.

F-100 IS BASIC FORM

Over recent years *Hacienda* has continued its attempt to simplify tax calculations. Under the present plan, income is divided in two parts. These are basically "earned" and "unearned" income. The section for "unearned" income is mis-called "savings" or *Ahorros*. This refers to income from investments, annuities, sale of property or shares, dividends, and even interest on bank accounts. It covers all forms of income not resulting from work, pensions, professional activities, or business profits. "Earned" income from work or pensions is declared in the other section of the F-100 form, called *general*.

SIMPLIFIED SYSTEM FOR WAGE EARNERS

Hacienda also keeps trying to bring the withholding tax on wages more into line with the tax the person actually owes, so that a greater number of workers do not have to make any tax declaration. If you are a salaried worker earning less than €22,000, you probably will not need to calculate a tax declaration on your own. *Hacienda,* the Tax Agency, will do it for you, on the *Renta Web*. As a result, almost 80 per cent of Spain's 20 million taxpayers do not need to file a return. This does not mean they are not paying income tax. It means that their withholding tax, taken out of their wage during the year, has been carefully calculated to match their liability by taking into account the number of dependants in the family and other factors.

Workers earning up to €22,000 a year can escape calculating the tax declaration under this plan, as long as their incomes have already been subject to withholding tax, and they are happy with the numbers the Tax Agency has used.

Regions Vary: We remind you that deductions and grants in

Spain's individual autonomous regions vary. For example, the Region of Madrid has varied its own local income tax scale. Other Autonomous Regions offer some different reductions so you must take advice locally to find out exactly. If you are resident in the Valencian Region or in Andalusia, the *Renta Web* system takes this into account.

FOREIGN RESIDENTS MUST DECLARE

Foreigners with incomes from outside Spain, but less than €22,000, should not get over-excited, however. Any foreign resident who has the right to apply a double taxation treaty cannot take advantage of the plan and this includes almost every foreigner who has retired in Spain and receives his pension from the UK or other country.

Another of the conditions for the €22,000 limit is that all the income must proceed from one source only, and it must have been subject to prior Spanish withholding tax.

This means that all *autónomo*, self-employed, workers must declare. Furthermore, the self-employed are required to make quarterly declarations, mainly to register the *IVA*, or value added tax, they have charged or suffered during the period.

The Spanish tax ministry, which is now known as the *Agencia Estatal de Administración Tributaria* — *Agencia Tributaria* for short — has been making efforts to ease the taxpayer's burden when he goes to declare.

The agency, which we still call *Hacienda*, has inaugurated new telephone information services and has beefed up its own assistance to taxpayers who declare early and use *Hacienda's* own computer programme.

You can take your pension receipts, your pay slips, your bank statement, the title deed and real estate tax receipt for your house directly to the tax office, where staffers will help you plug the data into the *Renta Web*, just as they did for millions of taxpayers last year.

You can rest assured that your declaration is in proper form and *Hacienda* also declares that users of the program will be first on the list to receive any refunds — *devolución* — coming to them. In many areas, taxpayers can make a previous appointment by telephone. You will be

DO IT THE EASY WAY

I have lived and worked in Spain for many years. I am now retired and receive a Spanish pension along with my royalty payments for the book you are holding. As a test, the other day I walked into the office of the tax consultant I have always used, with no papers at all. The tax consultant, who has electronic access to my Tax Agency file, entered my number and in five minutes, my mobile phone beeped with my results from *Renta Web*. We checked it and the consultant filed the declaration by Internet, remarking that I would get a few hundred euros back from the tax already withheld from my royalties. He then printed me a copy and I left happy. He charges very modestly for this.

assigned a time to meet with a staffer, who will help you to plug your declaration into the program. You must take all necessary papers with you (see below). In tourist areas, there is usually someone who speaks English.

The general number to telephone in order to make this appointment is 901-223344.

Furthermore, you don't have to go in person to your tax office. The forms can be presented directly at your bank, whether they require payment or not.

If your tax picture is complicated, however, do not hesitate to consult a Spanish tax consultant, the *asesor fiscal*, who will be able to advise you in detail on the circumstances of the foreign resident in Spain. Most of these tax consultants use the *Renta Web* program as well. You don't have to go the tax office to take advantage of it.

And, whether you are resident or non-resident, you can telephone *Hacienda's* own consultation number — 900 333 555 — to have your doubts settled by the tax man's own consultants. This telephone call is completely free, but users report that the number is often engaged. In other cases of telephone consultations, callers are sometimes asked to leave a message describing their problem, and *Hacienda* will call back with the answer. Try also 901 200 345.

All these user-friendly innovations at the tax ministry sound just fine, but they don't mean that *Hacienda* is not serious about enforcing the law and collecting its money. Let's sound a word of warning. Until recently, tax evasion was a way of life in Spain. People put ridiculously low values on their assets for property taxes, and anyone who talked about declaring his real income for tax was regarded as a kind of innocent fool.

Well, those good old days are gone forever. Spanish show business stars, football players and high-flying business tycoons find the taxman at their doors with a list of embarrassing questions. European Union regulations and treaties with non-EU countries have facilitated the free and automatic exchange of information. Corrupt officials with large bank accounts in fiscal paradises have been caught out. Some Scandinavian governments have informed the Spanish tax authorities that certain taxpayers have gone off their books and they have included specific income information.

The Spanish taxman has slammed the door on single-premium insurance policies and secret bank accounts; has exposed a gigantic ring of *IVA* (VAT) fraud; will tax offshore companies owning property in Spain when the ownership is not revealed; and requires a three per cent deposit when non-residents sell property.

Tax consultants and accountants who used to advise their clients to bury income and not declare dividends are now warning people that Big Brother, aided by the most modern computers in Madrid, really is watching everyone. This means you, so let's take a look at your possible tax obligations in Spain.

AVOIDING DOUBLE TAXATION

When you stay in Spain for 183 days in one calendar year, you become legally liable for Spanish income tax, whether or not you take out a formal residence permit. On the morning of the 184th day, the Spanish treasury ministry, *Hacienda*, considers you a resident for tax purposes, and this means income tax on all your income, wherever in the world it may arise. You also become liable for Spanish tax on your world wide income when you take out a residence card.

But what if you've just left the United Kingdom or Germany, where your pension has already been taxed? Do not worry too much. Spanish income tax regulations provide relief in cases where double taxation may arise. Spain has agreements with most countries to avoid double taxation and, where there is no specific agreement, relief is available through direct deduction of foreign tax paid or by a formula called *compensación extranjera,* or foreign compensation.

Even if you are not a resident of Spain and spend less than 183 days in the country, you are still liable for Spanish tax on any income arising in Spain, such as from the letting of your flat on the Costa Blanca. In this case, you may be taxed in Spain and will have to apply for relief when you pay income tax in your home country.

Scandinavians, Dutch and Belgians find Spanish income tax a relief. Most other Europeans will pay about the same as they paid at home. United States citizens will find that they still have to file for their US taxes because it is one of the few countries in the world which bases tax liability on nationality rather than on place of residence. Americans will also find that they have some Spanish income tax to pay on top of their US tax because Spanish rates are a bit higher than the American rates. They can, however, turn around and deduct most of the Spanish tax from their US tax.

The Spanish authorities make adjustments to avoid double taxation in this way: if you have already paid abroad a tax much higher than the one you would pay in Spain, you will not have to pay more. But if your income tax in your home country is less than it would be on the same income in Spain, you will have to pay the Spanish government the difference.

So you are taxed in Spain at Spanish rates. But you are not doubly taxed. It seems fair enough. These are general principles, and you can read all about them in a Spanish Ministry of the Treasury booklet called Taxation Regulations for Foreigners. You can also download Tax Agency information from the Internet.

If you are now liable to pay income tax in Spain, you will find that international agreements make all your income taxable, including your old-age pension, investments, interest, and any other source of income. The only exceptions to this are the pensions of civil servants.

They are taxable in the home country which pays them.

RETIRED CIVIL SERVANTS

However, the type of tax-free status varies from country to country because of the differences in Spain's treaties with each nation.

UK civil servant pensions were formerly tax-free in Spain. Now, under terms of the recently revised Spain-UK tax treaty, a retired civil servant will find that the amount of his civil service pension must be declared to the Tax Agency, which will add the sum of the pension to the declarer's other income, in order to calculate his tax percentage bracket. Then the amount of the pension will be deducted, but the remaining income will be taxed at the new and higher tax percentage. So the pension itself is not taxed, but this sneaky trick can still raise your tax bill.

These civil service pensions include the pensions of municipal employees as well. However, retired United Nations civil servants do not receive the benefits of this exemption, but they have formed an association to protest this apparent discrimination.

And so it goes, with other variations for other countries. If you are a retired civil servant, obtain a copy of your double taxation agreement with Spain in order to find your particular situation.

HOW TO AVOID DOUBLE TAXATION

For British citizens who have recently arrived to take up residence in Spain, a double taxation problem arises almost immediately.

The British tax inspector requires that a person be absent from the United Kingdom for a full tax year at least, before he is no longer liable for British income tax.

The UK tax year runs from April 6 to April 6. whereas the Spanish tax year is the natural year, from January 1 to January 1.

This overlapping of dates often means that a Briton is subject to tax both in the UK and in Spain during the first year of his Spanish residence.

If you have suffered income tax in both Spain and the UK, you can claim a return of your British tax from the HMRC by obtaining the S-1 (Spain-Individual) form through the HMRC web site or even by regular post from:

Inland Revenue, Inspector of Funds,
Lynwood Road, Thames Ditton,
Surrey KT7 0DP, England.

From this address you may also obtain forms on which to claim exemption from British income tax once you are an official resident of Spain. The form comes in both Spanish and English.

When you pay your Spanish tax, you present the two forms to *Hacienda* which stamps one for return to the British tax authorities as proof you have paid your Spanish tax.

You may also need to claim exemption for interest payments in the UK, where tax has been deducted at source, and on other investment income.

A number of shares and bonds are taxed differently when a Briton becomes non-resident in the UK. Great savings may be available if you get professional advice. Remember that you will not get any exemptions or reductions unless you apply for them.

WHO MUST DECLARE?

The only people not required to file a Spanish income tax declaration are those with incomes of less than €1,000 a year. Nevertheless, those with incomes around €12,450 will have no tax to pay, even though they are obliged to declare. This is because a wage under this figure has various deductions, plus the personal minimum exempt from tax of €5,550, leaving no tax base at all. These numbers are for tax year 2017, to be declared in May of 2018, remember. However, a person with this sort of low income almost certainly wants to declare. If his employer has withheld a percentage of his wage during the year and paid it to the Tax Agency, our low-income declarer will get a refund.

If you are running a business or working as a self-employed professional in Spain, you will have to declare no matter how low your income is.

Non-EU foreigners resident in Spain will need to present a Spanish tax declaration when they renew their residence card. Not to worry. You can present your declaration even if you do not owe any tax and this will meet the requirement.

FOREIGN RESIDENTS SHOULD DECLARE

All foreign residents, even if they have no income and do not owe any tax, should make a Spanish tax declaration each year. This declaration proves that they are tax residents in Spain, and thus are entitled to reductions and discounts when they sell their home or make a Spanish will.

Let us suppose that you are retired and a resident for tax purposes in Spain, and you are legally bound to make a tax declaration. In many cases, it is best to consult a tax adviser. This may be a lawyer who specialises in tax matters; an *asesor fiscal*, who is an accountant and tax consultant, or a *gestor* who is experienced in tax matters.

These advisers will be up to date on new regulations and current practice. They will charge you a fee ranging upwards from €100 for this service, depending on how complex your return is, but their advice can save you many times that.

HOW TO DECLARE

If your situation is simple and your income is from one basic source, such as a pension from your former employer, with perhaps a little income from stocks, you can do what millions of Spaniards do every spring, and walk into your local *Hacienda* office — which in major resort towns will be modern and well-equipped and staffed by young and helpful people — and ask for the *Información al contribuyente* section. Here you will probably find an English-speaking staffer who will advise on the preparation of your tax return and help you plug into the *PADRE* programme.

The usual dates for declaring Spanish income tax are from May 2 to June 30.

You need to present the following documents:

1. Your pension slips showing the amount of your income.

2. Your end-of-year bank statement, which will show any interest you have been paid because it forms part of your income.

3. Take any papers relating to deposit certificates, stocks or bonds or any other asset you own, wherever such assets may be located. Remember that you as a resident are subject to Spanish income tax on your worldwide income.

4. Of course you need your passport or your residence permit.

5. If you are claiming any deductions for invalid relatives living with you, for mortgage payments and interest on the purchase of your Spanish home, or for any other reason, take the appropriate documents.

6. If you have paid income tax in another country and are seeking relief from Spanish tax on that account, take the receipts or copies of your foreign declaration.

NO IMPUTED INCOME TAX ON PRINCIPAL RESIDENCE

Residents are no longer subject to the property owners' imputed income tax on their principal dwelling. For this tax, 2 per cent of the official rated value of your property, the *valor catastral*, is calculated as if it were income and added to your total. If your rated value has recently been raised sharply, the figure will be 1.1 per cent. This tax on imaginary income for the taxpayer's principal residence ended in 1999. If, however, you own two homes in Spain, you will have to pay the tax on the second residence.

Non-Resident Must Pay: Non-residents remain subject to the tax as, by definition, Spain is not their principal residence. They now file on Form 210 as described in the preceding chapter on Taxes on Property.

The 2 per cent or 1.1 per cent of value is not a tax. It is added to your other income just as if you had received the cash.

If your second property is valued at €120,000, for example, 2 per cent will be €2,400. If your income is modest, €12,000 a year, you add this sum to it. Now your income is €14,400.

You pay Spanish income tax at the minimum rate of 19 per cent, so the extra €2,400 of income produces an extra tax bill of just over €450. The EU non-resident pays Spanish tax at the same rate of 19 per cent, or 24 per cent if he is not an EU citizen. Some resident property owners have been surprised to discover that a garage they own is on a separate title deed from their home, and they must pay tax on their garage.

If you are fortunate enough to own two properties in Spain, take along your receipt for this year's *IBI*, the *Impuesto sobre Bienes Inmuebles*, the annual real estate tax. This slip shows the official rated value of the property which is not your principal residence, so the tax officials can calculate your imputed income tax.

The *Hacienda* staff will counsel you on the proper way to fill in the forms, on your basic deductions, any credit for foreign tax paid, and so forth. But they cannot work miracles for you and, if your situation is complicated, you may need the services of a professional tax consultant.

HOW MUCH IT WILL COST YOU

Spain has passed many areas of public administration to the individual regions. To pay for this, a part of the national income tax is also assigned directly to the autonomous regions. In order to simplify our calculations, however, we are not dividing the tax table into two sections because each Region has slightly different scales and deductions.

A series of former tax deductions, for medical expenses and others, has disappeared. They have been replaced by a reduction directly from income on the philosophy that each human being needs a minimum income simply to survive and that this survival minimum should not be subject to tax. For the 2017 tax year, this minimum is €5,550. A taxpayer over 65 increases his minimum by €1,150 €6,700. Over 75, he can take off €8,100 from his income.

The personal minimum also gives a break to the elderly pensioner. The Spanish income tax rates finally are similar to most European rates, though the complex system of taxing the difference between the successive rate bands is different.

To find your tax, consult the table. The first column lists your taxable income, after you have taken your reductions from your total income. The next column shows the maximum figure for that rate.

SPANISH INCOME TAX RATES for 2017
(in euros – rounded to nearest euro)

TAXABLE BASE	UP TO	RATE %
0	12,450	19
12,450	20,200	24
20,200	35,200	30
35,200	60,000	37
Excess		45

The tax table refers to the year 2017, payable in May and June, 2018. Income tax is divided into one share for the Spanish State and another share for each Autonomous Region, but we present the sum of the two. The final scale will vary in some Autonomous Regions.

The third column gives the percentage to apply. Once you go over the maximum for that rate, you apply the next higher rate to the excess and so on up the scale. Then you add the stages together for your total tax.

Sample calculation

It works like this:

If you are a married couple of pensioners with two pensions and a small investment income totalling, say, €30,000 a year, you will declare separately. First you consult the list of deductions.

If both of you are 66, your personal minimum is €5,550 plus €1,150, a total of €6,700 each. Times two gives €13,400. In fact, if you each receive income, you will make two separate tax declarations, but I am lumping them together to simplify. If your pensions are each over €14,500, you are also each entitled to the wage earner's deduction of €2,000 for "other expenses", together making €4,000, which gives total deductions of €17,400.

Deducting the €17,400 from €30,000 gives €12,600 taxable income.

You look at the table and see that a tax base up to €12,450 pays at 19 per cent, plus a very small amount above that, so you owe about €2,500 to the Spanish tax man. A final tax bill of €2,500 on an income of €30,000 means you are paying at a rate of less than 10 per cent.

DEDUCTIONS FROM INCOME

From your total income you can deduct:

The total amount of your payments into the Spanish Social Security system during this year.

Seventy-five per cent of any *plus valía* tax you may have paid during the year on a property transfer.

Your personal or family minimum exempt from tax. This minimum varies according to the person and the family. Deductions for children have been raised for 2015.

For example:

For the first child, €2,400.

For the second child, €2,700.

For the third child, €4,000

For the fourth child, €4,500.

Any further children, €4,500 each.

For any child under three years of age, a further €2,800.

There are more deductions for handicapped children, depending on the seriousness of the handicap. The children draw this deduction until they are 25 years old, as long as they are living at home and not earning themselves more than €8,000 in a year.

Any aged parents over 65 living in the family unit draw a deduction of €1,150 plus their personal minimum of €5,550 as long as they do not earn more than €8,000. Any person over 75 has an extra €2,250 added to his personal minimum of €5,550.

A handicapped person may have a personal minimum exempt from tax up to €8,000.

One-parent families and the handicapped have a higher range of all these deductions.

WAGE-EARNER DEDUCTIONS

There is also a separate wage-earner's reduction. On incomes of less than €12,000 the wage-earner can deduct €3,700 in addition to his other deductions. This deduction goes down on a sliding scale as income rises to €14,450, when it is fixed at €2,000.

Pension income counts as wage earnings, so nearly all pensioners would have the benefit of this deduction. If both husband and wife receive pensions, they each can deduct.

RATE FOR ANNUITIES

There are tax reductions for those who receive regular payments from lifetime annuities, called in Spanish *renta vitalicia*. Reductions depend on the age at which you begin receiving payments. Annuities for fixed time periods, such as 10 years, also have reductions.

The annuity income is taxed as "investment" income, meaning 20 per cent up to €6,000, 22 per cent to €50,000, and 24 per cent above that. The good part is that you are not taxed on the full amount of the income.

For lifetime annuities, the amount to be taxed goes by the following table:

40 per cent when the recipient began receiving payments at the age of 39 or less

35 per cent when he started between 40 and 49

28 per cent between 50 and 59

24 per cent between 60 and 65

20 per cent between 66 and 69

8 per cent from 70 onwards.

One big improvement here is that those receiving annuities over the age of 70 paid on 20 per cent of their income under the former system. They now pay only on 8 per cent.

So, if you began receiving your annuity payments at the age of 66, for example, you declare the entire amount but you are taxed on only 20 per cent of the income.

Fixed-Time Annuities: For payments received during this year, a five-year annuity pays on only 12 per cent of the income, a five to

10-year annuity on 16 per cent. An annuity of 11 to 15 years will be taxed on 20 per cent of the income, and an annuity of 16 to 20 years will be charged on 25 per cent of the payments.

MORTGAGE DEDUCTION ENDED

Spain's income tax deduction for mortgage payments ended as of January 1, 2013. Persons who are still in the middle of trying to pay off their mortgages retain the deduction but new buyers will have to pay full freight. The deduction is a maximum of €1,300 a year, but that is taken off your tax payable, so it has a large effect.

FOREIGN TAX DEDUCTION

If you have already paid income tax abroad, you can also deduct that from your Spanish tax bill. The procedure is to calculate the amount of Spanish tax you would pay on your income.

If you can show the amount of tax you have already paid abroad, this is entered as a possible deduction. But first, your tax consultant or adviser in *Hacienda* will make a little calculation, to find out what your *compensación extranjera* will be. It involves some complicated arithmetic.

This calculation is made by dividing your *base imponible*, or tax base, into your *cuota líquida*, the amount of tax actually payable, times 100.

This gives a percentage called the *tipo medio*, or average rate, which is then, in turn, applied to the tax base, giving a new tax payable figure. You then deduct from your Spanish income tax either the full amount of the tax you have paid abroad, or the results of the *compensación extranjera* calculation, whichever is less.

The reason for this tricky arithmetic is to make certain that the Spanish tax authorities do not find themselves in the position of having to refund to you tax money which, for example, you have paid to the Swedish Treasury.

Taxes in Sweden are higher than those of this country and Spain simply cannot permit you to deduct that very high payment, which would result in Spain having to pay you back money it had never received.

The application of that calculated *tipo medio* means that your Spanish tax payable never falls below zero.

This does not mean that people never get money back from the Spanish Treasury. Millions of people do every year, foreigners among them.

This refund is called a *devolución*, and about 80 per cent of all Spanish taxpayers get money back at the end of the year.

GLOSSARY

Agencia Estatal de Administración Tributaria – Spanish State Tax Agency
Base imponible – taxable base
Compensación extranjera – compensation for foreign tax paid
Contribuyente – tax payer
Cuota líquida – tax payable
Declaración de la Renta – income tax declaration
Devolución – refund
Devolución rápida – rapid refund plan
Hacienda – Ministry of the Economy
Impuesto sobre el Patrimonio – capital assets tax
IRPF (Impuesto sobre la Renta de las Personas Físicas) – income tax for individuals
PADRE – tax payers' help programme
Plus valía – municipal capital gains tax on property
Renta vitalicia – lifetime income, annuity
Saldo medio – average bank balance
Tipo medio – average tax rate
Valor catastral – rated value of property for tax purposes

Spanish Wills and Inheritance Tax

EU FORCES CHANGES IN SPANISH INHERITANCE TAX

In 2014 the European High Court ruled that Spain's practice of treating European Union citizens as foreigners for the purpose of inheritance tax reductions was contrary to EU rules and ordered the system changed. Because Spanish inheritance tax is administered by the individual Autonomous Regions, we really should say that the systems, all 17 of them, had to be changed.

Anyone who owns property in Spain or who inherits property must now look at his situation of residence. Are you a citizen of an EU country? Are you resident or non-resident in Spain? Is your inheritor an EU citizen or resident in an EU country? Or are you a non-EU citizen resident in a non-EU country? All these factors must be considered. If we take it case by case we can sort it out. Let's look at the various possibilities.

OWNER RESIDENT IN SPAIN

If the property owner is a tax resident in Spain, paying Spanish income tax as well as holding a residence permit or the Certificate of Residence of a European Union citizen in Spain, he has the right to most favourable treatment for taxing his property, applying the rules of the Region where the property is located. This also applies to an owner who is resident in any European Union country. His heirs however must also reside either in the same Autonomous Region or in a European Union country in order to obtain the Regional reductions.

HEIRS RESIDENT IN EU OR SPAIN

Thus, if a UK citizen who officially resides in Alicante leaves his principal residence to his son, who resides in Valencia, the heir has a 50 per cent reduction in his final inheritance tax bill. This reduction applies to a spouse or child over 21 years of age, as long as both are resident in the Valencia Region, or in any EU country.

If, however, the inheriting son is resident in a country outside the European Union, he will be taxed at the national inheritance tax scale, which has a miserable exemption of €16,000, no further reductions, and pays a higher percentage scale.

OWNER RESIDENT OUTSIDE EU

If an American or a Russian lives in his home country, outside the EU, and leaves his Spanish holiday home to his children, they will have to pay the national inheritance tax rates, even if they are official residents of Spain. This means they could be looking at a tax of around €40,000 to inherit a property valued at €250,000. Ouch.

Gift Tax: Similar regulations apply to donations. Spanish gift tax is also administered by the individual Regions, so do not think you can escape tax by making a gift of your Spanish property to your children before you die.

BREXIT BRINGS BAD NEWS FOR UK INHERITORS

Unless an unlikely deal is struck between Spain and the UK, British citizens will not enjoy the inheritance tax reductions available to European Union citizens in Spain since 2015. Once the UK is out of the EU, they will face higher inheritance tax rates and reduced exemptions unless they become official residents of Spain.

MAKE A SPANISH WILL

The short warning is:

1. If your heirs are non-resident in Spain or the EU, your Spanish property will almost certainly be subject to Spanish inheritance tax. Plan for it now.

2. Make a Spanish will. Make this will the same day you buy a property in Spain. It will save your inheritors time, trouble and expense. Be warned: If you die intestate, that is, without a will, Spanish law makes your children compulsory heirs.

Foreign property owners all over Spain are getting the impression that inheritance tax is being done away with. There is some basis for this idea because it has been discussed in Congress and new reductions are gradually coming into effect. These reductions, however, apply only to residents or non-residents who are European Union citizens.

The reductions for residents, in turn, depend on which Autonomous Region of Spain has jurisdiction over the property. Originally, there was only one Spanish State *Ley de Sucesiones y Donaciones*, the Law of Inheritance and Donations. This is the law that will be applied to non-residents. The same rate of tax applies to gifts as to inheritances, even among family members. Even worse, a gift does not have the benefit of any exemptions, except in some Autonomous Regions, and then only for residents of that Region. (See following section).

BIG NEWS: ANDALUCIA RAISES EXEMPTIONS TO ONE MILLION EUROS

The big news for 2018 is that the Andalusian regional government has raised the family exemptions on inheritance tax to one million euros per inheritor for children and spouses. Non-resident owners and inheritors benefit from this exemption if they are citizens of the European Union. Those inheritors who are not EU citizens will continue to pay inheritance tax at the much higher national rates, unless they are resident in Spain. The exemptions are in effect from January 1, 2018. This exemption replaces a former exemption on the first €250,000 of value for each individual family inheritor.

Spain, we must remember, is not a centralised single government. It is divided into seventeen individual regions, which have control over their health services, part of the income tax, and many other matters. These regions include Andalusia, the Valencian region, Catalonia, the Basque Country and others. Madrid, besides being the nation's capital, is an autonomous region unto itself.

For years most of the regions simply went along using the original inheritance tax system. Recently, however, they have begun to flex their legislative muscles and pass their own laws. These different systems of deductions, exemptions and tax rates give rise to a situation which the Spanish Registry of Tax Consultants calls "tremendously complex".

As an example, some of the regions, like Madrid, have basically done away with inheritance tax for their residents. Mainly, the regions achieve a zero or insignificant inheritance tax for their residents by the system of exemptions and deductions, rather than by annulling the law.

ONLY EU RESIDENTS GET TAX BREAKS

Let's see if we can simplify things a little.

Point One. If you are not an official resident of Spain or an EU country, your property will be subject to the existing State system of inheritance tax, which is always less favourable than the regional rules.

Point Two. If you are a resident, you want to be registered – "*empadronado*" — in the region where the property is located, in order to be entitled to the exemptions of that region. The same goes for Spaniards themselves.

Point Three. When speaking of total exemptions, this usually refers to the value of the principal residence of the deceased. He must have owned the property for a certain period, from three years to five years, depending on the region. In addition, the heirs must undertake not to sell the property for five years or ten years, depending on the region.

TIME RUNNING OUT TO RECLAIM TAX

As of January 1, 2019, the window closes for inheritors of Spanish property to reclaim overpaid inheritance tax. Here's why. In 2014, as we noted above, the European Court of Justice required Spain to put an end to this clear discrimination against EU citizens who own property in Spain. In response, Spain modified its inheritance and donation laws in favour of the non-resident, starting January 1, 2015. This opened the door for EU citizens to reclaim the amounts overpaid. Dozens of law firms offered no-win, no-fee services and thousands of inheritors were compensated for the over-payments. The opportunity ends, however, January 1, 2019, because the Spanish statute of limitations runs for four years from January 1, 2015.

Point Four. So the property owner must take legal advice in the region where his property is located and make his preparations according to the laws of that region.

A real forward planner would take up residence in one of the regions, like the Basque Country, with total exemption from IHT, a few years before he planned to die. He would consolidate all his assets there and his heirs would have no tax to pay when they inherit his estate.

But wait a moment. Most of the regions require that the heirs must be close family members and they themselves must also be residents in order to take advantage of the exemptions. Even better would be Portugal, which has no inheritance tax at all for spouses and children. But please do not tell anyone that you read it here.

NON-EU RESIDENT MUST PAY

If a non-resident leaves his holiday flat in Spain to his two children, also non-residents, the heirs must pay according to the basic national law. This means a miserable individual exemption of 16,000 euros. If a flat was valued at 200,000 euros, each child inherits 100,000 euros. Each applies his exemption of 16,000 euros and faces tax on 84,000 euros. This tax amounts to about 10,000 euros for each inheritor.

If the deceased lived as an official resident in Andalusia or in Valencia, had owned his principal residence there for three years, and left it to two children who were also residents, the exemption would be 99 per cent, meaning that the inheritors would pay no tax at all.

It looks complicated if we try to grasp all the differences in all the regional systems. However, if you take legal advice in the region where your property is located, your local lawyer or tax consultant can explain to you what your options are. Your professional can also calculate how much inheritance tax your property will attract, so you can prepare in advance.

SPANISH WILLS

There are four points to bear in mind in connection with Spanish wills:

1. You should make a Spanish will disposing of your Spanish property in order to avoid time-consuming and expensive legal problems for your heirs. Make a separate will disposing of assets located outside Spain.

2. As a foreigner, you will probably find that Spanish authorities do not oblige you to follow the Spanish law of compulsory heirs, in which you must leave two-thirds of your estate to your children. You can leave your estate to whomever you choose, as long as your own national law permits this. Your estate, however, will be subject to Spanish inheritance tax, which can be high when property is left by a non-resident to non-relatives.

3. There are very few ways around Spanish inheritance taxes and these legal ways require careful advance planning. Spanish national law provides no large exemption from inheritance tax, such as most countries have when the family home is transferred. The tax is due after the first €16,000 for each inheritor.

4. However, if you are an official resident of Spain leaving your property to a spouse or child who is also a resident, you may be eligible for a 95-per-cent reduction in the value of the property for inheritance tax calculation. Or maybe 50 per cent, or 99 per cent, depending on the Autonomous Region.

Let's look at these points in more detail.

SPANISH INHERITANCE LAWS

In order to protect the family and provide for the children, Spanish inheritance laws, like French or Scottish law, restrict the testator's freedom to leave his property to anyone he pleases.

It is almost impossible for a Spanish parent to make the classic threat that he will cut the no-good son out of his will. This is because Spanish law requires a parent to leave two-thirds of his estate to his children, even bypassing the surviving spouse.

In general, most people wish to provide for their children, so they have no problem in making a Spanish will in accordance with those provisions. But let us first establish just what the estate consists of when a person dies.

In Spanish law, a surviving spouse keeps all assets acquired before the marriage, half of the goods acquired during marriage, and all personal gifts or inheritances which have come directly to this spouse.

Assuming that most of the couple's assets were acquired during their marriage, this means that about half of their assets do not really form part of the deceased person's estate. Half of the property continues to belong to the surviving spouse.

This is particularly true of real estate. If the names of husband and wife both figure on the title deed of the property, each has one half of the ownership. Thus, when one dies, only half of the Spanish property is transmitted. The living spouse continues to own his or her half, with his or her name on the title deed.

CHILDREN ARE COMPULSORY HEIRS

Of the rest of the assets, only one-third can be freely disposed of, under the Spanish law of *herederos forzosos*, or obligatory heirs. When a person dies leaving children, the estate is divided into three equal parts.

One of these thirds must be left to the children in equal parts. Another third must also be left to the children, but the testator may decide how to divide it. That is, he can choose to leave all of this third to only one of his children or grandchildren. A surviving spouse has a life interest in this third. If the estate is a house or a piece of property, the child who inherits it cannot dispose of it freely until his surviving parent dies, because the surviving parent holds a usufruct over the property.

The final third of the estate can be freely willed to anyone the testator chooses.

DYING WITHOUT A WILL

If a foreign resident dies in Spain without a will, his estate in Spain will be distributed according to the Spanish laws of succession.

As an example, let us suppose that a husband and father dies, leaving a widow and three children. The only property is the house. The widow continues to own half the house, because her name is on the title deed as half-owner. The other half of the house constitutes the estate.

This is divided equally among the three children. When the estate is settled, each child will have one-third title to half of the house, meaning that each one now owns one-sixth of the house, and the title deed has four names on it, the widow and each of the three children. The widow also holds a usufruct (*usufructo*) on the children's share. This means she can use their half of the property until she dies, as well as her own half. They must all agree and sign the deed if the house is to be sold.

It is this provision of the inheritance law that causes the situation frequently seen in the Spanish countryside and villages, where six brothers are part owners of a *finca* or a *pueblo* house.

Dying without a will can cause time-consuming and expensive legal procedures for your survivors, so if you really want to care for them and if you have any definite ideas about how you want your estate distributed, you must make a Spanish will. It's easy and you will feel more secure.

NOTE: All our tax rates and exemptions here refer to the national inheritance law, which will apply to all non-EU residents. Residents will find regional differences. If you live in Aragon, for example, it is half of the estate which must go to children, not two-thirds. If you live in the Basque country, you probably will pay no inheritance tax at all. Check locally for details.

In most of the Regions, unmarried couples and same-sex couples who are registered with the Regional registry of de facto couples, or *parejas de hecho*, can also take advantage of family reductions.

SOME REGIONAL DIFFERENCES

Madrid has tax-free Donations and Inheritance: Madrid is both a city and an autonomous region. The region offers an exemption of 99 per cent off the value when a family member donates assets to another close family member. They must both reside in Madrid. This is important because the same national law covers both inheritance and donation and they are taxed at the same rate. The law in fact is called "*Ley de Sucesiones y Donaciones*", the Law of Inheritnce and Gifts. In Madrid a parent can donate his property to a child while still living and thus avoid gift tax. He does not have to worry about inheritance because a child who is also resident in Madrid will pay no tax at all. In some other regions, even a family member who receives a donation pays the same tax as if he inherited.

Valencian Region: The Valencian region offers a tax-free exemption on the first €100,000 of valuation, for children, spouse and parents, or €156,000 if the inheritor is a child under 21 years of age. Above that exemption, family members have a reduction of 50 per cent of the tax applied. All must reside in the Valencian region, or, as we have noted before, in another European Country.

Balearic Islands: The Balearic Islands, which constitute an Autonomous Region, have severely reduced inheritance tax for family members who are residents of the islands. First, each family inheritor has an exemption of €25,000 on his or her part of the inheritance. They have also made their own tax scale. The Balearics scale taxes close family inheritors at one per cent up to €700,000, at eight per cent above that up to one million euros, at 11 per cent up to two million euros, at 15 per cent to three million, and twenty per cent above that. The principal residence also has an exemption of 100 per cent up to a value of €600,000 for a spouse or children who have lived with the testator.

Catalonia: The surviving spouse has an exemption of 99% on the tax due, and inheriting children have exemptions that start at 99 per cent but are gradually reduced as the value of the inheritance rises. Only 84.60 per cent is exempt on an inheritance of one million euros, for example. Also, 95 per cent of the family residence is exempt up to a maximum of half a million euros.

Andalusia Donations: Among measures that ease inheritance and donation tax in the Andalusian Region are:

If an individual owner or professional leaves the family business to a child, who keeps it for five years, there is an exemption of 99 per cent.

A parent can donate up to €120,000 tax-free to a child, in order to buy the child's first residence. The child must be under 35 years old and must purchase a first residence in Andalusia within one month, to avoid the tax.

ARE YOU BOUND BY SPANISH LAW?

The Spanish law of obligatory heirs in theory applies to foreigners with property in Spain, restricting the disposal of this property just as it restricts such disposal for Spaniards. This is because most nations apply the law of the place where the property is located.

However, Article 9 of the Spanish Civil Code provides that, when a foreign property owner dies, even if he holds an official residence permit, the disposal of any assets he has in Spain will be governed by his own national law, not Spanish law.

If his own country's law permits free disposal of the estate, this frees him from the Spanish law of "compulsory heirs" explained above. English law and United States law provide free disposition of assets. German law and Scottish law require that some portion of the estate go to surviving children. You must check your own national law here.

This article does not free the foreigner from Spanish inheritance taxes, however.

This freedom applies only when such foreigner has an existing foreign will or Spanish will. If he dies intestate, without having made a will, Spanish law will be applied to his assets in Spain and they will be divided equally among his children.

This is a powerful argument for making a Spanish will disposing of your assets in Spain according to your wishes.

EUROPEAN CERTIFICATE OF SUCCESSION

In a world where people move around from country to country, we might find an Australian who resides officially in France and who owns property in Spain. His will could present some tricky cross-border legal questions about what law to apply to which property. As a result the European Union has produced EU Regulation 650/2012, which went into effect July 4, 2012. This law creates the European Certificate of Succession, which is a form of will that allows the testator to choose which law to apply to his entire estate. He can choose the law of the country where he officially resides or the law of his nationality. The various EU countries where his assets are located are obligated to follow the will. Real property will always be taxed, however, in the country where it is located. The bad news is that the UK and Denmark have not opted in to this law.

For citizens of the United Kingdom, the first complication arises here. A number of countries, including Great Britain, have laws stating that the disposition of real property such as land, houses and apartments will be governed by the law of the country where such property is located. English law — which applies to Wales and Northern Ireland in this case, but not to Scotland — also states that other assets, such as investments, will be governed by the law of the country where the deceased is legally domiciled at the time of his death.

So Spanish law says that English law will apply, and English law sends the ball right back, saying that Spanish law will apply, because that is where the property is located. An Englishman in theory is subject to the Spanish law, which may mean he can freely dispose of only one-third of his assets in Spain.

A number of other countries have laws similar to the English law. Investigate in your home country to find out what law applies to the disposition of real estate, the law of your home country or the law of the country where the immovable asset is located.

All this is the theory but what happens in real life?

MOST FOREIGNERS HAVE FREE DISPOSITION

In practice, any foreigner can make a Spanish will bequeathing his Spanish property to any person of his choice as long as his own national law is ruled by the principle of free disposition of property by testament. The Spanish registrar of wills accepts this. When the time comes, the will is executed and the inheritor takes possession of his new property. Spanish lawyers routinely make such wills.

This means that, even if you are British, you can make a Spanish will leaving your Spanish property to whomever you choose.

The law also says that any foreigner officially resident in Spain is subject to Spanish inheritance law on his world-wide estate.

In practice the authorities simply do not ask whether the testator is an official resident or not. They accept as valid the Spanish will disposing of only the Spanish property. The only requirement enforced by Spain is the payment of Spanish inheritance tax on property or assets located in Spain.

So most foreigners will find no problem in making a separate Spanish will to dispose of their immovable property in Spain, even though the law seems to say otherwise, whether they are residents or non-residents.

LEGITIMATE INHERITORS CAN CONTEST SPANISH WILL

One note of warning: All of the above relating to the foreigner's making a will that permits him to leave his Spanish property to anyone he chooses, thus avoiding Spanish inheritance law which requires him to leave at least two-thirds of his estate to his children, works perfectly well in most cases.

But, as we have said, it is not exactly in agreement with the law as written. It is more a matter of the Spanish authorities choosing not to enforce their own laws too strictly.

This means that, if you write your Spanish will leaving your lovely villa to your favourite daughter and cutting out your no-good son entirely, that son could get expert Spanish legal advice, contest the will on the grounds that the law stipulates that half of the inheritance is his, and win his case, thus getting title to half the villa.

So, if you foresee any possible challenge from one of Spain's legitimate inheritors, such as a child or a spouse, you should make other arrangements, such as transferring the title of the property to your chosen heir while you are still alive. You can always maintain the usufruct over the property, which gives you the right to use it as long as you are still living, although the title has formally passed to another person.

If you are quite certain that no possibility exists of successfully contesting it, then go ahead and make your Spanish will as you choose in the confidence that it will be executed as you have written it.

You also need to make a foreign will disposing of any assets you have in other countries. Be sure that any foreign will states clearly that it disposes only of your assets in that country and make sure to say in your Spanish will that it disposes only of your assets in Spain.

There have been unfortunate cases where a person has made one will in Spain stating that all assets are left to one inheritor and another will later made in Germany or Australia, saying the same thing, but leaving "everything" to a different person.

In one particular case, the testator intended to leave all her German assets to family members and her Spanish villa to the friend who had looked after her for years. She made a Spanish will leaving everything to her friend in Spain and then made a German will, dated after the Spanish will, also leaving "everything" to her

German family members. These inheritors later had the German will translated and legalised in Spain, and took possession of the Spanish property as well.

They were able to do this because the German will made no distinction of country and it was dated after the Spanish will, so it took precedence. So, the testator's wishes were not carried out and the faithful friend who had looked after the ill and dying person in Spain did not inherit the villa as she was supposed to.

This story is a good argument for taking legal advice when you make your Spanish will.

FOREIGN WILL IS VALID IN SPAIN

Legally, it is not absolutely necessary for you to make a Spanish will to dispose of your assets in Spain. A Briton who owns property in Spain can bequeath his Spanish apartment in the same British will he uses to dispose of his property in England, and his will can be probated in Spain. However, there are a number of steps which must take place in order to do this.

If you have lived in Spain for a long time, it may be necessary for you to re-create a legal domicile in your home country for purposes of making a will. You may be able to do this by filing an official "letter of intent" with your lawyers. This letter states that, even though you hold a Spanish residence permit now, you really intend to return to your home country in the end. This should be sufficient for establishing a legal domicile in your home country and will allow its laws to apply.

Let us suppose that you do this. Your foreign will (which can be made at your consulate in Spain as long as the proper formalities are observed) must go through the following process before it can dispose of your Spanish assets:

1. A certified copy of the grant of probate must be legalised by the Spanish consul in the testator's home country, and a Spanish translation of this certified copy prepared. A Spanish lawyer must then be empowered to prepare a list of the assets in Spain, see that the Spanish inheritance taxes are paid, and handle the rest of the paperwork involved in distributing the assets.

2. Two lawyers registered in your home country, or a Notary, or a Spanish consul-general in your home country, must prepare a certificate of law, a *Certificado de Ley*, which affirms that the testator had the legal capacity to make a will; that the will is valid; that the Spanish law of obligatory heirs and the dispositions relating to property of spouses do not exist in the law of your country; that the will has been duly proved, and that the trustees named have the correct legal powers to administer the estate.

3. Finally, your will is declared effective to dispose of your assets in Spain, and your Spanish lawyer can carry this out.

It's a complicated, time-consuming and expensive process, and it is clearly better to make a Spanish will disposing of your assets in Spain.

MAKING A SPANISH WILL

You go to see a Spanish lawyer and explain your wishes to him. In the case of the death of one spouse, for example, you may wish to leave all possible assets directly to the other spouse, without any inheritance to the children. As a foreigner, you should be able to do this.

Even if surviving children inherit their legal portion, it is not usually necessary for the house to be sold and the proceeds divided, for example. The surviving spouse continues to live in the house and administer it for the good of the children still at home. If the house is later sold, the children can then get their legal share of the price.

The lawyer will advise you as to how the will should read in order to carry out your intentions. People sometimes say that they want their Spanish flat sold and the proceeds divided among the children, for example. Your lawyer will tell you that you cannot do this. You must leave the flat to the children in equal parts. They can then sell it and divide the proceeds, but you cannot order its sale in your will. There may be other provisions on which your lawyer can advise.

The will is made out in two columns, one in Spanish and one in English, or in whatever language the testator prefers. The will is then checked by the Notario and signed in his presence. Witnesses are not necessary. This is called a *testamento abierto,* an open will, which is the usual form. The Notary keeps the original in his files, gives you an authorised copy and sends a notification to the central registry in Madrid, called the *Registro Central de Ultima Voluntad*.

The certification numbers of all Spanish wills are kept on file here

> **ONE MORE TAX: MUNICIPAL *PLUS VALÍA***
>
> If you have read the chapter on the sale and purchase of property, you will have seen that the Town Hall charges a tax on any transfer of property in its municipality. Guess what. This includes a transfer of ownership by inheritance. The *Plus Valía* tax is based on the rated value of the property, charging a percentage that rises with the number of years since it last changed hands. The tax varies widely from town to town, and there are various exemptions for family members living in the property. You can find out at your Town Hall just how much the tax will be.

to ensure that a legal copy can always be found. If the will is lost or if you do not know whether the deceased person has made a Spanish will or not, you can apply to the central registry to find out if a Spanish will exists under that name. If it does exist, the registry will give you the number and the name of the Notary who made it in the first place. You can get a copy of the will from the Notary. Having a Spanish will certainly speeds up the legal processes of inheritance.

The Notary will charge around €100 for the will and the lawyer's fee could be about the same, a total of €200, although this could go much higher if the will is complicated or involves large sums of money.

Remember that husband and wife must each make separate wills, as they each own property separately.

You can also find out almost exactly how much inheritance tax your Spanish estate will attract. Your lawyer will consult the table of rates and then you will know what to expect.

All too often, the existence of Spanish inheritance tax seems to come as a complete surprise to foreign property owners. This tax is charged even when the inheritance is between spouses, with only a minimum exemption.

SECRET WILLS

Should you wish to keep secret the provisions of your will, you can also execute a *testamento cerrado*, a closed will. It is, of course, important to have a Spanish lawyer advise you to make sure your wishes square with Spanish law. Otherwise, you might find your desires cannot lawfully be carried out. You take this closed will, in an envelope, to the *Notario*, who seals the envelope and signs it. He then files it, just as with the open will.

Other types of wills are also valid. You can make a holographic will, in your own handwriting, but this later has to be authenticated as genuine before a judge, which means more time, trouble and expense. You can even make a verbal will, in the presence of five witnesses. Each of the five witnesses then has to testify to the Notario that these are truly the wishes of the deceased. The *Notario* then prepares a written will and certifies it.

INHERITANCE TAX IN SPAIN

Spain's *Ley de Sucesiones* provides no large exemption from inheritance tax when property is passed to a spouse or to family members, so many foreign property owners are dismayed to discover that some tax will be due. The present law provides a total exemption from taxes only for legacies under €16,000. To be exact, the exemption is €15,956.87. This long number results from the addition of yearly inflation to an original round number, plus the conversion from pesetas into euros. We shall call it simply €16,000.

The €16,000 exemption seems rather small, but it applies to each inheritor, not to the total estate. So, if you have a property worth €120,000, your half equals an estate valued at €60,000, and you leave it equally divided among your spouse and three children, each will receive an inheritance worth €15,000, and the bequest will attract no tax at all.

In addition, an inheritor under the age of 21 can have an exemption of up to €48,000. For each year younger than 21, he deducts €4,000 more, until he arrives at the maximum exemption at the age of 13.

This exemption applies to bequests between parents, children, spouses and brothers and sisters. For uncles, cousins and nephews, the exemption is cut by half to €8,000. For more distant relatives, or those not related at all, there is no exemption.

95 PER CENT REDUCTION ON INHERITING HOME

Official residents of Spain leaving their principal residence to wife or children, who are also official residents, may be eligible for a 95 per cent reduction in their tax base under the National Law, even if they are not EU citizens.

There are three conditions to be eligible for this reduction:

1. You must have held an official residence permit for at least three years.

2. The home you transmit must be your principal residence and you must have lived in it for at least three years.

3. The inheritors must undertake not to sell the property for 10 years or for five years in many Regions. If they do, they are subject to tax.

This reduction applies only up to a maximum of €120,000. If your inheritance is a property worth €120,000, you can reduce this total by 95 per cent, taking off €114,000. So you pay tax on only €6,000, meaning no tax at all.

But if your family home in Spain has a market value of €360,000, then half of that is €180,000. Your reduction stops at the maximum of €120,000, meaning you must pay Spanish inheritance tax on €60,000, which comes to just over €6,000 in tax.

This reduction is also available for a principal dwelling left to a brother or sister over 65 years of age who has been living with the testator for the previous two years.

The reduction does not apply to any other property, such as a car or a yacht or shares in companies, only to the home itself.

The inheritor, in turn, must keep the property for at least five or ten years, depending on your Regional rules. If he/she attempts to sell it, he/she will have to pay any tax due on the original inheritance.

This measure forms part of a package of laws designed to help small family businesses rather than retired foreigners. Many small businesses in Spain have failed on the death of the founder because his inheritors were unable to deal with the inheritance tax on the property, such as a shop or a small factory. Now the children can freely inherit, as long as they continue to operate the business for 10 years.

That is the reason behind the 10-year requirement, which then causes problems for the foreign children who want to sell the property rather than keep it.

Retired foreign couples can also benefit, as described above, because the family home is included in the law. When one half of the couple dies, his or her share of the house or flat will be just about tax-free to the surviving partner.

Non-residents cannot take advantage of this reduction.

SETTING TAX VALUES

Spain has a set system for evaluating assets for purposes of inheritance tax. These are:

Real estate: Property is valued either at market price, or at the valor catastral, the rated value, or at the value set by *Hacienda* for purposes of wealth tax, whichever is greater. So, in almost all cases, you will find that the declared sales price on your title deed, or today's market value, will be the value used. That is, if you bought your flat 20 years ago for €60,000, and it is worth €150,000 on the market today, Spain's Tax Agency will value it at €150,000 for purposes of calculating inheritance tax.

When you make your inheritance tax declaration, if you declare the flat as worth only €120,000, you might get away with it, or you might get a notice from Hacienda that they have valued it at €150,000 and you must pay tax on €30,000 more.

DEDUCT UNPAID MORTGAGE

Of course you also deduct the amount of any outstanding mortgage against the property. If your villa is valued at €300,000 and you still have an unpaid mortgage amount of €150,000, this reduces the value of the inherited property to €150,000.

Remember that *Hacienda* has its own office of valuation and is perfectly aware of the market price of real estate. They will not fine you, but they will charge you the extra tax. They do this frequently.

If you disagree with their valuation, you can request an independent survey, a *tasación*.

Here is a useful tip when deciding what value to use when you wish to make your own inheritance tax calculation. Most autonomous regions maintain a valuation department. If you consult their web site, it will give you an acceptable value for your location.

The Andalusian regional government, for example, sets values at the following web site. http://www.juntadeandalucia.es/economiayhacienda/ov/tributos/valoracion/val_urbana.htm

You may be pleasantly surprised to find that their acceptable value is actually lower than today's real market price.

In many areas, the regional government sets values as a multiple of the property's rated value, or *valor catastral*, which is always lower than the market value. In Málaga, for example, they use three times the *valor catastral* as the lower limit to declare for inheritance tax.

Personal effects: The furniture, clothing, personal possessions and so on of the deceased are called the *ajuar*. For inheritance tax purposes they are routinely valued at 3 per cent of the price of the property. If valuable works of art or antique furniture pieces are included, they may be valued separately. In general, add 3 per cent of the property value to your estate.

Automobiles: Most property owners have automobiles, and these are included separately in the estate. Spain's Tax Agency publishes tables each year for the value of used cars. Other items, such as yachts or airplanes, will be valued separately.

Stocks and shares: Stocks and shares in companies or mutual funds or other investments are valued at their price on the day of the person's death.

Life insurance: If received by children, the total amount is added to the estate, after a reduction of €9,000. If received by surviving spouse, half of the amount is added to the estate, and the other half is taxed as a capital gain in the spouse's yearly income tax. Spouse also has reduction of €9,000.

Bank accounts: The balance on the day of death is added to the estate.

CALCULATE YOUR OWN TAX

You can calculate your own inheritance tax by using the tables shown here.

1. Figure total value: Figure your total value by referring to the section above on valuations.

SPANISH INHERITANCE TAX RATES 2018
(in euros – rounding céntimos)

TAX BASE	TAX	MARGINAL PERCENTAGE
0.00	0.00	7.65
7,993	611	8.50
15,980	1,290	9.35
23,968	2,037	10.20
31,955	2,852	11.05
39,943	3,735	11.90
47,930	4,685	12.75
55,918	5,703	13.60
63,905	6,790	14.45
71,893	7,944	15.30
79,880	9,166	16.15
119,757	15,606	18.70
159,634	23,063	21.25
239,389	40,011	25.50
398,777	80,655	29.75
797,555	199,291	34.00

2. Reductions: You can then subtract from this amount any debts owed by the deceased. This would include a mortgage still unpaid on the property, for example. You can also deduct the expenses of the last illness and the funeral and burial.

3. Refusal of inheritance: In cases where the debts of an estate are greater than the assets, which could happen when a small business constitutes the estate, for example, the inheritors can refuse to accept the inheritance, thus being free of their parents´ debts.

4. Calculation: After you have made any deductions allowed you for the inheritance tax, such as your basic exemption of €15,956.87, if the estate is passing to close family, let's suppose that your final taxable inheritance is about €42,000.

Look at the table to find the nearest figure below that amount. In this case it is €39,943. The tax due on that amount is €3,735.

Now you need to consult the marginal percentage list, for the rate charged on the difference between the steps. In your case you find that you must pay 11.90 per cent of the difference between €39,943 and your inheritance of €42,000.

The difference is €2,057. Multiply this by 11.90 percent and this gives you another €244.78. Add the two together and you have a total tax of €3,980, a little less than 10 per cent of your base.

These numbers were originally nice round numbers like five million in pesetas, but they have been increased according to inflation since the law was originally passed, and even more decimals arose when they were converted directly and exactly into euros.

RICH PAY MORE

From this table, it looks as if 34 per cent is the absolute top rate of Spanish inheritance tax. This is true when the estate is passed in direct line of descent or between spouses. But it can be much higher when bequests are made to more distant relatives or to non-relatives. And it can be even higher when the inheritor is already wealthy. Remember that the sliding scale of Spanish inheritance tax is designed to favour the poor and soak the rich.

This scale provides multiplying coefficients for the degree of relationship and also for the amount of existing wealth of the inheritor. To get the amount of tax due from those who are more

(in euros – rounding céntimos)			
ASSETS	**SPOUSES CHILDREN**	**COUSINS UNCLES**	**UNRE-LATED**
0 to €402,678	1.0000	1.5882	2.0000
€402,678 to €2,007,380	1.0500	1.6676	2.1000
€2,007,388 to €4,020,770	1.1000	1.7471	2.2000
More than €4,020,770	1.2000	1.9059	2.4000

distant relatives or non-related and those who already have sizeable fortunes, you must multiply the basic tax rates above by the coefficients given in the table on the next page.

So, if you are fortunate enough to possess assets in Spain worth more than four million euros, and you inherit more than €797,555 from someone who is not related to you, the Spanish tax ministry will multiply the 34 per cent by the 2.4 coefficient and will demand a tax from you of 81.6 per cent.

This system penalises inheritance to non-relations because it is designed to protect the family structure as well as the poor. It has caused problems for same-sex couples and for couples who may have lived together for many years in a stable relationship but are not married.

CAN YOU AVOID SPANISH TAX?

The high rate of inheritance tax and low exemptions in Spain cause many to seek ways round paying it, some of which are legal, some not.

POWER OF ATTORNEY

A note of warning: Many foreigners have been misled by the reference in English to an "Enduring Power of Attorney".

Such a power of attorney does not mean that the power endures beyond the death of the person who grants it. A power of attorney dies with its maker, in Spain and in the UK. The "enduring" simply means that it has no other fixed date of expiry.

People sometimes think that such a power of attorney will allow them to dispose of property, such as a villa in Spain, after the death of the owner, thus avoiding the formalities of a will and inheritance tax.

This is not so. The power of attorney legally expires when the maker of it dies. Some people have used the trick of failing to inform the authorities of the death and then using the power of attorney to sell a property.

If swiftly done, the authorities are not likely to catch you, but it is against the law. Further, if someone had reason to protest such a sale, they could have it annulled as a fraudulent act.

Family trust: Among the perfectly legal possibilities is the formation of a family corporation or trust, in which the family's wealth passes into the hands of the company, with each family member becoming a director of the company. So when one member of the family dies, it involves only a reorganisation of the board of directors and a transfer of some of the company shares, attracting very little tax. In Spain this is not properly a trust because the trust does not exist in Spanish law. It is a Spanish company.

Equity release, reverse mortgage: The idea of taking a loan against your property to obtain immediate cash or income has been slow to take root in Spain. However, a wide variety of plans is now available from international and Spanish lenders. In one plan you might borrow, say, half the value of the property and pay back nothing until the property is sold or you die, at which time the full amount plus interest becomes due. Your heirs can pay the loan and take possession of the property or sell the property, pay the loan, and split what is left. As the loan is a charge against the property, the inheritance tax is greatly reduced. In the meantime, you have spent the rest. See section on mortgages for more details.

Off-shore company: For non-Spaniards, the constitution of a Gibraltar-based company or other offshore operation in order to own real property in Spain has been another way to avoid Spanish inheritance taxes. In this case, when the founder of the company dies he leaves his shares in the company to whomever he chooses, in a will made outside Spain. But as far as Spain is concerned, the same company continues to own the property and no transfer has taken place, hence there is no tax. See chapter on taxes for more information, but be warned that Spain has placed a special tax on properties owned by companies registered in off-shore tax havens. You will need expert legal advice on your individual circumstances and the possible disadvantages of this offshore ownership before you decide.

Four-year limit: Another trick takes advantage of the fact that the statute of limitations on inheritance tax, and all other taxes, runs out after four years. That is, the state cannot collect the tax once four years have elapsed. So the scheme is to "lose" the deceased's will for four years, not declaring the property for inheritance. At the end of four years, the inheritor "discovers" the will and applies to register the property, free of any inheritance tax. Where the estate is large and the tax is high, this plan can be worth it.

Be warned, however, that Spanish law requires that an inheritance be declared within six months of the death. And, if you are found out, you can be subject to a surcharge of 25 per cent on the tax due, or even higher penalties if the Spanish authorities rule that deliberate fraud is involved.

Also be warned that the six-month period is included in the statute of limitations, so you really have to wait four years and six months for *prescripción*, the Spanish term for statute of limitations.

Gift: You can also make a gift of the property to your inheritors while you are still living, perhaps reserving the right to inhabit the flat as long as you live, but remember that the Spanish gift tax is exactly the same as the inheritance tax. The law in fact is called the Law on Inheritance and Gifts. Furthermore, a gift does not draw any exemption, even the 16,000-euro basic one, so you must examine your Regional rules.

"Sell" property now: Or you might "sell" your property to your heir, again reserving the *usufructo* or lifetime right to inhabit it yourself. At property transfer costs of around 10 per cent, this could save your inheritor a sizeable sum when the valuation is more than €50,000 and the inheritor is a non-relative.

You have to go on living for at least five years after you carry out this operation, however, or the state will assume that you did it only to avoid tax and will charge you the full amount.

This particular method has many attractions for same-sex couples where one party owns the property and wishes to leave it to the other, without suffering the very high rate of taxation applied to non-relatives.

Each case needs individual study so it makes sense to consult a Spanish lawyer when making your will.

GLOSSARY

Ajuar – the contents of a home, furnishings and equipment
Certificado de Ley – Certificate of Law, usually certifying that the law of another country is applicable
Exención – exemption
Herederos forzosos – compulsory heirs
Pareja de hecho – unmarried couple living together as man and wife
Poder – power of attorney
Prescripción – time limit on legal action, statute of limitations
Registro Central de Ultima Voluntad – Central Registry of Wills
Tasación – valuation, of property or other asset
Testamento – will, testament
Testamento cerrado – secret, closed will
Ultima voluntad – last will and testament
Usufructo – usufruct, right to enjoy
Valor catastral – officially rated value of property

SECTION

4

On the Road in Spain

On the Road in Spain

SECTION ONE – YOU AND YOUR CAR

When you move to Spain, do you sell your old car and buy a Spanish one?

Can you take your present car with you and keep it in Spain on its UK or other European registration?

If you do, what happens after you've spent some time in Spain? Can you import the car and register it in Spain?

Can you keep your foreign-plated car in Spain to use on your holiday visits?

If you become a resident, do you have to have a car on Spanish registration?

Let's look at these questions one by one.

CARS WITH FOREIGN REGISTRATION

Let's suppose that you already own a car with British or German registration. If you are a tourist in Spain, you can operate such a car for six months in a calendar year with no formalities.

You can even keep your foreign-registered car in Spain permanently, but you will have to garage it for six months of each year. You can only drive it on Spanish roads for six months.

With Spain's entry into the EU, the international insurance certificate, or so-called "green card", is no longer necessary, but you may find that your individual policy gives only minimum coverage when you are outside your country without it, so check to be sure.

If you are not a European Union citizen, your driving licence from your home country will be acceptable for up to six months of your stay in Spain, though authorities recommend that you have either an international driving licence or an official translation of your licence, which you can get from the Spanish consulate in your home country.

Neither the translation nor the international licence is necessary if you are an EU citizen. For more on licences, see the next chapter.

If you own a vacation home in Spain which you visit at Christmas time and in the summer, you can freely operate your foreign-registered car, using your foreign driving licence, with no further problems, as long as your total visits to Spain don't pass six months in any calendar year. The six months need not be continuous. It could be three visits of two months each, for example.

FOREIGN-PLATED CAR MUST BE ROAD-LEGAL

There is one catch to keeping your old UK vehicle year-round in Spain to use on your holiday visits. The car must be road-legal in its country of registration. This means that a UK car, for example, must have a current MOT. This sticker can only be obtained in the UK. A Spanish vehicle inspection station will be happy to check your car and issue the Spanish ITV sticker, but this does not make the car legal in the UK. So you must take the car back to the UK for its MOT. A number of owners have been caught in this way. You have been warned.

Because this period lies in a calendar year, it has this peculiarity: if the visitor enters Spain after June 30, he can keep and operate his foreign-registered car for the last six months of that year, and the first six months of the following year.

The six-month period is based on the stay of the person himself in the country, rather than on the length of stay of the car. That is, a European who stays in Spain for four months without a car, then decides to return to his home country and bring his car back with him, can only operate the car in Spain for another two months. He can keep it in Spain but he can't legally drive it.

So how do they know whether or not you are driving the car? Good question. For European Union citizens, there really is no effective way to know whether the car is being driven or not. They formerly were required to have the car officially "sealed" for six months of each year, but EU citizens no longer have to do this.

WARNING: POLICE CHECK FOREIGN-PLATE CARS IN SPAIN

We all know that many Europeans really live full-time in Spain without legally establishing residence, perhaps working illegally as well, and continue to operate their cars on non-Spanish plates.

The Spanish traffic police have been very lenient about these cars but they are now starting to crack down. In some areas where many foreigners live, they have stopped the cars they see regularly on the road and politely asked the drivers to clarify their situation.

When the EU driver says that he comes and goes and that he is never in Spain for more than six months in one year, the police politely ask him for documentary evidence.

They understand that it is difficult to produce a passport stamp inside the EU these days, so they will accept practically any paper, such as a recently dated airline ticket or train ticket or any other evidence that the person has travelled within the last six months.

If you are coming to Spain by car, we advise you to take all the trouble necessary to obtain an exit stamp from your home country. Even if you have to go and search for a border official, take the time and do it. This proof of your date of departure can be very handy later.

The police are also interested in whether the car is insured in its country of origin, or whether it is insured by one of the international companies. EU legislation requires that a car be insured in its country of registration. This means that no Spanish company can insure a vehicle registered in another country. This is a problem because your home country's insurance companies will not insure the car without a valid inspection certificate. And you cannot obtain this because your car is in Spain. The Spanish vehicle inspection is not legally valid in your home country, although some international insurance companies will accept it.

The police also observe the last date of the vehicle inspection. If it is a UK car, and its last MOT in Britain dates from 10 years ago, this would arouse suspicion. The law says that a foreign-registered car may stay in Spain as long as it is road-legal in its home country. This means that a UK car must have a current MOT. Some owners have been caught out and fined.

If the car has been inspected in Spain, in order to obtain the insurance, this is another piece of evidence. If the driver cannot produce any documents to prove his own absence from Spain, they have levied fines of €1,800 and more. They then require that the car be either imported into Spain and issued with Spanish registration, or immediately taken out of the country. You have been warned.

Non-Eu Citizens Subject to Sealing: Non-EU citizens, such as Americans and Canadians, are still subject to the sealing requirement if they wish to keep their foreign-registered cars permanently in

Spain. It works like this:

If you decide to stay in Spain after your six-month period is up, and you do not wish to drive your car out of the country, you can ask the Spanish customs officials to "seal" the car for you until you wish to remove it.

To have your car sealed, or *precintado*, you notify the customs officials, *Aduana*. They in turn notify the *Guardia Civil*, who will come, fill out the forms, and put some strips of tape across the steering wheel of the car, designed to ensure that you do not use it. The process is not expensive.

When you are ready to depart with the car, contact the customs office again; they will unseal the car.

You can then use the car six months, have it sealed until the end of the year, and use it again for the first six months of the following year. This sealing provision is useful for people who wish to keep their foreign-registered car in Spain all year round, but who only operate the car during their visits here.

Further, if you are not an EU citizen, you are required to have the car sealed if you leave it in Spain for more than two months while you yourself are absent. This sealing procedure applies only to non-EU citizens.

This is all very well, you say, for a tourist or a regular visitor, but I intend to take up full-time residence in Spain, and I want to know if I can keep my foreign-registered car with me and use it on Spanish roads.

No, you can't. An official resident of Spain must operate a car on full and normal Spanish registration. There is no way around this. After all, a Spaniard living and working in the UK would not be allowed to keep his Spanish-registered car forever either.

TAX-FREE IMPORTATION

Anyone, EU or non-EU, moving to Spain to take up official residence gets a break if they want to bring with them a car they already own.

This car will be exempt from import duties, from Spanish IVA of 21 per cent, and from Spain's own special "ecological" registration tax, ranging from 4.75 per cent to 14.75 per cent, depending on the level of emissions from the vehicle.

For Europeans, of course, there are no duties in any case, but for other nationalities the exemption from Spain's 10-per-cent import duty comes in handy.

The conditions for the exemption are that you must have owned the car for at least six months, you must have paid VAT in the country of origin and you must obtain a certificate of *baja de residencia*, a certificate of non-residence, from the country you are leaving.

Some nationalities can obtain this certificate from the town hall where they live. It can also consist of a declaration made to the Spanish consulate in your home country, declaring your intention to leave your residence and reside officially in Spain. Or you can make the declaration to your own consulate inside Spain after you arrive, stating that you are taking up residence in Spain.

The consulate will then issue the certificate, allowing you to apply for tax-exempt importation of your car.

Warning: Procedures to import a car this way must be started within one month from the date of issue of the residence permit. Non-EU citizens must take care here because the actual residence permit, which you must present, often arrives several months after the issue date stamped on it.

Really, it is best to apply for the car exemption at the same time you apply for your residence card. Because of this complication and the rest of the red tape involved in this application, you will need the services of an expert *gestor* — but it can be done.

For EU citizens, the process is now a little less complicated. When they apply for their Registration Certificate as an EU resident in Spain, this is immediately issued to them, and they can apply for their tax-free importation.

Citizens of most countries must also report to their home country traffic department that their vehicle is being permanently exported. This will avoid their being charged road tax in their home country for a vehicle which is no longer registered there.

The bad news is that, even without paying any taxes, the procedure will cost you around €700 for the various papers involved.

Remember that any concession on the duty-free import of cars applies only to people who take out an official residence permit. Such persons have always been able to import their household effects and furniture into Spain free of duty (see section on "Importing Your Possessions"), but automobiles formerly were not included.

CARS ON TOURIST PLATES

Real savings are available to non-EU persons who remain non-residents and purchase a new car on Spanish tourist plates.

This is the "export" registration provided by a number of countries. An American tourist, for example, can purchase his Mercedes-Benz directly from the factory in Germany, drive it around Europe for six months on the "Z" plates issued to him, without paying any of the normal German taxes. He will finally import the car into the United States, pay duty on a used car, and have it definitively registered.

This registration is designed, by its nature, to be temporary, lasting only until the car is taken to its new home, where taxes are paid.

An American who buys a €30,000 vehicle on Spanish tourist plates can save himself almost €10,000 by skipping Spain's total taxes of 28 per cent. He can have the car to use for a total of six months in any calendar year. These six months need not be continuous. He can make several visits as long as the total time does not exceed six months.

He is also required to have this tourist-plate car *precintado*, or sealed, if he is absent from Spain for more than two months (see above).

If he wishes to have the car available for use twelve months of the year, he can renew this tourist registration every year indefinitely.

One *gestoría* cited a total cost, including their fees, of around €600 for each renewal. This means twice a year. If the tourist plate has expired, the renewal fee is much higher. If you keep the car permanently in one town, they will charge you annual municipal vehicle tax as well.

The only requirements are that the car must be purchased with foreign currency and it cannot be bought on hire purchase.

BUYING A CAR ON SPANISH PLATES

Buying a car on Spanish plates, just the way Spaniards do, can save a lot of complications and has certain advantages. You do not have to pay in foreign currency and you can purchase on the instalment plan.

Britons in particular will find that new Spanish cars are priced lower than the same models in the UK.

A foreigner may buy a car on Spanish plates if he meets one of the following qualifications:

1. He holds an official residence permit or the EU Certificate of Registration.
2. He presents the *escritura* (title deed) to a home he owns in Spain. The deed must be for a dwelling, not a place of business, and it must be in the personal name of the foreigner, not in the name of a company, especially an offshore company;

3. He presents a *Certificado de Empadronamiento*, a certificate showing that he is a registered inhabitant of the municipality whose town hall issues the document. This is not a residence permit; it is only a registration certificate showing that the person lives in that municipality. You get this certificate by presenting your passport, a title deed or rental contract at your town hall.

4. He presents a rental contract of one year's duration.

Note of caution: If you are a non-resident and from a non-EU country and you buy a car on Spanish registration, make sure that you obtain one of the following documents:

1. An International Driving Permit to carry in addition to your home country licence.

2. An official translation of your driving licence, often available through the Spanish Consulate in your home country.

3. A *Certificado de Equivalencia,* (a Certificate of Equivalence) which is prepared by Spain's Royal Automobile Club, the RACE.

The reason for the exercise is that Spanish traffic police want somebody who is regularly on Spanish roads and not merely a tourist visitor to carry a licence they can read and understand. You can be fined €300 if you do not comply.

"ECOLOGICAL TAX" PENALISES HIGH-EMISSION VEHICLES

As of January 1, 2008, large four-wheel-drive vehicles with big engines that emit high quantities of carbon dioxide into the atmosphere face extra taxes in Spain. The new tax scheme replaces Spain's former special registration tax of seven per cent on smaller engines and 12 per cent on larger engines.

The good news is that smaller and cleaner engines now pay no special registration tax at all. After that, the tax rises from four per cent to 14 per cent on a sliding scale.

The basis is carbon dioxide emitted per kilometre driven. Under120 grammes, there is no tax. Above 200 grammes, the top rate of 14.79 per cent kicks in.

As a rough guide:

Gasoline engines under 1,000cc, diesel under 1,500cc – 0 tax

Gasoline engines under1,600cc, diesel under 2,000cc – 4.75%

Gasoline engines under 2,000cc, diesel over 2,000cc – 9.75%

Figures are approximate as emissions vary. Top rate – 14.75%

When you make the rounds of auto dealers in your part of Spain, collecting brochures and comparing prices, you will find many makes and models available, at prices in some cases a little lower than in the rest of Europe. Renaults, Fords, Opels, Seats, Citroëns, all manufactured in Spain, are among the best sellers. Dealers compete in offering guarantees, financing terms and special sales.

Besides these Spanish-manufactured cars, you can also find dealers specialising in imported cars on Spanish plates. Imported cars have actually captured 25 per cent of the Spanish market.

If you are a new arrival and don't own property, you may be asked to provide some financial certification that you can pay for the car, or even be required to find a Spanish co-signer to guarantee your payments.

You make a deposit on the car, which will vary from dealer to dealer, and agree terms from one to four years. Interest rates have come down on these plans as competition grows keener.

If you decide on a two-year scheme, for example, you will make your down payment and then sign a series of 24 *letras*, or bills of exchange, for the instalments. These *letras* oblige you to make the payments and are often addressed directly to your bank account for payment.

GOVERNMENT CONTINUES "PIVE" PLAN

The government has continued the PIVE plan, designed to encourage the scrapping of old cars circulating on Spanish roads. The plan offers substantial discounts to owners who officially scrap a car 10 years old to purchase a new Spanish car or even a relatively new used car. The initials stand for the Plan for Incentives for Efficient Vehicles. At this writing, it looks as if the plan for 2018 will subsidise only hybrid or electric vehicles but be sure to ask your dealer.

MUNICIPAL VEHICLE TAX

You pay your vehicle tax each year at the town hall. If you are not paid up, you will not be able to sell or trade in the car later.

This is the *Impuesto Municipal Sobre Vehículos De Tracción Mecánica,* a municipal tax on vehicles registered in each town. Formerly this tax was charged at a single rate all over Spain, but now each municipality is free to charge whatever rate it sees fit, so the tax varies from town to town.

It is based on the *potencia fiscal* of the car, its horsepower as rated for tax purposes. Small cars pay around €50 and large cars €100 and even more. Motorcycles also pay this tax each year.

Your car will go on the books of the town where you live as soon as you are registered as the owner of the car with the traffic authorities in the provincial capital.

To pay the tax go into the town hall and ask for the appropriate window. April and May are the usual times to pay, but this varies from town to town. You will not necessarily receive an individual notification, but announcements will appear in banks, in the

> **Be advised that you should take all your car papers into your *ayuntamiento* (town hall) when you purchase a new or used car to register for the tax. The Traffic Department is supposed to inform the town halls but it is best to be sure. The same applies when you sell or scrap your car. Make sure that you de-register your car at the town hall, or you will be charged tax for the following year.**

newspaper and on the municipal notice-board. It's best to ask when the tax is due. Late payment will draw a surcharge.

Many municipalities are now offering local taxpayers a carrot-and-stick programme, in which those who pay their taxes early get a discount. You can also arrange to have the tax paid by standing order at your bank.

This vehicle circulation tax receipt is one of the papers you should keep with you in your car, along with the car's official registration papers and insurance receipt, as the police may ask to see it at any time.

You cannot sell your car or trade it in for a new model without the paid-up vehicle tax receipt.

USED CARS

There is an active market in used cars in Spain, with many makes and models available. Used-car dealers can be found in all towns of any size and the new-car dealers have departments where they recondition and sell older cars taken as trade-ins for new ones. Dealers offer widely varying guarantees, prices and service, so be sure to shop around.

A resident can purchase a second-hand car on Spanish plates, just as if he were a Spaniard. You may be unpleasantly surprised at the high prices for second-hand cars, but that is the way the market is in Spain. As we have seen, taxes on automobiles are higher than in most other European countries, and in most parts of Spain the good weather ensures that cars deteriorate less rapidly than they do in many other parts of the world.

Many of the used cars available here are former rental cars. The Costa del Sol in fact may be the world's capital of hire cars, as those thousands of tourists who pick up their cars every week at Málaga airport attest.

Sometimes you can find a real bargain directly from a car hire company disposing of its two-year-old cars, and sometimes you find a real lemon being passed off by a dealer as a privately owned car. Be alert.

The dealer who sells you your second-hand car will probably be quite happy to arrange the transfer of title to you for a small fee. In a private sale, you and the seller can go to a *gestoría* which handles automobile transfers.

You can also go directly to the *Jefatura de Tráfico*, the motor vehicle department in your province, and handle the whole thing yourself, thus saving any intermediary's fees.

TAKE CARE WITH TRANSFER

To do this, you will need:

1. The transfer application form which you obtain at the provincial Traffic Department.

2. The circulation permit of the vehicle, with the transfer of owners listed on the back, including the seller's signature.

3. The paid-up municipal vehicle tax receipt, along with a photocopy.

4. Receipt for the payment of the vehicle transfer tax, charged at 4 per cent on the sale of second-hand vehicles. This tax is paid to the Spanish Tax Agency on Form 620.

5. A current ITV report and photocopy. This is the Inspección Técnica de Vehículos, the vehicle inspection certificate.

6. Residence card and photocopy.

7. Payment of €40 fee.

Present all your documentation at the Traffic Department.

Only the transfer form, signed by both seller and buyer, and stamped by the Traffic Department is proof of the change of ownership. If both parties go to *Trafico* and complete the transaction, fine. If someone else handles the transfer, even a dealership, do not deliver the vehicle until you see that the transfer has been registered with the Traffic Department.

Otherwise, you may find that the new owner conveniently forgets to register the car in his own name, which leaves you as the still-registered owner liable for any parking tickets or road taxes that come due on the car.

If you fear that this may be the case, you must then have the vehicle de-registered in your name. This is called a *baja de matrícula.*

Again, you obtain the form from the Traffic Department, and you must present the receipt for the current year's municipal vehicle tax. If you no longer have the circulation permit and the inspection certificate, because they are with the new owner, you can make a sworn declaration of this.

You must also make this application for *baja* when you scrap an old car. Sometimes you think that the car is off the road when it has in fact been repaired and someone totally unknown to you is illegally operating it.

Make the de-registration and you will be protected from later consequences.

VEHICLE INSPECTION REQUIRED

Vehicle inspection is compulsory for Spanish-registered cars more than four years old. Be alert when purchasing an older car, and ask for the *ITV* (*Inspección Técnica de Vehículos*) certificate. If the car doesn't have one, you have to have the car tested yourself if you want to use it on public roads, and there's no guarantee it will pass the test. When you hear Spaniards say *ITV*, they mean MOT.

JUNK YOUR OLD CAR

Spain is now fulfilling the terms of a European Union directive that requires old cars to be scrapped with a minimum of waste and contamination to the environment.

Authorised centres for this disposal of scrapped vehicles are opening around the country. Generally you must go the centre with your car and its registration documents. Some centres will come and pick up your old car and take it away. They will scrap the vehicle

DOWNLOAD FORMS FROM TRÁFICO WEB SITE

The Spanish Traffic Department, the *Dirección General de Tráfico*, maintains a very useful web site that offers a great deal of information on all subjects having to do with cars, roads, and driving. You can even fill in and download many of the forms necessary for various transactions with them. The web site is **www.dgt.es**.

At this same web site you can also consult a list of outstanding traffic fines to see if your name appears. This is much easier than getting a copy of the official provincial bulletin. Then you can be sure that you have not missed any notification sent by post.

in a proper manner and give you a certificate of its authorised destruction.

You should then take this certificate to your town hall and de-register the vehicle to avoid their charging you further municipal vehicle tax.

BUYING USED CARS IN EUROPE

Even though Spanish new car prices tend to be lower than new car prices in other EU countries, Spain's used cars tend to be rather more expensive, especially in the Mediterranean coastal areas. Perhaps they simply hold their value better in a sunny climate.

This situation has given rise to a thriving market in used cars imported into Spain from Germany or Belgium. One estimate calculates that a mid-level BMW about two years old can be bought and imported from Germany at a savings of around 25 per cent.

Be warned, however, that there is plenty of paperwork and delay. Experienced gestores report that the process can take more than three months The various testing and registration fees can easily reach €600, in addition to the special tax.

They also advise the prospective importer to make sure the original factory invoice for the car is available and to have the vehicle inspected and certified roadworthy in its country of origin even before it enters Spain.

Boats: You can enter a Spanish port with your foreign-registered yacht and keep it here and use it in Spanish waters for six months of a calendar year, just as with cars. The six-month period need not be continuous — an advantage for people who want to keep their yacht in a Spanish port but can only use it for a month or two at a time on extended visits. The customs authorities in the marina can seal the boat (*precintar*) while its owner is away, and unseal it when he wishes to use it. Thus, the non-resident can keep his boat in a Spanish port all year and use it for six months of that year.

Like cars, yachts are also available from dealers in Spain on a Spanish tourist flag registration, under which they do not pay normal Spanish taxes. Such a yacht can be used six months of the year, and an extension of its tourist registration requested each year to permit its owner to use it all year.

One useful provision of the sealing process for the non-resident yacht owner is that he can have his boat sealed for the last six months of the year and continue to live aboard it. He may not sail it out of the harbour, but he can use it as his home.

Import duties on a used yacht still come to something more than half the value of the boat, depending on the evaluation the customs authorities make. In addition, you can only import the boat if you are taking up official residence in Spain.

A Spanish resident will also need to obtain Spanish marine certification to operate his yacht in Spanish waters.

Caravans: Caravans are treated almost exactly like cars. That is, if you enter Spain with your caravan pulled by your car, you have six months in the calendar year to circulate freely as a tourist. You can also have the caravan sealed by the customs officials should you wish to leave it behind and drive out with your car.

Be warned: you cannot import from the UK into Spain most right-hand-drive vans and auto-caravan vehicles. This is because the law allows importation of a right-hand drive vehicle that has a full field of vision of 360 degrees (like most cars), but it prohibits the importation of right-hand drive vehicles (like camping vans) which have some rear and side vision blocked. This is on safety grounds.

Motorcycles: Motorcycles (*motos*) with engines of more than 49cc are treated exactly like cars, with the same six-month time limit.

The small 49cc machines are a different story. You do not need a *Certificado de Empadronamiento* or any other document to purchase one, and you can even import your foreign-registered bike duty-free as part of your personal possessions when you take up residence in Spain.

Initially your foreign licence and, later, your foreign licence with its translation, or an international permit, will be valid for these bikes. Your Spanish driving licence will also be valid.

If, like some people, you have no driving licence at all but want to operate one of these convenient little bikes for dashing around town, you can get a special licence to do so by taking a simple examination. Most driving schools can steer you through the process for a small fee.

Until recently even a youngster of 14 could ride a 49cc machine legally. No longer. Today the minimum age to get any moto licence is 15. At 18, your boy or girl can get a regular driving licence.

Don't forget to warn the child that he must wear a helmet both in town and on the highway or risk a fine.

INSURING YOUR CAR

If you are visiting Spain as a tourist driving your foreign-registered car, all the auto insurance you need is the coverage by your insurance company in your home country, extended to cover travel in Spain. Your own company can issue you a "green card", as the international insurance certificate is popularly known. If you are from an EU country, you no longer need this but it is still a good idea because some insurance companies limit their coverage to the legal minimum outside their own national borders unless the policy holder has arranged for his green card.

SPANISH CARS

Let's suppose that you have just purchased your Spanish car, on tourist plates or on normal Spanish registration, new or second-hand. The dealer who sells it to you will either have an insurance company representative as part of his organisation or will be happy to steer you to his brother-in-law who sells auto insurance. His brother-in-law's company may be fine, but it also pays to shop around, or at least ask among other foreign residents in your area to recommend a company.

If you are buying a new car on instalments, you may have little choice in what insurance you want. The dealer usually requires you to have full-coverage insurance on the car until it is paid off.

NOT NECESSARY TO CARRY INSURANCE RECEIPT IN CAR

As of 2008, it is no longer necessary to carry your paid-up automobile insurance receipt with you at all times in the car. It is a good idea but it is no longer a punishable violation of the traffic law. Spain's traffic department feels that their computer system is now fully on line to tell officers just about everything to do with your automobile registration and driving licence. As of 2017, however, you will need the receipt when you take your car for the inspection.

Competition among Spanish auto insurance companies has become fierce in recent years, so almost any figure we mention here can probably be beaten if you check a number of companies.

But all-risk insurance – *todo riesgo* – for a small car can cost you less than €500 a year if you are a woman of mature years. If you are an excitable young man, the same insurance may cost you €1,800. The cheapest rates are usually found from those companies offering their policies via the Internet.

You can also drive legally for less than €400 a year, or even less with a no-claims discount of 50 per cent, if you choose the basic obligatory insurance, required by Spanish law. This covers you only for claims by third parties but it will pay out up to 30 million euros for bodily harm and 10 million euros for damages.

A "third party" is anyone who makes a claim against you for injury or damage suffered as a result of the use of your car. It includes driver and passengers in another car with which you may collide. It may include even passengers in your own car who are not members of your family. It includes pedestrians, and the owners of any property you may damage. If you drive your car into someone's wall and knock it down, the wall's owner can make a claim against you.

DRIVING WITHOUT INSURANCE CAN SEND YOU TO JAIL

Since May 1, 2008, drivers who operate their cars on Spanish roads without insurance can be sent to jail for up to six months, as well as being charged with heavy fines.

This is part of the reform of the Penal Code for stricter traffic enforcement.

This minimum insurance does not cover you or your car at all. It covers only other persons and their property. This coverage is the legal minimum.

If you are injured by a driver who has no insurance at all, the Spanish insurance consortium, which backs the entire industry, will pay. Each company contributes to the fund, operated by the State.

If you want further coverage, you can take out additional insurance, and most people do. For a few hundred euros more, you can get the same third-party coverage, but up to much higher sums or even unlimited, which means no ceiling on what the company will pay in the case of a terrible accident with very high claims.

You can choose just what you need to insure. Such as yourself and your family, for example, who do not count as third parties, or your shiny new car. You can buy coverage against theft, fire, damage, death or injury, and even insurance to pay for legal costs involved in court proceedings brought against you or which you have to bring against another driver when claiming damages. You can get comprehensive insurance covering all these, or a policy covering only part.

Let's look at a few possibilities. Total coverage can cost you €1,000 or more, depending on the size and age of your car, but you can

get quite a lot of protection by taking out a policy under which you yourself pay the first €200 or so of any small damage to your car. This exemption is called a *franquicia*. Because you promise to pay this much, the company saves expense in administration and paperwork, and you get your major coverage more cheaply.
A typical policy might be one in which you pay the first €300 of any claim against you and you are insured for:

1. The full value of the car in case of fire or accident.

2. Up to 80 per cent of its value in case of theft.

3. Coverage for you and your family in case of death or permanent injury.

4. Coverage of legal expenses.

5. Unlimited coverage for third-party claims against you.

This could cost around €600 a year or even less for a mid-sized car.

FOREIGN CARS IN SPAIN

Many foreigners stay for long periods in Spain as non-residents, keeping their foreign-plated cars with them.

Legally, a foreign-registered car can stay on Spanish roads for six months in a calendar year without any formalities at all. In fact, the car itself can remain in Spain permanently, although it can only be operated on the road for six months of that year and must be garaged for the other six months.

The problem for these cars comes from European Union regulations which require that all cars be insured in their country of registration. Formerly, the owners of these British or other cars simply insured them with Spanish companies. They can no longer do this. Nor can they obtain insurance from the UK because the car has never been returned for its MOT and it is no longer a UK resident, as it were.

Some insurance companies have come up with a sort of off-shore insurance that will cover the car in any country except its original home. If you are in this situation, ask your insurance broker. With the European liberalisation of insurance companies, there are also Spanish branches of UK companies which will insure the car on UK plates.

These companies will require your car to pass the Spanish vehicle safety inspection, the *ITV*, to make sure it is in sound operating condition. You get your *ITV* sticker, which satisfies the insurance company but has no other legal force. Your car, if it is British-registered, remains illegal in the UK because it has no British MOT. Technically, the car is not legal in Spain either without its UK MOT, but police seldom ask. If you take it back to the UK, you will have to pass the MOT immediately.

What you really want to know is: what happens when you make a claim? Will the Spanish insurance company pay you? The short answer is, Spanish insurance companies are just as reluctant to pay out as most other companies, but they are also prepared to live up to their legal obligations.

If you have full coverage and someone dents your new car in the parking lot and departs without leaving his name, you will probably find that your insurance company pays up quickly and without a murmur for the repairs. But you may lose any credit you have been getting as a no-claims bonus. If the claim is not your fault, many companies will continue your credit.

On the other hand, if there is an accident and you feel the other driver is at fault, but he chooses to contest this, you may have to wait as long as three years for a court decision in back-logged Spanish courts.

IF YOU HAVE AN ACCIDENT

So some idiot has darted out of a side street without looking and pranged your new car. Or perhaps you yourself were careless, followed another vehicle too closely and banged into it.

In Spain procedures to follow after an accident are much the same as in any country. The police may appear and take all the details of both drivers. Or, in the case of smaller accidents, the two drivers can settle the matter between themselves. If there is no personal injury, it is not necessary to inform the police.

The two drivers can fill in the standard European Union form for a mutual agreement. This is called a *Declaración Amistosa*, a friendly declaration, in Spanish.

See "What To Do" section regarding an accident.

Keep in mind the two basic principles.

1. Do not admit any fault, even if your own actions are clearly the cause of the accident. Such admission can even give your insurance company a reason not to pay out.

2. Do not sign the mutual agreement form. Once signed, it is powerful evidence in court and can work against you if you have not understood it perfectly.

You must be sure to get the licence number, the name and the insurance company of the other driver. Do not be intimidated by any shouted threats. It is an upsetting situation, but try to keep your wits about you.

Remember that you have two months to bring a charge against the other driver. If you are sure that he is at fault, it is better to do this immediately, but it is not absolutely necessary.

If you live in Spain, the normal procedure will be to contact your insurance agent quickly. He will lead you through the process.

If you wish to make a charge, you go to the local police station, make a declaration and then let the insurance companies sort it out. Even if it seems clear that the fault is yours, do not be too quick to admit it. Again, let the insurance company handle it.

The Spanish courts do function, eventually. A friend of mine saw a car back into her own car in a parking lot, crumpling the door. The offending driver fled, but she was able to get the car's licence number. She traced the owner through this number, went to the police station and made a charge against him. Two years later she was summoned to a court hearing, where the other driver denied everything. The court ruled in her favour, however, and ordered the other driver to pay for all damages plus court costs, which his insurance company paid.

Two years was a long time to wait, but there is a satisfaction when justice is done.

Section Two
On the Road in Spain

A genuine European Union tourist visiting Spain and driving either his own car from his own country or a Spanish rental car can do so on the licence issued to him in his home country. He needs no translation or official certification to do this, and the privilege is good for a visit up to six months. A non-EU tourist will need an international driving licence to accompany his home country permit.

WHO NEEDS WHAT LICENCE?

EU citizen, non-resident

For the first six months of your stay in Spain, driving your car on European Union registration or a Spanish rental car, you can use your home country licence with no problem. If you operate your UK or other foreign-registered vehicle for more than six months, however, you can be fined or even have the vehicle impounded. This is about the vehicle, however, not about the driving licence.

EU citizen, resident, can use his licence

1. EU citizens who hold the European-style plastic licence, valid for 10 years or five years if you are more than 65 years old, can continue to use their EU home-country driving licence in Spain until it expires, even when they hold a Spanish residence certificate. Before the 10-year licence expires the holder must exchange it for a Spanish permit. These EU-style licences have the same format in all EU countries. Even the UK has issued plastic licences since 1998.

2. Or the EU citizen can exchange his permit for a Spanish driving licence. It is easy now to exchange your EU driving licence for a Spanish permit. If the holder of the EU-style licences goes voluntarily to the local traffic department, he can even be exempt from the medical exam. However, you will need to go in person to the traffic office with your present licence and two photos, for your original exchange. This exchange procedure is called a *canje*.

German, French, Belgian, "Lifetime Licence"
Holders of "lifetime" licences, with no date of expiry, such as the German, French, Belgian or Austrian permits, including the UK permits valid to the age of 70, have a special set of rules. Once the holder of a "lifetime" permit takes up residence in Spain, he can use it for only two years. After that, he must take his licence to the *Trafico* department and exchange it for a Spanish permit.

POINTS OFF YOUR UK LICENCE

If you break the traffic laws, you can have points taken off your German or French licence. In fact, if a holder of a UK 10-year permit exceeds the number of Spanish points allowed, Spain can take his licence, exchange it for a Spanish licence, annul the Spanish licence, and leave the offender without a driving permit. In addition, Spain will inform the home country that the person's driving licence has been cancelled.

LICENCE RENEWAL

The Spanish system is becoming more user-friendly. The licence renewal and medical exam have been combined into one procedure. A driver goes to the authorised medical centre, passes his exam, and has his renewal request processed on the spot in the medical centre. He needs his current licence and two photos, although most of the medical centres will make the photos on the spot. He pays the fee for the medical exam and the renewal fee. Prices vary somewhat but each is around 30 euros. The exam centre sends his renewal and medical form in to the traffic department, which then mails the new licence to the driver. This avoids a trip to the traffic department for the driver. If you later return to your home country, you can re-exchange your Spanish licence for a home country licence, just as you did here, only in reverse.

Non-EU, non-resident: For the first six months of your stay in Spain, driving your car on its home country registration, or driving a rental car, you can simply use your home country licence with no problem.

If you are driving a vehicle which you own, on Spanish registration, you must have an International Driving Permit to carry in addition to your home country licence.

Non-EU citizen, resident: Now things start to get tough for the non-European Union citizen. He absolutely must have a Spanish driving licence when he becomes a resident of Spain. There is no alternative.

Furthermore, he cannot exchange his home country licence for a Spanish one. Because the European Union is still working out its international agreements on driving licences, very few non-EU licences can be exchanged at this time, and for the immediate future.

This means that Americans, Australians, South Africans and so on must take the Spanish driving examination, both written and practical, just as beginning Spanish drivers do.

Furthermore, they must take the written exam in Spanish, except in some provinces, such as Málaga. Formerly the exam could be taken in several languages but now it is only in Spanish in most areas. Really, it is only logical. A person who does not know that *peligro* means "danger" could get into trouble.

Check driving schools in your area to see if you are among the lucky ones. The non-EU citizen must attend a Spanish driving school, and pay its fees, in order to take the exam. The Spanish *autoescuelas* have got a hammerlock on the system and have become semi-official bodies. You cannot go for the exam without the school.

A rock-bottom price for a few classes on the rules of the road, and a few driving classes, plus the exam cost, would be about €500.

And of course you must take the eye and reaction test as well.

The minimum age for a B licence, the most usual sort, is 18 and the maximum age is 65, if you have never held a licence before.

If you are 68 years old when you arrive in Spain, don't worry. The 65-year figure applies only to first-timers. You can continue to renew your existing Spanish permit as long as you are physically able to drive safely.

LAW OF ROAD SAFETY

Spain's traffic department has made a number of revisions in the rules. Here is a summary of the present Law of Traffic Safety, as of 2018.

50% DISCOUNT FOR PROMPT PAYMENT

The authorities have been fiddling with Spain's traffic regulations every year for the past few years, adjusting the points system for driving infractions, changing the schedule of fines, and making it easier to pay.

If you go 130 kilometres an hour in a 100-kilometer zone, your fine will be 100 euros. If you go up to 150 kph on a highway zoned for 120 kph, your fine will be the same 100 euros, for exceeding the speed limit by about one-third.

If you pay the fine within 20 days, you get a discount of 50 per cent, thus paying only 50 euros. You can even pay the fine on the spot by credit card, if the police car is equipped for it.

On the other hand, the new Road Safety Law makes it more difficult for offenders to escape their fines entirely. Formerly, the Traffic Department had only one year to collect a fine. Now they can pursue the violator for up to four years. Under the previous system, authorities estimate that about one-fourth of all traffic fines were never paid.

Another innovation is the use of "average-speed" devices, where two separate cameras measure the time it takes a car to travel between two points. This system has been installed in several tunnels on Spanish highways.

Parking in a space reserved for the handicapped has been elevated to the level of "serious" offence, and a new addition to the "serious" category is having a licence plate that is bent or darkened so that the camera cannot read it effectively.

Radar Detectors: Radar detectors are legal on Spanish roads, but the use of a radar-jamming device is not legal and constitutes a "very serious" violation with a fine of 600 euros or more and the loss of six points.

The Revised Code continues to divide infractions into "minor", "serious" and "very serious" categories. In Spanish these are called "*leves*", "*graves*" y "*muy graves*".

The fines assigned to these infractions are €100, €200, and €600. In our example above, the speeder who exceeded limit by a small amount was fined €100 for a "minor infraction". If he had been detected speeding at 80 kph in a road limited to 30 kph, more than double the limit, he would have fallen into the "very serious"

> **TAKE INSURANCE TO ITV**
>
> Vehicle inspection stations will now be empowered to demand the car's insurance document before they inspect it. Under the new rules, the insurance card need not be carried in the car, but the *ITV* will now be a place where you need it.

category and been charged a fine of €600 as well as losing six points. The infractions of three points and up fall into the "serious" and "very serious" categories. They will draw fines of €300 or €600 as well as the loss of points.

Keep in mind that even stiffer penalties, including time in prison, can be issued to drivers who persist in driving without a licence or who cause death by reckless operation, and other extremely serious offences. These penalties include confiscation of the offender's vehicle. He does not get it back.

If you feel that you have been unfairly charged, you have the right to appeal the fine and loss of points. We recommend that you use a Spanish lawyer or one of the firms that specialise in these cases to assist you in your appeal.

How the system works: Drivers are assigned 12 points. New drivers, with less than three years of experience, begin with only eight points. If the beginner drives for two years with no infractions, he gets four additional points to bring him up to twelve

Safe drivers are awarded two more points after three years without an infraction. After another three years they get one more extra point, making a total of 15 possible points.

Check your points: A driver can check on his number of points by going to the Traffic Department web site. The department is the *Dirección General de Tráfico* and the web site is www.dgt.es. The site also contains much more useful information.

When a driver loses points, he can recover up to four points by passing a course of driver safety education that consists of 15 hours of instruction. You can only do this once every two years. If a driver

POINTS SYSTEM

Two points off

For exceeding the posted speed limit, you can lose two, four or six points, depending on your speed over the limit.

Three points off

- Improper turn to change direction, which specifically means u-turns where not permitted.
- Use of mobile phone, headset or other attention-distracting device, such as a navigator, while in movement.
- Failure to use seat belt, helmet or other required safety device, such as adequate child seat.

Four points off

- Driving without proper licence or with suspended licence.
- Throwing from the car any object which could cause fire or accident.
- Failure to obey traffic signs, such as running a red light or Stop sign.
- Passing on a curve or where visibility is reduced.
- Endangering bicyclists when overtaking them.
- Failure to keep a safe distance.
- Failure to obey the orders of traffic officers.

Six points off

- Driving when over the legal alcohol limit.
- Driving under the influence of drugs.
- Refusing alcohol or drug test.
- Reckless operation.
- Driving a vehicle which has a radar jamming system.
- For professionals, exceeding their maximum driving time by 50 per cent.

ENFORCEMENT LEAVES SOMETHING TO BE DESIRED

Unfortunately, the enforcement of the points system leaves something to be desired. The Traffic Department reported that more than 5,000 drivers who had lost all their points are still on the road, quite legally because the loss of licence had not been officially notified to them by the courts.

loses all his 12 points, he must wait six months until he can attend the safety course. He must also pass a theoretical exam. If a driver loses his licence for a second time, he must wait one year without a driving permit before he can attend the course.

Lost Points Recovered: If a driver has lost points but then drives safely for two years, with no infractions, the points will be returned to his record.

DOCUMENTS TO CARRY IN CAR AT ALL TIMES

1. *Permiso de Circulación* — car's registration paper
2. *Tarjeta de Inspección Técnica* — shows *ITV* (MOT to you)
3. Valid driving licence, Spanish or EU
4. Medical exam certificate when necessary
5. Insurance document and receipt of payment
6. Municipal vehicle tax — not necessary, but good

The traffic code puts stricter controls on infants and children in cars and on motorcycles. A child up to three years old cannot ride in the front seat under any circumstances. It must ride in the back, in a seat with restraints designed for its size.

A child from four to 12 years old who is shorter than 1.5 metres may ride in the front seat with a special seat or belt system. If none is available, the child must ride in the rear seat.

A child of 12 taller than 1.5 metres can use the adult seat belt in the front passenger seat. Any person shorter than 1.5 metres must be treated the same as the child.

The revised law makes parents of minor children responsible for paying fines incurred when these children operate motor-bikes, which they can do at 16 years of age, although they must wait until they are 18 to obtain a normal driving licence.

Children under 12 are not permitted to ride as passengers on motorbikes. In exceptional circumstances children seven years old may accompany a parent.

And, yes, in this nation of tailgaters a driver is required to maintain a safe distance behind the vehicle he is following, and he is obliged to leave enough space for another vehicle safely to pass him and pull in.

If you have ever thought of reporting a driver who follows too closely, you are perfectly within your rights. Any citizen may report a traffic violation. You must be prepared to testify in court, however, to make your accusation stick.

All Spanish cars must be fitted with seat-belts and they must be worn. All cars must be fitted with rear seat belts as well.

If the traffic police have reason to think a driver has been drinking they can require him to take a breath test to analyse the amount of alcohol in his blood. If it exceeds the minimum permitted, he can be heavily fined and have his licence revoked. It is your right to demand a blood test as well, if you feel the breath test is wrong.

Refusal to take the breath test can lead to a charge of disobeying a police officer, which can bring a penalty of six months in gaol.

NON-RESIDENTS CAN BE FINED ON THE SPOT

If you are a non-resident tourist driving through Spain, you may be disturbed to discover that the Spanish police are authorised to demand payment on the spot for any traffic violation you commit.

The police can order your car impounded if you are unable to pay up. This is because their orders require them to take the steps necessary to ensure that the fine will be paid.

As a tourist has no property or other assets in Spain, which could be seized if he does not pay the fine, the agents can order that his vehicle be detained if he does not pay. Most police cars are now equipped to accept payment by credit card.

If you feel that you have been unfairly charged and wish to protest, you will have to pay the fine first, but you can fill in the space for contesting the ticket and mark garantía in the area where your payment is noted. This means that you consider your payment only a guarantee, necessary for the policeman to permit you to continue your trip, but that you intend to contest the ticket.

Just like the resident, you will be informed after a few months, when your court hearing is scheduled. You will have to list an address inside Spain for this purpose. You can then go to the Spanish court and make your case.

GLOSSARY

Aduana – customs
Baja de matrícula – de-registration of motor vehicle
Baja de residencia – non-residence certificate required for duty-free import
Canje – exchange of EU driving permit for Spanish permit
Certificado de Empadronamiento – registration in municipality
Coche – car, automobile
Franquicia – automobile insurance policy excluding first part of claim
Impuesto Municipal Sobre Vehículos De Tracción Mecánica – Municipal motor vehicle tax
Inspección Técnica de Vehículos – vehicle inspection, MOT
Jefatura de Tráfico – Traffic Department headquarters
Letra – bill of exchange, signed for monthly car payments
Matrícula – registration
Matrícula turística – tax-free tourist registration
Multa – fine, traffic or otherwise
Permiso de circulación – permit for vehicle to circulate on public roads
Permiso de conducir – driving licence
Potencia fiscal – tax-rated horsepower
Precintar – to seal, as in automobile or yacht
Todo riesgo – comprehensive insurance covering all risks

SECTION

5

Community of Property Owners

You and Your Community

When you buy a property in Spain — as more than one million foreigners already have — you automatically become a member of a legally constituted Community of Property Owners. Whether you like it or not. Whether the property is your retirement home or a holiday flat, whether it is an apartment, a townhouse or a detached villa on an urbanisation, you will find your own interests affected by the community and the decisions of your neighbours. You will pay your community fees every year, and you will meet with your neighbours at the Annual General Meeting to argue about whether to paint the outside of the building or whether to fire the gardener. You will cast your vote on these issues.

If your building or urbanisation is new, you may even take part in the original organisation of the community, with all its problems of drafting the statutes, electing a president, fixing the amount of community fees, planning the budget and defining the relation of the property promoter and his still unsold properties to the rest of the community.

Only those who buy an individual house in a town street or a farmhouse on a large tract of rural land will not have to deal with belonging to a Spanish *Comunidad de Propietarios*. A well-run community can add thousands of euros of value to an otherwise unremarkable house, and a poorly run community can cut thousands off the value of even a very nice apartment.

Before you buy any Spanish property, find out as much as you can about the operations of the community. See the list of questions to ask in the Capsule Guide that follows.

Over the years problems arising from community life have produced hundreds of letters to my magazine columns and many, many telephone calls to my radio programme. People want to know if the annual general meeting can be held in English, how to fire an administrator who is not properly serving the interests of all the owners, how to form a legal community on an unregistered urbanisation, how to collect community fees from non-payers, and hundreds of other matters.

This guide and the following two chapters aim to answer these questions and:

- To help you understand your rights and obligations as a member of the community of property owners.
- To show you how to participate effectively in community life, both in and out of the annual general meeting.
- To make suggestions for dealing with problems that most frequently arise.
- To provide a ready reference to the complete English translation of Spain's Law of Horizontal Property, the law which regulates communities of property owners.

Beware, however. If the law itself were perfectly clear to the normal citizen, we would not need lawyers to help us interpret it. This is just as true of Spanish law as it is of any other country's law.

So we have provided explanatory comments for each article of the law, telling how the rules work out in practice.

Keep in mind also that the English translation of the law is only informative. The real law is the one in Spanish.

Remember also that this book can only guide you in a general way. If there are serious disputes within your community which involve legal action, do not hesitate to obtain the services of a Spanish lawyer skilled in community matters. Often, a group of members can share the expenses. The courts of law are not an appropriate arena for the do-it-yourselfer.

WHAT IS A COMMUNITY?

The Community of Property Owners - *Comunidad de Propietarios* - is the Spanish system for regulating the joint ownership of common property. In an apartment building this means the entranceway, the staircases, the lift, the roof space, the grounds and any other shared spaces used by all the owners. On an urbanisation it will include the roads, gardens, communal pools, lighting system, drains and other services.

This type of ownership is often called "condominium" in English, for co-ownership. The community sets out the manner in which all the co-owners manage their joint affairs for the best administration of the shared property. The co-owners must decide how much money they want to pay for the maintenance and management of their building, and how this money will be spent.

The law which regulates this system is called the Law of Horizontal Property *(La Ley de Propiedad Horizontal)*. This law, originally passed in 1960 and amended in April, 1999, and again in 2003, and again in 2013, is actually more vertical than horizontal because it applies mainly to apartment buildings, although it also covers townhouse developments of attached units.

Communities of owners on urbanisations of detached villas do not come directly under the original Horizontal Law but amendments to the 1999 law make it easier for detached villas to use the Horizontal Law's protection.

Urbanisations are regulated by other laws included in several sections of the Land Law, the *Ley del Suelo*. These communities may be of several sorts, but the most effective are called *Entidad Urbanística Colaboradora de Gestión y Conservación*. This mouthful translates as "collaborating urbanistic entity of management and maintenance," and is often shortened to EUC. Estates of detached villas may require a different body of law because they present different problems. The roads, drains and lighting installations of the urbanisation may serve the public as well as the residents, thus having a quasi-public aspect which requires collaboration between the urbanisation owners and the Town Hall authorities. This interaction between the town and the estate demands extra regulation not needed in the case of apartment buildings.
But in both cases the idea of the law is the same: to provide a framework in which the community becomes a legal force. It can go to court, enforce the payment of community fees and make contracts. It can also be sued itself. Many problems have arisen in communities of detached villas because they were not originally formed according to the correct laws.

SEE: *Law of Horizontal Property, Articles 1 through 5, Article 24, and Legal Communities for Urbanisations.*

BEFORE YOU BUY

When you buy property in Spain, you become a member of the Community of Property Owners. You should know five things about this community before you sign any purchase contract.

Ask these five questions:

1. How much will I have to pay each year in community charges?

Whether you buy an apartment, a townhouse or a detached villa, the property will have a participation share assigned to it, the cuota, which determines the amount of the yearly fees for community expenses. This can vary from as little as €50 a month in a modest apartment building up to €400 a month and even more on a luxurious urbanisation with many services to maintain.

These fees can be expected to rise with the general cost of living. The community members may have unexpected expenses, such as repairing the lift or the roof, or they may vote improvements which will add to the costs.

Keep in mind that community fees only cover the operating and maintenance of the building or estate. In addition, you will have to pay your individual annual real estate taxes and your water and electricity bills.

Ask your seller for his last paid-up community fee receipt. He is obligated by law to justify this or to declare the amount of the debt. If this is not possible, you can find out your property's share by asking the promoter of the building or the president of the community.

2. Are the community fees paid up to date?

The Horizontal Law requires the president of the community to produce a certificate stating that the property's fees are paid up, or listing the amount of the debt owed. The seller of the property should arrange for this. Formerly the buyer could be held liable only for the community fees of this year and last year but under the revised 2013 law he will have to pay the fees for the three preceding years.

The law makes the seller responsible for unpaid community fees and for concealing any hidden debt which may attach to the property.

3. Can I see the Community Statutes?

Of course you can, and you can learn many things from them about life in your new property. Remember that the regulations of the statutes will be binding on you as a member of the community. If they prohibit dogs, you will not be able to keep Rover, for example.

Many sales contracts contain a clause in which the buyer states that he accepts the statutes of the community, understands them and agrees to abide by them. Even when there is not such a reference, the buyer is legally bound when he becomes the owner of the property. He cannot refuse to join a community which legally exists.

Ask your seller, the president of the community, or the real estate promoter of a new building for a copy of the Statutes. If they are not available, it may mean problems ahead for you, which brings us to the next question.

4. Does the community legally exist?

Sometimes a community of property owners does not have a proper legal existence, even when required by law. This can occur in a new building or urbanisation when sales are not yet completed and the community has not yet been constituted and its statutes registered with the Property Registry, in the case of apartment buildings, or the Registry of Conservation Entities, in the case of an urbanisation. Yes, a properly constituted community is registered in the Property Registry. After all, it owns property, such as the garden spaces or the roads.

This legal vacuum can also occur when an established urbanisation either is illegal and unregistered or when the owners have formed their association under laws not properly designed for communities of property owners. Unless these associations of owners are registered and the new buyers agree in their contracts to abide by the statutes, their rules may not be legally enforceable. This does not mean that you don't have to pay your community charges. Spanish courts have often ruled that such associations have a de facto existence, and a right to collect the fees for the common good.

Ask to see the legal registration of the community in one of the registries listed above.

If the community does not yet exist or is not properly registered, you will sooner or later have problems to sort out, either in the formation of the community or in making it a legal body. In either case, lawyers will be involved and there will be fees to pay.

5. Is the community in debt? Check the minutes book

If the community has had to borrow money in order to pay for unexpected repairs on the building, you will assume your share of this debt when you become a member. Inform yourself in advance. You can find out this and many other things by looking at the official minutes of the last Annual General Meeting of the community, along with the accounts. Your seller should have a copy of the minutes, called the *Libro de Actas*, and the accounts. If he has not, you can obtain them from the president of the community or from the promoter of the real estate where you are purchasing.

A reading of the minutes will give you an idea of the sort of problems and expenses that arise in this particular community. It should contain a record of the voting as well, so that you can see if one individual has voted the proxies of many others, as often happens in communities where many of the owners are absent from their properties much of the time.

If the minutes show that the principal business of the last meeting was how to deal with the persistent water problems or with the backlog of unpaid fees, you will know you have trouble ahead.

These official minutes will be in Spanish, but it will be well worth your time to have at least a rough translation made. The administrator or president of the community is obliged by law to keep these records at the disposal of the members.

SEE: *For proper registration of community, Law of Horizontal Property, Articles 5 and 6, and Urban Regulations of the Land Law, Articles 25 and 26.*

For community fees, see Amendment to Article 9 of Horizontal Law. For minutes of the meeting, see Law of Horizontal Property, Article 17.

YOUR RIGHTS AND OBLIGATIONS

As a member of the community of property owners, you have the right to attend the annual general meeting, and any other meetings of the community, along with the right to be properly informed in advance of the dates and the order of business of any meeting called. If you are not correctly informed, you can protest and even have the results of the meeting annulled by a court.

At the meeting you have the right to voice your opinion, the right to vote, and to present motions for the vote of the other members.

You have the right to be elected and to hold office in the community. You may be the president, the vice-president or the secretary. You may be charged with administrating the affairs of the community.

You have the right to see all of the documentation and records of the community. The administrator or other officers are legally bound to keep these records and accounts at the disposal of the members. If they refuse to show them to you, you can obtain a court order to see the documents.

You have the right to hold and to vote proxies issued by other members who are absent from the meeting. This is common practice in communities where the foreign owners are absent much of the time. Most communities in fact have a standard proxy form on which an absent member can delegate his vote to another member. In fact, you may even give your proxy to a non-member of the community.

If you feel that a decision voted by the majority of the community is illegal or contrary to the statutes, you, acting alone, can ask the local court to rule on the matter. If you feel that the decision is legal, but seriously prejudicial to your own interests, and you can unite 25 per cent of the owners and shares, you can petition the court to have the decision annulled, or you can oblige the president to call an extraordinary general meeting. You will need skilled legal counsel for either of these actions.

You are obligated to pay the *cuotas* — community fees which have been properly voted by the members at the annual general meeting. If you do not pay, the community can claim the debt in court and even have your property sold at auction.

You are obligated to abide by the statutes of the community. If these statutes require all owners to paint their properties white and forbid owners to keep dogs, then you must paint your property white and you may not keep a dog. If you violate the statutes, the community members can vote to ask the court to issue an injunction which will forbid you from entering your property for a period of up to two years. This seldom occurs but the threat is there and it has been carried out in a few isolated cases.

Both the Law of Horizontal Property and the statutes of most communities make provision for maintaining your property in good condition so that it does not cause damage to the other owners, and permitting workmen to enter your property when it is necessary for repairs on the building.

SEE: *Law of Horizontal Property, Articles 9 and 10. For violation of statutes, Article 19.*

THE PRESIDENT

The only community officer required by law is the president. He must be elected from among the members of the community, and he can carry out all the administrative work if no other officers are elected or appointed.

The president acts as the legal representative of the community in action. He signs contracts and cheques and can bring lawsuits in the name of the community when he is authorised by the vote of the general meeting. He himself can be sued by the community if the members feel his actions have prejudiced their interests. If the community is sued, perhaps by someone who fell through a badly maintained balustrade, the president, acting through a lawyer, will be their representative in court. The president gives orders to the administrator.

The president will prepare the notices of general meetings, along with the order of business. He will see that the notices are sent out well in advance. He will oversee the preparation of the accounts of expenditures and income and he will prepare the budget for the coming year. He makes sure that the minutes of the meeting are carefully kept and notarised. He presides over the meeting and informs the absent members in writing of the decisions taken. If they do not register any protest within 30 days, their agreement to the decisions is assumed.

The president, when acting as the sole officer of the community, will oversee the management of the common elements of the property, will hear the complaints of the community members, and has full responsibility for the operation of the community, subject only to the approval of the annual general meeting.

The president is so important that the law says the community must never be without one. The usual term of office is one year, although the statutes may specify other time periods. If the community does not act to elect a new president when the time is up, the old one continues in office until a new president is elected.

Many small communities where the president is the only officer find difficulty in persuading one of the members to take on this time-consuming responsibility. In many buildings, the flat owners take it in turn each year to be the president. Under the revised 1999 law, the president can even be paid for his services.

SEE: *For duties of the president, Law of Horizontal Property, Article 13.*

THE ADMINISTRATOR

Because so many details demand the attention of the person who runs a community, most communities choose to name a professional administrator for this job. The administrator is contracted to manage the services of the community and is paid a regular fee for this service. Although many communities choose to employ a licensed *Administrador de Fincas*, or professional property administrator, or a licensed tax consultant or accountant, the community administrator need not hold any official title.

Many people think that the professional administrator is an elected officer of the community. This is not so. He is a hired professional, usually contracted for a period of one year. The community may vote to renew his contract, vary his payment, or name a new administrator at the annual general meeting. In extreme circumstances the president may terminate the services of the administrator at any time if he feels that the administrator is not carrying out the duties specified in his contract. This decision must be submitted to the general meeting for approval, but this can take place after the action.

Relations between communities and their professional administrators have caused many problems. The administrator's contract must be very carefully drafted to make sure that both parties know their rights and duties.

The administrator's duties are the normal ones of seeing to the proper management of the common elements of the community. Unless otherwise specified in the statutes of a particular community, the horizontal law says that the administrator shall prepare the budget and present it to the meeting; maintain the building; inform the owners of his activities and carry out any other function conferred by the general meeting.

Many administrators carry out the work of the community effectively and rapidly, doing their best to keep all of the owners satisfied and well informed. They charge a reasonable fee for their services and they present the community members with clear accounts each year at the general meeting. These administrators are treasures.

In other cases, members complain that the administrators do not carry out the work for which they are responsible, that they arrange community affairs to suit themselves rather than the members, and that their accounts are vague and confusing. This leads the members to worry about where the money has gone. These administrators should be replaced.

Replacing the administrator, like electing the president, is an important step and will require the majority vote of the community members. This brings us to the annual general meeting, discussed below.

SEE: *For duties of the Administrator, Law of Horizontal Property, Article 20.*

ANNUAL GENERAL MEETING

The annual general meeting is the maximum authority of the community of property owners, who are required by law to meet at least once each year to elect a president, discuss issues affecting the community, to examine and approve the accounts of expenditures of the previous year. They must decide upon the budget - and the fees each member will pay - for the coming year.

The minutes book (*libro de actas*), which records details of the meeting and voting, is an official legal document which can be used in Spanish court proceedings. It must be stamped as authentic by a notary or a judge. This book establishes the right of the community president in court to bring a lawsuit against a community member who has not paid his fees, the cuotas. It should record the names of members who voted in favour of a measure, either in person or by proxy, and the names of those who voted against each measure. This listing is often ignored in practice but communities should take the trouble to do it.

The record of votes becomes important when a minority of community members wish to bring a legal protest against the decision of the majority, claiming that their interests have been seriously damaged, even though the majority vote was otherwise quite in order. In a court case, the dissenting minority must bring action against the majority. So the minutes book, as a legal document, establishes the names of those who voted on either side. The book is evidence in court, and decisions made by the community are serious matters.

Before you attend your first meeting, you should try to meet the president and the administrator of your community, as well as other members, to get an idea of the problems facing the community. If you already have a motion that you want passed by community vote, you must request in writing that the motion be placed on the official agenda of the meeting. You can also begin to assemble the proxy votes of members who support your position and who will be absent from the meeting. This proxy can be a simple written authorisation that enables you to cast the vote of the absentee.

You must be notified at least eight days in advance of the meeting's date, time and place. You should also receive a written agenda, the order of business to be transacted. This agenda is very important because the members can only vote on proposals listed on it. The members can bring up any new business they wish at the meeting, but only for discussion. The idea is that the members should have advance notice and time to consider any new proposal.

At the meeting, you will register your attendance, and any proxies you will vote, with the secretary or keeper of the minutes book. The president will preside over the meeting. The first item will be the reading and voting to approve the minutes of the previous meeting. If the minutes do not meet with your approval, either because they are false or incomplete, you can vote against accepting them. Your protest will be registered in the book and can serve as evidence in court if you wish to make a claim.

The accounts of the previous year's income and expenditures will then be presented for the members' approval. You should have received your copy of these accounts before the meeting. Sometimes they are perfectly clear and other times they are quite incomprehensible. Ask the president, administrator or treasurer to explain any points not clear to you.

Then discussion will start on proposed plans and expenses for the coming year. Many issues can arise. Perhaps one group wishes to paint the building or to install a swimming pool, but others protest that this will raise the fees too high.

Tempers can run high at community meetings. They often degenerate into multilingual shouting matches when not properly managed. Even in the best of circumstances, meetings tend to be longwinded, as different members insist on discussing minor details. One community I know voted unanimously to limit each member's speaking time to five minutes, and to limit each member to two speeches.

When it is time to vote, you will vote according to your *cuota*, or community share. This *cuota*, based on the size of your property, determines both your share of community fees and the weight of your vote. Usually, the majority of members is also the majority of the *cuotas*, but sometimes a few members with large properties can dominate the workings of a community. This can happen on an urbanisation where the developer still controls the votes of the unsold parcels of land and runs the community to suit himself.

The votes of the members will be recorded in the minutes book and action will be taken accordingly. A new president will be elected by majority vote and the building will be painted or not, according to the majority decision. There is always the possibility of protest, remember, when a minority of members feel they have been mistreated by the majority.

If a decision requires a unanimous vote, such as a change in the statutes or a construction project which will alter the participation shares of the community members, this unanimity can be achieved by informing any absent members of the decision. If they do not respond negatively within one month the motion is considered as passed unanimously.

One recent amendment to the horizontal law provides that the installation of ramps and other facilities for the handicapped requires only a three-fifths majority, even when such an alteration of the building would normally need a unanimous vote. This does not exactly give the handicapped a free rein, but it does improve their negotiating position. The new law came from a court case in which one person in a building had blocked the installation of ramps. This was perfectly legal although not very nice, and the Spanish Congress voted, in July 1990, to amend the law.

Finally the meeting will be adjourned, with some members pleased and others not pleased at all. This is truly democracy in action, with all its advantages and disadvantages.

When people are unhappy with their community, they refer to it as "they." The community is never "they". It is always "we".

SEE: *For proxy votes, Law of Horizontal Property, Article 15, for annual general meeting, Article 14, For Minutes Book, Article 19.*

The Law of Horizontal Property In English

Horizontal Law Revised 2013

New Text of Law 49/1960 of July 21, as amended by Law 8/1999 of April 6, published in the Official State Bulletin April 8, 1999, and modified by Law 51/2003 of Equality of Opportunities, and modified by Law 8/2013, of June 26, of Urban Rehabilitation, Regeneration and Renovation, published in the Official State Bulletin Number 153 of June 27, 2013, article one of the First Final Dispostion.

CHAPTER I: GENERAL DISPOSITIONS

Article 1

The purpose of the present Law is the regulation of the special form of property ownership set out in Article 396 of the Civil Code, called horizontal property.

For the purposes of this Law, any part of a building which may be subject to independent use by virtue of an entrance either to the public thoroughfare or to a common area of the building itself shall be considered as "premises".

Article 2

This Law shall apply to:

a) Communities of Owners constituted under the provisions of Article 5.

b) Communities which fulfil the requirements established in Article 396 but which have not filed their charter or constitution as horizontal property. These communities shall be governed, in any case, by the dispositions of this Law in matters regarding the legal framework of ownership of the property, of its individual parts and of its common elements, as well as matters referring to the reciprocal rights and obligations of the community members.

c) Private real estate complexes (urbanisations or estates), in the terms

established in this Law.
d) Subcommunities, by which is meant, as disposed in the basic charter, that various owners, as a Community and for their exclusive use and enjoyment, dispose of certain common elements and services which have their own unity and a functional and economic independence.
e) Urbanistic conservation entities, in such cases where their Statutes so dispose.

What it means

The 1999 law allowed urbanisations, or private housing estates, to be governed by the Horizontal Law, even if they never registered their statutes or constituted themselves legally as communities. If they meet the terms of Article 396 of the Civil Code, which basically means that the community shares some common elements, they can obtain the full force of the law in compelling the payment of debts and enforcing their rules.

Formerly, the only way for such non-registered urbanisations to obtain full legal status was through the complicated process of creating a Collaborating Urbanistic Entity. This still is necessary in some cases but the revised law now permits most urbanisations to function as real communities.

The 2013 revisions remove the need for unanimous vote in order to facilitate works that improve the accessibility or energy efficiency of the building.

CHAPTER II: REGARDING THE SYSTEM OF OWNERSHIP BY FLATS OR BUSINESS PREMISES.

Article 3

In the system of ownership set forth in Article 396 of the Civil Code, the owner of each flat or business premises shall have:
a) The unique and exclusive ownership rights over an adequately delimited area subject to independent usage, along with the architectural features and all types of installations, apparent or not, which may be included within its boundaries and which serve the owner exclusively, as well as any ancillary property expressly mentioned in the property deed, even when they are located outside the delimited area.

b) Co-ownership, with the other owners of flats and premises, of the remaining common areas, appurtenances and services.
To each flat or commercial premises there will be assigned a share of participation (cuota) relative to the total value of the property, expressed as a percentage of it. Said share (cuota) will serve as a basis to determine participation in the expenses and earnings of the community. The improvements or deterioration of each flat or premises will not alter the assigned share, which can only be changed under the terms established in Articles 10 and 17 of this law.
Each owner may freely dispose of his property right, but he may not separate the elements composing it and any transmission of the property right shall not affect the obligations arising from this system of property ownership.

What it means

The provisions of Article 3 are quite clear, setting out the terms of separate individual ownership of flats and the joint ownership of the common elements of the building. In paragraph A, the reference to "ancillary properties" means such things as garages or storage space in the basement which go with each apartment.

The final section of paragraph B establishes the principle that an owner may not subdivide his property. Later we shall see that he can indeed divide his property into smaller units, but this requires the consent of the community, as it will affect the participation shares.

Article 4

The action of division shall not proceed to terminate the situation regulated by this Law. It can only be effected by each co-owner in regard to one flat or premises, is limited to that property, and providing that the joint ownership has not been established intentionally for the common service or use of all the owners.

What it means

Article 4 makes it clear that any further action of subdivision of the property will not affect the scheme of Horizontal Property regulating the building in general. The last line means, for example, that a gardener who is given a flat in the building for his own use may not subdivide it. This action of division usually occurs when a property is inherited by several owners.

Article 5

The charter of constitution of the condominium (ownership by flats or premises) will describe, besides the property as a whole, each one of those units to which a correlative number is assigned. The description of the overall property must express the details required by the mortgage legislation and the services and installations belonging to it. The description of each flat or premises will express its area, boundaries, the floor on which it is located, and any ancillary properties such as garage, attic or basement.

This same charter shall determine the share of participation that pertains to each flat or premises, to be set by the sole owner of the building at the beginning of its sale by flats, by the agreement of all existing owners, by arbitration, or by court order. For this determination, the useful surface area of each flat or premises relative to the total area of the building, its exterior or interior emplacement, its situation, and the use it can reasonably be assumed to make of the common services and installations shall be taken as a basis.

The charter may also contain regulations for the establishment and exercise of this property right and other dispositions not prohibited by law relating to the use and purpose of the building, its various flats or premises, installations and services, expenses, administration and management, insurance, maintenance and repairs, forming private statutes which shall not prejudice third parties if they have not been registered in the Registry of Property.

In any modification of the property title and apart from what is disposed regarding the validity of community decisions, the same requirements shall be applied as for the charter of constitution.

What it means

In Article 5 we find several important points about the constitution of the community of owners. In the first paragraph the method of describing the property is set out. In the second paragraph, we find that each owner's *cuota*, or participation share, is fixed when the community is legally constituted and registered. Afterwards it can only be changed by unanimous vote of all members.

This paragraph also notes that the use each property makes of the common services shall be taken into account when setting the *cuotas*. This provision allows variation between flats and commercial premises, for example. Sometimes commercial premises pay a cuota per square metre higher than that of flats, on the grounds that the people they attract make extra use of common elements. In one case, the promoter of the building (who can set the *cuotas* when the flats are first sold) provided in the statutes of the community that the commercial premises would pay no *cuotas* at all until they were sold. This is because the flats always sell first and the commercial premises sometimes remain vacant for a year, or even more. By this means the promoter avoided paying any *cuotas* on his unsold business premises, and the community of owners had a lower income than they otherwise would expect.

This provision in the statutes — written by the promoter — is perfectly legal, even if unfair to the other new flat-buyers, and is only one of the little tricks available to the promoter when he constitutes the community. It is always wise to read the statutes of the building or urbanisation where you are going to purchase.

In the case of the community cited above, the flat owners were preparing to vote against the promoter's rule in the statutes, charging that their interests were prejudiced by it.

Article 5 continues to note that the private statutes of the community will not be binding unless they are registered in the Registry of Property as part of the registration of the building itself

It is perfectly possible for a community to exist without private statutes, which means that it will be regulated only by the terms set out here in the Horizontal Property Law. These regulations are sufficient for the orderly government of the community, but most buildings also require some special statutes to suit their individual circumstances.

Article 6

In order to regulate the details of their co-existence and the proper usage of the services and common elements and within the limits established by the Law and the statutes, the body of proprietors shall be able to make internal rules binding on all owners unless they are modified in the manner set forth for making decisions regarding administration.

What it means

Article 6 is clear in itself. It allows the members of the community to make internal rules by majority vote. This would include matters such as the banning of pets or a requirement to make all awnings the same colour. This is the Horizontal Law for flats. In most urbanisations, such internal rules may only be enforceable when the new purchasers have specifically agreed to accept the statutes in their purchase contract.

However, as we shall see, the revised 1999 law allows urbanisations to register their communities under the terms of the Horizontal Law, making their rules binding on the members.

Article 7

1. *The owner of each flat or business premises may modify the architectural features, installations and services of the flat, so long as it does not diminish or alter the safety of the building, its general structure, its form or its exterior condition nor prejudice the rights of another owner, reporting such alterations beforehand to the representative of the community.*

In the rest of the building he may not make any alteration whatsoever and if he observes the need for any urgent repairs, he should communicate this to the administrator without delay.

2. *The owner and the occupant of the flat or business premises are forbidden to carry on in the flat or in the rest of the building any activities which are not permitted in the statutes, which damage the property, or which violate laws regulating activities that are a nuisance, unhealthy, noxious, dangerous, or illegal.*

The President of the community, either on his own initiative, or at the request of any of the owners or occupants, shall require the immediate ceasing of any of the activities prohibited in this section, under warning of appropriate legal action.

If the offender persists in his conduct, the President, upon authorisation by the General Assembly, duly convened for this purpose, can seek a court injunction against him, which, where not expressly provided in this section, shall proceed according to the "Ordinary Judgement" regulations.

Once the action is brought, along with the accreditation of formal notification to the offender and the certification of the resolution voted by the General Assembly, the court, as a precautionary measure, may order the

immediate ceasing of the prohibited activity, warning that non-compliance will constitute contempt of court. The court may likewise order as many such immediate measures as deemed necessary to ensure the effectiveness of the cease and desist order. The action must be brought against the owner of the property or, in such case, against the occupant.
If the sentence is in favour of the plaintiff, the court may order, as well as the final ending of the prohibited activity and the awarding of damages involved, the deprival of the defendant's right to use the flat or premises for a period not to exceed three years, depending on the seriousness of the violation and the damages caused to the community. If the offender is not the owner, the sentence can terminate all the offender's rights over the flat or premises as well as order his immediate eviction.

What it means

Paragraph 2 of Article 7 sets forth the manner in which the community can protect itself from truly antisocial elements in its midst.

If one of the owners or his tenants is brewing poisons in his kitchen, with nasty fumes in the air vents, or if they insist on making loud noises all night long, or if they scatter garbage through the halls, the community can go to court against them and obtain an injunction order to cease the offending activity.

The community can also seek cash damages for the problems and suffering involved.

If the offender does not obey the order, he can be considered as in contempt of court, and ordered to leave the property for up to three years.

If he is a tenant, he can be evicted immediately, as well as losing any contractual rights he has over the property.

Included in the list of banned activities are those forbidden by the statutes. Thus, dogs may be prohibited, for example, and owners must abide by this.

If an owner ignores the statutory prohibition, the community, by majority vote, may take legal action against him. Article 7 also limits the owner's right to alter his property to interior elements only, and only when it does not threaten the structural soundness of the building or alter its appearance. One problem that arises here is the closing-in of the terraces. Because the enclosure of the terrace with glass panels alters the exterior form of the building and would change the pattern of participation shares because of the greater enclosed area, it is strictly prohibited by this article.

So, when an owner goes to the community president and asks for permission to glass in his terrace, this must be denied. As you may notice, however, about 75 per cent of all the terraces in Spain have been glassed in. You guessed it. None of these owners asked anyone's permission. They just went ahead and did it. If neither the community nor the town hall presents any complaint, the terrace remains enclosed. The possibility of protest does exist, however.

ARTICLE 8 IS ABOLISHED

Article 9

The obligations of each owner shall be:

***a)** To respect the general installations of the community and any other common elements, whether for general or private use by any of the owners, whether or not they are included in his unit, making appropriate use of them and avoiding any damage or deterioration at all times.*

***b)** To maintain his own flat and private installations in a good state of order in conditions that do not prejudice the community or the other owners, making good any damages caused by his lack of care or that of any persons for whom he is responsible.*

***c)** To permit in his flat or premises the repairs required for the service of the building and to permit in his flat the necessary rights of passage required for works or the creation of common services of general interest, carried out or agreed according to the terms of this law, having the right to be indemnified by the community for any damage and prejudice caused.*

***d)** To allow entry into his flat for the purposes stated in the three preceding paragraphs.*

***e)** To contribute, according to the participation share(cuota) determined in his property title or according to any system especially established, to the general expenses for the proper upkeep of the building, its services, taxes, charges and responsibilities that are not subject to individual allocation. Amounts due to the community deriving from the obligation to contribute to the payment of the general expenses which correspond to the fees assessed for the period up to date of the current year and for the previous three* *years shall be deemed preferential debts under the terms of Article 1923 of the Civil Code and take preference for their settlement over those listed in paragraphs 3, 4, and 5 of that law without prejudice to the preference in favour of salary debts established in the revised text of the Workers' Law, approved by Legislative Royal Decree 1/1995 of March 24.*

Any person acquiring a dwelling unit or commercial premises in the system of horizontal property, even with a title inscribed in the Property Registry, is held responsible, with the acquired property as guaranty, for the amounts owed by previous owners to the community for the payment of general expenses up to the limit of fees charged for the period to date of the year in which the acquisition took place and for the preceding three natural years. The property itself is legally encumbered for the fulfilment of this obligation.

In the public contract or deed of sale by which the property is transferred in any way, the seller must declare that he is up to date with payment for general expenses of the community, or he must list what he owes. The seller must present certification of the state of his balance with the community, coinciding with this declaration, without which no public title can be authorised, unless the buyer should expressly waive the seller from this obligation. This certification shall be issued in a maximum of seven days from the request by the person acting as Secretary of the Community, with the authorisation of the President. In the case of fault or negligence, they shall be held liable for the accuracy of the information and for damages caused by delay in its issue.

***f)** To contribute, according to their respective participation shares (cuotas), to the reserve fund which shall exist in the community for the maintenance and repair of the property and, when necessary, for works of rehabilitation. The reserve fund, which is held by the community to all effects, shall be supplied with an amount that in no case shall be less than five per cent of the last ordinary budget.*

The community may use the reserve fund to take out an insurance policy covering damages to the property or to undertake a permanent maintenance contract for the building and its general installations.

***g)** To observe due care in the use of the property and in their relations with the other owners and to be responsible to them for any infractions committed or damages caused.*

***h)** To notify the person acting as Community Secretary, by any means which allows evidence of service, of their domicile in Spain for the* *purpose of receiving citations and notifications of any sort related to the Community. In the absence of this notification, the flat or premises in the Community shall be considered the domicile for receiving communications from the Community, and delivery to its occupant shall constitute full legal notification.*

Should notification to the owner prove impossible at the place indicated in the previous paragraph, it shall be deemed to have taken place if the notice is posted on the notice board of the community, or in a visible place set aside for this purpose, indicating the date and the reasons for which this form of notification has been employed, signed by the person acting as Community Secretary and endorsed by the President. Notice served in this way shall produce full legal effect in three days.

i) *To notify the person acting as Secretary of the Community, by any means providing certification of delivery, of any change in ownership of the unit. Any owner who fails to comply with this obligation will be held liable to the Community jointly with the new owner for debts incurred after the transfer, without prejudicing his right to claim repayment from the new owner. These terms shall not apply when any of the governing bodies of the community established in Article 13 have been notified of the change of owners by any other means or by definite actions of the new owner or when the transfer is publicly known.*

2. *For the application of the preceding regulations, expenses will be deemed as general when they are not imputable to one or several flats, nor shall the non-usage of a service bring exemption from the fulfilment of the corresponding obligations, subject to the terms of Article 17.4 of this Law.*

What it means

The first paragraphs of this article set out owners' obligations clearly enough.

Paragraph E tells us that the new buyer in a community is held responsible for the community fees of this year and the three preceding years, with the property itself acting as the final guaranty for payment. The previous law made the new buyer responsible for only one year's back charges. When you buy, you want to be sure the fees are paid up, or you will have to pay them.

This paragraph also tells us that the seller is obliged to present certification of payment up to date or the amount of his debt at the time of signing the contract, which means at the Spanish Notary's office. The president of the community must vouch for this certification.

Further, without the certification of payment or debt, the notary will not stamp the contract of sale, unless the buyer specifically waives the requirement.

Paragraph F provides for the establishment of a reserve fund in all communities, which must be at least 5 per cent of the normal operating budget, and sets out the obligation of each owner to contribute to this fund. The fund can be used for an insurance policy or a maintenance contract, thus protecting the installations.

Paragraph H requires every member to notify the community of the address in Spain where he wishes to receive any legal notices. One way to do this is to use the Burofax system of the Spanish postal service. They will certify both the content of the message and its delivery. Lacking an address, the community can notify the owner at the property itself, and, if for some reason this cannot be done, simply posting the notice on the notice board will take full legal effect within three days.

This is a big change from previous practice, which made the notification so complicated that communities just gave up trying. The procedure used to be so difficult and time-consuming that it was hardly worthwhile in most cases. The community had to prove that the defaulter had received in a certified manner each of the unpaid bills, and that he had been informed of the debt and had acknowledged receipt, and every stage of the process was complex.

The last paragraph of this article settles another common dispute. Sometimes an owner will declare that, because he does not use the swimming pool, which he voted against in the meeting, he will not pay this portion of his community charges. This line says he is obliged to pay, abiding by the majority decision.

Even so, in many communities, the members will vote to exempt non-users from the payment for a particular amenity.

The final paragraph refers to Article 17.4, which sets out who has to pay for what in more detailed terms.

Article 10

1. *The following actions shall be obligatory and shall not require the previous agreement by vote of the General Meeting, whether or not they involve the modification of the basic constitution or the Statutes, and they are imposed by organs of Public Administration or requested by the owners:*
a) *Works and actions necessary for the proper upkeep and fulfilment of the duty of maintenance of the building and its common services and installations, including in all cases those necessary to satisfy the basic requirements of safety, habitability, and universal accessibility, as well as the condition of the ornamentation and any others derived from the imposition by the Public Administration of the legal duty of maintenance.*
b) *Works and actions necessary to guarantee reasonable adjustments with regard to universal accessibility and in any case those required at the instance of the owners in whose dwellings or commercial premises handicapped persons or persons over seventy years old live, work or voluntarily lend their services, with the purpose of assuring to them a usage adequate to their needs of the common elements, such as ramps, elevators or other mechanical or electronic devices which improve the orientation or access to the exterior, given always that the annual cost of these works, after any public grants or subsidies are discounted, does not exceed the amount of twelve ordinary monthly payments towards the general expenses. If the remainder of the cost, beyond the above-cited monthly amounts, is assumed by the owners who have requested the works, this fact does not eliminate the obligatory nature of the works.*
c) *The occupation of common elements of the building or the private real estate complex during the time it takes to carry out the actions described in the preceding paragraphs.*
d) *The construction of new works and any other alteration of the structure or fabric of the building or the common elements, as well as the constitution of a real estate complex, as set out in Article 17.4 of the revised text of the Land Law, approved by Royal Legislative Decree 2/2008 of June 20, which are required as a result of the inclusion of the building within the scope of an action of urban rehabilitation or regeneration and renovation.*
e) *The acts of material division of flats or premises and their annexes to form other, smaller independent units, an increase in size by aggregating bordering units in the same building, or a decrease in size by segregating a part of the unit, at the desire and instance of their owners, when such actions are possible as a result of the inclusion of the building within the*

scope of an action of rehabilitation or urban regeneration and renovation.
2. *Taking into account the necessary or obligatory nature of the actions referred to in paragraphs a) to d) of the preceding article, the following shall proceed:*
a) *The works shall be paid by the owners of the Community or group of Communities and the decision of the AGM shall be limited to the distribution of the pertinent expense and the determination of the terms of payment.*
b) *Owners who oppose or unjustifiably delay the execution of orders issued by the competent authority shall be held liable individually for any fines or penalties imposed by the administration.*
c) *The flats or premises shall be liable to pay the costs deriving from the execution of such works or actions under the same terms and conditions as those set out in Article 9 for the general expenses.*
3. *In all cases, administrative authorisation shall be required:*
a) *For the constitution and modification of the real estate complex referred to in Article 17.6 of the revised text of the Land Law, approved by Royal Legislative Decree 2/2008 of June 20, under the same terms.*
b) *When, the material division of the flats or premises and their annexes to form other smaller independent units, the increase of surface area by aggregating other bordering properties of the same building or the reduction of the unit by segregating some part of it; new construction and any other alteration of the structure or fabric of the building, including the enclosure of terraces and the modification of the exterior covering of the building in order to improve energy efficiency, or of the common elements when they meet the requisites set out in Article 17.6 of the revised text of the Land Law, approved by Royal Legislative Decree 2/2008 of June 20, when it has been requested after approval by three fifths of the owners who in turn represent three fifths of the participation shares.*
In these instances the consent of the affected owners shall be registered and the General Assembly of Proprietors, by common agreement with these owners and by a majority vote of three fifths shall determine the indemnity payments that apply for damage and prejudice. Setting the new participation shares, as well as the determination of the nature of the works to be carried out shall require, in the case of any disagreement, the timely approval of the General Assembly, by the same majority. With regard to this situation the interested parties may request arbitration or a technical report under the terms established in the Law.

What it means

Article 10 requires the Community, as owner of the building and installations, to maintain them in a safe and useable condition. The Community may also be required by law to ensure accessibility for handicapped or elderly persons. The big change here for 2013 is that, when a person over 70 or who is handicapped requests an improvement, the Community must react and no vote of the AGM is required. If the improvement is ordered by public authority, then a unanimous vote of the Community is not required. In fact, the approval of the AGM is not necessary at all when the works are ordered because the Community is included in a rehabilitation and regeneration plan ordered by the government. When the Article refers to "public authority", it means that a Town Hall, for example, can order the Community to make repairs that are necessary for the public safety or improved accessibility. If part of the building collapses due to lack of maintenance, the Community will be held liable. Even one member of the Community can go to court and seek an order to compel the Community to make necessary repairs. See next Article for more details.

ARTICLE 11 IS ABOLISHED

ARTICLE 12 IS ABOLISHED

Article 13

1. *The governing bodies of the Community shall be the following:*

a) The General Assembly of owners.

b) The President and, when applicable, the Vice-Presidents

c) The Secretary

d) The Administrator

The Statutes or a majority vote by the General Assembly may establish other governing bodies for the Community but these may not detract from the functions and responsibilities with regard to third parties which this Law confers on those mentioned above.

2. *The President shall be chosen from among the owners in the Community by election or by turns in rotation or by drawing lots. Acceptance shall be compulsory, although the designated owner may request the Court to relieve him of the office, within one month of taking office, citing his reasons*

for it. The Court, following the procedure established in Article 17.3, will rule on the matter, designating in the same ruling which of the owners will substitute for the President in the office, until a new President is chosen in a time set by the Judge.
Likewise, the Court may be approached when it has proved impossible for the Assembly to choose a President for some reason.
3. *The President legally represents the Community both in and out of court and in all matters affecting it.*
4. *The existence of Vice-Presidents is voluntary. They shall be chosen by the same procedure established for the designation of the President. The Vice-President or Vice-Presidents in the order prescribed, shall replace the President in cases of absence, vacancy or incapacity and assist him in carrying out his duties according to the terms established by the General Assembly.*
5. *The functions of secretary and administrator shall be carried out by the President of the Community, except when the Statutes or the General Assembly, by majority vote, provide that such office be held separately from the presidency.*
6. *The posts of Secretary and Administrator may be vested in the same person or separately chosen.*
The posts of administrator or secretary-administrator may be held by any owner or by individuals with sufficient professional qualifications or legally licensed to carry out such functions. The post can also go to a company or other corporate entity in the terms set out by law.
7. *Unless otherwise provided by Community Statutes, the term of office of all governing bodies will be for one year.*
The persons designated to can be removed from their offices before the expiry of their terms by a resolution of the General Assembly, convoked for an extraordinary meeting.
8. *When the number of owners in the community is no more than four, they can govern themselves by the administrative system of Article 398 of the Civil Code, if their Statutes expressly establish this.*

What it means

Article 13 states that the president must be a member of the community. A simple majority vote in the annual general meeting suffices to elect him, and a simple majority vote can put him out, along with any other officer of the community.

There is nothing in the rule book that says the president must speak Spanish, or be Spanish, or even an official full-time resident of Spain. It would be difficult for an absentee president to serve his community well, of course, but the only requirement is that the president be a member of the community.

By law, the president is the only officer that a community must elect. He can combine in himself the duties of the secretary, treasurer and administrator, and in many smaller communities this is the case. In larger blocks — sometimes numbering more than 100 members — communities may elect a vice-president to stand in for the president when he is absent, a secretary to keep the official minutes book of the meetings, a treasurer to take charge of the funds, and appoint a professional administrator to handle the maintenance of the property. The professional administrator, paid for his services, may not in principle be a member of the community as this would be an obvious conflict of interests.

The community can see that the president's expenses are covered and they can even pay him a wage if they choose.

The president's responsibilities include:

Convening the annual general meeting, giving reasonable advance notice, along with the order of business. Any owner who was not properly notified of the meeting can later protest and have the results of the meeting annulled by a judge.

Presiding over the general meeting, seeing that the order of business is followed and making sure that each person gets a fair hearing. This can be a very arduous task.

Representing the community in its relations with the individual members. That is, if you have a complaint about water dripping from the terrace of your upstairs neighbour, you take this complaint to the president.

Representing the community to all third parties, which would include the company contracted to paint the building. It is the president who signs the contract in the name of the community.

Carrying out any legal action for which he has been authorised by the majority vote of the owners assembled in the general meeting.

It is a serious matter to be president of a legally-registered community of property owners. The president cannot simply resign his office, for example, if things do not go well. He officially holds the post until a new president is elected. This is because the community can never be without a legal representative. So, if the president wants out, he must convene an extraordinary general meeting for the election of his successor or petition the court to relieve him.

Further, if the community members feel that the president, through negligence or error, has seriously damaged their interests, they can bring suit against him for monetary damages.

Normally the president is elected for one year, unless the community statutes specify a longer term of office. At the end of this year, his mandate will continue unless the general meeting votes to replace him. So it is perfectly possible for a president to continue in office year after year without any new elections.

If any member of the community wants to contest this continuance, he can either ask for an election notice to be included in the agenda of the meeting, or he can call for elections in the meeting itself. Remember that the annual general meeting is the supreme authority of the community. It can, by majority vote, elect a new president whenever it desires to do so. The normal procedure would be to convoke an extraordinary general meeting for this purpose. Remember also that, whenever 25 per cent of the members agree, they can call for such an extraordinary general meeting.

This unpaid job of president is often so unrewarding that, in some buildings, rather than actually hold elections, the community members agree to take the post in turns, with a different member taking up the task each year. When your turn comes, you are unanimously "elected" and this is shown in the minutes book.

If the community chooses to contract a paid professional administrator, the president can hire and fire this administrator, subject always to the specific contract made, giving account later to the community.

Sometimes community presidents act in a high-handed manner, spending the funds incorrectly and favouring one group of owners over another. This might happen when one member controls many votes. Far more often the president is a civic-minded spirit who is willing to take his turn at handling the problems which arise in any community, only to discover that his co-owners find fault with every decision he makes and are utterly ungrateful for his efforts to help the common good. So he is vastly relieved when his term of office ends and he absolutely refuses to be elected again.

If the community chooses to name a secretary, his function will be the normal work of a secretary in any organisation: to send or deliver the notices of meetings; to take the minutes of the meeting and see that they are recorded in the official minutes book, which is stamped by the Notary; to keep the records, correspondence and documents of the community and to show these to any member who wishes to inspect them, and to send out notification of the decisions taken in the annual general meeting to any absent members. This is obligatory. Members who were absent from any meeting must be reliably informed of any decisions taken at that meeting. They then have 30 days starting from the date they received the notification, in which to make a protest if they are opposed to the decision. If they do not make a written protest, they are considered as accepting any action taken by the meeting. If the meeting has adopted a measure needed unanimous approval, the non-reply of the absentees is included as approval, thus making the vote "unanimous".

Although the law of horizontal property does not require a vice-president or a treasurer, the community statutes can provide for the election of these officers, or the members may vote at the annual general meeting to create the offices and elect members to carry them out. The treasurer would prepare the proposed budget of expenses for the forthcoming year for the approval of the meeting; would collect and keep the funds of the community; would be responsible for the accounts, and make payments and prepare the yearly accounting for the members' approval. He might also order an independent auditing of the accounts, especially if the community is a large one with important sums of money coming in and going out.

An important point to note about a possible vice-president in a community is that this office must be specifically mentioned, with its powers, in the statutes or in the official minutes book of the community. If not, the vice-president will not be empowered to use the faculties of the president in his absence. He will not be able to sign cheques, represent the community or take legal action.

Article 13 closes with a mention of Article 398 of the Civil Code, which provides a much simpler legal framework for organizing the affairs of communities with four or fewer members.

Article 14

The functions of the Annual General Meeting are:
a) *To appoint and to remove the persons who hold the official posts mentioned in the preceding article and to settle any complaints which the property owners may bring against their actions.*
b) *To approve the budget of foreseeable expenses and income and the pertinent accounts.*
c) *To approve bids and the carrying out of all repair work on the property, whether ordinary or extraordinary, and to be informed of any urgent measures taken by the Administrator in accordance with the terms of Article 20, paragraph C.*
d) *To approve or change the statutes and to make bylaws for internal management.*
e) *To be informed and to decide on the other matters of general interest to the community, taking any necessary or advisable measures for the best common service.*

What it means

Article 14 states the basic functions of the annual general meeting. The general meeting, ordinary or extraordinary, is the supreme authority of the community. Its decisions, either by majority vote or unanimous vote when necessary, are binding on all officers and members of the community.

Majority vote will elect the officers and also put them out if necessary. If the members are unhappy with the president, for example, they themselves can convoke an extraordinary general meeting, and vote him out. If they have contracted a professional administrator for one year, they can vote at the meeting not to renew his contract.

The meeting will hear the budget of expenses prepared for the coming year. They must approve the expenses or the officials will not be empowered to spend the money. It is here that the fighting often starts. Does the community need a full-time gardener? Should they paint the building or let it go another year? Each point of view will have its backers. They present their opposing arguments, a vote is called, and majority rules. If a dissenter feels his own private interests are seriously damaged by a decision of the majority, he has the power to protest before a court.

The community must also approve the accounts presented for the preceding year. Here again there are often many protests, as some presidents and even some professional administrators often fail to keep adequate records. This is sometimes due to concealment of payments to the administrator but more often results from careless bookkeeping. Many larger communities are beginning to require an independent audit of the accounts as a regular yearly practice.

The third item of the functions of the annual general meeting is probably the one that causes most fireworks: the execution of extraordinary works and the necessary funding. In every community there is someone who wants a swimming pool, or a new lighting system, or satellite television. And in every community there is someone who does not want these things and says he will refuse to pay for them.

Remember that a dissenter can refuse to pay — legally — if the improvement is not "necessary" and if his share of it comes to more than a three months' *cuota*.

The annual general meeting has the power to change the statutes, but only by unanimous vote, and to make internal regulations. These would include things like the prohibition of pets in the building, for example, or the denial of permission to hang out laundry on the roof terrace.

Of course the members must have information in order to decide matters of general interest to the community, as noted in the final section. This means that the administrator and president must present complete information to the meeting. It is their legal obligation to allow community members to examine the community's accounts and documents.

Paragraph C makes special mention of the assembly's right to be informed by the administrator of any urgent measures he has taken. Administrators sometimes treat communities as their own property and fail to keep the members well informed of their actions.

Article 15

1. *Attendance at the general meeting of owners shall be in person or by legal or voluntary representation, a written authorisation signed by the owner being sufficient to accredit this representation.*

If a flat belongs jointly to several owners, these shall name one representative to attend and to vote in the meetings.

If the flat is held in usufruct, the attendance and the vote belong to the original owner who, except for his manifestation to the contrary, shall be held to be represented by the holder of the usufruct, this representation requiring to be specifically expressed when the vote is on the matters referred to in the First paragraph of Article 17 or on extraordinary works or improvements.

2. *Owners who at the time of the Assembly are not current in the payment of all their debts owed to the Community, and who have not legally challenged these debts or deposited the amount of them in court shall be allowed to take part in discussion but shall not have the right to vote. The minutes of the meeting will show the names of the owners deprived of their voting rights and neither the person nor the participation share shall be computed when calculating the majorities required by this Law.*

What it means

The first paragraph of Article 15 makes provision for the representation of a community member by proxy if he cannot attend in person.

A simple "written authorisation" is sufficient to establish this proxy legally. There is no specific form required. All it need say is that you authorise such-and-such a person to vote in your name at the meeting of the community on such-and-such a day, and it should include the phrase "any postponement of that meeting". This is because very often the community does not have a full quorum when the meeting is first called and so it will be held on the 'second convocation", usually specified as half an hour later.

This sort of open proxy can be dangerous if you do not fully trust the person exercising it. He can vote against your best interests if he chooses. You can also make a specific and detailed proxy, which authorises its holder to cast your vote only in certain ways. That is, the proxy can declare that its holder must vote "yes" on items three and five of the meeting agenda and can vote "no" on items one and four, and that he must abstain from voting on the other issues. The secretary of the meeting will ask to see the proxy forms when he registers each member's attendance at the meeting, so he will know this.

Most communities have proxy forms already printed and available from the secretary, but they are the open sort, so you must make your own if you want to be specific. There is no provision for absentee voting by post.

The holder and voter of your proxy does not have to be a community member. He can be anyone you choose to name.

Proxies have caused many problems in communities. Foreign owners absent from Spain tend to give their proxy to some influential person in the community. This person is often the developer of the building, who still has unsold units, and so is a member of the community. He votes the shares of the unsold flats still in his name, along with the proxies he has been given, and can often control the operations of the community in this way. Or it may be the president who keeps himself in office with these proxies. In one case, it was the representative of a rental agency which owned some flats in a building and managed others. With the proxies the agency controlled, they ran the building to suit the renters and to the disadvantage of the permanent residents. So there are many tricks available with proxies.

Article 15 also refers to flats held in usufruct. This means that the owner has granted the right to occupy the flat to another person, as sometimes happens when the property is held in the name of a son or daughter. The son or daughter, by a legal document, grants to the parent the lifetime right, the usufruct, to inhabit the property. This is sometimes done in order to skip over one generation of inheritance taxes. When the parent dies, the son or daughter simply takes possession of the property which has always been his. The holder of this usufruct is considered the owner's representative at the community meeting for all normal matters. If, however, the community is voting to change its statutes or to authorise extraordinary works, then the holder of the usufruct will need a specific written authorisation from the owner of record.

Paragraph 2 of the article contains the real change in the revised law. For the first time, community debtors are both deprived of the right to vote and are listed for all to see. Unless these debtors have impugned the court decision against them and deposited the funds, they cannot vote.

Article 16

The General Meeting of proprietors will be held at least once a year to approve the budgets and accounts and at any other time the President considers it advisable or when one quarter of the owners request it, or any number of owners who represent at least 25 per cent of the participation shares.
The President shall convoke the meeting and, in the absence of this, the promoters of the meeting, giving notice of the agenda of business, the time, day and place of the meeting for the first call, and, when applicable, the second call. Notification shall be given in the form set out in Article 9. The notice of meeting shall contain a list of the owners who are not current in the payment of debts to the Community and will warn of the loss of the right to vote under the conditions expressed in Article 15.2
Any owner can request the General Meeting to examine and resolve on any matter of interest to the Community.
For this purpose he should present to the President in writing the clearly specified points he wishes dealt with. The President shall include them in the agenda of the following General Meeting.
If the majority of owners, representing at the same time the majority of participation shares (cuotas) are not present at the time of the first call, the meeting shall be convened again on second call, without the need for a quorum. The meeting shall be held on the second call at the time, date and place indicated in the first notification. It can be held on the same day, as long as at least half an hour has passed since the first call.
Failing this, it shall be convened again, according to the forms established in this Article, within eight days following the meeting not held. In such case, notification must be made at least three days before the meeting.
3. Notification of the ordinary Annual General Meeting will be given at least six days beforehand and, for extraordinary meetings with as much advance notice as possible so that it can come to the attention of all the parties involved. The general meeting can lawfully take place even without the convocation of the President, providing that all of the proprietors agree and decide this.

What it means

Article 16 states that, by law, a general meeting must be held at least once a year. The only item of business legally required is the approval by the members of the accounts and budget. It is not strictly necessary to hold elections for a new president because the old one will continue in office until he is replaced by majority vote.

But the expenses must be approved by a legally-registered vote of the community members. It is perfectly possible for them to decide that they will not pay out any money for the next year. This means, of course, that the electric company will cut off the lights and the building's insurance policy will lapse. But no money can be spent without the majority vote of the members.

The president prepares the official Agenda of the AGM. It should be distributed before the meeting for the information of the members. The Agenda is important because, in strict terms, only the items that appear on it can be voted and decided. That is, if some member presents a proposal at the meeting itself and everyone agrees to pass it, that is all right. But if even one member complains that he was not properly informed in advance, the vote can be annulled.

This annual general meeting is the ordinary meeting. Other meetings, known as extraordinary meetings, may also take place. The president may call such a meeting at any time, giving adequate notice. This question of what constitutes "adequate" notification is a little tricky, especially when three quarters of the members of the community are residing in another country at any particular moment, but any president will try to give sufficient notice because he knows that a member who feels he has not been correctly warned of the meeting can protest and a court may rule the results of the meeting void.

An extraordinary meeting can also be called whenever one quarter of the members of the community, or people who represent one-quarter of the participation shares, request it. The president is then obligated to convene the meeting. In the case of the president's absence or incapacitation, the promoters of the meeting may also convoke it.

The law mentions one-quarter of the participation shares, or *cuotas*, because in many cases one or two owners may control a much larger share of the building than the owner of a single flat. One such example would be a large department store that holds more than one-quarter of the *cuotas* all on its own. Another would be the developer himself, who controls and votes all the shares of the unsold flats. This situation, in which one owner holds great voting power, has caused problems in more than one community.

It is common practice for the second calling of the meeting to appear on the original notification, usually set for a half hour after the first calling.

This means that, if a majority of members or *cuotas* is not present — and often it isn't — the meeting can still take place, no matter how few owners or shares are present. Their decisions will be perfectly valid if not protested by the other owners within 30 days after they are notified of the actions.

Article 17

Decisions of the general meeting shall be subject to the following rules:
1. *The installation of common infrastructures for access to telecommunication services regulated by Royal Decree Law 1/1998 of February 27, regarding common infrastructures in buildings for access to telecommunication services or for the adaptation of those already existing, as well as the installation of common or private systems for the use of renewable energy, and also for the necessary infrastructures to access new collective energy supplies can be agreed, at the petition of any owner, by one-third of the members of the community, who in turn represent one-third of the participation shares.*

The community may not charge the cost of the installation or adaptation of the aforesaid common infrastructures nor those derived from their following conservation and maintenance to the owners who have not expressly voted at the General Meeting in favour of the agreement. Nevertheless, if they should later request access to the telecommunication services or to the energy supply, and this requires the use of the new infrastructure or the adaptations made to the pre-existing system, this can be granted them, with the provision that they pay the amount which would have been apportioned to them, properly brought up to date, applying the appropriate legal interest rate.

Regardless of the dispositions of the preceding paragraph with respect to expenses for conservation and maintenance, the new infrastructure installed shall have the consideration for the effects established in this Law, of a common element.

2. Without prejudice to the dispositions of Article 10. 1. B, the execution of works or the establishment of new common services with the purpose of doing away with architectonic barriers which impede the access or mobility of handicapped persons, and in any case, the establishment of lift services, even when this means the modification of the Constitution Tile or the Statutes, shall require the favourable vote of the majority of owners, which in turn represents the majority of the participation shares.

When decisions are correctly taken for the execution of works of accessibility, the Community shall be obligated for the payment of expenses, even when the annual amount exceeds twelve ordinary monthly payments for common expenses.

3. *The establishment or suppression of services of doorman, porter or vigilance, or other common services of general interest, whether or not this involves the modification of the Constitution Title or the Statutes, shall require the favourable vote of three-fifths of the owners, which in turn represent three-fifths of the participation shares.*

The same system shall apply to the rental of common elements which have no specific purpose assigned to them in the building, and to the establishment or suppression of equipment and systems, not mentioned in Paragraph 1, whose purpose is to improve the hydraulic or energy efficiency of the building. In this last case, decisions correctly taken with regard to this regulation shall be binding on all owners. Nevertheless, if the equipment or systems have a private usage, the favourable vote of one-third of the Community members who represent in turn one-third of the participation shares, shall be sufficient, applying in this case the assignment of costs established in the aforesaid paragraph.

4. *No owner can demand new installations, services or improvements which are not necessary for the adequate conservation or liveability safety and accessibility of the building, according to its nature and characteristics. Nevertheless, when decisions are correctly taken by the favourable vote of three-fifths of the total number of owners who in turn represent three-fifths of the participation shares, to carry out innovations, new installations, services or improvements not required for the adequate conservation, liveability, safety and accessibility of the building, which have not been demanded, and whose cost of installation exceeds the amount of three* *ordinary monthly payments for common expenses, the dissident shall not be obligated, nor his share payment modified, even in the case where he cannot be deprived of the improvement or advantage. If the dissident desires, at any time, to participate in the advantages of the innovation, he will have to pay his part of the expenses of the execution and maintenance, duly brought up to date by the application of the corresponding legal interest.*

Innovations which render any part of the building unserviceable for the use and enjoyment of one owner may not be carried out without his registered and express consent.

5. *The installation of a station to recharge electric-powered vehicles for private use in the parking area of the building, given that this point is located in the individual parking spot in the garage, shall require only a previous communication to the Community. The cost of such installation and the consumption of electricity shall be fully for the account of the interested owner or owners.*

6. *Decisions not regulated expressly in this article which imply the approval or modification of rules contained in the Constitution Title of Horizontal Property or the Statutes of the Community shall require the unanimous vote of all the owners who represent the total of the participation shares to be valid.*

7. *The vote of the majority of owners who in turn represent the majority of participation shares shall be sufficient for the validity of other decisions. At the second calling of the meeting decisions taken by the majority of those present who in turn represent the majority of participation shares shall be valid.*

When a majority cannot be achieved by the procedures established in the preceding articles, the Judge, at the petition of an interested party in the month following the date of the Second Calling of the meeting, and after hearing the litigants previously summoned, shall rule in equity on the course to be followed within twenty days, counting from the original petition, and pronouncing on the payment of costs.

8. *Except in the cases expressly provided in which the cost of the services may not be charged to the owners who did not expressly vote in favour of the resolution at the AGM or in the cases where the reform or modification is made for private use, the votes of those duly informed owners who were absent from the meeting shall be counted as favourable if they did not declare their disagreement to the person exercising the function of Secretary*

of the Community by any certified means within 30 natural days of being informed of the resolution taken by those present in accordance with the procedure established in Article 9.
9. *Decisions correctly taken under the terms of this Article shall obligate all of the owners.*
10. *Disagreements regarding the nature of the works to be executed shall be resolved by the AGM. Interested parties may also apply for arbitration or a technical report in the terms established in the Law.*
11. *Expenses for the payment of improvements made or to be made in the building shall be for the account of the owner at the time when the expenses for the payment of the improvements fall due.*

What it means

Under the previous Law of Horizontal Property, a unanimous vote was required for any modification of the building, which led to necessary and useful action being blocked by one or two dissenters.

The new law sets out very carefully the sort of actions which now require only a three-fifths majority.

It also notes that your vote will be counted as favourable if you were absent from the meeting and did not protest within 30 days of being informed, and you will then be bound by the decision of those present at the meeting.

Sometimes a very small number of owners really make the decisions for the community.

If you are baffled by references in this article to access to telecommunications, don't worry. They mean communal television aerials, which require only a one-third vote in order to bind all of the owners. The same goes for work to install any renewable energy source.

All other community votes require only a simple majority, including the election of the president.

And if you are puzzled by the requirement that this majority must be a majority of the number of owners present as well as a majority of the amounts of participation shares, or *cuotas*, this is understandable.

The law stipulates this double majority because a conflict can arise when one owner controls many shares because he owns 10 apartments in the building or for some other reason. Spanish courts usually rule in favour of the number of owners rather than the amount of *cuotas* when deciding a contested vote.

Article 18

1. *Decisions voted by the Annual General Meeting may be challenged in court, following the provisions of the general procedural law, in the following situations:*

a) When such decisions are contrary to the law or to the Community Statutes.

b) When they are seriously damaging to the interests of the Community itself and benefit one or several owners.

c) When they cause serious harm to an owner who has no legal obligation to suffer this harm, or when the decisions have been made by abusing the law.

2. *Owners who expressly registered a dissenting vote in the meeting, those who were absent for any reason, and those who were incorrectly deprived of their right to vote are legally entitled to impugn these decisions. To challenge a resolution of the Meeting, an owner must be current in his payment of debts owed to the Community or he must deposit the amount of the debt with the Court beforehand. This rule shall not apply when challenging a decision regarding the establishment or alteration of the participation shares referred to in Article 9.*

3. *The action lapses three months after the decision taken by the general meeting unless the decision is contrary to law or to the Community Statutes, in which case the period is one year. For those owners who were absent this period is counted from the date of notification of the decision according to the procedure set out in Article 9.*

4. *Impugning a decision of the general meeting does not suspend its being put into force unless the Court orders so, as a precautionary measure, at the petition of the plaintiff and having heard the community of owners.*

What it means

Article 18 means that even one owner can challenge a community decision in court, if it seriously harms the interests of one of the members, or if it seems to benefit a few people to the detriment of the community as a whole, or if it is contrary to law or the statutes of the community.

Dissenters, be warned that you should have your vote against the measure reflected in the official minutes book if you want to impugn the decision.

Absentees have three months in most cases, and they had better have their fees paid up.

Article 19

1. *Decisions of the general meeting shall be recorded in a book of minutes stamped and validated by the Property Registrar in the form set out by law.*

2. *The minutes of each meeting must express at least the following circumstances:*

a) The date and place of the meeting

b) The name of the caller of the meeting, or the names of the owners who promoted it.

c) Whether it was ordinary or extraordinary and whether it was held on first or second call.

d) List of all those attending and their respective offices, as well as those owners represented by proxy, with the cuotas of each one.

e) The agenda for the meeting.

f) Decisions taken, showing, where it is relevant for the validity of the decision, the names of those owners who voted in favour and those who voted against them, as well as the participation shares they respectively represent.

3. *The minutes book should close with the signatures of the president and the secretary at the end of the meeting or within 10 days after. At the signing of the minutes book, the resolutions of the meeting shall be in force, unless the law disposes otherwise.*

The minutes shall be sent to the absent owners, following the procedure set out in Article 9.

Errors or defects in the minutes are rectifiable, provided that the book unmistakably indicates the date and place of the meeting, the owners in attendance, either present or represented by proxy, the decisions taken, with notation of the votes for and against, as well as the participation shares represented and that the book has been signed by the president and secretary. Said rectification should be made before the following general assembly, which must ratify the corrections.

4. *The Secretary will keep the minutes books of the general meeting. He will likewise retain, during a period of five years, the convocations,* *communications, powers of attorney and other documents relating to the meetings.*

What it means

The official minutes book described here must be kept in Spanish because it is a legal document, registering the acts of the community. This *libro de actas* must be stamped by the Registrar of Property and its contents can be cited in court.

The book must record the names of the members present and the proxies present at the meeting; tell who presided; when and where the meeting was held; give the agenda for the meeting; mention the main points of view discussed in the debate; list the resolutions taken and record the voting results.

If any member or group wishes to contest a resolution of the community, either in person or by certified post, this also should be recorded.

This minutes book establishes the powers of the president and any other officer to act for the community, and justifies the actions by its recording of the community's votes.

The annual general meeting usually begins with the reading of the minutes of the previous meeting, which must be approved by the members. If any member has a protest against the book, it must be registered officially in the book itself. It sometimes happens that the official record does not agree with one person's version of what actually happened, so it is necessary to be attentive.

Article 20

It is the function of the administrator:

a) To ensure the proper management of the house, its installations and services and, to this effect, provide the owners with timely information and warnings.

b) To prepare the budget of anticipated expenses sufficiently in advance and submit it to the general meeting, proposing the necessary measures to cover the expenses.

c) To attend to the conservation and maintenance of the building, arranging for the ordinary repairs and taking urgent measures regarding extraordinary repairs, giving an immediate report to the general meeting or, as the case may be, to the property owners.

d) To carry out resolutions taken regarding works and to make any payments and receive any monies as properly disposed.
e) To act, when the case arises, as secretary of the general meeting and to keep custody, at the disposition of the owners, of the documentation of the community.
f) Any other functions conferred by the general meeting.

What it means

Contrary to popular belief, the administrator, when he is a paid professional, is not an elected officer of the community. He is contracted for his services, usually for one year, and the community may choose not to renew his contract at its termination, and to employ another paid professional administrator.

Of course, a community member, the president or another, may carry out the many duties of administrating the building, and he may even be paid for it.

Article 20 lists the functions of the administrator. He must run the building properly and keep the owners informed about it. If there is no treasurer, the administrator prepares the budget for the coming year, attends to repairs in the building, makes payments and receives money, acts as secretary and keeps the community records safe and at the disposition of the members, and any other functions voted to him by the community.

Because the administrator may be a volunteer member of the community, the law sets no requirement for carrying out this mission. The administrator needs no professional title or special qualifications. He does not have to be Spanish or even to speak Spanish.

Nevertheless, many of the paid professional administrators hold titles as lawyers, gestors or, best of all, as an *administrador de fincas*, a professional property management expert.

Most administrators try to give good service to the community, charge reasonable fees, and put up with many petty complaints from the members. But others are not so honest, and more than one community has had bad experiences with administrators who seem to feel that the community works for them, rather than the other way around.

Sometimes promoters, in order to maintain their influence in the community, even have the names of administrators written into the original community statutes when they register the building. They are counting on the fact that any change in the statutes requires a unanimous vote, which is very difficult to achieve, so the members could not put out the administrator. Their legal position here is quite shaky, though, as the law also says that the annual general meeting has the power to change the president and the administrator.

In any case, if the community feels that the administrator is not presenting proper accounts, or his fees are too high, or he has purchased supplies from his cousin when he could have got them more cheaply from another source, they can vote him out.

The administrator, whether professional or volunteer, can also be sued in court for damages caused by his misconduct or negligence in office.

Article 21

1. *The obligations referred to in paragraphs e) and f) of Article 9 must be fulfilled by the owner of the flat or premises in the time and form determined by the General Meeting. If not, the President or the Administrator, if so disposed by the General Meeting, can seek legal redress by the procedure established for the "Proceso Monitorio" (Rapid Judgement).*

2. *Use of the Monitorio procedure will require the prior notification of the decision of the General Meeting approving the claim of the debt with the Community by the person acting as Secretary, with the endorsement of the President, providing that this decision has been notified to the owners affected in the form set out in Article 9.*

3. *Expenses involved in the notification to pay, when the notification is officially registered and the justification of such expenses accompanies the request, can be added to the original amount being claimed under terms of the previous section.*

4. *When the previous owner of the dwelling or premises remains liable to respond jointly for the payment of the debt, the initial demand can be brought against him, without prejudicing the right to repeat the demand against the present owner. Likewise, the claim can be brought against the registered owner, with the same right as mentioned above.*

In all these cases, the initial claim can be made against any one of those liable to pay or against all of them jointly.

5. When the debtor contests the original claim of the Monitorio process, the creditor can seek a preventive embargo of his goods sufficient to cover the quantity claimed as well as interest and costs.
In any case, the Court will order the preventive embargo without the necessity for the creditor to post a precautionary bond for the amount claimed. Nevertheless, the debtor can avoid the embargo by posting a bank guarantee for the amount claimed from him.
6. When the professional services of lawyer and procurator are used in the initial claim of the Monitorio process to reclaim money owed to the Community, the debtor shall be required, subject to the limits established in section three of Article 394 of the Code of Civil Judgement, to pay the fees for both of their actions, even when these refer only to the demand for payment and even if they do not appear before the Court.
In those cases which are contested, the general rules for payment of costs shall be followed. If the creditor obtains a ruling totally favourable to his claim, the fees of the lawyer and procurator shall be included, even when the appearance of the lawyer and procurator is not required by law.

What it means

This article sets out some important changes to the original law which at last put real teeth into the community's ability to compel payment of debt.

The community can now certify the debt and go immediately into court for a lien against the debtor's property. If the debtor does not pay up, the court will order some of his assets seized to pay the debt. If the debtor chooses to fight the bill, he himself must put up either his assets or a bank guarantee for the amount. Formerly, the community was required to make a deposit with the court when they sought to collect the back fees. No longer.

For a description of the "*Proceso Monitorio*" see the section on You and the Spanish Authorities under "Lawsuit without Lawyer". This procedure is something like Small Claims Court and makes it relatively simple for someone, including communities, to act legally to collect a debt.

Formerly, any community debts that accumulated during the procedure could be simply added into the original debt. This is no longer possible under the new system.

If the debtor fights in court to drag out the case, he will be liable for legal costs if he loses.

Article 22

1. *The Community of Property Owners will be liable with all its assets and credits for any debt to third parties. In addition, the creditor can act against each individual owner who took part in the process for his proportional share of the unpaid amount, after serving a demand for payment on such owners.*

2. *Any owner can oppose the claim by justifying that he is fully current in the payment of all debts due to the community at the time the demand referred to above was made.*

If the debtor immediately pays the demand, he will be charged the proportional part of the costs involved.

What it means

It happens with a certain frequency that communities of property owners cannot pay their debts to suppliers or service providers simply because their members have not paid their annual community fees.

This article gives community creditors a handle on direct action. They can proceed against the members themselves as individuals. Those members who are fully paid up cannot be made to pay.

Article 23

The legal structure of horizontal property (condominium) is terminated:

1. *By the destruction of the building, unless there is agreement to the contrary.*

Such destruction shall be deemed to exist when the cost of rebuilding exceeds 50 per cent of the value of the property at the time the event occurs, unless the amount in excess of the aforesaid cost is covered by insurance.

2. *By conversion into ordinary ownership or joint ownership.*

What it means

Clearly, the horizontal property scheme must be terminated when the building is destroyed. By fire, for example. The second paragraph refers to the sale of the building to one owner or several joint owners.

Yes, the community can even vote — unanimously, of course — to sell itself and divide the cash among the owners.

CHAPTER III: REGARDING PRIVATE REAL ESTATE COMPLEXES

Article 24

1. *The special scheme of property ownership set out in Article 396 of the Civil Code shall be applicable to those private real estate complexes which meet the following requirements:*

a) Being made up of two or more buildings or independent plots whose principal use is dwellings or commercial premises.

b) The owners of these buildings or properties or of the units into which they are divided horizontally, with an inherent nature for this right, participate in an indivisible co-ownership of other real estate elements, such as roads, installations or services.

2. *Private real estate complexes referred to in the previous Number may:*

a) Constitute themselves as one only Community of Owners by means of any of the procedures established in the second paragraph of Article 5. In this case they will be subject to the dispositions of this Law, which will be fully applied to them.

b) Constitute themselves as a grouping of Communities of Owners. To this effect, the Charter of Constitution of the new grouped Community must be granted by the only and single owner of the complex or by the Presidents of all the Communities to compose it, previously authorised by majority vote of their respective general meetings. The Charter of Constitution will contain the description of the real estate complex in its setting and descriptions of the elements, roads, installations and common services. Likewise, it will fix the participation shares (cuotas) of each of the component Communities, which will be jointly liable for the obligation to contribute to the general expenses of the group macro-community. This title of charter and the Statutes of the Community can be inscribed in the Property Registry.

3. *The grouping of Communities referred to above shall, to all effects, enjoy the same legal situation as Communities of Owners and will be governed by the dispositions of this Law, with the following special provisions:*

a) The general assembly of owners, unless otherwise agreed, will be composed of the Presidents of the communities forming the group, who will represent the individual owners of each Community .

b) The making of decisions for which the Law requires qualified majorities will require, in all cases, the prior vote of the majority required in each of the individual Communities that compose the grouping.
c) Except by agreement of the general meeting otherwise, the dispositions of Article 9 of this Law regarding the reserve fund shall not apply to the group community.
The jurisdiction of the governing organs of the group community cover only the real estate elements, roads, installations and common services. In no case shall their decisions prejudice the faculties corresponding to the governing bodies of the Communities of Owners which make up the grouping of Communities.
4. *The dispositions of this Law, with the same special provisions, shall be applicable to those private real estate complexes which do not adopt any of the legal forms indicated in Number 2 as a complement to agreements made by the co-owners among themselves*

What it means

This is the big one. The Horizontal Law now takes account of urbanisations of detached houses, or groupings of townhouses, flats and detached villas.

The full protection of the new Horizontal Law is available for these urbanisations, with very little effort on their part. They can vote for it, write themselves a set of statutes, and go straight to the Property Registry.

Previously, urbanisations had to form themselves as Collaborating Urbanistic Entities, a complex process which often proved extremely expensive for the owners and involved long and tortuous negotiations with the town hall.

Sometimes the formation of an EUC will be the only possibility for an urbanisation, but many of them will now find their way smoothed to legality and the power to enforce debt collection.

ADDITIONAL DISPOSITION

1. *Without prejudice to any dispositions which, using the powers conferred on them, the Regional Governments may make, the constitution of the reserve fund regulated in Article 9.1.f) shall comply with the following*

rules:
a) The fund must be created when the General Meeting approves the ordinary yearly budget, corresponding to the year immediately following the putting into effect of this Law.
New Communities shall create the fund when they approve their first ordinary budget.
b)When constituted, the fund shall be endowed with no less than 2.5 per cent of the ordinary budget of the Community. To this effect, the owners must make in advance the necessary contributions proportionally to their participation shares.
c) When the ordinary budget for the financial year following that in which the fund was established is passed, the amount of the reserve fund should reach the minimum quantity established in Article 9.
2. *The amount of the reserve fund at no time during the budget period shall be less than the minimum legally established.*
Amounts drawn from the reserve fund during the budget period in order to pay the expenses on maintenance and repairs of the property permitted by the present law shall be computed as an integral part of the fund for purposes of calculating its minimum amount.
At the beginning of the following financial year there shall be made the contributions necessary to cover the amounts drawn from the reserve fund in accordance with the terms of the preceding paragraph.

What it means

The last disposition requires communities to establish and maintain a reserve fund to deal with any emergencies.

Communities of Detached Villas

Those who live in urbanisations of detached villas have a more complicated set of problems than those living in flats. Before 1978 it was very difficult for them to form any sort of community with the legal power to enforce its statutes and compel payment of fees.

The inhabitants of these housing estates, or urbanisations, a rather new invention in Spain at that time, had to find ways of financing their roads, lighting, security, gardens, etc, as well as establishing the basic services of water, electric power and rubbish collection.

Even when they can now come under the protection of the Horizontal Law, they still have these basic problems not related to the pure legality of their existence.

In addition, the urbanisations often had complex relations with the town hall of their municipality. If the road passing through the estate continues on to other properties and is used by the general public, who pays for its maintenance? Can the inhabitants cut this road and seal off the community, or are they obliged to permit the public to use it? Will the town hall rubbish collectors enter the estate, or must all rubbish be placed at a central point for collection? A thousand questions arise.

What is basically important for the formation of a community is Royal Decree 3288/1978 of August 25, which sets forth the regulations for urban administration based on the existing *Ley del Suelo,* the Land Law. Even the 1978 regulations are complex and confusing, but they can provide a framework for setting up an effective community.

These regulations establish the figure of the *Entidad Urbanística Colaboradora de Gestión y Conservación*, the Collaborating Urbanistic Entity of Maintenance and Management. A real mouthful to describe the quasi-public functions of the urbanisation of detached villas. This is often shortened today to EUC.

In a perfect world, you would find that your dream villa was located on an urbanisation where all roads, lighting and services were carefully provided by a benevolent and foresighted municipal administration, just as they are in many countries. But you are more likely to encounter a situation where the developer is no longer maintaining the roads and services, where the town hall refuses to help because all the requirements in the original building permission were not fulfilled by the developers, and the owners are unable to establish an effective community.

You need to start with Article 25 of the 1978 regulations. If you are lucky, your situation will come under Section 3 of this law which provides for the forming of collaborating entities which group all owners in a certain zone, whether they want to join or not. Without the power to compel all owners to belong to the entity, it would be meaningless.

Then you can study Article 67, which provides that the town hall will take charge of maintaining and providing all normal services once these have been ceded to the town hall. That is, the association of owners or the developer will transfer the roads, sewage, lighting and perhaps some common green zone to the town hall.

The catch here is that the town hall may very well refuse to accept this transfer until the roads and other services have been put into good condition. Guess who must pay for this. Right. Either the developer, or the owners as a group. Some parts of the regulations can even oblige the urbanisation to pay all costs for establishing connections to the nearest town roads, sewers and lighting systems.

The great advantage of the collaborating entity is that the urbanisation then becomes a normal part of the municipality for the provision of basic services, and, if one of the members refuses to pay his share of community fees, the town hall itself may act against him with the threat to seize his property or bank account to satisfy the unpaid debt. This procedure is much more effective and rapid than going through the courts.

So you begin to see that the collaborating entity must work closely with the municipal authorities because the urbanisation is not separated from the rest of the world the way an apartment building is. In fact, the authorisation of the town hall is required for the formation of this entity.

All these negotiations between the owners and the municipal authorities will require the counsel and representation of a Spanish lawyer or property administrator who is knowledgeable in this area. In one recent case on the Costa del Sol, the backers of a very large estate worked closely with the existing owners and the town hall. First the existing owners voted unanimously to form an association. Then the developers, acting on the requirements of the town hall, put all the services in good order. Costs were shared by the owners and the developer. Then the backers had to pay the town hall a fine of €120,000 for not fulfilling all their original obligations. (The town hall first wanted €480,000, but were argued into the lower figure.) Finally, the town hall accepted the transfer of the roads and other services, and authorised the formation of a collaborating urban entity. This was properly registered in the registry of such entities, which exists at the provincial urban office, giving it a legal personality.

Any new purchaser in this zone must now become a member of the entity by virtue of his purchase. This is clearly stated in each sales contract. Both the developer and the present owners have bound themselves to include such a clause in any sales deed. Even if they didn't, the legal personality of the entity requires it.

Now the members only have to squabble among themselves about how much to pay for the security patrol, whether they want an extra tennis court and how to act against the owner with the barking dogs. Of course they also have to fight with their new partners in the town hall about the size of their assessment for the sewage repairs, compared to the urbanisation just down the road. The problems will never end, but at least they have a clear and coherent system for dealing with them.

These particular members are now up in arms because they feel they are being charged twice for municipal services. That is because they pay their annual real estate taxes to the town hall, the IBI, just like other owners. But they also pay their annual fees to the EUC, which, they argue, covers basically the same services, so they are being forced to pay twice. The argument is still going on.

Things can be much worse in a situation where the owners cannot agree at the beginning and where the developer is not willing to help. But if the whole thing seems like too much trouble, remember that a well-run community can add thousands of euros to your property's value and a poorly maintained urbanisation can cut thousands off your price.

The following section contains an English translation of the Spanish national legislation affecting the formation of conservation entities. It is not complete because many different bodies of law can come into play. The Land Law is frequently modified and each region, such as Valencia or Andalusia, has its own land law as well. Nevertheless, the basic 1978 law still gives a good idea of the legislation.

LAW FOR DETACHED VILLAS
Land Law Regulations III
Regulations of Urban Administration
TITLE I General Dispositions CHAPTER 1. Subjects and Means of Administration SECTION 6.

ARTICLE 24

1. *Affected parties may participate in urban administration through the creation of Collaborating Urban Entities.*

2. *Collaborating Urban Entities are:*

a) Compensation Boards.

b) Administrative Associations of owners in the co-operation system.

c) Entities of Conservation.

3. *Collaborating Urban Entities will be governed by their Statutes and by the dispositions of this section, without prejudice to the application of* *the specific precepts contained in Chapters 11 and III of Title V of these Regulations for Compensation Boards and Administrative Associations of owners in the co-operation system, nor to the provisions established in Chapter 1-V of Title III for the conservation of the works of urbanisation.*

What it means

These regulations establish a legal basis for private citizens to participate in public administration. Keep in mind that streets, lighting, main drains, sewage systems and electric conduits passing through the land of the urbanisation to the next property will be of public nature. It is not like a building of flats, in which the services are simply connected and do not pass on to other properties.

This article of the regulations allows private persons to share administration of these services with the municipal authorities through the formation of one of three types of collaborating urban entities.

The first mentioned, the compensation board, is created when land is being re-zoned or subdivided and where several owners may be involved. The situation can get complicated. Imagine an area which includes a large working farm, a small factory with lots of land around it, nine or 10 homes built on large rural plots, and maybe a developer who has bought a big tract which he wants to urbanise. The nearby town is expanding and a new road is being put in. The entire zone will be declared building land.

The compensation board is the legal structure created for the purpose of sorting out all the problems that will arise and for seeing that each participant is fairly treated. The town hall is represented, too, as it will be expropriating land from some of the owners for the road and other services. The members of the board will squabble and negotiate until they agree on each party's share of the rights and obligations. This is one form of urban entity.

The compensation board operates principally as a forum to ensure the equitable distribution of problems and profits in such a re-zoning situation. But what happens after the subdivision is complete?

One scheme set up in law is the second structure mentioned in this article: the administrative association of owners in the co-operation system. Here the owners co-operate with each other and with the town hall to organise smooth functioning of the services in the area they share. This is much like the conservation entity, but its legal underpinnings are different, involving several different ownerships.

Both the compensation board and the administrative association are designed to serve in the early stages of a transformation in the ownership pattern of land. Either of them can be changed into a conservation entity, the legal framework for the ongoing maintenance of an established urbanisation.

Article 25

1. *The constitution of the Compensation Boards and of the Administrative Associations of owners in the co-operation system shall be adapted to the provisions of the regulations contained in the respective schemes of action.*

2. *Entities of conservation of the works of urbanisation may be constituted as a result of the transformation of some pre-existing Entity of those set out in the previous number or, specifically for these purposes, without previously having constituted any Entity for the execution of the works of urbanisation.*

3. *The constitution of a conservation Entity will be obligatory whenever the duty of conservation of the works of urbanisation falls upon the owners included in a determined zone or unit of action by virtue of the dispositions of the town urban Plan or the bases of the urban action programme or if it results expressly from legal dispositions. In such cases membership in the conservation Entity will be obligatory for all owners included in its territorial range.*

What it means

The big news comes here in the last sentence of paragraph 3, which provides that membership in the conservation entity shall be obligatory for all owners in the zone, and that the formation of the conservation entity shall be obligatory when provided by law, meaning that it may be set out in the town urban development plan, or in a Plan of Urbanistic Action, a development plan for a restricted area, or it may simply be a regulation passed by the Town Council.

Any legal disposition will suffice.

In practice this means some urbanisations will find that the law requires them to form a conservation entity and that all must be members, and other urbanisations will find it is not legally necessary for them to do so.

Article 26

1. *Collaborating urbanistic entities shall have an administrative character and shall be dependent in this order on the acting urbanistic Administration.*

2. *The legal personality of collaborating urbanistic entities shall be understood as acquired from the moment of their inscription in the corresponding Registry.*

What it means

The first paragraph of this article grants to these entities powers to act legally, and notes that this power depends on the entity's relation to the public administration involved, which would usually be the municipality, though it could also be the province or a special authority ruling some particular piece of terrain.

The second paragraph reminds us that there exists a special Registry for these entities and they cannot act with legal force, to compel payment of debts, for example, until the entity is properly registered.

Article 27

1. *The constitution of collaborating urban entities, as well as their Statutes, must be approved by the acting urban Administration.*

2. *The document approving this constitution shall be entered in the Registry of Collaborating Urban Entities which is kept by the respective Provincial Urban Commissions, where likewise shall be kept an example of the statutes of the entity authorised by the competent official.*

3. *The appointments and dismissals of the persons charged with governing and administrating the entity shall also be inscribed in said Registry.*

4. *Modification of the statutes shall require the approval of the acting* *urban Administration. The respective resolutions, with the content of the modification, in such case, must be entered in the Registry.*

What it means

This article points up the importance of the co-operation required of the local town hall or other urban administration body which has competence over the zone. These official bodies must approve the formation of the entity and its statutes.

The names of its officers, and any changes in its rules, must be registered in the Registry. Any major changes of the statutes will require approval from the municipal authorities.

Article 28

The transfer of title which determines membership in any of the types of collaborating urbanistic entities shall carry with it the termination of the rights and obligations of the transferring party and the acquirer shall be understood as incorporated into the Entity from the time of transfer.

What it means

This of course applies only when the Entity is legally constituted and registered. If the owner's community is not an Entity, but only a civil association, then each new buyer's contract must contain a clause stating that he joins the community and agrees to abide by its statutes.

Article 29

Resolutions of Collaborating Urbanistic Entities shall be adopted by simple majority of participation shares, unless a special quorum is established in the Statutes or other regulations for certain cases. Such resolutions can be impugned in appeal to the acting urbanistic Administration.

What it means

Each urban entity can make its own statutes with provisions on where unanimous vote may be required. If they do not, this article of the regulations will apply and a simple majority decision will be sufficient to take action. Any owner who feels his interests have been prejudiced can appeal the vote to the town hall or other official administration acting in the case.

ARTICLES 30 THROUGH 57 are of a highly technical nature and do not bear directly on the formation of communities.

Article 58

The owners of properties affected by an urbanistic action programme shall be obliged to pay the costs of urbanisation specified in the following articles in proportion to the area of their respective properties, or, as the case may be, to the area figuring in the documents referred to in Article 53 of these regulations.

What it means

This means that owners shall be assessed payment participation shares according to the size of their properties. Big properties pay more, small properties pay less. The Article 53 referred to relates to various forms of documenting property ownership, such as the *Registro de la Propiedad*, and others.

Article 59

1. *The cost of works of urbanisation which are charged to the account of the owners of a determined zone or unit of action shall include the following:*
a) Street works, including works of levelling, compacting and paving of roadways, construction and kerbing of pavements and channelling which must be constructed in the subsurface of the public way for services.
b) Sanitation works, which include general and partial collectors, connections, sewers and culverts for rain-waters and purification installations, in the proportion that they affect the action unit or zone.
c) Water supply, in which is included works of obtaining the water, when such are necessary, the distribution to homes of potable water, of irrigation water and of fluid for fire-fighting.
d) Supply of electrical current, including its conduction and distribution and public lighting.
e) Gardening and tree-planting in parks, gardens and public ways.
2. *Private parties involved in works of urbanisation in a zone or urban*

action unit may be reimbursed for the expenses of installation of the networks of supply of water and electricity, charged to the concession-holding companies, to the extent that, according to the regulation of such services, these expenses must not be charged to the users. The costs of installation shall be accredited by certification issued by the acting administration.

What it means

Have they left anything out? The owners on an urbanisation can find themselves liable for any of the expenses mentioned here. If the developer has failed to carry out all requirements set by the town hall, either in the urban plan itself or other subsidiary legislation, the owners can be stuck for it in most cases. It pays to check up first.

Article 60

Any indemnities owed to the owners and renters of buildings or constructions of any sort which must be knocked down for the correct execution of the plan, as well as indemnity payments arising from the destruction of plantings, works or installations incompatible with the plan being carried out shall likewise be charged to the account of the property owners in the proportions set out in Article 58.

What it means

Yes, they left something out. Owners are also liable for any payments made to persons suffering loss from the execution of the urbanisation plan.

Article 61

Also for the account of the owners of land included in the zone or relevant action unit shall be the cost of preparing and processing the Plan of plots and the projects of urbanisation and the total cost of expenses of subdivision or compensation.

What it means

This expense would fall on the owners of land which is in the process of being subdivided, and will produce profits for them when they sell. It is not likely to affect purchasers on an already-established urbanisation; but be alert because legal expenses can also be charged to the owners.

Article 62

If agreement exists between the Administration and the affected owners, the payment of all or part of the expenses noted in the three previous articles can be made by the owners ceding to the Administration, for no consideration and free of all charges, buildable land in the amount deemed sufficient for the compensation of such expenses, whose value shall be determined in the agreement itself.

What it means

That's good of the administration. If you can't pay, they will accept your valuable land instead. In fact, this situation normally arises when the town itself is re-zoning land. The new building permissions mean large profits for the existing owners so it is expected they pay for it, either in cash or by the transfer of part of the land to the town hall.

Article 63

Owners of non-programmed developable land which is the object of a Programme of urbanistic action, besides paying the costs of urbanisation set out in the previous articles and satisfying any supplementary charges which the programme may impose on them, must pay for the complete execution or the supplement necessary for the exterior works of infrastructure on which the urbanistic action is based, such as road networks connecting with population centres, installation or amplification of the channels of services of water supply, drains and sewage, purification stations, supply of electricity and any other services necessary for the land subject to the urbanistic action programme to be duly connected through these general systems with the structure of the Municipality in which the programme is carried out.

What it means

Owners of land which is improved or made more valuable by any action of the town hall can find themselves liable even for these expenses.

ARTICLE 64 has been left out, as it does not bear directly on communities.

Article 65

Incompliance by the owners of the land with the obligations and charges established in these Regulations will give rise to:

a) The collection of the urbanisation costs by executive order under threat of embargo and legal seizure of the property.

b) Expropriation by the Administration of the lands affected by compliance with the charges, the Administration itself, or the Compensation Board, as the case may be, being beneficiaries of the expropriation.

What it means

This article is what makes the conservation entity such an effective form for communities of owners of detached villas in an urbanisation. The executive order to seize property of non-payers is a far easier and swifter process than going to court against them, which can take many months, and even years.

ARTICLE 66 has been left out, as it does not bear directly on communities.

CHAPTER IV - MAINTENANCE OF THE URBANISATION

Article 67

The conservation of the works of urbanisation and the maintenance of the equipment and installations of the public services will be the charge of the acting administration, once the transfer of these services has been made.

What it means

Yes, this is the dream paradise in which the town hall provides and maintains all the basic services of the urbanisation. This article obliges them to do so. The catch is that they have to accept the transfer of these services from the private developer or urbanisation first. And they will not accept — and have not done so in many cases — these services until everything is properly installed and functioning. Sometimes this works quite well and the community, the services and the town hall co-operate in harmony happily ever after, with the occasional non-payer of fees being forced to produce the money by the threat of executive order. Far more often, the town hall finds many deficiencies in the installations and services and will not take over their administration and maintenance until the owners' community has put them right, at great expense. Be warned.

Article 68

1. *Regardless of the dispositions of the preceding article, the owners of the land included in the zone or action unit will be subject to the aforesaid obligation when it is imposed on them by the Urban Zoning Plan, or by the bases of a programme of urban action or results expressly from legal dispositions.*

2. *In the case of the preceding number, the owners must form themselves into an Entity of Conservation.*

What it means

Even though it is clear from both principle and law that the owners will be obliged to maintain the installations, this article exists to remind us of that fact. Even when no specific provision is made for this, that last phrase of Article 68 paragraph 1 — "results expressly from legal dispositions" — gives the town hall the power to pass a resolution requiring the owners to maintain their roads in good repair, and the community will be bound by law.

Article 69

1. *The participation of the owners in the obligation of conservation and maintenance of the works of urbanisation, equipment and installations of the public services, when this is not the charge of the acting administration, shall be determined as a function of the participation share set for them by the Compensation Board, in the subdivision plan, or, as the case may be, in the share specified in the Entity of Conservation.*

2. *If systems of horizontal property have been constituted over the properties, the contribution of the owners to said obligation of conservation and maintenance shall be determined by the participation share (cuota)* *with relation to the total value of the property which is assigned in each community.*

What it means

This article determines the way in which each owner's share of the payment is calculated, and provides also for calculating the shares of apartment dwellers who already have horizontal property systems operating in their buildings located on the parent urbanisation.

Article 70

1. *Whosoever shall be the subject to whom corresponds the obligation of maintenance referred to in the preceding articles, the Town Hall or the acting administration, in its condition as owner of the lands of public domain, works, equipment and installations of obligatory cession, may require by executive order under threat of embargo the payment of the shares owed, whether acting on its own initiative or at the instance of the collaborating urbanistic entity.*

2. *The amount of the payment share will be delivered by the Town Hall or acting administration to the entity charged with the conservation, when this obligation does not pertain to the Administration.*

What it means

Paragraph 1 here repeats the power of the town hall to carry out an executive order of garnishment or embargo in order to compel payment of participation share fees. It notes that the town hall may do this either on its own initiative or when requested by the conservation entity. Paragraph 2 makes it clear that the town hall is to deliver this money to the conservation entity, unless the town hall itself is charged with the maintenance of the services. This means the town hall can collect the money and provide the services, or collect part of the money and provide part of the services.

Because the town hall itself is often a member of the entity, because of its own installations on the 10 per cent of the land which the promoter must transfer to the Town, this gives rise to a situation where the town hall may have to collect debts from itself.

"Legality" of communities

A final note here on the "legality" of communities. Throughout this text we refer to the inscription of the community in the Property Registry or Registry of Conservation Entities. We point out that the Statutes must be registered in order to be fully legal, and we insist on every point of the law being observed.

This is all well and good. In the real world, however, we find groups of houses built in the property boom that do not really make up an urbanisation, where the owners have simply agreed to organise and pay for some basic services among themselves. We find urbanisations that were never registered as such, where no community statutes exist, but the owners hold annual meetings and pay dues. We find other urbanisations, where the community has formal statutes and regulations, but these are not registered.

Are all these other forms of communities "legal"?

Well, in one sense they are not legal because they are not registered. But if you, as an owner in one of these situations, think you can get away with not paying your fees, perhaps you should think again.

Spanish courts have ruled on a number of occasions that these communities, although not registered, have acquired a legal personality simply by existing through the years, that they function for the benefit of the owners and society in general, and so they can in fact compel the payment of fees and bring a case against a non-payer, even seizing his property and having it sold at auction.

Index

D

S

T

U

V

W

Y

Printed in Great Britain
by Amazon

72467143R00249

Heart Shoots

An anthology to aid the work of
MACMILLAN CANCER SUPPORT

Indigo Dreams Publishing

First Edition: Heart Shoots
First published in Great Britain in 2013 by:
Indigo Dreams Publishing Ltd
132 Hinckley Road
Stoney Stanton
Leics
LE9 4LN
www.indigodreams.co.uk

ISBN 978-1-909357-05-1

British Library Cataloguing in Publication Data. A CIP record for this book can be obtained from the British Library.

Designed and typeset in Palatino Linotype by Indigo Dreams.
Cover photo by Dru Marland: drusilla.marland@btopenworld.com
Cover design by Ronnie Goodyer at Indigo Dreams.

Printed and bound in Great Britain by Imprint Academic, Exeter.

Papers used by Indigo Dreams are recyclable products made from wood grown in sustainable forests following the guidance of the Forest Stewardship Council.

Heart Shoots is dedicated to the brave people who are fighting or have beaten cancer and all those who care for and help them along the way.

His Royal Highness has asked me to wish you every success.

Mark Leishman, Private Secretary to TRH The Prince of Wales

The Prime Minister greatly appreciates the excellent work of Macmillan Cancer Support and hopes that the anthology is a great success.

Matthew Style, Private Secretary to Rt Hon David Cameron, MP

I wish you every success with fundraising. "Never give up on hope, it can be your 12th man right up until the 93rd minute!"

Sir Alex Ferguson CBE, Manager, Manchester United F.C.

I know only too well the effects of cancer having lost my own mum to lung cancer. I am delighted to give my support to Indigo Dreams Publishing; I hope it exceeds all expectations for Macmillan Cancer Support.

Gaby Roslin

Heart Shoots is the successor to *Soul Feathers,* the 2011 anthology initiated by Annie Morgan and co-edited by Annie and Ronnie Goodyer.

Heart Shoots has retained the ethos of publishing poems from the newcomer to the internationally famous.

about the editor

Ronnie Goodyer is an experienced publisher and director of Indigo Dreams Publishing Ltd which he runs with his partner, Dawn Bauling. IDP publishes poetry collections, anthologies, fiction, non-fiction and three poetry and prose magazines: *Reach Poetry* monthly (now in its 15th year), *Sarasvati* bi-monthly and *The Dawntreader* quarterly. It also runs competitions for prizes and publication. Indigo Dreams Publishing was the Poetry Sponsor of the Brit Writers Awards, 2012.

Ronnie ran his own Celebrity Management company and published Uri Geller's first novel *Shawn* and England cricketer-turned artist Jack Russell's *A Cricketer's Art*.

He is a widely-published poet and his poetry has been selected for numerous anthologies, including *Peace In Our Time* for the Red Cross; *Dancing Through The Pain (plus sketches)* and *Off The Wall* for MIND; *Flowers On A Shoestring* for the ONE-TO-ONE Children's Fund; *Review of Contemporary Poetry* for The Stroke Association; *Earth Love* for Conservation charities; *Pulling Funny Faces at the Dog* for NSPCC; *People's Poet book of Book of Muddy Paws* for animal sanctuaries; and *Listening To The Birth of Crystals* in aid of deaf children (he also designed the cover for this). Solo collections include *Within The Silence, Indigo Dreams, Lizard Reality, New Words From An Old Hat, The Way of the Dance* and *Indigo Dreams Revisited.*

He is an experienced poetry adjudicator and was invited to be on the BBC Judging Panel for their *Off By Heart* competition screened in May 2009.

Ronnie lives with his partner Dawn and senior border collie Soxx and hopes to relocate home and business back to Cornwall, UK, later this year.

a note from Indigo Dreams

All authors/artists whose work is included in Heart Shoots and those who granted permission for work to be used in this anthology have donated their time, energy and talent for the benefit of Macmillan Cancer Support.

We at Indigo Dreams Publishing Ltd would like to applaud and thank each one of them.

Macmillan Cancer Support
January 2013

One in three of us will get cancer and it's the toughest thing most of us will ever face. If you've been diagnosed with cancer, or a loved one has, you'll want a team of people in your corner supporting you every step of the way; that's who Macmillan Cancer Support are.

We are the nurses and therapists helping you through treatment. The experts on the end of the phone. The advisers telling you which benefit you're entitled to. The volunteers giving you a hand with the everyday things. The campaigners improving cancer care. The community supporting you online, any time. The fundraisers who make it all possible.

The number of people with cancer is growing every day. We want to reach and improve the lives of every one of those people. To do this we rely on the generosity of supporters. The publishers of *Heart Shoots* have waived profit to enable its retail price, and for every copy sold £2 (inclusive of VAT) will be paid to Macmillan Cancer Support (charity registered in England and Wales (261017) and in Scotland (SCO39907). Thank you supporting Macmillan by purchasing *Heart Shoots*.

If you'd like any information about how to access our support or hear more about you can get involved please contact

0808 808 0000 www.macmillan.org.uk

CONTENTS

Heart Shoots

True Love – Sharon Olds

In the middle of the night, when we get up
after making love, we look at each other in
complete friendship, we know so fully
what the other has been doing. Bound to each other
like mountaineers coming down from a mountain,
bound with the tie of the delivery-room,
we wander down the hall to the bathroom, I can
hardly walk, I hobble through the granular
shadowless air, I know where you are
with my eyes closed, we are bound to each other
with huge invisible threads, our sexes
muted, exhausted, crushed, the whole
body a sex—surely this
is the most blessed time of my life,
our children asleep in their beds, each fate
like a vein of abiding mineral
not discovered yet. I sit
on the toilet in the night, you are somewhere in the room,
I open the window and snow has fallen in a
steep drift, against the pane, I
look up, into it,
a wall of cold crystals, silent
and glistening, I quietly call to you
and you come and hold my hand and I say
I cannot see beyond it. I cannot see beyond it.

First Love – John Clare

I ne'er was struck before that hour
With love so sudden and so sweet,
Her face it bloomed like a sweet flower
And stole my heart away complete.
My face turned pale as deadly pale.
My legs refused to walk away,
And when she looked, what could I ail?
My life and all seemed turned to clay.

And then my blood rushed to my face
And took my eyesight quite away,
The trees and bushes round the place
Seemed midnight at noonday.
I could not see a single thing,
Words from my eyes did start —
They spoke as chords do from the string,
And blood burnt round my heart.

Are flowers the winter's choice?
Is love's bed always snow?
She seemed to hear my silent voice,
Not love's appeals to know.
I never saw so sweet a face
As that I stood before.
My heart has left its dwelling-place
And can return no more.

Roses – George Eliot

You love the roses – so do I. I wish
The sky would rain down roses, as they rain
From off the shaken bush. Why will it not?
Then all the valley would be pink and white
And soft to tread on. They would fall as light
As feathers, smelling sweet; and it would be
Like sleeping and like waking, all at once!

Still A Woman – Claire Knight

I watch you playing with the kids –
my grandchildren – your face returning
to who you were, glimpses of familiarity.

The tell-tale signs of the past year, however,
are still evident: your short curly hair
you call the 'chemo perm'; the scar
below your collar bone, just visible when
you wear a strappy top... you are young
and fashion conscious after all; the cold
metal 'port' in your chest, used every
three weeks for drug therapy.

Your amazing bra hides what has been
taken away. I cannot imagine
how that felt to the woman in you, to the mother
and lover...

You have just completed the 'Race for Life',
5 kilometres of walking in a pink t-shirt with
hundreds of woman, all shapes and sizes,
knowing how it feels.

Your hair is bleached blond now, a statement
that you are still very much here,
and you are still a woman, a vibrant, strong,
changed woman....I'm so proud.

lump – Samantha Newbury

I object to your existence;
Your, quite unnecessary, invasion
of my personal space.
I will not dignify you
with underlining or capitals.

You will not,
with your sneaky, snichty cells,
steal one more millimetre
than the thirteen
you have already stolen.

And don't even think
about a surreptitious diversion
into my lymph glands;
I guarantee, if you do,
you will be sorry.

I am serving you
with three week's notice
of eviction.
You will be, forcibly,
removed.

Make sure you pack
all your belongings;
There will be no
other possibilities
for you, here.

Afterglow – Oz Hardwick

Where are you? There
in the weeds, in the reeds
at the lip of the lake, babbling
like a smiling Ophelia, embracing
almond blossom, celandine.

The water is so clear
it's invisible beneath you,
flying, cotton-winged,
hair streaming above
sunken bullion koi.

This is how it should be:
air like new milk, splashing
ripples into upturned hands,
cold below and palms glowing.

Village Hall – Mandy Sutter

I'd like to live in a village hall
lie down on pale cool floor boards
made safe by the dark tread of farmers,
wake under the gaze of high windows
in the presence of a hundred chairs
waiting. I'll do as the no-smoking sign

says, refrain from drinking
on the premises, trust the fire door
to tell me all I need to know about coming
and going. The stage curtains can be kept
closed, the spotlights off. News will come
to the notice board, but not often.

Give me dust and echoes and old smells
and all the shades of maroon
I could ever dream of, coat hooks
and pelmets and wedges
to hold doors open on hot nights.
Give me time for questions and requests

and room to notice the things that move:
spiders and woodlice, the second hand
of the clock, the squares of light
that bloom and fade on the floor,
like carriages of an enchanted train
forever travelling.

Last light – Helen Addy

With cancer she is a child again,
the drive to the hospital lit
by her pale face tilting at trees,
her voice proclaiming
everything clean and bright.
Her handbag lies open on her lap,
Turkish delight spilling out,
whitening the seats.
The *darling* she gives to her daughter's name,
glistens like a wedding band, its yellow
piercing her final night like a star.
Her hands lie youthful against the sheets,
a fan scatters summer across her brow,
and the silence of the heart monitor
is a good husband's promise of sleep.

The Visiting – Pippa Little

The sky is blue all day.
Your sweet peas and tomatoes, antique roses,
all leap their own length and longer.
We prop the back door open from early to late.

Every day before the visiting
I walk to the end of the harbour wall,
curl up in its last hollow, ungainly bird
out-growing the nest, like those

the cat brought in to offer you:
all summer that ugly, matted animal
you'd push off your knee, swear at, even kick
on occasion – stalks in and out, bereft without you,

mouth blooded with longings

Peelings – Alison Brackenbury

What am I good at? Useless things.
Listening to strangers on slow Scottish trains.
Did you know they had square sausages?
Standing on one leg- Not Yoga; muddy years of
Wellingtons.
And peeling parsnips. Cooking grand Christmas dinner,
amongst dried cranberries, asparagus,
my daughter passed the knife, then was surprised
my awkward hands whipped smoothly down each root,
flicked pale gold slivers, thin, to save the flesh
which frost and soil had left as sweet as nuts,
which you may understand. And I remember
in tea's cold desert, though the saucepans steamed,
caught in a creaking visit once, I said,
(mouth full) 'These are good parsnips! Did you grow them?'
'Yes', said my father, shrunk to eighty years,
nodded with dignity, like his tall father.
We were not good with words. Each time my hand
slips down, as sharp as winter, and casts off
a pale coat, I am grateful, still, to parsnips.

In The Study – Todd Swift

How my books silence you engages me
So that I find myself here reading you
As you read many books upon these shelves;
I read your subtle lips that do not move;

And become a critic of what writes love –
A maker silent as the ease of light
That strikes the eye to print so words can see.
It is not difficult to prove that flight

Is not fancy when it comes to desire
On which no lofty treatise can improve.
As fire lifts air so that it rises up
An unseen heat is hand to my basket –

Balloon above the quiet of your thought
So my soft shadow looks across your face
And dares not gently descend quite so soon
So as to lose your place but land my kiss.

Clocks – David Coldwell

Holding hands, we balance and hop
in silence through the long grass so as
not to wake the farm dogs.
The metal field gate resists my push
and prints a leaf green pattern on my coat
whilst I shoulder it wide into the land. You're riding high,
holding tightly until thin pink wellingtons skid
off and your cry wakes the dogs.

This day, this walk, this place where we rest
is bottled heart shaped in the spring light.
Your cry subsides to a murmur and a big bottom lip
slowly disappears as I hand you the flower,

the seed head that you take tightly in your hand;
never letting go as though life depended on it.
The blow ball slowly disappears to the wind,
dissolving to nothing as the hours fizz away.

You're now ahead of me
bending at the knees to pick a bunch,
spinning and singing as you watch each magic dance;
feathered angels that slowly part and fade away.

Time is against us but I show you the game:
we count with each forced breath
until there is nothing left
but the bare green stem, held tightly.

Make a wish, you shout
with excited eyes of something only you know.
I take back your hand, swinging as you skip
I already have, I say, as you break free.

Home Thoughts, From Abroad – Robert Browning

Oh, to be in England
Now that April's there,
And whoever wakes in England
Sees, some morning, unaware,
That the lowest boughs and the brushwood sheaf
Round the elm-tree bole are in tiny leaf,
While the chaffinch sings on the orchard bough
In England—now!

And after April, when May follows,
And the whitethroat builds, and all the swallows!
Hark, where my blossomed pear-tree in the hedge
Leans to the field and scatters on the clover
Blossoms and dewdrops—at the bent spray's edge—
That's the wise thrush; he sings each song twice over,
Lest you should think he never could recapture
The first fine careless rapture!
And though the fields look rough with hoary dew,
All will be gay when noontide wakes anew
The buttercups, the little children's dower
—Far brighter than this gaudy melon-flower!

Chime – Geoffrey Winch

Sister? – how I envisage you,
our mother's desire – for you
she would have declared the truth

but all too late she told me
how close we once had been , so close
we could not have been told apart.
Yet all too soon – probably

the day the sirens wailed
as the enemy holed the town's arcade –
you slipped through the world –
silently protesting about discord?

For a time all bells were muffled
so I never heard your urging,
then when they began to ring again
I failed to know your voice.

Sister – there's always been a reason
why bells have appealed, but only
of late I've heard your bell-words
telling me how she's made her peace.

At Home – Pat Simmons

For Hugh

The man across the ward has a pot plant
and a television set and now his wife
has brought a little reading lamp. They close
his curtains and sit quiet in their fantasy home.

It must be cosy in there: the trolleys' clanging
muffled, and the bleeps of chemo machines
pushed to a far distance, to another world,
where they have chosen not to live.

We do not have such organising energy.
We're scared to gather a fabric tomb around us.

So we sit, me skewed and awkward, neck cricked
by hospital furniture arrangements,
you curled in the whispering womb of the ripple bed.
And we hold each other's hands, our only home

in this new grey land where we did not choose to live.
Between our palms we hold our privacy, the space
where love and warmth can nestle and a thousand
little jokes we do not need to tell.

And when I leave there are no walls to hide
the fierce and gentle glory of our kiss.

From *Cracking On: poems on ageing by older women*, (Grey Hen Press, 2009)

Keeping Faith – Angela Topping

i.m. Matt Simpson & Michael Murphy

Very well, old friend, I will keep faith with you.
On our last walk together you showed me
the long grass where you scattered seeds for Michael
not knowing whether they would grow or fail.

Those seeds had not been in the ground a month
when you yourself had parted with your breath
and we were left bereft without your love.

You'd made promises to look for him
as sparks of flowers under summer skies
where specks of larks ascend and zephyrs blow.

On such a day as that I will arise
and take the path again that we two shared
to see the weeds that hopefully you sowed,
and scour the skies for one high-flying bird.

From *I Sing Of Bricks* (Salt, 2011)

Familiar – R V Bailey

Call it unfortunate if you will - I
Can certainly understand why -
But love is so *persistent*. It just goes on
After, you might reasonably say, its usefulness is done,
However silent the house, empty the bed,
Obsequies long since over, long since buried the dead...

Love is a damaged thing, trailing absurd,
Forlorn and pathetic as a dressing-gown cord.
Intimate as breath, loyal as a shadow, close as a cry,
Nothing will shake it off.
                                        Nor should you try.

From *The Losing Game*, (Mariscat Press, 2010)

A Minor Role – U A Fanthorpe

I'm best observed on stage,
Propping a spear, or making endless
Exits and entrances with my servant's patter,
Yes, sir. O no, sir. If I get
These midget moments wrong, the monstrous fabric
Shrinks to unwanted sniggers.

But my heart's in the unobtrusive,
The waiting-room roles: driving to hospitals,
Parking at hospitals. Holding hands under
Veteran magazines; making sense
Of consultants' monologues; asking pointed
Questions politely; checking dosages,
Dates; getting on terms with receptionists;
Sustaining the background music of civility.

At home in the street you may see me
Walking fast in case anyone stops:
O, getting on, getting better my formula
For well-meant intrusiveness.

At home,

Thinking ahead: Bed? A good idea!
(Bed solves a lot); answer the phone,
Be wary what I say to it, but grateful always;
Contrive meals for a hunger-striker; track down
Whimsical soft-centred happy-all-the-way-through novels;
Find the cat (mysteriously reassuring);
Cancel things, tidy things; pretend all's well,
Admit it's not.

Learn to conjugate all the genres of misery:
Tears, torpor, boredom, lassitude, yearnings
For a simpler illness, like a broken leg.

Enduring ceremonial delays. Being referred
Somewhere else. Consultant's holiday. Saying Thank you
For anything to everyone.
                                        Not the star part,
And who would want it? I jettison the spear,
The servant's tray, the terrible drone of Chorus:
Yet to my thinking this act was ill-advised
*It would have been better to die)**. No, it wouldn't!

I am here to make you believe in life.

**Chorus: from Oedipus Rex (trans. E. F. Watling)*

Alicia's Diary – John Stocks

Meet me and I shall know you, light and shadow
A formless, fantastic distillation,
Confection of smoke and fogs and gaslight.

Meet me and I'll watch you as you wander
Dreamily up pea-souped side streets,
Long neck hidden by black buttoned collar,
Your exhaled breath a ghostly miasma,
Drifting past the clanking city tram-cars,
The news boy who teases you, calling out your name.

Meet me on Fargate, waiting at Cole's corner,
Top hat and tailed, tapping with my cane,
Yours for all eternity my darling,
Yours beyond the final cutting edge of time.

Late for your theatre tea, warm hands wrapped in velvet,
Hat pulled down over your pert, pink ears,
Your diary shows me all your sweet conceits,
And makes me long to hold you- snug as the grave.

First published in *Other Poetry* magazine

Remembrance – Maya Angelou

Your hands easy
weight, teasing the bees
hived in my hair, your smile at the
slope of my cheek. On the
occasion, you press
above me, glowing, spouting
readiness, mystery rapes
my reason

When you have withdrawn
your self and the magic, when
only the smell of your
love lingers between
my breasts, then, only
then, can I greedily consume
your presence.

From *The Complete Collected Poems Of Maya Angelou* (Virago, an imprint of Little, Brown Book Group)

Coruscation – Angus Ogilvy

Light accentuates dark.

In winter dawns
I turn on my lamp
and morning rolls over to midnight.

Dark accentuates light.

Relinquishing gloom
I am dazzled
by the lustre of the universe.

It doesn't matter that
the house burns down in the night
in a pre-emptive attack on murk.

It doesn't matter that
hope's slim candle splutters
on its see-saw dance with dread.

Only my light,
which accentuates
and is accentuated
by dark,
shall pass.

Previously published in *Lights in the Constellation of the Crab* (Hermit Crab 2012)

Opening Up The Possibility Of Perfect – K V Skene

only to ride that memory-go-round
while all our painted horses
gallop into summerhaze, impervious
to the rise and fall of small iridescent voices,
flutter of pony tails, flying high-fives
that cover the thud of hooves
hooked on fairground music; slightly too loud,
too innocent, too beautiful, too
sad – so much of you is part of me
and yet ...
                                        and yet
you were dying to be told
what I thought you should never have been told
swung from gynaecology, oncology, radiology, theology
with a stubborn smile
opening up the possibility of perfect
as sunset, a slivered moon, our sleepy children
all get carried away
to wherever they must go – but it's all right now
it's all over.

Previously published in *Reach Poetry* magazine #155

Butterflies – Sue Johnson

The Thames laps the moss-covered wall
and I know that soon
the tide will carry you away from me

I don't know which tide yet
no one can say whether this or the next

It's hard to think of dying when the sun's shining
I try to cast out the fear of death
that lingers from my childhood
hoping instead
you'll turn into a butterfly
and your soul will take wings and soar into a cloudless sky.

I draw strength from the colours I see from the train –
a pink scooter leaning against
a corrugated iron shed painted lilac and purple
white shirts flapping on a balcony
where a blue butterfly flirts with scarlet geraniums

My mobile rings and I sense the tide has turned
imagine you happy and flying free.

Lift Home – Fred Beake

So, she tearfully discusses it with me
now news of the treatment has come
(as three or four others I have known)
because she has to discuss it with someone.

We talk of the things that might be done
– to help the healing, vitamins,
videos and music to distract her fear.
I mention others I have known.

She tells me about her brother
– his pain and weakness, and the degradations
of hospital; mentions he was a boxer –
says she does not mind death

but only this pain that has begun
already. We go back to videos.
She says she can watch Titanic
over and over again.

I glance out at the wind-blown hedges
along this country lane
down which I daily drive a short cut home,
think how many leaves must have been undone

but the trees continue on
– for a while at least,
and with all this rain, and now abrupt sun
the emerald meadows flame.

Previously published in the *London Magazine* and the collection *"The Old Outlaw"* (Shoestring Press)

The Good-Morrow – John Donne

I wonder by my troth, what thou and I
Did, till we loved ? were we not wean'd till then ?
But suck'd on country pleasures, childishly ?
Or snorted we in the Seven Sleepers' den ?
'Twas so ; but this, all pleasures fancies be ;
If ever any beauty I did see,
Which I desired, and got, 'twas but a dream of thee.

And now good-morrow to our waking souls,
Which watch not one another out of fear ;
For love all love of other sights controls,
And makes one little room an everywhere.
Let sea-discoverers to new worlds have gone ;
Let maps to other, worlds on worlds have shown ;
Let us possess one world ; each hath one, and is one.

My face in thine eye, thine in mine appears,
And true plain hearts do in the faces rest ;
Where can we find two better hemispheres
Without sharp north, without declining west ?
Whatever dies, was not mix'd equally ;
If our two loves be one, or thou and I
Love so alike that none can slacken, none can die.

Ultrasound – Elaine Trevitt

The sonographer sweeps the probe
the length of my belly
and exclaims.

She finds the moon
has slipped from its orbit
as a heavenly body

and landed in mine
in an uncharted transit across my liver
bright curve tight under my diaphragm

luminous and full, and ominous
but better the moon, I think
than an endless sea.

I think of the moon landings
and ponder my own
giant leap

wonder how my landing may be
at the end of the journey
I am only just beginning

We Refugees – Benjamin Zephaniah

I come from a musical place
Where they shoot me for my song
And my brother has been tortured
By my brother in my land.

I come from a beautiful place
Where they hate my shade of skin
They don't like the way I pray
And they ban free poetry.

I come from a beautiful place
Where girls cannot go to school
There you are told what to believe
And even young boys must grow beards.

I come from a great old forest
I think it is now a field
And the people I once knew
Are not there now.

We can all be refugees
Nobody is safe,
All it takes is a mad leader
Or no rain to bring forth food,
We can all be refugees
We can all be told to go,
We can be hated by someone
For being someone.

I come from a beautiful place
Where the valley floods each year
And each year the hurricane tells us
That we must keep moving on.

I come from an ancient place
All my family were born there
And I would like to go there
But I really want to live.

I come from a sunny, sandy place
Where tourists go to darken skin
And dealers like to sell guns there
I just can't tell you what's the price.

I am told I have no country now
I am told I am a lie
I am told that modern history books
May forget my name.

We can all be refugees
Sometimes it only takes a day,
Sometimes it only takes a handshake
Or a paper that is signed.
We all came from refugees
Nobody simply just appeared,
Nobody's here without a struggle,
And why should we live in fear
Of the weather or the troubles?
We all came here from somewhere.

From *Wicked World* (Puffin, 2000) with kind permission.

Phone Call – Margaret Beston

I hold your voice in my hand, picture
jet-black hair glossy from the shower -

you, listening to Lorca on a gramophone
in the Paris flat we shared in the 60s.

Your words struggle through my fingers,
jolt me into the present, as you grapple

with a new vocabulary, its harsh
consonants hawking in your throat.

My voice stumbles over alien sounds
like a stranger in an unfamiliar house,

pushes aside altered images, elbows past
men and babies, different cities,

until it finds you. And for a moment
we're back, laughing as we soak up sun

on our tiny balcony, long before rogue cells
invaded. When there was only future.

Night song – Moira Andrew

Radio 4 says nightingales
are in danger – surely they've
got that wrong?
I remember its scalpel song
slicing the summer night,
of la Vayssiere.

I remember the wide bed,
how it complained as we
rolled helpless
into the middle, feeling for
one another in a spiral of
luminous dark.

I remember your grim joke,
determined grimace, when pain
twisted your heart,
me thinking how temperamental
mobiles could be in this
godforsaken valley.

But this time round your spray
worked its magic and we made
frantic love
while from deep in the patch-
work woods, rose an unbroken
thread of song.

(First published in *Firebird*, Indigo Dreams Publishing, 2011)

Tomorrow I will remember – Emer Davis

Tomorrow I will remember,
remember the times
I followed your gaze,
the time I felt your eyes
covering every inch of me,
as we moved through the crowd.

Tomorrow I will gather you up
and take you with me
across the fields of our youth
shrouded in rhododendrons
I remember the time
we showered ourselves in pink petals.

Tomorrow I will remember,
remember the times
I bathed your feet
in a sea of blue
crystallised in salted memories,
we watched our shadows disappear.

Tomorrow I will take you
to that resting place of ours,
and spread your speckled dust
across the white ripples
surging towards me
as we say goodbye.

Tortoise Valentine – Norman Bissett

O, my beautiful, iron-clad love,
my *testudo elephantopus,*
my gentle juggernaut,
my ponderous, sweet, sagacious giantess,
preceding me slowly across Galapagos
on square-cut mahogany feet,
you set my heart a-flutter
as coyly you crane your leather neck
for succulent titbits of cactus.

Ah, but your neck is comely,
like swamp-coloured parchment.
In your glittering eye
lurks the wisdom of the ages.
That you appear impregnable
challenges me, mightily.
Come, let me shelter and shade you
beneath my millennium dome.
Let us grow geriatric together.

No Crying – Jacquie Swift

It is dark outside, but there is no crying.
The moon is creeping its pathway along the sea
and the stars pepper the ink soaked sky.
But there is still no crying.

Nor is there crying as the sun
steers itself over the brightening edge,
paints the rippled, angle of the earth's planes
with its languid, spreading glaze.

There can be no crying for it is too big.
This impending erasure, this stealing
of world, self, family, sons
is too hard a lesson to accept, but
there can be no crying for today
and none for yesterday.

These are to be treasured, savoured, now.
There is a deep longing in my breast
for what is here, this passing moment,
things, flowers, loved possessions
gathered over so many years.

But, for the loss of all those longed for tomorrows
there can be no crying
for it is too big
and the tears would never end.

'C' and Faith – Anne Dunford

This thing 'C'
It really tests faith alright.
That Don Cupitt,
he talked about the Sea of Faith.
Me, I've just had problems with
'C' and faith.

How come someone,
only half way through
a normal life-span
finds they've got a relationship,
an all too close relationship,
with big 'C'.

All too soon that relationship ends
and so does their life.
Why them?
What did they do to deserve that?
Who has the answers?
'Have faith my son.'
Show me the faith that
can give me a good answer.

Bath – Myra Schneider

Kindness, an Irish lilt in her voice,
spares me the effort of running the water
and supports my elbow when, stripped
of everything but wound dressings,
I take a giant step into the tub.

Warm water wells into my crotch,
unlocks spine, lullabies stomach.
Is it because I've passed through
extremity that this comfort is intense
as the yellow daffodils trumpet?

Yesterday - my raw body stranded
by the basin, chill sprouting on my skin
while a Chinese student nurse
conscientiously dabbed each
helpless area - is miles away.

Dimly, I remember a stark room
and the high-sided saltwater bath
I was dipped in a few days
after giving birth. As Kindness
babies my back with a pink flannel

I'm reborn though maimed, ageing.
And this pool of bliss can no more
be explained than the song that pours
from a lark as it disappears into
stitchless blue, the seed circles

that cram a sunflower's calyx,
day splashing crimsons
and apricot golds across the sky
before it seeps into the silence
of night, the way love fountains.

From *Writing My Way Through Cancer* (Jessica Kingsley, 2003)
and *Multiplying The Moon* (Enitharmon 2008)

Pleasure Beach – Paul McDonald

We came of age one weekend in Blackpool:
sixteen and on the lam, too young for the vodka
and quarter ounce of resin. Your dad would have

murdered me then crucified the corpse.
We partied at Man Fridays,
mirror ball freckling our embrace,

drove our neighbours nuts in the guest house.
At the Pleasure Beach we breakfasted on Bombay mix.
I bought a flick-knife comb;

you lost your Alice band around the Revolution.
With a rifle and a row of ducks I bagged a teddy bear
who sat and watched our second night of love,

then became your pillow for the coach ride home.
He lives beside a suitcase on the wardrobe now:
thirty three this summer, still looking horror struck.

Migrant Hawker – Caroline Gill

You skim through my hair on this dragonfly day,
zig-zagging along as you harvest my thoughts,
to bind them in bands on your rainbow today.

You soar with red admirals, hover with honey bees;
pausing, then drifting, and scattering dreams
of turquoise and bronze on this harlequin day.

Oak leaves are rustling and summer is ending:
your teneral frame proves that more is to come,
but your presence alone will suffice for today.

Who knows how you came to alight on my trellis,
preferring the warmth of my buddleia's bloom
to the whisper of reeds on this pivotal day?

Your wings gather gold from an updraft of current
as sunlight emerges through shadows of cloud,
restraining those equinox blues for today.

My Mother's Ashes – Carrie Etter

I wanted to get naked, dip a finger
in water, dip a finger in you,
and begin painting my skin till
it was half me, half you in
a more accurate self-representation.
I wanted to upend the urn
like you said I toppled the sugar jar
at two: I reached up and its crystal grains
spilled over me, over the counter;
you walked in and I called, "Hi, Moddy,"
as though nothing were amiss.
(Nothing was.) In the night I wanted
to dig a hole in the back yard
and crawl in after you.
In the day I wanted to Victorianize,
have your ashes sealed in a clear
glass locket to rest an inch below
my larynx, a surrogate voice.
I wanted to sprinkle a little
into flour, egg and cocoa
and feed the cake of you to everyone.
I wanted to sit with my four sisters,
your twelve grandchildren, and say
"her own recipe" and "it's the best cake
I'll ever make."

First published in *Poetry Review*

Celery Soup – Maggie Sawkins

I fetch the chair from the formica table
to reach into the cupboard

take the butterfly opener
from the drawer and turn and turn
till the ragged edge lifts.

The creamy liquid plops into the pan
and I stir in a figure of eight
the way she taught me to.

I lay the tray with salt and pepper
arrange triangles of sliced white bread.

I carry it up to her bedroom
where she is propped against the pillow,
steam warms her face but she doesn't smile
because every Friday they burn her skin
and they've taken her breast away.

It feels like a dream

except my footprints are still there
embedded in the blueness
of a blue kitchen chair.

Spots – Sharon Larkin

Experts say sunspots
on eleven year cycles
relate to global temperatures.
Lots of spots there
make it warmer here.
Cynics might dismiss
carbon emissions
in comparison.

This morning
when spring cleaning
I found fly dirt on the light bulb
in the middle of the ceiling
with correlations to the quantity
of bluebottle droppings
on the lampshade.
But with strong detergent
in a little water
I washed it all off.

Last week X-rays disclosed
a shadow on your lung
possibly a reflection
of exposure to asbestos.
Can't scrub that away.
Can't pooh pooh that.
Can't pretend you're not
at the core of my universe.

Luck of the draw – Alwyn Marriage

I heard today of someone's mother,
rising a hundred in a few months' time,
who's blind and lives alone,
smokes forty cigarettes a day,
drinks two whole bottles of neat gin each week,
which in itself is something of a feat.

I also met a man whose overweight
body, just three short years ago,
was riddled with disease,
and yet who, thanks to the NHS
escaped death's clutches and now lives
largely in the unhealthy way he did before.

And yet, over the last few years
I've lost two friends through cancer:
both light-drinking, active, slim non-smokers,
cheerful women, who faced their fears
courageously and fought the mad,
exponential cells with hope and determination.

Clearly some strike lucky
while others are defeated,
but it's difficult in the circumstances
not to react with anger in the face
of such injustice,
or at the very least
feel cheated.

You All In White – Leonard Cohen

Whatever cities are brought down,
I will always bring you poems,
and the fruit of orchards
I pass by.

Strangers in your bed,
excluded by our grief,
listening to sleep-whispering,
will hear their passion beautifully explained,
and weep because they cannot kiss
your distant face.

Lovers of my beloved,
watch how my words put on her lips like clothes,
how they wear her body like a rare shawl.
Fruit is pyramided on the window-sill,
songs flutter against the disappearing wall.

The sky of the city
is washed in the fire
of Lebanese cedar and gold.
In smoky filigree cages
the apes and peacocks fret.
Now the cages do not hold,
in the burning street man and animal
perish in each other's arms,
peacocks drown around the melting throne.

Is it the king
who lies beside you listening?
Is it Solomon or David
or stuttering Charlemagne?

Is that his crown
in the suitcase beside your bed?
When we meet again,
you all in white,
I smelling of orchards,
when we meet—

But now you awaken,
and you are tired of this dream.
Turn toward the sad-eyed man.
He stayed by you all the night.
You will have something
to say to him.

Plainsong – Deborah Harvey

for TCH

I was bringing in the washing,
folding laundered clothes and bedding,
all woven with the warmth of early summer,
when I noticed the new leaves on the creeper,
how in their gleaming
they were the colours of carnival glass.

That night the rain in the crab apple tree,
the plainsong of ring doves
and thinking of you kept me from sleeping,
while the moon brimmed with fire mined from the dark,
light finally freed of its mantle of rock.
It was numinous, perfect.

From *Communion* (Indigo Dreams Publishing, 2011)

Hospital Song – Penelope Shuttle

I'm my own nurse,
my own cardiologist,
my own operating theatre,
my own MRSA

I'm the visitor
with her smile of disbelief

I'm the one in the next bed
swiftly hidden behind screens,
dying in a panic-scrum of doctors

I'm the hospital
sleepless all night,
the consent form,
the morgue

I'm the pain and the salve,
the stricken one yelling -
          get me out of here

I'm my own heartbeat
pounding on and on
but why?
long after yours has stopped

By kind permission of The Manhattan Review and Bloodaxe Books

Spider – Chrys Salt

i.m Caroline Bingham

After submitting to therapy
at London Zoo
you showed me the photograph
and a certificate to prove it
you and the massive spider
in wary proximity.
Not exactly befriended you said
but cautiously tolerated
his bee-soft furriness
low-slung between knobble-kneed, articulated
hairy legs - crouched on your lapel
like an oversized brooch.

Having once relieved your hand basin
of a skittering country cousin
while you Miss Muffeted in the kitchen,
refusing point blank to pee
until I declared the bathroom a spider-free
zone - I was impressed.

After the cancer came back
I always wrote
'To Caroline, my conqueror of spiders'
on all my cards and letters.
A mantra of wishful thinking,
a coded note
addressed to your certificated courage
a cross fingered spell
against that other spider
deadly on your coat.

Blue Vein – Geraldine Green

I showed you my blue vein,
a think skein with green running through.

I showed you my greenblue vein that runs from my heart
finger all the way up my arm, takes in the camber of my elbow,

my greenblue vein runs like a stream to my shoulder, curves
and rests somewhere close to my breast.

I know what it means
you know what it means

but we don't speak of it.

Originally published in *Passio'* (Flarestack Publishing)

As If I Were Winter Itself – Pascale Petit

When I enter the hospital where my mother is lying

I will bring a flask of water collected from Lethe
and a flask from the Mnemosyne.

I will sip from each.
This will feel like swallowing shafts of sunlight.

I'll take deep breaths, hungry for canyon air.

A porter will rub fox-fire on my face
for the ride in the luminous lift.

Corridor walls will be translucent,
I'll see the trees imprisoned inside –

blue branches with old wounds as leaves,
red trees with raptor-roots.

Are you ready for the truth?

Ward Sister will ask, releasing
lemon-yellow and saffron butterflies.

They are the first flurry of winter
I'll reply, addressing

Mother's forgetting eye
and her remembering eye.

Then I'll say everything I always wanted to say to her.

The butterflies will mass on her bed,

rays streaming through the window
will wash us both.

Her hands will shake but that won't stop me.

From *Heart of a Deer* (Enitharmon, 1998)

Kate – Pippa McCathie

(for my niece)

I walked in a snow storm
to the edge of the sea
and I saw you dancing,
arms high above your head,
you turned, turned,
in the glow of the smile
that lit your face.

I wanted to catch you,
keep you beside me,
watch your silk gold hair
play with the wind,
hear your clear voice sing
or your man and your daughter.

I pleaded with you
to hold on till morning,
but you waved as you ran,
skip danced down the sand
into the sea
and away.

Originally published in *Reach Poetry* magazine

To My Wife Asleep – Philip Lyons

Years from now when we are both long dead
I hope there'll be an echo of this scene:
a man and woman lying in a bed,
the wife asleep, the husband curled around her,
and in the darkness just the sound of rain.

I lie here trying not to think of work.
Your heart is beating underneath my arm,
your body's warmth a comfort. Worries lurk
inside my skull like coils too tightly wound,
but till the morning they can do no harm.

The world will bark its orders soon enough.
For now I am content to be awake
and know that what I feel for you is love,
the common sort: two human beings bound
together by a bond that does not break.

From *Like It Is* (Poetry Space, 2011)

Anymore – Dennis Locorriere

She sold his old records, burned every book
Gave his good clothes to the poor
He made the most of what little he took
And never looked back anymore

She spent all the money, swept up the ashes
Plenty of closet space free
The pictures come back in sharp, blinding flashes
But, lately, they fade a lot faster
Where they used to cause total disaster
Now, they disappear almost immediately

It's not about him. It's all about her.
It's not about them...that's for sure
It's just about time she got through her head
She doesn't have a side of the bed

anymore

She sets her alarm clock for 6:45
Even on weekends these days
She's up and she's out, there's things she can do
And dreaming just seems like a waste

But, when she returns, puts her key in the door
The silence is shocking and deep
She counts every step on the polished wood floor
Fixes a drink that she never enjoys
Switches the radio on, for the noise
And, desperately, hopes that she'll soon be asleep

It's not about him. It's all about her.
It's not about love...what a bore!
It's about letting go. Everyone does
Nothing is anything near what it was

anymore

From *Whatever's Burning Now* (Indigo Dreams Publishing, 2011)

Washing my mother's hair – Char March

It's role-reversal time
she's bird-thin
fragile as her brittle smile
her teeth suddenly too big for her mouth
lips thinned, clumsy with Vaseline
to stop the cracks
showing

Only last summer
she broke the world record
for Running For The Bus
carrier bags thumping at her varicose legs
then fanned herself with the Radio Times
all the fifteen stops
home

Now her spine
is hooked
into a question mark
from which her head tries to look up
she doesn't have to bend at all to get her hair
into the wash
basin

For the first time
in my life, and hers,
I pour the warm water
the baby shampoo the best conditioner I could buy
rub the blushing whiteness of her scalp gently
while she holds her
flannel

clamped to her eyes
like she taught me to
and she says *Oh that's lovely.*
Just what I need, love. That's right, give it a good rub
Oh that's just lovely. I'll be a new woman.
and I rub and chat
quietly

and joke with her in a
put-on voice
Has Madam done her numbers for the lottery yet?
and *Will it be Torremolinos again this year, Madam?*
and the other things that mind-numbed hairdressers
say to their
ladies

and nothing at all
about how
much I love her
and how very strange it is to be feeling her wet hair
between my fingers for the very first time and how
worried I am by the
deepness

of the scoops in her neck
framed by
stirrups of collarbone and how
I've never seen her breasts before and how
surprisingly plump they are sitting on the stark
twin ladders of her
ribs

But she still has plenty
of reserve left
and asks me to call
the nurse to see to her b.t.m. – the bedsores and the simple
wearing thin of herself – but as I help her
into a clean
nightie

I catch sight of
her mons
hairless and pink
and looking so strangely new and suddenly I'm glad
to go and get the nurse because suddenly I can't
speak and I can't
see

where I'm going
and my Mum
is dying and I've
got to come to terms with it
and be sensible
    and look after my Dad
        and all I want is for her to wash my hair
            and tell me a bedtime story
                and not be
                    this very old bent lady with teeth
                        that are suddenly
                            too big
                                for her mouth.

From:
The Thousand Natural Shocks (Indigo Dreams Publishing, 2011)

My Mother's Shoes – Denise Bennett

For Ada aged 100

At five my mother wore loose boots
her brothers had worn, stuffed with rags
or torn paper; two sizes too big,
filled with the history of their lives.
Each day she skidded over fields,
to the village school.

In mid-life she had a fetish
for sexy black stilettos,
tap-clacking on lino or polished floors
of dance-halls, her feet taut as arrows.
Each night she teetered on spindle heels,
grew to five foot three.

In old age she bought comfort shoes
from charity shops:
satin pumps, *worn once for a wedding,*
red lace-ups, low heeled suede slip-ons.
Each day she trudged round the town
wearing down the weight of other lives.

At ninety eight, when she craved
something pretty,
I got her soft leather, silver slippers.
For one brief moment, I was Dandini,
she was Cinderella.
They nestle *unworn,* in her wardrobe.

She rarely gets out of bed now

Who Goes Amid the Green Wood – James Joyce

Who goes amid the green wood
With springtide all adorning her?
Who goes amid the merry green wood
To make it merrier?

Who passes in the sunlight
By ways that know the light footfall?
Who passes in the sweet sunlight
With mien so virginal?

The ways of all the woodland
Gleam with a soft and golden fire -- -
For whom does all the sunny woodland
Carry so brave attire?

O, it is for my true love
The woods their rich apparel wear -- -
O, it is for my own true love,
That is so young and fair.

Woodland Friend – Wendy Webb

I need a friend just now, and that friend's you,
to show the path that I've lost; there where she
is glistering in early morning dew.
For this is that place I would like to be.

I need a confidante, though it must seem
like I've a brightness, stumbling pebbles small
as you could tap aside. Your cobwebs dream
my shadowlands, where saplings rise up tall.

Do you know where I wander? Where and how
to find a startled deer of woodland glade
and then still trembling heartbeat to your Now.
You are a dream I had once, long replayed

into those yesterdays, when I was young.
Yet, for some time, I have not felt so strong.

Notes from the Balcony – Lynn Woollacott

The *Eucalyptus globulous* trees sway
as a green wall lizard quivers
on the wooden slats of the balcony,
he pauses, lifts one leg and dares
to hop onto my red nail polished toes,
and slither the peak of arch on my foot.
He stretches his neck to the sun and says,
I was lazing on a rocky slab
when my world loomed with shade,
the sky blackened,
the sun was eclipsed by a dark shadow,
all the birds fell silent
and the sea resounded,
a moment later it was light again.

The lizard slips down my foot
his cold belly and feet imprinting
his tiny proportioned touch. He begins
to feast on foraging ants,
chewing them open mouthed
as if about to spit out their exoskeletons,
but he won't wait to be photographed.
The essence of him leaves a needy presence
quite unlike the scars that struck
a random path that shimmer
across my sister's back and chest,
she smiles on the sun bed, scratches patchy,
auburn hair, and makes an exaggerated
reptile pose for my camera.

blood and bone – Julie Maclean

You feed the garden now
Remember that day
our first bird camouflaged
in the dusty feathers of the Cootamundra
Pinky cap nodding   Seeds appearing
for the first time   You fed bacon scraps
to the maggies   Your scaly fingers
clawed in the shadow of the hammer's grip
Hands, by the way, I love

You planted stakes in the west
Grosse Lisse were Aquarian children
Laterals were dreadlocks
You would not tame them
Murder you said

Three springs ago it was a moonscape
then grasses nosed through
Lines of purpling beetroot
Slicks of onion   Squatting mignon

I love to watch you work
The way you kneel,
gathering everything
up into the core of you
Intense   Silver-quick
One eye on the clock

Your back is stiffening
There's harvest in the making
It wasn't always this way

Autumn leaves – Julian Jordon

Mottled, like Autumn leaves,
her delicate skin, that once
drew admiring glances.

Mellow mists
those eyes that sparkled
at uniforms
home from the horrors.

Mere twigs, her limbs:
legs that ran
to the corner shop
for rationed sugar,
arms that held me safe.

She lies now,
curled on her side,
like a tiny question mark
on a linen page.

The tiny gold band
slips around her fading finger
as she clutches
the clinical chrome cot-side
of the bed
she will never leave,
still breathing.

It seems but a single tick
of the ceaseless clock
since 'that nice young doctor',
staring at his shoes,
had mumbled a prognosis.

The room had held its breath
as she stared for a moment
into the well of her memories,
then reached out to steady
the doctor's trembling hand,
and apologised
for the inconvenience.

Snapshots From Sheila's Life – Pauline Brehony

In memory of Sheila Waddington

Petite pupil with neat bob and brown uniform
stands beside the grand piano
auditioning for Iolanthe…
a serious child, eleven years old
with unassuming, valiant manner,
endearing smile —
my first encounter.

Decades later
there she is across the lounge
enjoying the music, poetry, company,
at Alma's elegant soiree.
Recognition. Conversation. Reminiscence.
And when the poetry is over:
"I'll drive you home!"
and, on the way:
"I'd love to come for Singing Lessons!"
"Then, *do*. Next week," I say.

"I'm creating cards for Christmas.
Like to come? I've all the gear."
And this I do;
And under her skilful tutelage
create a card for grandchild Rosie
of geisha girl and blossoming cherry tree.
Then, at my gate: "Loved seeing you," she says; —
Embracing me as though it were
for the last time.

It wasn't — quite.
I visit again, but with my son…
"You do know she will be changed," he warns,
And indeed she was —
I saw this as she flung the door ajar
(smiling…always smiling).
Body ravaged now and thin,
but spirit strong as The Phoenix.
She adjusts, sporadically,
a dark brown wig.
"A friend has purchased my house" she says;
"but, I may stay, until — !"

Hushed church, where candlelight creates
Rembrantian luminosity and shade. Taped music.
Advent of white coffin along the central aisle; —
funereal ship sailing The Styx.

Mourners minds teem with memories. And I recall
Her tutoring the Chinese Martial Art, Xi Gong —
And my laughter every time she said:
"Doctor Who is flying over from China and will stay with me."
A master of Xi Gong; and incredibly — his name!

Eulogy now, praising her talents, abundant qualities.
My son whispers: "Have you seen what's on top of the coffin?"
I hadn't. So now, I look. And, in place of a wreath,
I see — her white, skating boots!

I flip my brochure — and there she is, at an ice rink:
my former pupil, beloved friend (smiling…always smiling),
as with certainty she'll be
on the spiritual dimension her daring soul
has truly earned.

Certain Small Things – Cathy Bryant

i.m. Sarah Richards

Certain small things -
a way of laughing
like yours, quick and wry.
A Moomin mug.
Mauve woollen hand-knits.
Self deprecation.
White wine. Secret tears.
Quirky books, swift temper.
- some of them slip away
on oblivious nights or
busy afternoons.
Was it coffee you liked, or tea?
What colour were your eyes?
Why do some deaths touch
so much more than others,
yet details blur?
In guilt and grief
it's time to recall the list,
the litany of small things
still binding, still true.
The way you bit into cake.
Your silent offering of your heart.
A brown top with
a plunge neckline you wore
with a bold necklace
and your hair up.
Bravery. Some sort of stew.
Not liking to eat fruit.
The laughs we had
when you were at chemo.
A loathing of artsy fartsyness.

You were one of those who
quietly clear up at the end of things.
A blanket. A scarf. Your name.

So We'll Go No More a-Roving – Lord Byron

So we'll go no more a-roving
So late into the night,
Though the heart still be as loving,
And the moon still be as bright.

For the sword outwears its sheath,
And the soul outwears the breast,
And the heart must pause to breathe,
And love itself have rest.

Though the night was made for loving,
And the day returns too soon,
Yet we'll go no more a-roving
By the light of the moon.

Love Song of the Boatman – Eileen Carney Hulme

At the old boathouse
after you'd shown me
your stone skimming skills
I say we're in danger

As you breathe orange-blossom
secrets on the bare of my neck
we are unwrapping summer
like children at the coast

Kidnapping the sun
building invisible sand castles
treading barefoot over rocks
slip sliding on dreams

You say angels once lived here
watching over the boatmen
– for a second we are still
listening for their presence

On wooden beams we scroll
hieroglyphs of lovers long travelled
water hums and your fingers are feathers
beating the drum of my heart

The Way You – Gill McEvoy

It was the way you seemed to bounce
across Front Square as if your body held
some inner joy; the way you wouldn't dance
at parties but sat there, pipe in mouth,
considering the quainter follies
of the human race.

The way, later, you referred to me always
as "*my* wife", not "the *wife*"
as some men do.

It was all of these.
And I wanted it to last
forever.

First published on the online site, *Ink sweat and tears*

21 Orde Lane – Elaine Booth-Leigh

That first winter in Wallsend
the wind walked booming
into our lives – we could not
sleep in dawn-dipped chill.

You were sweet to kiss,
buffeted breath and sweat
from riding into gale and air,
hair blow-waved, set by sea salt.

We ate no meat and my oven
was a cardboard box, foil-lined.
You brought treasures: lentils
and *A Kumquat for John Keats*.

Divided by a Common Language – Liz Loxley

Never more foreign
than when she is cooking
vegetable pasta,
her nouns, her inflections:
'erbs -- tom*ato*, or*eg*ano,
b*as*il -- she peels zucchini,
steadies an eggplant,
fingers straddling
its purple belly.

At the table, she pours
two glasses of Mer*lot,*
watches it eddy
in its cut glass bowl,
inhales its fruit tang.

'Do you know' she says
'the name Mer*lot*
is thought to derive
from the Old French word
for young blackbird: Mer*lot,*
a diminutive of merle.'

Never less foreign
than when she's in bed,
where I unpeel her,
smooth the eggplants
of her breasts, breathe in
the Merlot of her skin.

Hallowe'en – Harry Owen

i.m. Judith Thwaite

Silence rings in the ears.
An orange grin stares down her mind
as children shriek in memory
and grey figures, mist-thin, swirl
like ectoplasm from the solid dark
until coffee dissolves them.

This room is thick with soft tissue.
Veins of thought circulate
the feculence of evening;
she toys with a séance of half-meaning,
dips sophisticated fingers
into a mess of superstitious nonsense,
knowing that none of this is true,
or all of it.

She smiles and nods as the end draws near,
but her skin whispers awkward incantations
to the air while shadows flicker
and the night nurse reads quietly on.

First published in the collection *The Music of Ourselves* (Cheshire County Council, 2004)

Communicating with the Comatose – Helen Victoria Anderson

If hearing is the last sense to go, you'll know I love you.
Not one for sentimental tripe, my tone was mocking, ironic,
but those nurses can tut-tut all they like–
I kid you not.

If hearing is the last sense to go, you'll know the baby's fine.
A bruiser boy – thirteen pounds – lumbered with your
gangly legs, your baldy head, your greedy guts
for life.

If hearing is the last sense to go, you'll know I see now,
it wasn't that straightforward. I judged harshly,
in angry adolescent monochrome. Grown-ups
forgive in colour.

If hearing is the last sense to go, you'll know I'll keep
this chit-chat torture up for days. Man of few words,
you'll long for a minute's peace or preferably
the Boro results.

If hearing is the last sense to go, you'll know it's time
to rage against their machines and refuse
to respire. Mum will never be alone
on my watch.

White Sunday – Pauline Kirk

Today is White Sunday.
Hawthorns open on verges,
in back yards, along railway sidings.
All this cool springtime
beauty has been held in store,
chilled for a late Whitsuntide.

Now even Stourbridge dazzles
through a diesel's dirty glass.
There is white everywhere:
cow parsley and daisies,
white dandelion clocks.
Every vacant plot
wears Whit Sunday dress.

Today, I saw the look of death
briefly on your face, but it passed.
For another summer, we will sit together
and laugh. The view from my train
is more lovely because of it.
White and cool and sharp, it hurts,
a sprig of hawthorn across my cheek.

Published in *Pennine Platform* and *Poetry Monash* (Australia)

Love in the Rain – Joan Sheridan Smith

Recalled, one birthday.
We were to meet some friends
for a boat trip and a picnic
In Regent's Park.

As the train left the station it grew dark.
A crack of thunder and a jagged knife
of lightning, sudden rain
cascading down the window.
We had the whole compartment to ourselves-
We were Dido and Aeneas in the cave.

No boats on the Serpentine.
Our friends, holed up in College rooms,
gave us a picnic on the floor,
and later, when it cleared
we took a bus to Richmond
and walked beside the river, eating
cherries from a paper bag.
He hung some round my ears.

But to him I was only a diversion.
I wanted something more.

Another time, again in summer rain,
We're walking, hair in rat-tails, muddy boots,
and thinking of the comfort of a pub,
of tea and toasted tea-cakes, and a bath.
A later love that lasted sixty years.

Climbing The Malverns – Greg Freeman

Picking strawberries, soft fruit caking jeans,
socks nibbled by something in the barn at night.
On a free Saturday, after Friday night revels,
accompanied by hangovers we climbed the Malverns,
all Herefordshire and Worcestershire beneath our feet.

You were a schoolmate I didn't know too well.
I bowed to your knowledge of British blues bands,
admired your cool. We tried it on with the Irish girls,
then walked on the beacon, wind wiping
school slate clean, landscape misting in the distance.

I had this plan of hitching to Cornwall;
you had it all mapped, a job in cartography.
Children of the suburbs and the Kingston bypass.
White boys' blues from the Thames delta;
black magic guitar of New Malden's Peter Green.

Life happened to you. The early wedding:
I look at the picture, the long-gone friends.
Afterwards you headed west. Occasional news.
Children, divorce, another marriage, more kids.
Out of the blue, a school reunion; that old, lazy smile.

A few years later, another message came. Now,
in first flush of our son's vows, we find ourselves
climbing the Malverns in apple harvest time.
Confetti showers of October leaves. The love
we saw in their faces. Albatross on the pub jukebox.
I raise my glass of cider, Kevin, remembering you.

Myfanwy – John Betjeman

Kind o'er the *kinderbank* leans my Myfanwy,
White o'er the playpen the sheen of her dress,
Fresh from the bathroom and soft in the nursery
Soap scented fingers I long to caress.

Were you a prefect and head of your dormit'ry?
Were you a hockey girl, tennis or gym?
Who was your favourite? Who had a crush on you?
Which were the baths where they taught you to swim?

Smooth down the Avenue glitters the bicycle,
Black-stockinged legs under navy blue serge,
Home and Colonial, Star, International,
Balancing bicycle leant on the verge.

Trace me your wheel-tracks, you fortunate bicycle,
Out of the shopping and into the dark,
Back down the avenue, back to the pottingshed,
Back to the house on the fringe of the park.

Golden the light on the locks of Myfanwy,
Golden the light on the book on her knee,
Finger marked pages of Rackham's Hans Anderson,
Time for the children to come down to tea.

Oh! Fullers angel-cake, Robertson's marmalade,
Liberty lampshade, come shine on us all,
My! what a spread for the friends of Myfanwy,
Some in the alcove and some in the hall.

Then what sardines in half-lighted passages!
Locking of fingers in long hide-and-seek.
You will protect me, my silken Myfanwy,
Ring leader, tom-boy, and chum to the weak.

First published in *Old Lights For New Chancels* (John Murray 1940) With kind permission of the publishers.

Where the heart is – John Webber

I thought of you today
in a way I had not thought
of you before.
I was in that house with you
but still unborn,
while you quietly went
about its rooms,
imagining the future,
enjoying the peace
while it lasted.

I must have heard you talking,
singing to yourself,
in that house, bought to house
my birth, my infancy.
All new to you this space,
motherhood, husband,
an unknown life ahead
with hope at the helm
and I was with you,
feeding on your hope.

I breathed the air you gave me,
synchronized my heart with yours
while you wondered
what the colour of my room should be.
And when you rested, tired from the labour
of me in your body,

I dreamed your dreams,
and wondered what this house would bring,
when I would be outside you,
but so very much within.

To my mum, Pam, who died from cancer 42 years later.

From *Stan's Highway* (UKA Press, 2013)

A Private Man – Eleanor Dent

Don't tell your colleagues
your husband has cancer
for I am a private man.

Don't tell your sisters
your lover has cancer
for I am a private man.

Don't tell your friends
that your best friend has cancer
for I am a private man.

Don't tell our son
that his father has cancer
for I am a private man.

We will go through this
together
but
in private.

River – Sophie Wellstood

i.m. Suzy Barratt 1964 – 2007

It was just so:
suddenly the air was soft mown grass
although the tower blocks
the shouting and the dogs
held the evening ugly

A smile pulled my face and then
I stepped into an afternoon and we were there
beside the hawthorn and warm cow parsley

I saw you leap the gate, I saw you
leave your shoes and run
through thistles in the cowpat field
the sun and you and birdsong in me

These are not my feet walking
this is not my mouth speaking
this is not my shadow, my shiver
I am in the fields with you, by the river

The Embroidered Cottage – Sue Moules

A thatched cottage with stepping stone path,
a garden and flowers around the door,
embroidered on brown linen, dated 1954.
Did we buy it at the Victoria Hall auction
or the British Legion jumble sale?

Too chocolate-box to be real,
yet such craft and skill .
We hung it in our council home
where the kids threw stones,
trampled on our runner beans:
"this is council, not yours" they'd say
as they jumped into the garden
to collect their footballs.

That picture
stitched by a woman long dead,
I fold in bubble wrap
as we clear your house
put in the charity box,
take out again,
ask my daughter:
"May I keep this?"

on the morning of my death – Jim Bennett

the buses will still run into Lime Street
people will get off and make their way to the Library
museum and Art gallery
and all the paintings, books and objects
I looked at touched read
and loved will still be there
for everybody else to see

people will sit in cafes and bars in Liverpool 1
discuss news   plan holidays
lives together or figure out how to say goodbye
others will watch them scribble notes for poems
later try and find the right words
to write up their vicarious lives

flags will fly at mast top
people will dance   sing   make love
the concert that I had tickets for will go ahead
the one or two empty seats unremarked
there will be no announcement from stage
few people will notice

the ferry will still cross the Mersey
playing Gerry over and over again
a whole bunch of things I always intended to do
will have to be done by someone else
that is how it will be
no clash of thunder final trump of angels
just another day on the morning of my death

His tweed suit – Anna Kisby

passes me on the street today
hung on an elderly gent, natural as a pelt.

I want to call it Dunkirk-green –
he *was* there – but it's more a camouflage
for heroism. A gentle man's cloth –

for all he could bare-handed hold
pots of potatoes straight from the stove.
Here's its good taint

of sweat long-settled into wool.
My cheek against its bristles
as good a thing as butter

spread against toast. The scratch
of dancing shins on which I learnt to balance.
My stride more stable

for the certainty of its good lap. Trousers hitched,
he sits with the News of the World
to form delicate birds that vanish

behind high shoulders
with a *Fly away Peter, fly away Paul!*
So that here in the street I mutter

an answer –
Come back Peter, come back Paul –
to the vanishing back of his suit.

I feel I should address you by your full name – Nicky Phillips

For Rita Plumb – friend and inspiration.

You first came into my consciousness
some long time ago, twenty years maybe.
I'd heard a bit about you before then
but our circles hadn't overlapped.
Then a good friend of mine grew close to you
but left without letting you sort things out.
She talked about you with such enthusiasm,
bright-eyed, radiant with expectation.
I learned from her about your work,
which I admire immensely;
it's everywhere these days.
You touch so many lives.
You're the sort my mum might have liked:
strong, focussed, the helpful type,
though with quite a destructive streak.
Mum was before your time but
things worked out well for her nevertheless.

Last week we met again, you and I.
We weren't formally introduced
but I sat in with you and my friend Charlie.
Much as I respect and am in awe of you,
I'd rather not get to know you well –
keep a distance, not become familiar.
So as I show appreciation of all you do,
I'll use your full name. Thank you, Chemotherapy.

Annabel Lee – Edgar Allan Poe

It was many and many a year ago,
In a kingdom by the sea,
That a maiden there lived whom you may know
By the name of ANNABEL LEE;
And this maiden she lived with no other thought
Than to love and be loved by me.

I was a child and she was a child,
In this kingdom by the sea;
But we loved with a love that was more than love –
I and my Annabel Lee;
With a love that the winged seraphs of heaven
Coveted her and me.

And this was the reason that, long ago,
In this kingdom by the sea,
A wind blew out of a cloud, chilling
My beautiful Annabel Lee;
So that her highborn kinsman came
And bore her away from me,
To shut her up in a sepulchre
In this kingdom by the sea.

The angels, not half so happy in heaven,
Went envying her and me –
Yes!– that was the reason (as all men know,
In this kingdom by the sea)
That the wind came out of the cloud by night,
Chilling and killing my Annabel Lee.

But our love it was stronger by far than the love
Of those who were older than we –
Of many far wiser than we –
And neither the angels in heaven above,
Nor the demons down under the sea,
Can ever dissever my soul from the soul
Of the beautiful Annabel Lee.

For the moon never beams without bringing me dreams
Of the beautiful Annabel Lee;
And the stars never rise but I feel the bright eyes
Of the beautiful Annabel Lee;
And so, all the night-tide, I lie down by the side
Of my darling- my darling- my life and my bride,
In the sepulchre there by the sea,
In her tomb by the sounding sea.

Effigies – John Mole

They lie side by side,
Her hand in his,
No hound at their feet
But a restless cat
That prowls the duvet
Until it discovers
The crook of his spare
Extended arm.

Two effigies, remembering
How they would wake
And turn to each other
When her body allowed,
But visited now
By a phantom embrace
No less in love
Than they ever were.

First published in *TLS*

Two Become One – Emma Lee

I'd be trapped: hands in washing up water
gazing over your garden (it was yours, not ours)
You'd stand behind, slip arms around my waist.
The window would reflect a couple back at us.

I feel that presence now, as if something
in my peripheral vision as there's one less
set of dishes to wash and no reflected couple
in the darkening window.

Originally published in *Under the Radar* magazine #10

Washed Clean – Jacqueline Pemberton

Baby clean; haloed by the
Pink haze of disinfectant,
Hair capped back,
Face blank.

I'm marked with the sign of the cross,
The place where the knife enters,
Cuts through bone and nerves.

The surgeon said the scar will be 'this big'
Stretching his hand, wide as it would go.

My unblemished skin mourns
Dancing frocks I will never wear.
Blue hospital nightdress folded
At the end of my bed,

Balloons into life with
Frayed white tags,
Mimicking modesty.

Three hours until theatre,
This is the unknowing time,
A dubious bliss of ignorance.

On waking I will be told
News I cannot
Refuse to hear.

Trees wave outside my window.
One nurse told me you can hear Blackpool Zoo;
Cries carry both ways by the wind.

Joining up the dots – Alison Lock

I juggle half shell to half shell.
A string of mucus
loosens, a swinging thread drifts
like a memory.

I see the tension in her arm, folding
in the flour, milk, tears,
while I push in my cutter, making
the shape of a star.

That night we look up at the loved ones
as they join up the dots,
sketching their ploughs
and bears and dragons until —

Up there!
she is pointing to a new arrival,
one that is pulling on a thread —
stitched into our hearts.

Dorothy's Doctor – Kate B Hall

Just home last night
front room full of unpacked stuff
Dorothy's doctor thinks
Dorothy has breast cancer
I can't think about anything else
I wander from room to room
Dorothy's doctor thinks
Dorothy has breast cancer
No, no I think
that can't be right
she's had children
did she breast feed?
did she used to smoke?
I didn't know her then
can't cry, can't concentrate
can't believe you won't be home
until tomorrow
outside some kid's crying itself hoarse
the way they do
and the April showers continue to shower
Dorothy's doctor thinks
Dorothy has breast cancer
and all I can think of to do
is write a fucking poem

February - a poem of hope – Ian Clarke

Close the curtains,
shut out the dark,
the fox hunted red raw,
keep out the wind ribbed sea,
a gale rinsing rock to shingle,
shingle to sand,

and look beyond snow saddled roofs,
beyond the earth's curve crusting,
to a green murmur on acres starved,
to a river nectar drowsy,
a damsel fly's blue cooling into flight,
and under the window shadow choked earth

thaws to pearl tears:
their light bowed moon dipped and brittle,
shadow scented and rising white,
winter's last breath drained to a shiver,
spring star bare and perfect
hatching between frost and roses.

From *A Slow Stirring* (Indigo Dreams Publishing 2012)

Love Is Just A Four-Letter Word – Bob Dylan

Seems like only yesterday
I left my mind behind
Down in the Gypsy Café
With a friend of a friend of mine
She sat with a baby heavy on her knee
Yet spoke of life most free from slavery
With eyes that showed no trace of misery
A phrase in connection first with she I heard
That love is just a four letter word

Outside a rambling storefront window
Cats meowed to the break of day
Me, I kept my mouth shut, too
To you I had no words to say
My experience was limited and underfed
You were talking while I hid
To the one who was the father of your kid
You probably didn't think I did, but I heard
You say that love is just a four letter word

I said goodbye unnoticed
Pushed towards things in my own games
Drifting in and out of lifetimes
Unmentionable by name
Searching for my double, looking for
Complete evaporation to the core
Though I tried and failed at finding any door
I must have thought that there was nothing more
Absurd than that love is just a four letter word

Though I never knew just what you meant
When you were speaking to your man
I can only think in terms of me
And now I understand
After waking enough times to think I see
The Holy Kiss that's supposed to last eternity
Blow up in smoke, its destiny
Falls on strangers, travels free
Yes, I know now, traps are only set by me
And I do not really need to be
Assured that love is just a four letter word

River Exe mussels with chilli, tomato and parsley at Rick Stein's Café – Dawn Bauling

The foreplay is with warm bread and olive oil:
you drip, I lick my lips like a cat.
Then the mussels arrive
with just-opened steam
and a light dandruff of parsley.
You drool slightly before choosing,
teasing the dark, hard lips
to reveal a first soft pearl.
You suck its sweetness,
leaving a light aftermath
of garlic.

The Exe has done its work well.

I cross my legs
whilst you pluck and prick
with your perfect poet fingers,
slipping them between
teeth and tongue tip,
dipping into lemon and water
oil slick –
in out, out in, dripping
frivolity, necessity hidden.

O lucky bowl.
O lucky tongue.

You will spoon the juice slowly
saying the spice is just right
the flavours lingering:
"Just hot enough."
If only you knew.

We refuse dessert.

Let's Not Go Out On This Winter Day – Ronnie Goodyer

Let's not go out on this winter day,
the wind is shouting at the walls,
the fire won't take that long to catch,
the softness of the sofa calls.

Let's not go out on this winter day,
let's both hold still and think of ways
to travel worlds inside our heads,
refuse the places winter stays.

Let's walk through books, let's walk through poems,
visit Fern Hill and Dover Beach;
to Yeats' Lake Isle of Innisfree,
Frost's America, Homer's Greece.

Let's drink too much and let's laugh too loud,
let's find what sheer indulgence brings!
Let's clink our glasses while we can
and catch each other's hiccupping!

Then let our music resound from rooms,
as we struggle to sing as one,
Strawberry Fields, Forever Young,
Redemption Song, Here Comes The Sun.

Let's not go out on this winter day
but well before the flames expire,
let's sink into each others arms,
make love before our winter fire.

The Song Of Wandering Aengus – W B Yeats

I went out to the hazel wood,
Because a fire was in my head,
And cut and peeled a hazel wand,
And hooked a berry to a thread;
And when white moths were on the wing,
And moth-like stars were flickering out,
I dropped the berry in a stream
And caught a little silver trout.

When I had laid it on the floor
I went to blow the fire a-flame,
But something rustled on the floor,
And some one called me by my name:
It had become a glimmering girl
With apple blossom in her hair
Who called me by my name and ran
And faded through the brightening air.

Though I am old with wandering
Through hollow lands and hilly lands,
I will find out where she has gone,
And kiss her lips and take her hands;
And walk among long dappled grass,
And pluck till time and times are done
The silver apples of the moon,
The golden apples of the sun.

With grateful thanks and acknowledgement to the Estate of W.B. Yeats. From *The Collected Poems Of W.B. Yeats*.

Souvenir – Catherine Graham

Flashbacks
polished like prized bric-à-brac.

The lustre of love
longed for like sleep, sleep
for the insomniac.

When do memories become souvenirs,
trophies
tarnished by quicksilver tears?

If, when all is said
and inevitably done,
we pay the piper, we call the tune

then it's the pure gold shine of your love
I'll remember –
your mouth, your kiss, your atomic number.

From her collection *Things I Will Put In My Mother's Pocket*
(Indigo Dreams Publishing 2013)

Butterfly at Parthenay – Tina Negus

Feathers and bones of a dry, dead swallow
on the stone flags inside the doorway.
Living
symbol of the summer sun,
flying into this ancient church some seasons past,
chasing insects, perhaps, for a brood of young
beneath the window's arch outside.
Visitors closed the door,
departing,
unaware.

Death,
in this place of life.

The rough now empty coffins left against the wall,
tell less of death than this frail form.
A butterfly brightly dancing in the beams of light
along the nave, will also die,
and lying, dry, in some dim dusty corner,
speak,
to future visitors.

Embers – Sophia Argyris

I remember your eyes
as they were at certain times;
when sunlight tilted in them,
emotions or desires lit them
into darker fires. Then you
bring a warmth of flames
stroking smoke into cool dark air.
Youth and stillness,
things we cannot keep,
everything I cannot rekindle.

Nothing burns now but time,
withering to ash and floating.
But I don't mind the scent
of charcoal so very much.
I breathe it in, hold it
in my mouth for moments,
taste the memory, remnants of heat,
the syllables of your name
until it fades and I am cold again.

Mind Games – Alison Michell

In the kitchen you hopscotch
with ingredients, juggle recipes -
this year the marmalade won't set.
Grandmother's footsteps sneak to the car,
safety lecture falling on deaf ears
so we play hide and seek with keys. I hate
these games, the way wily memories
shadow-box, sidestepping out of reach.

Except that the holiday in Brodick 1934
is Box Brownie sharp. You climb Goat Fell,
beat your favourite brother three and two
skipping all the bunkers. Still on the course
approaching ninety, a bit the worse
for wear with pacemaker and low
blood pressure, let me be your ball
of string to keep the way secure.

From *Look well to this day* (Bookmark Publications, 2012)

Trinity Ball – Catherine Higgins-Moore

A bleary eyed young couple
walked
3.5 miles
from Front Arch to Palmerstown Park.
Her
in last night's chiffon frock
protected
from the fresh wind
by an oversized tuxedo jacket,
silver high-heels in hand.
Him
still swigging from a bottle
of Jameson's.
Bow-tie lost
in the rose bush
beside the Graduates Memorial Building?
Love is a piggy-back
over a gravelly footpath,
a home-cooked breakfast,
the whole day spent in bed
with the rose
he picked as fresh
as the moment
he gave it.
Saved
in a makeshift vase
between
Whitman and Joyce.

First Night – David Mark Williams

Not sleepless, it's that both of you
cannot close your eyes to this
wrapt contemplation of each other,
lying side by side, face to face,
the room lit by a white moon.
Around you, the whole place hums,
wired and monitored.
This is where they cut you apart.
You're adrift now, separate,
no longer sharing the same body,
the same breath.
What is beginning is a slow
unravelling, as the heart demands
to be held tight.

Love on a Turkish Ferry – Angela Christopher

Sun bleaches lego-brick houses,
the sea is a moving silver net,
light rides waves, white boats trail foam.
Linked hands are everywhere. A girl's
pink watch and lime vest are caressed,
fingers linger on her bra strap.

Seagulls dive for thrown bread,
auburn hair is hugged by a beard.
Last night, I felt your razor sharp
stubble, your warm legs over mine.
Now couples pose for photographs,
babies suck bread, dark glasses shine.

A girl with hennaed hands laughs,
her face inside a man's black cap.
I feel the dizzy, strange fever
of our early love, the urgent
need to hold onto each other,
on that camping trip in Scotland.

Yesterday, in the yellow hotel room,
on a wide scarlet bed, our slow
kisses still had a kernel of fire.
Surrounded by youth, I go back,
see my young self in each girl's
trance-like glowing face.

Waiting – Jackie Wills

Where's my lover?

Not in the wind
banging on windows,
or clouds,
so slow
to turn pink and grey.

If I whistle
will he rush to me
over the Downs?

I long for Antarctica's days,
endless
as queues for bread,
squatters reclaiming wasteland.

Children wait for kisses,
mothers stand by graves
until the Resurrection.

In three hours,
I meet them all.

Together
we stare
into the next minute

hoping land and light
will break our fall
and cushion us, soft as silt.

From *Commandments* (Arc 2007) by Jackie Wills

The Truth About Hearts – Susan Jane Sims

For Chris

Tell me the truth about hearts,
not any of that tosh
about giving them away
as if we really could do that and live.

Tell me only
that if I live an average life
my heart will beat
two and a half billion times.

That's all I need to know; that
and the fact that my heart will recognise
what it loves and grow.

Detritus – Vivien Jones

for Laurence who died October 2011

You waved by the car,
that last time
see you soon, I'll phone.
no caption on the moment
to say, fix your face now
because you will phone
to say, *sorry, a bit sore,*
and that was the last time
before today.

Your DNA is on our recorders,
sorry about that you laughed,
your saliva now our treasure.
What was that last harmony,
an end-of-piece chord,
three notes that made us smile ?
What of the *luter's detritus;* strings, music,
chamois, pencils, erasers, footrest
and tuner,
that creative mess at your feet,
even at concerts.

rise,
sit,
kneel,
Bell rings
respond,
sing,
reflect,
pray,
your shell in a box.

Somewhere in my mind
your perfect plucked note pierces
through; a memory of shared bliss
in a wood lined palace,
a lute in your hands,
sound rushing along passages,
up chimneys, a floor away
I hear a note and its decay,
part of your essential detritus.

Legacy – Robyn Bolam

In memory of Frank and Irene Lomax

We don't know where we'll go when we set off on the journey;
we leave with the tide, trusting it will bring us home.

Remember that we can't always see the birds in winter trees
but a trembling twig sometimes sings.

We keep faith that life will sail through death
though we find ourselves in strange waters.

Remember, we are sea and sky, flowers on the water,
and love in your hearts like hidden birds singing.

And when you thought – Marilyn Ricci

Dedicated to: Hannah Jutson

it was long gone, here it is,
up your sleeve, in your pocket,
tucked under a sleeping cat.

You pull it out, let it fall,
drape it over both arms,
admire its improbability

a thin-air hammock, woven in light,
          to be flung up
                    between
a cold house and a home,
harsh words and a smile.

Lie in it. It will hold you.

Published in *Smiths Knoll*, issue 41, 2007 and *Rebuilding A Number 39*, pamphlet (Happenstance Press, 2008)

Sunset and Match – Geoff Stevens

Eyes starry, and pointing to the Pole
you enfold me
like a warm summer night
the fireflies sparking from your hair
cloy me in your embrace
our breaths squeezed out
as night air diminishes
in our busy mouths.
And we ignite
a naked breeze cooling the sweat
upon our brows
your eager hands
glued around my neck.
And behind all this
our horizon is a last touch of fire
like a trace of strontium
on a spectrograph
crimson in its desire to propagate.

From *Sleeping With You and other night-time adventures* (Indigo Dreams Publishing 2012)

Agonist – Lesley Carty

Close to the heartroot, a cell divides.
Eyes contracting and widening in the dark
with that rainbow-flash of the cat patrolling
her boundaries. Tones of voice convey
the chromatics of fear and need; a flick of the tail,
a purr outside the range of perceptible sound
trembling beneath the fingers.
Inside the locked cell, love survives.

The seed sends out a shoot whose ramifications reach below
the superficial veins of the soil, a heat-seeking missile
to unearth and neutralise each source of hurt,
each remembered and forgotten blow.

This substance, for many years our kindest friend,
has helped us guard the borders, bar the door,
and stay alert to danger. It will not easily let us go.
But prison is no place to raise the child we found
and held, so like and yet unlike our own. The choice today
is stark. Either we must break strong bonds of loyalty,
or break the one we love, for whom to fail
is not an option. Controlling pain is not the end.

Ma’s Cook Book – Sallie Durham

All the best recipes were in her
little brown book, with the
stained cover like a map of Africa.
Banana bread and devilled chicken,
the trifles she assembled –
glazed cherries, and the upflung
arms of ghost-green angelica
were tiny drowning men in seas of cream.

I don’t know how she found the time
to write them down, those flawless
pencilled loops, rubbed to crumbs
by a decade in a dark drawer –
secreted away like love letters.
Every recipe a rainy afternoon,
a kiss, a glimpse of lifting elbows,
hands gloved in gunk, her laugh.

For my mother, Kay Gee, who died of lung cancer on January 25th 2000

The day she left home – Jan Harris

I made chilli, in a pot two arms wide
with sweet peppers, tomatoes red as a beating heart,
glorious curls of onion.

There were brothers, father, boyfriend of course
to carry the wardrobe we picked
when she was just handle-tall,
the boxes of belongings gathered over years;
she didn't need me to do that

so I made chilli.
They came home later
ate it all in big hungry mouthfuls.

More things to move tomorrow

perhaps I'll bake a cake.

A High White Bed – Jenna Plewes

Everything is far away
doll's house small
she's looking down
a long, long way down
through the wrong lens

she holds the bare white room
in the palm of her hand
picks up the metal bed
with finger and thumb
gentles the little figure
into her other hand

bends her head to her cupped palm
listens
the small child is quiet now
her fight to breathe is over.

Like great white moths

snowflakes settle

on her empty hands

Adlestrop – Edward Thomas

Yes, I remember Adlestrop –
The name, because one afternoon
Of heat the express-train drew up there
Unwontedly. It was late June.

The steam hissed. Someone cleared his throat.
No one left and no one came
On the bare platform. What I saw
Was Adlestrop – only the name

And willows, willow-herb, and grass,
And meadowsweet, and haycocks dry,
No whit less still and lonely fair
Than the high cloudlets in the sky.

And for that minute a blackbird sang
Close by, and round him, mistier,
Farther and farther, all the birds
Of Oxfordshire and Gloucestershire.

List Before Departure – Maggie Norton

I'll put it on the list: that in the yard
I saw in the dawn mist
sweet jasmine open its twists
of trumpets that the bees frisked

and beyond the door leading to the lane
pink foxglove urged its store
of nectar up to light, poured
out leaves for rough tongues to core

and Painted Ladies danced over windfalls
in tipsy innocence,
doing ballet on the chance
of an orchestra of ants.

Yes, head all lists with this: in the backyard
I smile in a dawn mist
as jasmine opens its twists
of trumpets for bees to kiss.

From *Onions and Other Intentions* (Indigo Dreams Publishing, 2012)

Birthday Wishes – Thelma Laycock

She lifts the receiver,
puts it back,
today is the day
if she leaves it until tomorrow
she won't ring.
she picks up again
dialling the strange number
who will answer?
on the third ring it is his voice
husky as an old man's yet
exuding the same gentleness
she speaks in English, clipped
against his singing language,
a flock of birds.
yes, he remembers her
his health is not too bad
nor his wife's
like old friends they talk
then end the call
as she wishes him 'Happy Birthday'.

at night in her hotel room
the dragon of love and desire
deep in his thirty year tomb
strikes up, an unexpected cruel backlash;
she paces the room seeing dawn
over deep snow, pink and yellow
against the buildings of his city;
she settles her briefcase ready for the airport
but her mind is in an English garden,
green eyes, dark hair, white blossom above her.

The Quiet Life – Alexander Pope

Happy the man whose wish and care
A few paternal acres bound,
Content to breath his native air
In his own ground.
Whose herds with milk, whose fields with bread,
Whose flocks supply him with attire,
Whose trees in summer yield him shade,
In winter fire.
Blest who can unconcern'dly find
Hours, days and years slide soft away,
In health of body, peace of mind,
Quiet by day,
Sound sleep by night; study and ease,
Together mixt; sweet recreation;
And innocence, which most does please
With meditation.
Thus let me live, unseen, unknown,
Thus unlamented let me die,
Steal from the world, and not a stone
Tell where I lie.

Let us pray – Jo Peters

When, by stealth, cancer crept up on us
and caught you by the throat, fear told me, 'Pray'.
But I'd lost contact, mislaid the address,
might say, 'You bastard, don't take him away'.
So others still in touch promised their prayers,
and I took books and tissues to the ward,
remembered to bring post and newspapers;
too late to beg for favours from the Lord.

But sometimes as I sat there while you slept,
new expert in drugs, therapies and scans,
I'd look down at my hands, by now adept
at giving liquid feeds, those wilful hands,
pocketing my pride, laced in dumb prayer,
pleaded that the outlook might be fair.

First published in *The Interpreter's House* magazine.

Fistful Of Dreams – Linus H L Łyszkowska

For Marie who died too soon

At the back of a deep drawer
In the old kitchen dresser
A treasure beyond price lies hidden,
Swaddled in a silken knotted handkerchief,
A child's fistful of dreams, a handful of
Tiny, pale green, ocean-polished pebbles,
Cherished memories of two sisters
Walking hand in hand
Along the summer-blessed shore
Of a holy Hebridean island,
One day when we were young.

Loveliest of Trees, the Cherry Now – A E Housman

Loveliest of trees, the cherry now
Is hung with bloom along the bough,
And stands about the woodland ride
Wearing white for Eastertide.

Now, of my threescore years and ten,
Twenty will not come again,
And take from seventy springs a score,
It only leaves me fifty more.

And since to look at things in bloom
Fifty springs are little room,
About the woodlands I will go
To see the cherry hung with snow.

She Walks in Beauty – Lord Byron

She walks in beauty, like the night
  Of cloudless climes and starry skies;
And all that's best of dark and bright
  Meet in her aspect and her eyes:
Thus mellowed to that tender light
  Which heaven to gaudy day denies.

One shade the more, one ray the less,
  Had half impaired the nameless grace
Which waves in every raven tress,
  Or softly lightens o'er her face;
Where thoughts serenely sweet express,
  How pure, how dear their dwelling-place.

And on that cheek, and o'er that brow,
  So soft, so calm, yet eloquent,
The smiles that win, the tints that glow,
  But tell of days in goodness spent,
A mind at peace with all below,
  A heart whose love is innocent!

Lovers on Aran – Seamus Heaney

The timeless waves, bright, sifting, broken glass,
Came dazzling around, into the rocks,
Came glinting, sifting from the Americas

To posess Aran. Or did Aran rush
to throw wide arms of rock around a tide
That yielded with an ebb, with a soft crash?

Did sea define the land or land the sea?
Each drew new meaning from the waves' collision.
Sea broke on land to full identity.

By kind permission of the author, from *Death of a Naturalist*
(Faber & Faber, 1966)

Amelia – Joni Mitchell

I was driving across the burning desert
When I spotted six jet planes
Leaving six white vapor trails across the bleak terrain
It was the hexagram of the heavens
it was the strings of my guitar
Amelia it was just a false alarm

The drone of flying engines
Is a song so wild and blue
It scrambles time and seasons if it gets thru to you
Then your life becomes a travelogue
Of picture post card charms
Amelia it was just a false alarm

People will tell you where they've gone
They'll tell you where to go
But till you get there yourself you never really know
Where some have found their paradise
Other's just come to harm
Oh, Amelia it was just a false alarm

I wish that he was here tonight
It's so hard to obey
His sad request of me to kindly stay away
So this is how I hide the hurt
As the road leads cursed and charmed
I tell Amelia it was just a false alarm

A ghost of aviation
She was swallowed by the sky
Or by the sea like me she had a dream to fly
Like Icarus ascending
On beautiful foolish arms
Amelia it was just a false alarm

Maybe I've never really loved
I guess that is the truth
I've spent my whole life in clouds at icy altitude
And looking down on everything
I crashed into his arms
Amelia it was just a false alarm

I pulled into the Cactus Tree Motel
To shower off the dust
And I slept on the strange pillows of my wanderlust
I dreamed of 747s
Over geometric farms
Dreams Amelia – dreams and false alarms

Well worn – Michelle Sorrell

Orbiting separate hemispheres
Sitting with knees bent,
Being in your presence
Gracefully by consent.

In the attic are dinners, roses,
Memories of long nights,
Albums and Moses basket
Shielded from the stark daylight.

Who names what we have made?
Romance, a malleable form,
Is well used, love's like
Old pebbles, rough shined and worn

Listen! – Sarah James

Why do you only see the moon
through flickering shadows?

How come light ripples off water
to drip through your clasped hands?

Is everyone's sun a wilting daisy
or egg yolk broken as it hits the pan?

When you put a lit match to your lips,
why let its flame gust, then die?

Can your eyes' grey skies explain
clouds weighting you down inside?

Which leaf here is your hope?
Could we make its greenness grow?

Will you notice now for me tonight
how your life glistens with moonlight.

Maps and Lockets and Imagining Your Face – Adele C Geraghty

Could I but touch the silken lines
of your face once more, drawn in pastel sunset rivers,
across the definitive horizon of your eyes,

I would, Braille reading , quench my thirst for recollection
in a mind map, double and triple folded;
compressed for safety in gentle, muted chambers,

ready to open on any occasion, when the treacherous loss
of touch and liquid melody of sound are far beyond my
feeble conception. An ocean's depth between us.

I would keep you, if I could, like a locket, close to my breast,
warmed by it's gold and heartened by it's presence;
never allowing hands to wrench you from me.

Yet even if, as a map or a locket, you might be taken from me,
my own cunning deception would quell the pain of loss;
there are always maps to be found and lockets to be had.

But flesh is not so easily replaced, nor do maps or pictures
touch my heart or fill the space, in a magnitude
of miles and time, left by the absence of your face.

Neck Lump – Roger Elkin

for Helen

Felt it before she saw it, fingers
lingering as circling its rise and swell,
then pincering but not pinching skin,
just sensing, as if testing whether
there was any give in it. Certainly nothing
she could name as hurt or pain, but a dulled
muscle-pull, or under-bruise, barely there.
Not much to worry about, she thought,
though mirrors confirmed she'd better
have it checked.

And did.

The excision would leave its giveaway
snail trail: that thinned down carmine pink
she could conceal behind filigree chain
whose intricate links would divert looks,
bring praise
or, for special days, a garlanded
scarf wreathed in practiced casualness
and satisfying others eyes
unless, of course,
she really felt the need to advertise how she'd
survived the lump, the knife, the chemo-fix

then she'd plump for going open-necked,
a defiant, self-confessing cut above the rest.

Sonnets from the Portuguese, XIII – Elizabeth Barrett Browning

And wilt thou have me fashion into speech
The love I bear thee, finding words enough,
And hold the torch out, while the winds are rough,
Between our faces, to cast light upon each?

I drop it at thy feet. I cannot teach
My hand to hold my spirit so far off
From myself.. me.. that I should bring thee proof,
In words of love hid in me... out of reach.

Nay, let the silence of my womanhood
Commend my woman-love to thy belief,
Seeing that I stand unwon (however wooed)
And rend the garment of my life in brief
By a most dauntless, voiceless fortitude,
Lest one touch of this heart convey its grief.

Wondrous Moment – Alexander Sergeyevich Pushkin

The wondrous moment of our meeting . . .
I well remember you appear
Before me like a vision fleeting,
A beauty's angel pure and clear.

In hopeless ennui surrounding
The worldly bustle, to my ear
For long your tender voice kept sounding,
For long in dreams came features dear.

Time passed. Unruly storms confounded
Old dreams, and I from year to year
Forgot how tender you had sounded,
Your heavenly features once so dear.

My backwoods days dragged slow and quiet —
Dull fence around, dark vault above —
Devoid of God and uninspired,
Devoid of tears, of fire, of love.

Sleep from my soul began retreating,
And here you once again appear
Before me like a vision fleeting,
A beauty's angel pure and clear.

In ecstasy the heart is beating,
Old joys for it anew revive;
Inspired and God-filled, it is greeting
The fire, and tears, and love alive.

Chemo Women – Connie Ramsay Bott

It's one of those days,
taking the kids to the public pool,
the older two in the "boys" side,
hopefully looking after themselves,
the three year old boy with me,
in the "girls" side.
I'm trying to keep track of swimsuits,
locker keys, towels, water wings,
my attempts at control and planning
turning to pandemonium
and I'm thinking, "I hate this."
If I wasn't trying to be a good mother
I'd never come near a public pool.

There's a lot of splashing,
too much shrieking, some serious fun,
(not mine) and we get through the hour,
return wet and chilly to the locker rooms,
dress for the real world.

In reception we pass two women,
both bald, thin, with an ethereal look.
I know in an instant that they are survivors
trying to build themselves up
or working to re-enter the world
that they came close to leaving.

I want to hug my sons,
want to cry for the ladies
and rejoice in my day,
my good luck and the happy chaos
that I live in.
I'm not a survivor, like them.

I'm just a fortunate mum with three boys
who's had a light brush
with someone else's nightmare.

Devotion – David Norris-Kay

What love the world cannot destroy
Is linked between our eyes?
What door leads to the garden
Where true devotion lies?

No greater understanding
Can lace our darkened years:
No mystery more eternal
Than love's abundance here.

Embracing all, in quiet words,
When first your shadow touched my heart,
And still remembrance here beheld
Of painful moments thrown apart . . .

And if fate's destiny is death,
Devotion still remains a whole,
Uniting love and life beyond,
Unbroken thought which binds the soul.

And when prayer fails to bring solace
From troubled words and jest,
I seek devotion harboured in
The hollow of your breast.

Unchanging in affection,
This love, eternal lies,
In the shallow of our sunlight,
And deepness of our eyes.

Promises - A Love Song – Barbara Robinson

If you see no Angels
then I will sculpt them for you.
If you see no sun
I will shine a light for you

— and if you see no heaven
I will take you in my arms,
kiss you, awaken your soul.
We'll drift into forever,
beyond the triumph of stars
where paradise awaits.

The passing of a thousand Springs
cannot compare to my love.
As the lotus flower blossoms,
petals turned towards the sun,
so you will flourish

— wrapped within my arms,
discovering the joy
of each new born day.
A triumph of hearts entwined;
our two souls reborn.

Home Movie – Carolyn Oulton

I can see the faces twice
through and above
the square inch of glass.
I start talking to it,
remembering myself.

Of course they don't hear
the hoarseness of hand on bark,
the flaying of blunt, uneven
flesh. Woodpecker faces
jabber from the mouth of an old tree.

A child in a hollow tree
waving or not waving?
where a man is standing
by a hollow tree
watching the face of a child.

When I Have Fears – John Keats

When I have fears that I may cease to be
Before my pen has glean'd my teeming brain,
Before high-piled books, in charactery,
Hold like rich garners the full ripen'd grain;
When I behold, upon the night's starr'd face,
Huge cloudy symbols of a high romance,
And think that I may never live to trace
Their shadows, with the magic hand of chance;
And when I feel, fair creature of an hour,
That I shall never look upon thee more,
Never have relish in the faery power
Of unreflecting love;--then on the shore
Of the wide world I stand alone, and think
Till love and fame to nothingness do sink.

After Cancer – Lucinda Carey

Knew he had been ill,
but I'd always thought of him secretly
as Gimli,
a doughty short tempered dwarf
with definite views.

(I know I shouldn't have, but you can't help your thoughts)
This was confirmed by his vociferous, avid
consumption of chilli cheese.

His house cut into the underside of a cliff,
containing rare rock slivers displayed
on the cavernous mantelpiece beside fossils.

With stubborn tenacity he laughs,
resumes his place amongst his
companions, questing energy.

But he seems too frail to
wield the weighty pickaxe.
Yet still he delves a lode
of poems.

Yellow Jacket – Pippa Munro Hebden

For my husband George who died of cancer September 2008

I kept your bright yellow sailing jacket.
It was much too useful to give away.
Double zipped and waterproof with a hood,
it keeps me dry as I trudge through the fields.
I think of you pacing the wooden decks,
your blue eyes scrunched against the salty wind,
flapping sheets of canvas above your head,
the rigging snapping and the prow dipping.
My seas are grass tracks with sandbanks of mud.
A black leather leash lies coiled in my hand.
A tall butterscotch hound pads silently
behind me, just as you always used to do:
I turn around to check that she's still there.
I caress her fur, softer than your beard.
Her chestnut eyes are puzzled by my tears.
I thrust my hand deep into one pocket.
Your folded handkerchief is always there.

Painting for the Nodes – Kate North

for J.N.

It's a hot one
today
when I call
and you sound relieved
picking up.

Thanks
you declare
before even asking;
it's obvious
I will,
we all will.

I arrive
at yours alive
and ask.
You show me
to the spare room.

Walls and skirting,
if it's not too much.
Stop
when you've had enough,
you say.

And you disappear
downstairs
to the floor boards.
The house is full
of helpers
useful and useless.

I make my way
with rollers,
paint.
This is my first
brush with emulsion.

Your spare room
is a suntrap
in the afternoons.
I stand, hoping
in a glare of light,
that this will make a difference.

Earlier
our Mother told me
in confidence
that she wanted
to place her hand on your neck
claw inside
pull out the decay
place it in her mouth
and swallow.
When you come to check,
to declare my skill and diligence,
parade your happiness,
my gaze flickers
between yours
and the neck.
It is getting bigger
and I revert
to kneeling and smoothing the gloss
on the skirting.

Left alone
I decide to tackle the door.

Not on your list
but obviously required.
As I daub at wood panels
sweat merges with tear
high on my cheek.
I annoy myself with the inappropriate,
memories that prove
we don't always get along.

And now I'm left
painting
offering lifts
making calls of concern
reading up
having late night chats
with all those people
who have come out to care;
for what it's worth.

Once It Was The Colour Of Saying – Dylan Thomas

Once it was the colour of saying
Soaked my table the uglier side of a hill
With a capsized field where a school sat still
And a black and white patch of girls grew playing;
The gentle seaslides of saying I must undo
That all the charmingly drowned arise to cockcrow and kill.
When I whistled with mitching boys through a reservoir park
Where at night we stoned the cold and cuckoo
Lovers in the dirt of their leafy beds,
The shade of their trees was a word of many shades
And a lamp of lightning for the poor in the dark;
Now my saying shall be my undoing,
And every stone I wind off like a reel.

Train, water, geese – Sue Vickerman

You don't say goodbye, you say –
watch for that view across the water
Philip Larkin wrote about; email me your thoughts.
At the barrier your eyes swivel away,
look at anything, run along the length of the train.
Later I'm not sure if your soft
un-puckered lips almost brushed me.

So here they are: the Humber Bridge harp-like
in this hazy light, water flatter than any
I have ever seen, sealed closed, lidded,
white as the sky, but not skin – not alive
like skin, less human, no pulse
ever so slightly visible beneath it,
this view you brought me home to look at
too smooth and pristine to visualise ships here,
their bitty twig-masts criss-crossing

though you've been telling me all day
how ships packed with spices, fresh fruit, booty,
would push into the estuary; this day of wanting you
more than good food, more than water
you could have tugged me in, you could have harboured me
but we did not so much as bump gently
like little boats do.

Your beloved panorama becomes houses,
light industry, small rail stations on the dull plain,
but always, somewhere, water, mirroring.
My hands on the train's window trace wetlands
that lie too quiet, expressionless.
If I could puncture that deadpan face

with the snapped back of a bull-rush; if you would
skid onto the water like those Canada geese just did,
your feet scuffing up a brilliant shower…

From *Thin Bones Like Wish-bones* (Indigo Dreams Publishing, 2013)

Branching Out – June English

The cherry tree centres the garden. Its shade
reaches out, touches your vacant chair,
sneaks in through the bay window flecking
the piano. I lift the lid, finger the ivory keys,
touch middle C and suddenly it's Chopin,
sadly-hopeful, tender-true: a prelude

to low-key my grief. The sun steeples,
fills the room. Its warmth relaxes me,
and in this altered state I feel you near,
hear you call my name, watch you pattern
and re-pattern sun-specks of household dust
into a consonance of light and shade,
a gentle nocturne from the shadowlands.
There's a butterfly in the cherry tree.

First published in *The Sorcerer's Arc* (Hearing Eye)

Augury – Roselle Angwin

for Annie

That day we sat on the hand-hewn crude
oak bench in mild September sun
at the top of the Teign: Hunters' Wood,

where the rowans splashed crimson
the slant light's opaline threshold,
a prefiguring of the blood

which we didn't see then
would have to be shed, where you'd need
to be strong to survive the descent

into holy darkness. I remember leaves
crisp underfoot; the voice of the river;
and I remember the single white deer

almost not glimpsed as she, brief visitor,
flowed into and out of our world
as if to answer a promise

you'd made at your birth,
as if you'd come back to find her.

From *All The Missing Names Of Love* (Indigo Dreams Publishing, 2012)

Solitaire – Valerie Morton

The bar's still there at the Gare du Nord,
tucked in that moody corner; I'm upset
at how it's tarted up and a new decor

illuminates the table where we met,
breathless together in the Paris air.
You're the way I see you - I can't forget:

smoking your pipe, with time to spare -
one hour until your journey to Marseilles.
You offer me my very first Sancerre

and through the bowl of every glass I see
your face distort in its mellow glow.
I smile - as sure as any girl can be.

It's time to leave you here. But before I go
I breathe the steam and hear a whistle blow.

Shades of grey – Poul Webb

Can you see the tasteful greys,
the pearl grey walls that surround you,
the dove grey blanket against your parchment skin?
Feather-like breath like goose wing or swan's down.
Dipping your toe into the shallow end of the night.
Can you see the starlings gathering to roost
in the pale grey evening light?

Soon the impending darkness will embrace you,
and having unravelled your allotted skein of time,
you can venture further out into the murky depths
that look so inviting by the light of the stars...
And, when you are so far away
that I can no longer see you,
I will assume that you have safely reached
your finite shade of grey.

From the collection *Shades of Grey* (Boho Press 2006)

Your name – Karen Dennison

I couldn't speak your name
but wrote it on a sky
so empty it hurt.

Fields were open palms
of forgiveness
while still horses
breathed out wishes.

I held your memory
like it was a child
and like a child
it grew too large to hold.

Yellow poppies flowered
where you fell,
sang your name
until it rang from my mouth
like a bell.

Truce – Patrick B Osada

Deep in this winter without love,
no gentleness can touch my will.
The summer sun and calling dove
are frozen out, ice holds me still.

There are no harsh words left unsaid,
our silences are ripped and sore,
your rebukes echo in my head –
can you still love me anymore?

Our common ground is scorched and brown,
here bitterness alone takes root;
I face each day wearing a frown
and search in vain for love's green shoots.

To end this impasse and endure
will take a kindness beyond hurt :
give me your hand, affect a cure,
with graciousness we'll sooth torn hearts.

Desideria – William Wordsworth

Surprised by joy--impatient as the Wind
I turned to share the transport--O! with whom
...But Thee, deep buried in the silent tomb,
That spot which no vicissitude can find?
Love, faithful love, recall'd thee to my mind--
...But how could I forget thee? Through what power,
...Even for the least division of an hour,
Have I been so beguiled as to be blind
To my most grievous loss?--That thought's return
...Was the worst pang that sorrow ever bore,
Save one, one only, when I stood forlorn,
...Knowing my heart's best treasure was no more;
That neither present time, nor years unborn
...Could to my sight that heavenly face restore.

On First Looking into Chapman's Homer – John Keats

Much have I travell'd in the realms of gold,
And many goodly states and kingdoms seen;
Round many western islands have I been
Which bards in fealty to Apollo hold.
Oft of one wide expanse had I been told
That deep-browed Homer ruled as his demesne;
Yet did I never breathe its pure serene
Till I heard Chapman speak out loud and bold:
Then felt I like some watcher of the skies
When a new planet swims into his ken;
Or like stout Cortez when with eagle eyes
He star'd at the Pacific — and all his men
Look'd at each other with a wild surmise —
Silent, upon a peak in Darien.

Survival – Kate Scott

For J.W.

It will take you shielding yourself
against the darkness
that blinds your heart
and punctures your lungs
so your breath draws quick and bleak and cold.

It will take you listening out hard,
as one listens for deer in the deep-leaved woods,
to the words of courage and love that come your way
falling through the thick branches like spells of light.

It will take you straining to hear these words
against the cacophony of the inane,
the well-meaning-but-clumsy pats of comfort,
the callous, tactless happiness
that bumps into you without looking
as you try to find your way alone.

It will take you seeing your friends,
forgiving them not always understanding,
not always offering
the right words, the right actions,
which you hardly know yourself,
so deep are you among these lonely trees
as you try every path
and see him nowhere.

It will take
the seasoning of trees,
the circles wider round the loss,

the light further from the dark.
It will take growing from the ground,
following the turning days,
taking flight
past the tips of the trees,
finding
new leaves,
life.

Something Happened – Maitreyabandhu

Something happened in the dark,
the dark of your closed eyes,
early after the moon had set
behind the blackened pines.

Your body ached; your head was bowed
but not towards his face.
A heron flew up from your sleep
to find a better place.

It was cold and you were tired.
Half-dreams came and went
while you made your way below
to where the heart relents.

First published in The Crumb Road (Bloodaxe Books, 2013)
With kind permission of the publishers.

A Birthday – Christina Rossetti

My heart is like a singing bird
  Whose nest is in a water'd shoot;
My heart is like an apple-tree
  Whose boughs are bent with thick-set fruit;
My heart is like a rainbow shell
  That paddles in a halcyon sea;
My heart is gladder than all these,
  Because my love is come to me.

Raise me a daïs of silk and down;
  Hang it with vair and purple dyes;
Carve it in doves and pomegranates,
  And peacocks with a hundred eyes;
Work it in gold and silver grapes,
  In leaves and silver fleurs-de-lys;
Because the birthday of my life
  Is come, my love is come to me.

INDEX

A

B

C

D

E

F

G

H

J

K

L

M

N

O

P

R

S

T

V

W

Y

Z

Indigo Dreams Publishing Ltd
132 Hinckley Road
Stoney Stanton
Leicestershire
UK

www.indigodreams.co.uk